NORWAY'S EU EXPERIENCE AND LESSONS FOR THE UK

This book examines Norway's affiliation to the EU and systematically assesses the potential suitability of this arrangement for the UK as a viable EU affiliation post-Brexit.

Framing the book within the framework of the broader European context, the authors ask how much autonomy and room to manoeuvre tightly integrated non-member states have under this arrangement. They present an in-depth assessment of Norway's close EU affiliation and provide insight into what this may reveal to us about the post-Brexit European political order. The book's analytical framework centred on autonomy under complex interdependence has relevance well beyond the confines of the Norway case. This includes the UK, not least since the EU–UK Trade and Cooperation Agreement (TCA) leaves considerable uncertainty. It contains transitory elements; there will be implementation reviews, and there may be many more bilateral and multilateral agreements before the trade relationship is fully defined.

This book will be of key interest to scholars and students of European Union politics, Norwegian politics, British politics, European integration, and, more broadly, to European studies and international relations.

John Erik Fossum is Professor at ARENA Centre for European Studies, University of Oslo, Norway.

Christopher Lord is Professor at ARENA Centre for European Studies, University of Oslo, Norway.

Fay Madeleine Farstad is Senior Researcher at CICERO – Center for International Climate Research, Norway.

Arild Aurvåg Farsund is Professor at the Department of Government, University of Bergen, Norway.

Merethe Dotterud Leiren is Research Director at CICERO – Center for International Climate Research, Norway.

Espen D. H. Olsen is Professor at Oslo Metropolitan University, Norway, and Senior Researcher at ARENA Centre for European Studies, University of Oslo, Norway.

Marianne Riddervold is Professor of Political Science at the Inland Norway University of Applied Sciences, Researcher at NUPI, and Senior Fellow at the UC Berkeley Institute for European Studies.

Johanne Døhlie Saltnes is Lecturer and Visiting Researcher at the University of Brasilia, Brazil, and Affiliated Researcher at ARENA Centre for European Studies, University of Oslo, Norway.

Øyvind Svendsen is Senior Researcher at the Norwegian Institute of International Affairs (NUPI) and Associate Professor at the Inland Norway University of Applied Sciences.

Jarle Trondal is Professor at Department of Political Science and Management, University of Agder, Norway; Professor at ARENA Centre for European Studies, University of Oslo, Norway; and Senior Fellow at Institute of European Studies, University of California, Berkeley, US.

Dealing with Europe

Series editors: John Erik Fossum

University of Oslo, Norway, and Christopher Lord, University of Oslo, Norway.

This mini-series offers books which respectively examine the potential modes of affiliation adopted by key countries with the EU, systematically assessing the potential suitability of each arrangement as a viable EU affiliation post-Brexit model for the UK against the revealing backdrop of the domestic political context of each country. It clarifies which actors and factors are supportive of such arrangements in each country; which actors and factors are the main challenges; what form of balance there is and how precarious that is. Finally, each country case study considers what would happen should the UK try to adopt such a model.

Switzerland-EU Relations
Lessons for the UK after Brexit?
Edited by Paolo Dardanelli and Oscar Mazzoleni

Norway's EU Experience and Lessons for the UK
On Autonomy and Wriggle Room
John Erik Fossum, Christopher Lord, Fay Madeleine Farstad, Arild Aurvåg Farsund, Merethe Dotterud Leiren, Espen D. H. Olsen, Marianne Riddervold, Johanne Døhlie Saltnes, Øyvind Svendsen, and Jarle Trondal

NORWAY'S EU EXPERIENCE AND LESSONS FOR THE UK

On Autonomy and Wriggle Room

*John Erik Fossum, Christopher Lord,
Fay Madeleine Farstad, Arild Aurvåg Farsund,
Merethe Dotterud Leiren, Espen D. H. Olsen,
Marianne Riddervold, Johanne Døhlie Saltnes,
Øyvind Svendsen, and Jarle Trondal*

LONDON AND NEW YORK

Designed cover image: © MarkRubens / iStock

First published 2024
by Routledge
4 Park Square, Milton Park, Abingdon, Oxon OX14 4RN

and by Routledge
605 Third Avenue, New York, NY 10158

Routledge is an imprint of the Taylor & Francis Group, an informa business

© 2024 John Erik Fossum, Christopher Lord, Fay Madeleine Farstad, Arild Aurvåg Farsund, Merethe Dotterud Leiren, Espen D. H. Olsen, Marianne Riddervold, Johanne Døhlie Saltnes, Øyvind Svendsen, and Jarle Trondal

The right of John Erik Fossum, Christopher Lord, Fay Madeleine Farstad, Arild Aurvåg Farsund, Merethe Dotterud Leiren, Espen D. H. Olsen, Marianne Riddervold, Johanne Døhlie Saltnes, Øyvind Svendsen, and Jarle Trondal to be identified as authors of this work has been asserted in accordance with sections 77 and 78 of the Copyright, Designs and Patents Act 1988.

All rights reserved. No part of this book may be reprinted or reproduced or utilised in any form or by any electronic, mechanical, or other means, now known or hereafter invented, including photocopying and recording, or in any information storage or retrieval system, without permission in writing from the publishers.

Trademark notice: Product or corporate names may be trademarks or registered trademarks, and are used only for identification and explanation without intent to infringe.

British Library Cataloguing-in-Publication Data
A catalogue record for this book is available from the British Library

ISBN: 978-1-032-16043-6 (hbk)
ISBN: 978-1-032-16067-2 (pbk)
ISBN: 978-1-003-24696-1 (ebk)

DOI: 10.4324/9781003246961

Typeset in Times New Roman
by Apex CoVantage, LLC

CONTENTS

Acknowledgements	ix
1 Introduction	1
2 Autonomy and wriggle room	23
3 Post-Brexit climate and energy policy in the EU, UK, and Norway: a new trilateral relationship?	48
4 Fisheries, aquaculture, and agriculture: autonomy and wriggle room in primary industry policies	69
5 Global trade and development: the challenge of translating legal wriggle room into autonomy	97
6 Flexible association in foreign, security, and defence policy: a case of gradually diminishing autonomy?	124
7 Citizenship, migration, and mobility	141
8 Autonomy under complex interdependence: the case of Norway and lessons for Brexit?	160
9 Not much wriggle room: Brexit and the Norway model	185

10 Conclusion 207

Britain and Norway lost on voyage: a postscript 218
Andrew Duff

Index *225*

ACKNOWLEDGEMENTS

This is a multi-authored book. The idea was to gather a group of experts who together would write a coherent book. This involved numerous meetings and extensive cooperation in the process of writing. Nevertheless, since the book has a range of substantive chapters, each author was assigned the task of writing a chapter on their specific field of expertise. We therefore specify who is the main author in charge of each chapter for two main reasons. One is to acknowledge the specialist expertise that has gone into the different chapters. The other is to offload the authors of collective responsibility for all the contents of the book. An initial draft of Chapter 1 was produced by John Erik Fossum and Chris Lord. An initial draft of Chapter 2 was presented by John Erik Fossum and Jarle Trondal. Both these drafts have been so extensively commented and revised as to make up a collective effort. Chapter 3 was the prime responsibility of Fay Madeleine Farstad and Merethe Dotterud Leiren. Chapter 4 was the prime responsibility of Arild Aurvåg Farsund. Chapter 5 was the prime responsibility of Johanne Døhlie Saltnes. Chapter 6 was the prime responsibility of Marianne Riddervold and Øyvind Svendsen. Chapter 7 was the prime responsibility of Espen D. H. Olsen. Chapter 8 was the prime responsibility of John Erik Fossum, with significant contributions from Jarle Trondal, especially. Chapter 9 was the prime responsibility of Chris Lord. Chapter 10 was a collective effort of the whole author group.

When preparing the book, we initially launched a policy dialogue where we invited a variety of stakeholders (civil servants, interest group participants, and academics) to share ideas on autonomy and wriggle room, particularly with the case of Norway in mind. This meeting took place 1 December 2021 in Oslo and provided much needed and valuable insights into the world of practice. We are grateful to the participants, who, through their reasoning about the topics, have contributed to improve the quality of our contributions. We are also thankful to the interviewees, who have shared their valuable time to respond to our queries. Many thanks also for excellent research assistance from Silva Hoffmann and Siri Katrine Helland Stai, who have helped in organising meetings and editing and formatting the manuscript.

We gratefully acknowledge financial support from the EU's Horizon 2020 programme (Societal Challenges 6: Europe in a changing world – Inclusive, innovative and reflective societies) under Grant Agreement no. 822419. The Research Council of Norway has also funded this work through the Research on international relations, foreign and security policy and Norwegian interests (BENCHMARK, project no. 289442).

Finally, we are thankful to Andrew Taylor, the editor at Routledge, for support and patience and for publishing our work.

1
INTRODUCTION

The United Kingdom's (UK) decision to leave the European Union (EU) in 2016 sparked a wide-ranging and highly politically charged debate on how the UK should organise its relationship with the EU after its formal exit ('Brexit'). No clear majority for any option was found,[1] prime ministers have gone and come,[2] and political tensions have run high within and between political parties, governing institutions, and UK nations. Precipitating this was an important shift in the British public debate: what had been a focus before the referendum on the Norway and Swiss models was replaced by a hardening of positions. Brexiters now insisted that any negotiated alternative to the UK's relationship with the EU should be based on the EU-Canada free-trade agreement (CETA).[3] That would involve less *polity* convergence on aspects of the EU's political and legal order than 'the Norway model' (see later), and less commitment to *policy* convergence over time than either Norway or Switzerland's relationship with the EU. It was the Canada model that ultimately shaped the EU-UK Trade and Cooperation Agreement (TCA).[4] How solid or entrenched this framework agreement remains shrouded in uncertainty as the parliamentary situation in the UK may change significantly. The uncertainty is, if anything, amplified by the Ukraine war, the ensuing energy crisis, and other serious fallouts from this devastating incident.

The UK's decision to leave the EU has generated massive scholarly and political interest in how the EU does and should relate to affiliated non-members (or third countries); what impact such arrangements have on the EU, its members, and systems of governance; and what impact such arrangements have on 'third countries'' systems of governing, including of course the UK itself.[5] Intrinsic to this debate is the issue of comparison and comparability. The UK's decision to leave the EU is the first case of a member state formally departing from the EU. This situates the UK in a new category of state in Europe, that of an ex-member state (Lord, 2015),

DOI: 10.4324/9781003246961-1

which brings up the issue of how distinctive such a status is. During the Brexit process, the UK's efforts to work out a bespoke arrangement with the EU gave a strong impetus to the scrutiny of existing EU affiliation arrangements, notably the Swiss, Norwegian (European Economic Area (EEA)-based), and Canadian (CETA-based) modes of affiliation. Both before and during the Brexit process, these were discussed as possible templates or models for how the UK might develop its own relationship with the EU post-Brexit. In this connection it is important to underline that the EEA Agreement, which forms the core of the Norway model, is the most binding and legally regulated relationship that the EU has formed with any third country (Gstöhl and Phinnemore, 2019). New possibilities might also emerge in the future. See, for example, Andrew Duff's (2013) proposal for a new form of association. Yet the EEA was also the EU's preferred choice for any relationship with the UK that involved its continued participation in the single market.[6]

The TCA signals that the UK is no longer in the Customs Union or the single market, and yet leaves quite a bit of openness and uncertainty as to the UK's future EU affiliation. The TCA contains transitory elements, there will be implementation reviews, and there may be many more bilateral and multilateral agreements before the trade relationship is fully defined. The TCA is, crucially, a governance arrangement. It is notable that the European Commission introduced the legislation establishing the TCA as an association agreement and not a trade agreement. The TCA is perhaps better understood not just as one more of the EU's 50+ trade agreements but, rather, as one of three ambitious governance arrangements the EU has attempted with non-members, one being the EEA, the other being the Swiss model.[7]

The sheer intensity of the UK's internal struggles to come up with a viable relationship with the rest of Europe post-Brexit shows that states that are deeply divided on the EU issue may need a prolonged period of political debate and negotiation to work out what form of EU arrangement they can settle on. The UK's experience underlines that the challenge is not simply that of finding a suitable mode of EU affiliation; we also need to understand the room for manoeuvre or wriggle room that is available in any affiliation with the EU. Further, there is a need to understand the ties that bind states and societies together in (asymmetrical) patterns of interdependence almost regardless of the formal mode of EU affiliation. And finally, we need to understand the *internal* conditions for accepting a given mode of EU affiliation, including the actors and factors that may sustain or undermine a given mode of EU affiliation *over time*. These internal conditions vary considerably across those states whose EU affiliations are the most relevant for the UK, that is, Switzerland, Norway, and Canada.

Academic assessments of possible models for the UK have provided important insights, albeit mainly with reference to legal and institutional arrangements.[8] Far less attention has been paid to how third countries' political systems, policies, economies, political cultures, and societies operate within and adapt to these arrangements in practice, and whether there are significant differences between countries and between sectors and issue-areas. The upshot is that analyses of formal and legal arrangements have thus far prevailed over political science analyses of power and domination, the reality of autonomy and wriggle room, comparative analyses across different types of policy substance, and political sociology analyses of aspects of culture and identity.

The book's main purpose outlined

The book's main purpose is to increase our understanding of the relationship between the EU and its affiliated non-member states and the implications of such relationships for different policy areas and, based on these insights, extract lessons for the UK. For this purpose, we, on the one hand, focus on the triangular relationship between Norway, the UK, and the EU, and, on the other hand, develop an analytical framework that helps to shed new light on EU–third country relations under conditions of complex interdependence.

The book's point of departure is that it is not sufficient to look at the relationship between Norway and the EU as a static point of comparison for the relationship between the EU and UK after Brexit. All three relationships – those between Norway and the EU, the EU and the UK, and Norway and the UK – change in relation to each other.

Further, the book develops a theoretical framework for analysing and learning lessons from EU–third country relations under conditions of *complex interdependence*. This framework is not only useful for discerning lessons from the cases that are studied here but is of relevance well beyond the cases explored in this volume. Key here is the concept of *autonomy*, which refers to having choices and an ability to will choices. The book aims to fill an important gap in the literature: to clarify the nature of and the conditions for autonomy in a context of complex interdependence. The European integration process creates a pattern of legally regulated complex interdependence that includes affiliated third countries. To capture the nature and scope for autonomy under such conditions of binding international collaboration, the book develops a subcategory of autonomy, which we label *wriggle room*. By wriggle room we mean the scope for autonomous choices within formal legal commitments and constraints. We apply this framework to explore the relationship between autonomy, broadly speaking, and wriggle room, more specifically with explicit reference to Norway's affiliations with the EU: how much wriggle room Norway has in its relationship with the EU, how Norway's wriggle room has been changed by Brexit, and what lessons follow for the UK.

The context of Brexit makes the focus on autonomy a natural choice given the slogan 'Taking Back Control' – which the UK Leave side used relentlessly. We may also add that we are induced to think about autonomy in terms of independence from the modern focus on sovereignty that is characteristic of 'seeing like a state' (Scott, 1999). Nevertheless, the choice to focus on the notion of autonomy over that of sovereignty and independence – as we will explain in further detail later – is because it lends itself better to understanding circumstances wherein states and their societies are bound together in patterns of complex interdependence. Under such circumstances, states very often face internal conditions and constraints that delimit the scope for independence in their external relations. Under these conditions, autonomy is a more useful term than independence because it is less concerned with demarcating bounds between the internal and the external and, instead, is more focused on what the state seeks to achieve and the means it has available for doing so. Autonomy (in contrast to independence) may thus also be enhanced (rather than reduced) through self-binding interstate collaboration marked by conditions of complex interdependence.

Sovereignty, independence, autonomy, and wriggle room

The book innovates on the state of the art in extant literature by developing the autonomy-oriented analytical framework and the special role of wriggle room therein. More specifically, the book asks how much autonomy and wriggle room tightly integrated non-member states such as Norway have under this arrangement and what implications we can draw for the UK from this. This volume thus makes a novel contribution by establishing the conceptual distinction between autonomy in a general sense as an ability to make and will choices and autonomy in the narrow sense as wriggle room within formal and legal relationships. No systematic assessment of Norway's wriggle room and autonomy has been conducted thus far. Norway's autonomy and wriggle room has, moreover, been a matter of contention within Norway. The issue of wriggle room has been raised in the UK debate on the merits and demerits of the 'Norway model'.

A mantra in the UK's Brexit debate was, as noted earlier, that of 'taking back control'. The Brexiteers underlined the imperative for the UK of escaping from what they saw as the shackles of EU control, whereas the Remainers argued that the UK had considerable scope for staking out its own desired course within the EU. These two positions resonate with the distinction between two concepts, which we find in the fields of international relations and social psychology: independence and autonomy.

As noted earlier, social science's propensity to think with and through state-based categories would lead us to place the emphasis on independence. With *independence* we refer to the absence of reliance or dependence on others. Independence needs to be distinguished from *sovereignty*, which refers to the legal right of final decision.[9] It is possible to have a legal right to final decision and yet be dependent on others. States all round the world have a legal right of final decision. Yet they vary greatly in their dependence on others. Thus, the strong emphasis on formal legal status suggests that sovereignty is binary (either you have it or not). Sovereignty, in contrast to independence and autonomy, is not tailored to power relations. It is simply a formal status that can be held by those who differ markedly in their power and independence. Unlike sovereignty, independence can be understood as a continuum or a scale from complete autarchy (no reliance on others) to complete dependence on others.

With *autonomy* we refer to the will and ability to pursue what an actor takes to be its preferences. This may or may not be under conditions of independence. Autonomy is useful for several reasons. The focus on goals and capacities means that the concept of autonomy is attentive to important aspects of the domestic politics of third states and how actors perceive and relate to the situation of complex interdependence. Further, autonomy is useful for studying complex interdependence since it recognises that an actor (a person, a state, an international organisation, etc.) may be reliant on others and yet still pursue an autonomous interest and course of action. The issue is how much space or scope the relationship provides for the pursuit of the actor's preferred choice or option.[10] It is at least arguable that the British debate has not fully engaged with questions of autonomy; or, in other words, with how much choice is available under alternative forms of non-membership – choice not only relating to the mode of EU affiliation but to state and societal capacity and capability. That, in turn, is a different question to that of sovereignty, which has been prominent in British thinking.

These brief remarks suggest that there is an overlap between what autonomy and independence signify. At the same time, the terms differ in how relevant they are for analysing the conditions facing states in today's Europe. In contemporary Europe the facts on the ground suggest that the relationship between independence and autonomy is highly lopsided given the high level of complex interdependence there is. But since so much of the political and scholarly debate has been couched in the terms of sovereignty and independence ('Taking Back Control') (HM Government, 2018), it follows that our understanding of the conditions for independence and the role and status of EU third countries would improve insofar as we clarify the nature of and scope for autonomy. Further, as we see in the case of the UK's Brexit debate, it is not simply a matter of independence versus dependence but of autonomy understood as will and ability to pursue an own course within the context of a legally regulated relationship with the EU.

The scope for autonomy, we argue, is shaped by each party's will and ability to pursue a course of its own choosing; it is also affected by the nature of the relationship: how binding or compelling it is, that is, if the contract is open-ended or highly specified, and whether it is symmetrical or asymmetrical. The EU is, legally speaking, a highly regulated political system.[11] This is reflected in the EU's relations with third countries in the sense that these are regulated by a wide range of association agreements that vary considerably in how legally binding they are. It appears, thus, that the more comprehensive and legally binding the agreement, and the more the agreement takes the EU's legal system as its basis, the more the third country forfeits or accepts constraints on its autonomy. Such an assumption does not, however, take into consideration the extent to which the agreement leaves action space or room for manoeuvre, that is, what we refer to as wriggle room.

Wriggle room, as the term is defined in this book, is a subcategory of the broader concept of autonomy. It refers to the scope or extent of action space that a state has within a legal framework, that is, the degree of flexibility, choice, and discretion that this relationship provides. This term will be further unpacked and its implications spelled out in Chapter 2. For our purposes, given our emphasis on Norway, and the fact that Norway sometimes finds itself squeezed between the EU and the UK, it is particularly interesting to do two things. For one, examine the wriggle room that is available within the legally regulated EU – Norway arrangement; and for two, whether and how that wriggle room has been affected by Brexit. We are interested in examining whether and to what extent the EEA Agreement (in particular) would be a legally regulated straitjacket for third countries, and to what extent there is leverage or scope for action for third countries within the context of this arrangement. Further, we examine if there are tangible changes post-Brexit given that there is a new and less binding UK-EU agreement, and a new UK-Norway agreement, which mirrors much of the TCA. Our understanding of wriggle room thus relates directly to the nature and implications of the legally regulated relationship between Norway and the EU, Norway and the UK, and the EU and the UK. Thus far no systematic examination of the relevant aspects of wriggle room in the EU-Norway relationship has been conducted; nor is there any systematic examination along the triangular Norway-EU-UK lines. This book fills these gaps.

What is also not much discussed in the literature is what form and scope for autonomy a third country has under such conditions of legally regulated albeit highly asymmetrical relations. Autonomy extends well beyond those easier-to-measure traits that wriggle room directs us to focus on and has an important *subjective* component: autonomy hinges on how much action space actors consider themselves to have. The overall scope for autonomy is therefore more difficult to measure than is the scope for wriggle room, and it is likely to be contested among different actors. Further, as noted, autonomy refers to the will and ability to pursue what one takes to be one's interest and stake out one's own future (beyond a state's action room within the legal framework); how and to what extent a third country is able to compensate for the negative effects of constraints imposed by the form and contents of the EU affiliation; and the capacities as well as social support that a third country has for staking out its own desired course regardless of the formal EU affiliation.

Finally, the discussion of autonomy has thus far focused on states and, as we develop further in Chapter 2, resonates with the literature on state autonomy and with the EU's focus on strategic autonomy. However, there is also a further body of literature on individual autonomy that is relevant here, not the least because the EEA Agreement effectively makes EEA-EFTA citizens economic citizens of the EU (Olsen, 2014). We develop this notion in Chapter 7, but the main thrust of this book is to discuss the state dimension of autonomy.

The list of traits to be associated with autonomy shows that, in addition to autonomy being a broad concept, several factors need to be accounted for in order to understand the implications of autonomy (in relation to states). Autonomy-relevant traits of third countries are, for instance, Norway's political system, its political culture, its public administration, and its society.

For Norway these observations suggest that the wriggle room the country may have within the context of the legally regulated EU affiliation is related to Norway's de facto autonomy of will (e.g., autonomous agenda-setting), which implies that Norway-internal factors need to be taken into account. Hence, we query whether or to what extent Norway has established a clear position on what it wants in relation to the EU. Along the same lines, Norway's autonomy of action (including Norway-generated and autonomous implementation and practicing of law) becomes important. Wriggle room is part of that but far from the whole story given that it is directed at the action space that is available within the context of the formal and legal Norway-EU affiliation. In addition, autonomy focuses on the de facto room of manoeuvre that institutions and actors may *actually* enjoy (as understood by an outside observer) and *perceive* themselves to enjoy. As such, we expect that empirical observations of autonomy can be de-coupled from the limitations of wriggle room.

Triangular relations and dynamics

A key feature of the book is the focus on triangular Norway-EU-UK relations. Unpacking this complex web of political, institutional, and economic relations, the triangle consists of i) relationships between all three (Norway-EU-UK); ii) three sets of bilateral relationships (EU-Norway, EU-UK, and Norway-UK); and iii) options all three have to 'go it alone' in specific policies, if not overall. In practice, of course, the EU and Norway have not chosen the unilateral option, which is only important as the counterfactual to the triangular and bilateral relationships that have been preferred.

In terms of power and influence, the EU-Norway relationship is highly asymmetrical and brings up the question of how much wriggle room there is for Norway in its EU-relation. Norway is small, also in comparison to the UK, although we cannot ignore possible variation across sectors, such as the energy sector where Norway, in the 2022 European energy crisis, played a critical role as Europe's largest single gas supplier (see Chapter 3).

Nevertheless, size matters, and this difference in size is, if anything, compounded by the fact that Norway is closely associated with the UK. Norway's UK relationship can have spillover effects on Norway's relationship with the EU, and Norway's relationship with the EU can have spillover effects on Norway's relationship with the UK. Hence, there is an inevitable need to adopt a triangular Norway-EU-UK focus. Norway, it has often been noted, is both 'inside' and 'outside' the EU at the same time (NOU 2012:2). The book provides an overview of the EEA Agreement and compares that with the TCA. Further, it examines triangular Norway-EU-UK relations in depth within a range of important issue-areas. This collection helps the reader to get a better sense of the range and the breadth of arrangements that make up Norway's EU affiliation. The issue-areas selected here are climate and energy (Chapter 3); fisheries and agriculture (Chapter 4); trade and development (Chapter 5); foreign, security, and defence policies (Chapter 6); and citizenship, mobility, and migration (Chapter 7).

The book demonstrates that even a non-member such as Norway is, in significant ways, internally organised for relationship(s) with the EU and is, at the same time, trying to reconcile that with its relationship with the UK.[12]

What are the defining features of Norway's EU affiliation?

There are at least three different ways of understanding or reading Norway's affiliation with the EU. This book sheds light on all three: i) the EEA Agreement, ii) the other agreements that Norway has with the EU, and iii) the domestic political and social context that these agreements are embedded within. This chapter focuses on the two first (legal) aspects, with explicit reference to the formal affiliation, in other words the various agreements that tie Norway to the EU.

The EEA Agreement is the most comprehensive association agreement that Norway has entered in modern times, and it enjoys considerable popular support (see Chapters Eight and Nine). Norway's distinct EU affiliation is often presented as a domestic depoliticising compromise: It has enabled EU membership opponents to keep Norway out of the EU, it has often kept the EU out of Norway's own politics, and at the same time it has provided EU membership proponents with guaranteed access to the EU's internal market and almost all EU programs (Egeberg and Trondal, 1999; Fossum, 2010; Rye, 2019). Norway entered the EEA Agreement with the EU before the 1994 EU membership referendum, where a small majority of the Norwegian population voted against EU membership. Therefore, the membership rejection had no bearing on the status of the EEA Agreement.

Overview of the agreements: the EEA

Norway is associated with the EU through a wide range of agreements. The White Paper that examined Norway's EU affiliation in 2012 reported well over 70 agreements (NOU 2012:2); there are now more than 100 (Kühn and Trondal, 2023). Substantively, these range from the internal market, Schengen association agreements, agreements on asylum and police cooperation (Dublin I, II, and III), agreements on foreign and security policy (Norway participates in the EU's battle groups), agreements on internal security and justice, and fisheries, to name a few. Through these agreements, Norway has incorporated roughly three-quarters of EU legislation compared to those EU member states that have incorporated everything (NOU 2012:2, pp. 2–3). Key areas that fall outside the scope of the cooperation are the euro, the Customs Union and foreign trade policy, the Common Agricultural Policy, the Common Fishery Policy, and taxation. However, even some of these areas are affected by the rules of the single market. Free movement of capital affects taxation rules, and a substantial number of veterinary and food safety rules are included in the agreement.

The most important single agreement by far here is the EEA Agreement which came into effect in 1994 (Lichtenstein's took effect 1 May 1995) and was intended to include the remainder of the EFTA[13] states in the EU's internal market. When the EEA Agreement took effect, the EEA-EFTA countries had to incorporate all relevant EU legislation that was in effect at the time of signing the agreement. The EEA Agreement is intended to ensure legal homogeneity within the entire 30-member EEA (the 27 EU members and Iceland, Lichtenstein, and Norway). The 'reward' for the EEA-EFTA states would be assured participation in the EU internal market basically on a par with an EU member state.

The main objective of the EEA Agreement was:

> to establish a dynamic and homogeneous European Economic Area, based on common rules and equal conditions of competition and providing for the adequate means of enforcement including at the judicial level, and achieved on the basis of equality and reciprocity and of an overall balance of benefits, rights and obligations for the Contracting Parties.
>
> *(Agreement on the European Economic Area, 1994)*[14]

Homogeneity refers to

> an economic area based on common rules and equal conditions of competition, and providing for the equivalent means of enforcement, including at the judicial level. Because it is dynamic, the homogeneity is also maintained when rules and interpretation of rules change in the EU.
>
> *(Fossum and Graver, 2018, p. xvii)*[15]

The EEA-EFTA countries participate in most aspects of the EU's internal market (the agriculture and fisheries sectors are formally speaking exempted, but even here there is a lot of Europeanisation) even if they are not part of the EU's Customs Union (that is also the case with Switzerland). In contrast to Switzerland's (broad range of) sectoral bilateral agreements, the EEA Agreement is a broad and dynamic multilateral agreement between the 27 post-Brexit EU member states and the three EFTA states, Iceland, Liechtenstein, and Norway.[16]

The fact that the EEA Agreement is dynamic is intended to ensure effective market participation. Each EEA-EFTA state's compliance with the evolving EEA rules is closely monitored by the EFTA Surveillance Authority (ESA). The Single Market Scoreboard reveals that the transposition deficit in the three EEA-EFTA countries is not higher than the EU member state average; for Norway's case at 0.4, it is considerably lower (European Commission, 2020).

Regarding the EEA Agreement, there has been considerable expansion into related flanking areas, such as, for example, environmental and social affairs. In addition, the dynamic nature of the EEA Agreement makes it difficult for a state to prevent areas that have been explicitly excluded from the agreement subsequently being pulled into its orbit. For Norway, a telling example is agriculture. It is politically very sensitive and was *explicitly excluded* from the initial EEA Agreement. At present, 40 per cent of the rules and regulations that Norway incorporates are in the field of foodstuffs (see Chapter 4). Important reasons for inclusion were the need for market access for fish and the sheer dynamics of horizontal expansion. These provisions are not confined to border-crossing activities but cover internal affairs:

> In practice today, this body of regulations makes up the main portion of all public regulation pertaining to production, sale, labelling, hygiene and so forth with regard to fish and agriculture in Norway and to a large extent sets the standards in both these sectors.
> *(NOU 2012:2, pp. 2, 646–647, authors' translation)*

The situation of agriculture for Norway shows how the affiliated non-member loses control over an issue-area that it explicitly sought to *remove* from the trade-off equation and testifies to how difficult it can be – within a dynamic process of EU integration – to fence off one particular policy or sector as an area of 'self-rule'. However, the Norwegian government maintains a system of subsidies that it has considered necessary to sustain thriving rural communities in a country where the conditions for large-scale farming are challenging.

EEA Article 105 states that the EEA Committee 'shall keep under constant review the development of the case law of the Court of Justice of the European Communities and the EFTA Court' and take measures 'to preserve the homogeneous interpretation of the Agreement' (Agreement between the EFTA States on the Establishment of a Surveillance Authority and a Court of Justice, 1994). Article 106 states that

> In order to ensure as uniform an interpretation as possible of this Agreement, in full deference to the independence of courts, a system of exchange of information concerning judgments by the EFTA Court, the Court of Justice of the European Communities and the Court of First Instance of the European Communities and the Courts of last instance of the EFTA States shall be set up by the EEA Joint Committee.
> *(Agreement between the EFTA States on the Establishment of a Surveillance Authority and a Court of Justice, 1994)*

In the event of differences or disputes over the interpretation of the agreement, EEA Article 111 empowers the EEA Joint Committee to settle the dispute according to principles laid down in that article. Thus, we see that in the final instance the settlement of disputes over interpretation is political and not judicial (Fossum and Graver, 2018, pp. 36–37).

Thus, the presentation shows that the EEA Agreement places the EEA-EFTA states in a quandary: they want and seek assured single market access whilst retaining national sovereignty. With assured market access comes a system of legal oversight and sanction that is clearly directed and operated by the EU. Even that does not ensure full homogeneity: when the EU undergoes a treaty change, there is no mechanism in the EEA Agreement to update its rules as a follow-up to such changes in the EU. A similar point applies to the fact that EU law develops through a dynamic interpretation by the Court of Justice of the European Union (CJEU), based on a teleological approach to the rules; or, in other words, an assumption by the CJEU that Union law is to be interpreted as aiming at an 'end' of European integration. The EFTA Court is anxious to ensure legal homogeneity and therefore relates to the new EU legislation (Fredriksen and Franklin, 2015, p. 649). The implication is that insofar as EEA rules are subsequently changed through legal interpretation, 'this means that legislation is changed without any collaboration from the EFTA countries' (Graver, 2016, p. 818).

The EEA Agreement's institutional structure is designed as a two-pillar structure with bridging institutions, as well as a court and a surveillance body.[17] This arrangement (with the exception of EU agencification, see Egeberg and Trondal, 2015) ensures formal sovereignty for the EEA-EFTA states. It does not, however, ensure autonomy, since the rule import is a one-way street, from the EU to the EEA-EFTA states. There is no mechanism for reciprocal rule export from the EEA-EFTA states to the EU. The institutional structure, to some extent, cloaks this; however, it does not alter the facts on the ground.

Overview of the other EU-Norway agreements: Schengen and beyond

The Schengen rules cover several areas, namely rules on checks on persons at the outer borders, harmonisation of the conditions of entry and of the rules on visas for short stays (up to three months), enhanced police cooperation (including rights of cross-border surveillance and hot pursuit), and stronger judicial cooperation on criminal cases through a faster extradition system and transfer of enforcement of criminal judgments on police cooperation. In addition, the agreement includes the establishment and development of the Schengen Information System (SIS). The SIS is a large-scale information system that supports external border control and law enforcement cooperation in the Schengen states. Schengen has its own institutional arrangements that differ from those of the EEA. The main institution is the Mixed Committee, which is made up of the EU member states, the European Commission, and the four associated countries: Norway, Iceland, Switzerland, and Liechtenstein. All Schengen relevant issues that arise in the ongoing cooperation are discussed in this committee. There is no common decision-making body as within the EEA. The agreement has a guillotine clause: should either Iceland or Norway decide not to adopt new Schengen legislation that has been enacted in the EU, the agreement shall be considered terminated with respect to Iceland or Norway, unless the Mixed Committee, after a careful examination of ways to continue the agreement, decides otherwise within 90 days.[18] The Schengen acquis is dynamic and develops by changes in the EU legislation that is included in the association agreement. There is no Schengen Court, and the EFTA Court is not empowered to deal with issues that arise under the Schengen agreements. Nevertheless, the Mixed Committee keeps a watchful eye on the development of the case law of the CJEU and the competent courts of Norway and Iceland relating to such provisions.

Norway has signed several additional parallel agreements with the EU, including, for example, agreements on asylum and police cooperation (Dublin I and II) and on foreign and security policy – Norwegian troops are at the disposal of the EU's battle groups. The Norwegian Official Report that produced the largest-ever assessment of the EEA Agreement estimated that around 75 per cent of all of the EU's laws and regulations apply to Norway (NOU 2012:2, p. 2).[19]

The dense form of affiliation that makes up the sum total of the Norway model generates its own pressures for contiguity in norms, rules, and interpretations, which show up in how domestic institutions operate. Two telling examples pertain to how the Norwegian Supreme Court, in the rulings Nye Kystlink and Bottolvs, voluntarily adapted to EU law and did so in issue-areas that were *not* regulated by the EEA Agreement (Fredriksen, 2015). In a situation of tight regulation coupled with 'regulatory gaps', rule contiguity becomes important. The institutions within a closely associated non-member will feel strong domestic pressures for filling in whatever 'gaps' there are between the different agreements that the country has signed with the EU (Fredriksen, 2015).

The onus on uniformity is not only to be found on the side of the EEA-EFTA countries. The recent CJEU Case C-897/19 I.N.:

> Strengthens the impression of the EEA/EFTA States as 'insiders' rather than 'outsiders' also in matters where the application of EEA law is affected by parts of EU law that fall outside the scope of the EEA Agreement, but which are covered by other agreements between the EEA/EFTA States and the EU.
>
> *(Fredriksen, 2020, p. 1)*

Decision-shaping and scope for political participation

The presentation thus far has shown that the EEA-EFTA states have extensive rights and obligations in relation to the EU, and their participation in the EU's internal market is so extensive that it is almost on a par with member states. This form of market participation, similar to de facto economic membership, does not, of course, extend to the political realm, because the EEA-EFTA states have only limited access to EU decision-making forums; they are barred from participation with co-decision rights in the European Council, the Council, COREPER, and the European Parliament (EP).

Within the framework of the EEA Agreement, Norway has a number of experts in EU bodies and committees, especially in the European Commission (NOU 2012:2, pp. 2, 824, 829–830). In issues regulated by the Schengen agreement, Norway has the right to participate in meetings (without voting rights) in the Council and has representatives in the committees under the Council.

The Norwegian Parliament has six representatives in the EEA Parliamentary Committee, gets access (through invitation) to the EU's system of interparliamentary coordination (COSAC), and has the right to be present in the interparliamentary committee on foreign and security policy. There are also explicit measures taken by Norway to get better access to the EU system. For instance, the Norwegian Parliament has an office in Brussels that is located within the European Parliament. The Norwegian EU Delegation in Brussels understands itself as a spokesperson for Norwegian interests, and Norwegian regions and local government bodies have representatives present in Brussels.[20] The same applies to various business and trade union interests.

The fact that the EEA-EFTA states have comprehensive rights and obligations without participation in EU decision-making suggests that the relationship is a matter of taxation without representation given that EEA-EFTA member states and Switzerland contribute to the EU budget and take part in EU programmes such as Horizon (2020) and Erasmus+ as a crucial part of their integration in the Internal Market. The EEA Agreement makes explicit this commitment: the EU and the EEA-EFTA States:

> [S]hall take the necessary steps to develop, strengthen or broaden cooperation on matters falling outside of the four freedoms, where such cooperation is considered likely to contribute to the attainment of the objectives of [the] Agreement, or is otherwise deemed by the Contracting Parties to be of mutual interest.
> *(EFTA, 2023)*

Under the EEA Agreement the financial contribution is calculated by applying a proportionality factor. Since 2011 the overall level of net contributions expressed in terms of commitments has increased. Under this scheme, Norway's contribution to the EU budget during the 2014–2019 period was 2,181,762,249 euros, whereas Switzerland's contribution for the same period was 2,196,864,781 euros (European Court of Auditors, 2021).

The earlier brief presentation of Norway's EU affiliations underlines the asymmetrical nature of the relationship. In effect, the structure posits the EU as hegemon, even if the EU is not designed to be such (Eriksen and Fossum, 2015). Nevertheless, on a strict interpretation of sovereignty, the EEA is sovereignty preserving: Norway formally does keep the legal right of final decision. The interesting question, then, is not to do with sovereignty, but with autonomy: is the EEA autonomy reducing, autonomy preserving, or even autonomy enhancing?

The EEA, arguably, both constrains choices and creates choices Norway would not otherwise have. Accordingly, our concern is less with formal sovereignty and more with actual influence, which we track along the lines of wriggle room and autonomy.

Comparing Norway and the UK's affiliation to the EU

The UK's affiliation with the EU after Brexit has received massive attention in the media and among researchers. On Christmas Eve of 2021 the EU and the UK announced that they had reached an agreement. The EU-UK Trade and Cooperation (TCA) agreement secures UK trade with the EU but is far less ambitious than the EEA Agreement. With Brexit, the UK exited both the EU's internal market and Customs Union, with some significant consequences for the trading relationship between the UK and the EU. With regards to trade, two consequences are worth considering in detail.

First, by exiting the single market and Customs Union, British products are no longer automatically accredited in the EU. A central characteristic of the EU's single market and Customs Union is the harmonisation of many product standards and the mutual recognition of many more standards between EU countries. Leaving the Customs Union adds the further difficulty that British products are now subject to documentation requirements from which they were previously exempt. Border controls and documentation requirements reduce and delay trade between the UK and the EU. They are prominent examples of how the removal of tariffs through the Trade and Cooperation Agreement still leaves non-tariff obstacles to trade. In comparison to the UK's new trading relationship under the TCA, Norway is far less exposed to non-tariff barriers to trade with the EU. Membership of the EEA Agreement means that it is part of the EU's single market (with the exception of fisheries and agriculture). It, therefore, operates much the same system of regulation and standards. Although, like the UK, Norway is not a part of the EU's Customs Union, that is less administratively burdensome in the Norwegian than the British case, given that Norway is already aligned with the EU through the single market and is more of a resource-based economy with far less non-EU input into the articles it produces.

The second noteworthy consequence is caused by the UK's exit from the Customs Union. Exiting the Customs Union allows the UK to negotiate its own trade agreements with third states and other trade blocs. Norway has already shown how that wriggle room can be used to shape its global trade policy either bilaterally or in consortium with the other EFTA states. Although the TCA gives UK exporters tariff and quota free access to the EU market, the exit from the Customs Union will have particular consequences for the UK. Most importantly, the TCA subjects EU and UK exports to rules of origin requirements. Rules of origin requirements ensure that the goods traded without tariffs originate in the UK or the EU and not from countries outside the UK and EU member states. Products without a qualifying level of processing in the UK or EU will be subject to tariffs. But perhaps even more important is that all goods are now being checked with regard to their origin, which has had particularly negative effects for the extensive trade in agricultural products and seafood (see Chapter 4).

This change with the TCA creates challenges for companies in the UK that formerly had tariff-free access to the EU market for their products. For instance, the car producer Nissan, which relies on the import of batteries from Asia, has announced that it will have to start producing its batteries in the UK at a larger expense to comply with the rules of origin requirements (see also Chapter 3) (Bailey, 2021). For Norwegian companies, this is a less pertinent problem as they have never been part of the EU's Customs Union and thus have complied with rules of origin requirements in their trade with the EU since the entry into force of the EEA Agreement. However, for UK businesses, the change from EU membership to TCA involves a complicated change in requirements for trade and loss of trade benefits.

The TCA also has consequences for the trilateral relationship between the EU-UK and Norway. Overlapping bilateral trade agreements are generally less beneficial than common agreements. The TCA has consequences for Norway and the EEA Agreement. The main reason for this is the earlier-mentioned rules of origin requirements which again may lead to stricter border controls and a larger demand for documentation of products traded between Norway, the EU, and UK.

The EEA Agreement secures Norway's participation in the EU's common market including the free movement of goods, services, capital, and persons. The TCA is a much less comprehensive agreement and focuses on free trade between the UK and the EU for goods that meet rule of origin requirements, some facilitation on trade in services, a framework for law enforcement and judicial cooperation in criminal and civil law matters, as well as a horizontal agreement on governance. The British exit from the Union enables British autonomy over several policy areas that have been politically important for policymakers, inter alia the ability to conclude bilateral trade agreements with third parties and the control over British migration policies. Yet the exit from the common market and Customs Union has led to a more complicated relationship between the European non-members and members of the Union, which we will explore further in the next chapters.

Before concluding, we will briefly outline the governance arrangements in the TCA. That is important for the question of autonomy. Two sets of considerations are key. One pertains to the scope and structure of the arrangement, the other to the role of politics versus law. The more the arrangement is operated through political negotiations rather than legally binding rules (and a court as overseer), the more we should think of this in terms of autonomy rather than wriggle room.

TCA governance arrangements

In the following we provide a brief overview of the governing arrangements built into the TCA. These are, in summary form:

Single Structure. By adopting the TCA, the UK has chosen to regulate its external affiliation with the EU through i) a single treaty, ii) a single over-arching institutional framework, and iii) a single dispute mechanism. Those 'singularities' are at least one way in which the TCA is closer to the EEA than to the Swiss model of multiple bilateral agreements. There is also a further commitment to try to keep to a single framework over time. Any further bilateral agreements the EU and UK conclude in the future will be supplementing agreements to the TCA unless provided otherwise.

Mutual Consent. The working of the agreement will be overseen by a Partnership Council (PC) co-chaired by a member of the Commission and a UK Government Minister. The PC will be supported by a system of joint committees: a trade committee, 10 specialised in trade matters and eight specialised on energy, air transport, aviation safety, road transport, social security coordination, fisheries, law enforcement and judicial cooperation, and Union programmes. At all levels decisions will require the mutual consent of the UK government and the EU.

Dynamic Elements. As seen, the TCA is mainly a commitment to create a free-trade area by removing tariffs at boundaries. That can be achieved through a largely static treaty. Now that the EU and UK have decided by treaty to remove tariffs at boundaries, they don't need to decide much more together. All they need is a body (the Partnership Council) to oversee that each separately implements what they have already agreed to remove tariffs, together with a mechanism to resolve disputes. In complete contrast, a single market – and, therefore, the EEA – seeks to remove barriers to trade behind borders. That really does require a dynamic treaty: a continuous commitment to go on adding to what was decided in the initial treaty by continuing to make further law together and to interpret and administer that law together. All that said, there are some clauses of the TCA that allow the scope of the cooperation to be expanded from 'within the agreement'.

Dispute Settlement. The TCA, and decisions taken under it by the PC, are legally binding on the EU and UK under public international law. Disputes on how the EU or UK should interpret or apply their obligations can, if not resolved by the parties themselves, be arbitrated by an independent tribunal. If either side fails to comply with an arbitration agreement, the other can suspend parts of the agreement with some scope for cross-retaliation. For example, tariffs can be imposed in response to other breaches.

Review and Exit. The TCA is due for review every five years, and either party can terminate the agreement with 12 months' notice. There is also a fast-track termination procedure that allows either party to terminate in 30 days if another is in breach of 'shared principles'. Those include democracy, human rights, the rule of law, and the fight against climate change. Either could terminate if the other does not keep to the Paris Accords, and, conceivably, either could terminate if the other withdrew from the ECHR.

This brief overview reveals that the TCA is a governing arrangement that is less comprehensive, less binding, and more subject to political negotiations than the EEA Agreement. That suggests that the relationship between autonomy and wriggle room is different in the two cases: more prominent and relevant for Norway than for the UK. Having said that, we need to see how the TCA develops over time, given that the agreement is built to develop.

The contents of the book

The present chapter introduces the key themes of the book. Chapter 2 is titled 'Autonomy and wriggle room' and provides the book's basic analytical framework. Chapter 3 titled 'Post-Brexit climate and energy policy in the EU, UK, and Norway: A new trilateral relationship?' is the first of five substantive chapters that assess the scope for autonomy and wriggle room in a range of key policy areas. Chapter 4 follows up with an in-depth study of the conditions for autonomy and wriggle room in the primary industries and is titled 'Fisheries, aquaculture, and agriculture: Autonomy and wriggle room in primary industry policies'. Chapter 5 focuses on 'Global trade and development' and complements the discussion of autonomy and wriggle room with the EU-external dimension. Chapter 6 is titled 'Flexible association in foreign, security, and defence policy: A case of gradually diminishing autonomy?' and, as the title suggests, taps into the situation in the important foreign, security, and defence fields. Chapter 7 is titled 'Citizenship, migration, and mobility'. It complements the other chapters' emphasis on state autonomy with the notion of personal autonomy that we associate with citizenship. Chapters 3 through 7 have focused on understanding the relationship between autonomy and wriggle room in a range of important policy areas. All of these chapters take Norway's affiliations with the EU as the point of departure and assesses wriggle room and autonomy from that vantage point. Chapter 8, titled 'Autonomy under complex interdependence – the case of Norway and lessons for Brexit?', shifts the focus to the Norwegian domestic situation and queries what aims the government and key political actors have in relation to the EU (autonomy of will), whether there is an active effort to expand autonomy by search for options, and what capabilities the state has to pursue its aims. Chapter 9, titled 'Not much wriggle room: Brexit and the Norway model', shifts the focus to the UK and examines the UK's reception of and discussion of the Norway model. Chapter 10 holds the conclusion.

The book provides a theoretical framework that it applies to the triangular Norway-EU-UK relations across a range of important issue-areas. The list of issue-areas is far from complete, but the issue-areas cover both the internal and external conditions for wriggle room and autonomy. The issue-areas we have selected also encompass the different portions of Norway's EU affiliation: the single market, Schengen, and foreign, security, and defence policy as well as the two important exceptions, agriculture and fisheries. The book also covers areas that have become increasingly politicised and have led to calls for increased autonomy in the UK, namely global trade relations and migration. Arguably, the issue-areas that have been selected are also the ones that have most frequently been debated in Norway-EU relations. These issue-areas are thus also important in the context of EU-UK relations.

Notes

1 Even the majority in the 2019 election was in seats, not votes. It also remains unclear how far the hard approach to Brexit taken after that election will correspond to a majority of British opinion in the long run.
2 David Cameron resigned as the prime minister after six years in office, 13 July 2016, after the British public took the decision to reject his entreaties and exit the EU. Theresa May entered office but stepped down 24 July 2019 as she repeatedly failed to achieve parliamentary support for the legislation needed to implement the Brexit withdrawal agreement. Her successor, Boris Johnson, in charge when the UK formally exited the Union on 31 January 2020, resigned 6 September 2022, after several scandals. Liz Truss took over but initiated economic reforms that proved unpopular and was followed by Rishi Sunak, who took over the office 25 October 2022.
3 EU Canada Trade Agreement (CETA)(2017) Available at: https://policy.trade.ec.europa.eu/eu-trade-relationships-country-and-region/countries-and-regions/canada/eu-canada-agreement_en (Accessed 9 February 2023).
4 The EU UK Trade and Cooperation Agreement (2021) Available at: https://commission.europa.eu/strategy-and-policy/relations-non-eu-countries/relations-united-kingdom/eu-uk-trade-and-cooperation-agreement_en (Accessed 9 February 2023). For a comparison of TCA and CETA, see Neuwahl (2020).
5 For UK government sources, see: Policy papers and consultations – GOV.UK (www.gov.uk). For a brief list of academic assessments, see Gstöhl and Phinnemore (2019) for an overview of third countries' EU affiliations; Svendsen (2022) on third countries security and defense; Fossum (2019) and Fossum and Graver (2018) on the Norway model; Dardanelli and Mazzoleni (2021) and Lavenex and Schwok (2015) and Lavenex and Veuthey (2023) on Switzerland; Jonsdottir (2013) on Iceland; Frommelt (2016, 2017, 2018) on Lichtenstein. Further, a useful source of information is: Home – UK in a changing Europe (ukandeu.ac.uk).
6 Consider the famous 'Barnier staircase'(Barnier, 2017).
7 There is some debate about whether the Sunak government gave some thought to the Swiss model on taking office in 2022. See the *Financial Times* 21 November 2022. www.ft.com/content/5bc9fd89-dd20-4848-b1ba-8abe646c643c.
8 For important assessments, see for instance Gstöhl and Phinnemore (2019); Frommelt (2016, 2017, 2018). Within Norway, the EEA has been mainly analysed from a legal perspective. See Arnesen et al. (2018). Clear gaps are lack of studies of the effects of Europeanisation on socio-economic models. The Nordic model is a case in point (Fossum, 2023).
9 There is a large body of literature on sovereignty. For different positions, see in particular Bartelson (1995); Jackson (2000); Holsti (2004). For critical assessments, see for instance Krasner (1999); McCormick (1999).

10 This definition dovetails with much of the state autonomy debate that took place in the 1980s. See for instance Nordlinger (1981); Skocpol (1985); Fossum (1997). It also resonates with current EU debates on strategic autonomy (see Chapter 2).
11 This is well reflected in the central role of law in fostering social integration. See the body of literature on 'integration through law' (Cappelletti et al., 1986; Stein, 1981).
12 See NOU (2012:2); Olsen (2002).
13 EFTA was established in 1960 and now has four members: Iceland, Liechtenstein, Norway, and Switzerland. Three of these countries are members of the EEA, but not Switzerland.
14 For a comprehensive overview of the specific provisions of the EEA Agreement, see Arnesen et al. (2018).
15 On the principle of dynamic homogeneity in EEA law, see Hreinsson (2015).
16 For overviews of Norway's relationship with the EU, see Claes and Tranøy (1999); Eriksen and Fossum (2014, 2015); Fossum (2019); Fossum and Graver (2018); NOU (2012:2); Sverdrup (1998). For Iceland's relationship, see Jonsdottir (2013); Thorhallsson (2004, 2019). For overviews of Lichtenstein's relations with the EU, see Frommelt (2016, 2017, 2018).
17 The first pillar is constituted by the EU institutions; the second one by the EEA-EFTA institutions. There are also joint bodies to implement the EEA Agreement. 'The two-pillar structure is necessary because the EEA-EFTA States have not transferred any legislative competences to the EU or to the joint EEA bodies. In addition, the EEA-EFTA States are also, [. . .] constitutionally unable to accept binding decisions made by the EU institutions directly' (Frommelt, 2019).
18 Council Decision of 17 May 1999 on Certain Arrangements for the Application of the Agreement Concluded by the Council of the European Union and the Republic of Iceland and the Kingdom of Norway concerning the association of those two states with the implementation, application and development of the Schengen (Acquis, 1999, art.8(4)).
19 For Iceland's agreements with the EU, see EU Commission (2023).
20 For an assessment of the role of such regional offices, see Haugen (2022).

References

Agreement between the EFTA States on the Establishment of a Surveillance Authority and a Court of Justice (1994) *Official Journal of the European Communities*, L 344/1, 31 December.

Agreement on the European Economic Area (1994) *Official Journal of the European Communities*, L 1/3, 3 January.

Arnesen, F., Fredriksen, H. H., Graver, H. P., Mestad, O. and Vedder, C. (eds) (2018) *Agreement on the European Economic Area – A Commentary*, Baden-Baden: Nomos.

Bailey, D. (2021) *Battery Production: A Challenge after Brexit*, UK in a Changing Europe. Available at: https://ukandeu.ac.uk/battery-production-a-challenge-after-brexit. (Accessed 24 January 2023; 8 February 2023).

Barnier, M. (2017) *Slide Presented by Michel Barnier, European Commission Chief Negotiator, to the Heads of State and Government at the European Council (Article 50) on 15 December 2017*. Available at: https://commission.europa.eu/publications/slide-presented-michel-barnier-european-commission-chief-negotiator-heads-state-and-government_en#details (Accessed 10 February 2023).

Bartelson, J. (1995) *A Genealogy of Sovereignty*, Cambridge: Cambridge University Press.

Cameron-Chileshe, J. and Thomas, D. (2022) *Rishi Sunak Rules Out Swiss-style Trade Deal with EU*. Available at: www.ft.com/content/5bc9fd89-dd20-4848-b1ba-8abe646c643c (Accessed 24 January 2023).

Cappelletti, M., Seccombe, M. and Weiler, J. H. H. (1986) *Integration Through Law*, Berlin: De Gruyter.
Claes, D. H., and Tranøy, B. S. (eds) (1999) *Utenfor, annerledes og suveren? Norge under EØS-avtalen*, Bergen: Fagbokforlaget.
Council Decision of 17 May 1999 on Certain Arrangements for the Application of the Agreement Concluded by the Council of the European Union and the Republic of Iceland and the Kingdom of Norway Concerning the Association of Those Two States with the Implementation, Application and Development of the Schengen Acquis (1999) *Official Journal of the European Communities*, L 176/31, 10 July.
Dardanelli, P. and Mazzoleni, O. (eds) (2021) *Dealing with Europe – What can the UK Learn from the Swiss Experience?*, London: Routledge.
Duff, A. (2013) 'The Case for an Associate Membership of the European Union', *LSE Blogs*, 3 March. Available at: http://blogs.lse.ac.uk/europpblog/2013/03/06/associate-eu-membership/(Accessed 8 February 2023).
EFTA (2023) *EU Programmes with EEA EFTA Participation*. Available at: www.efta.int/eea/eu-programmes (Accessed 24 January 2023).
Egeberg, E. and Trondal, J. (1999) 'Differentiated Integration in Europe: The Case of the EEA Country Norway', *Journal of Common Market Studies*, 37(1): 133–142.
Egeberg, M. and Trondal, J. (2015) 'National administrative sovereignty – under pressure', in Eriksen, E. O. and Fossum, J. E. (eds) *The European Union's Non-Members: Independence Under Hegemony?*, London: Routledge.
Eriksen, E. O. and Fossum, J. E. (eds) (2014) *Det norske paradoks – Om Norges forhold til Den europeiske union*, Oslo: Universitetsforlaget.
Eriksen, E. O. and Fossum, J. E. (eds) (2015) *The European Union's Non-Members: Independence under Hegemony?*, London: Routledge.
EU Commission (2023) *Iceland. EU Trade Relations with Iceland. Facts, Figures and Latest Developments*. Available at: https://policy.trade.ec.europa.eu/eu-trade-relationships-country-and-region/countries-and-regions/iceland_en (Accessed 24 January 2023).
European Commission (2020) *Single Market Scoreboard: Norway*. Available at: https://single-market-scoreboard.ec.europa.eu/countries/norway_en (Accessed 2 January 2023).
European Court of Auditors (2021) *Financial Contributions from Non-EU Countries to the EU and Member States*. Luxemburg: European Court of Auditors. Available at: Review N° 03/2021: Financial contributions from non-EU countries to the EU and Member States (europa.eu) (Accessed 2 January 2023).
Fossum, J. E. (1997) *Oil, the State and Federalism*, Toronto: Toronto University Press.
Fossum, J. E. (2010) 'Norway's European "Gag Rules"', *European Review*, 18(1): 73–92.
Fossum, J. E. (2019) 'Norway and the European Union', in *Oxford Research Encyclopedia, Politics*, Oxford: Oxford University Press.
Fossum, J. E. (2023) 'The Norway Model and the UK Post-Brexit', in Fossum, J. E. and Lord, C. (eds) *Handbook on the European Union and Brexit*, Cheltenham: Edward Elgar, pp. 362–383.
Fossum, J. E. and Graver, H. P. (2018) *Squaring the Circle on Brexit – Could the Norway Model Work?*, Bristol: Bristol University Press.
Fredriksen, H. H. (2020) 'A "Special Relationship" Built on a Patchwork – How the CJEU Sees the EEA EFTA States', *EFTA-Studies*. Available at: www.efta-studies.org/a-special-relationship (Accessed 2 January 2023).
Fredriksen, H. H. and Franklin, C. N. K. (2015) 'Of Pragmatism and Principles: The EEA Agreement 20 Years On', *Common Market Law Review*, 52(3): 629–684.

Frommelt, C. (2016) 'Liechtenstein's Tailor-Made Arrangements in the EEA: A Small State's Creative Solutions in European Integration', in Wolf, S. (ed) *State Size Matters*, Wiesbaden, Germany: VS Springer, pp. 131–162.

Frommelt, C. (2017) *In Search of Effective Differentiated Integration: Lessons from the European Economic Area (EEA)* (Unpublished doctoral dissertation). Zurich, Switzerland: University of Zurich.

Frommelt, C. (2018) 'Lichtenstein and the EEA', in Arnesen, F., Fredriksen, H. H., Graver, H. P., Mæstad, O. and Vedder, C. (eds) *Agreement on the European Economic Area: A Commentary*, Baden-Baden: Nomos, pp. 35–58.

Frommelt, C. (2019) *Institutional Challenges in the EEA. Analysis.* Available at: www.efta-studies.org/institutional-challenges (Accessed 2 January 2023).

Graver, H. P. (2016) 'Possibilities and Challenges of the EEA as an Option for the UK After Brexit', *European Papers (EP)*, 1(3): 803–821.

Gstöhl, S. and Phinnemore, D. S. (eds) (2019) *The Proliferation of Privileged Partnerships Between the European Union and Its Neighbours*, London: Routledge.

Haugen, M. C. (2022) 'Regional Presence in the EU – A Qualitative Study of Regional Offices' Activity in Brussels', *EU3D Report* 8/22, ARENA Centre for European Studies: University of Oslo.

HM Government (2018) *EU Exit: Taking Back Control of Our Borders, Money and Laws While Protecting Our Economy, Security and Union*. Available at: https://assets.publishing.service.gov.uk/government/uploads/system/uploads/attachment_data/file/759792/28_November_EU_Exit_-_Taking_back_control_of_our_borders__money_and_laws_while_protecting_our_economy__security_and_Union__1_.pdf (Accessed 24 January 2023).

Holsti, K. J. (2004) *Taming the Sovereigns: Institutional Change in International Politics*, Cambridge: Cambridge University Press.

Hreinsson, P. (2015) 'General Principles', in Baudenbacher, C. (ed) *The Handbook of EEA Law*, New York: Springer International Publishing, pp. 349–389.

Jackson, R. (2000) *The Global Covenant: Human Conduct in a World of States*, Oxford: Oxford University Press.

Jonsdottir, J. (2013) *Europeanization and the European Economic Area Iceland's Participation in the EU's Policy Process*, London: Routledge.

Krasner, S. D. (1999) *Sovereignty – Organised Hypocrisy*, Princeton: Princeton University Press.

Kühn, N. and Trondal, J. (2023) 'Living in Between: Consequences of Associated Membership', in Fromage, D. (ed) *(Re-)defining Membership: Differentiation in and Outside the European Union*, Oxford: Oxford University Press (forthcoming).

Lavenex, S. and Schwok, R. (2015) 'The Nature of Switzerland's Relationship with the EU', in Eriksen, E. O. and Fossum, J. E. (eds) *The European Union's Non-members: Independence under Hegemony?*, London: Routledge, pp 36–51.

Lavenex, S. and Veuthey, A. (2023) 'The Swiss Model in the Context of Brexit: From "Side-Street" to "Dead-End"?', in Fossum, J. E. and Lord, C. (eds) *Handbook on the European Union and Brexit*, Cheltenham: Edward Elgar, pp. 345–361.

Lord, C. (2015) 'The United Kingdom, a Once and Future (?) Non-member State', in Eriksen, E. O. and Fossum, J. E. (eds) *The European Union's Non-members: Independence Under Hegemony?*, London: Routledge, pp. 211–229.

McCormick, N. (1999) *Questioning Sovereignty*, Oxford: Oxford University Press.

Neuwahl, N. (2020) 'The 2020 EU-UK Trade and Cooperation Agreement as a Canada Style Agreement', *EU3D Working Paper* 4/2020, ARENA Centre for European Studies: University of Oslo.

Nordlinger, E. A. (1981) *On the Autonomy of the Democratic State*, Harvard: Harvard University Press.

NOU 2012:2 (2012) 'Utenfor og innenfor – Norges avtaler med EU' ['Outside and Inside: Norway's Agreements with the European Union'] [online], *Norwegian Ministry of Foreign Affairs*. Available at: www.regjeringen.no/no/dokumenter/nou-2012-2/id669368/ (Accessed 17 January 2022).

Olsen, E. D. H. (2014) '"Utenforskapets" paradoks: mot et depolitisert statsborgerskap?', in Eriksen, E. O. and Fossum, J. E. (eds) *Det norske paradoks: Om Norges forhold til den Europeiske Union*, Oslo: Universitetsforlaget.

Olsen, J. P. (2002) 'The Many Faces of Europeanization', *Journal of Common Market Studies*, 40(5): 921–952.

Rye, L. (2019) *Norge i Europa*, Trondheim: Fagbokforlaget.

Scott, J. C. (1999) *Seeing Like a State – How Certain Schemes to Improve the Human Condition Have Failed*, New Haven: Yale University Press.

Skocpol, T. (1985) 'Bringing the State Back In: Current Research', in Evans, P., Rueschemeyer, D. and Skocpol, T. (eds) *Bringing the State Back In*, Cambridge: Cambridge University Press.

Stein, E. (1981) 'Lawyers, Judges, and the Making of a Transnational Constitution', *American Journal of International Law*, 75(1): 1–27.

Svendsen, Ø. (2022) *The Politics of Third Countries in EU Security and Defence: Norway, Brexit and Beyond*, London: Palgrave MacMillan.

Sverdrup, U. (1998) 'Norway: An Adaptive Non-member', in Hanf, K. and Soetendorp, B. (eds) *Adapting to European Integration – Small States in the EU*, London: Longman Publisher.

Thorhallsson, B. (2004) 'Shackled by Smallness: A Weak Administration as a Determinant of Policy Choice', in Thorhallsson, B. (ed) *Iceland and European Integration: On the Edge*, London: Routledge.

Thorhallsson, B. (2019) *Small States and Shelter Theory – Iceland's External Affairs*, London: Routledge.

2
AUTONOMY AND WRIGGLE ROOM

Introduction

This chapter outlines the analytical framework for the book, whose main theoretical ambition is to increase our understanding of autonomy under conditions of complex interdependence. We focus on those legally regulated forms of complex interdependence that the EU has developed with third countries and place the emphasis on Norway and the UK. As noted in Chapter 1, we introduce the notion of wriggle room as a means for capturing how much autonomy states can obtain under various forms of legally binding interstate and supranational collaboration. The state's overall autonomy can then be summed up as a function of how much autonomy it has given up through entering a system of legally binding international collaboration; how much wriggle room that legally binding collaboration provides for; how much that legally binding international collaboration improves on the state's ability to pursue its goals; and how much residual autonomy the state has in terms of will and capacity.

Our focus on autonomy under legally regulated international collaboration has implications for the structure of this chapter. We start with outlining wriggle room and thereafter proceed to the broader issue of autonomy, because the legal affiliation a third country forms with the EU affects both the terms of will-formation and the nature and access to capacity and capability that the state will have.

The next part spells out the key analytical dimensions in wriggle room. The subsequent part focuses on the broader notion of autonomy and clarifies what is meant by will and capability and provides a brief overview of the various forms or sources of capability. The final part concludes.

Unpacking wriggle room

Wriggle room, as noted earlier, is confined to the scope for autonomous action within a set of legally regulated affiliations, with emphasis on the rules and arrangements governing these. The question is how tightly the rules regulate and direct behaviour towards certain more or less clearly defined ends. Note that this is not only about whether or the extent to which the rules prevent alternative courses of action; it is also about whether the rules prevent a state from doing more or going further than the rules prescribe.[1]

Empirically in this book, wriggle room refers to Norway's ability to operate within the constraints of its EU and UK legally regulated affiliations, at all stages.

We distinguish between EU-internal and EU-external forms of wriggle room[2] because we need to know whether the EU affiliation simply constrains third countries in their relations with the EU and its member states or whether the EU affiliation also constrains third countries in their relations with non-EU actors. The very notion of wriggle room prompts a two-way investigation: the nature and scope of EU constraining (and enabling) factors (as a top-down dynamic), and the third country's will and ability to maximise the action-space available (as a bottom-up as well as across-states dynamic).

The EU-internal dimension of wriggle room pertains to Norway's ability to affect EU decisions within the various aspects of Norway's EU affiliation, such as in the internal market, state support, Schengen, and so forth. A case in point is the scope for decision-shaping in the EEA. The EU-external dimension of wriggle room pertains to whether and the extent to which Norway is constrained in its current affiliation from forming agreements with other states independently of the EU.

The book's focus on triangular Norway-EU-UK relations shows that it may be difficult to keep the EU-internal dimension separate from the EU-external one, as reflected in the fact that post-Brexit Norway has a varied set of affiliations with, respectively, the EU and the UK. Strictly speaking, those aspects of the Norway-UK relation that have direct bearing on Norway-EU relations, we discuss under EU-internal given that the EU is an important determinant here. Those aspects of Norway's external affiliations that touch on non-EU countries and matters are discussed under the heading of EU-external. When there is an ambiguity pertaining to the UK, this is discussed in relation to EU-internal and, as such, restricts the category of EU-external to non-EU, non-UK matters for the sake of clarity.

The question is how the complex set of affiliations may affect Norway's wriggle room. The two affiliations: Norway-EU and Norway-UK may pull Norway in different directions, especially if there is a growing gap between the EU and the UK or if the EU-UK affiliation becomes less rule-bound and more unpredictable. This has bearing on the extent to which we talk about wriggle room or autonomy in general: the less rule-bound interstate relations are, the more the focus shifts from wriggle room to autonomy in general.

We unpack wriggle room through several steps. The first step is to clarify the nature and scope of Norway's affiliation with the EU and the UK. Norway's EU affiliation is highly complex and pertains to a wide range and composite of affiliations, as shown in Chapter 1. A relevant question is: how similar or different are these affiliations regarding wriggle room? Some of the affiliations involve decision-shaping (EEA and Schengen); others do not. Some are dynamic and thus semi-automatically updated; others require (re)negotiations.

The second step, focusing on those involving decision-shaping, we unpack with reference to the following list, which is tailored to the assessment of the framework of rules governing EU-Norway relations. The list includes both those rules and norms that are incorporated through legislative procedures and those that are not, such as, for instance, those that incorporate Norway in EU agencies. The unpacking of wriggle room involves seven relevant items or dimensions:

a) In terms of new legislation from the EU (and new terms of agreement with the UK)
b) In terms of existing legislation
c) In terms of 'dynamic homogeneity'
d) In terms of agencification and administrative interweaving
e) In terms of sanctioning and compliance mechanisms
f) In terms of the differences between the Norway-EU and the Norway-UK formal affiliations
g) In terms of a state exiting from the EU
h) In terms of the EU-external dimension

We unpack each of these in turn.

RE: a) Wriggle room in relation to new EU legislation

Given the unidirectional nature of Norway's EU-relationship, especially in the EEA and Schengen – with Norway adopting legislation that originates in the EU – the scope for wriggle room is of great importance. Thus, as the first step, we examine the scope for Norwegian influence in the different decision stages in the EU legislative process. These are policy initiatives, range of alternatives, involvement in actual decision-making, implementation and transposition, and feedback/learning.

With regard to decision-making influence, it is well known that the earlier an actor is able to enter the decision process, the more ability one has to shape the final outcomes. The first stage of the decision-making process is labelled **initiative** and is about the ability to set a decision-making process in motion by gaining acceptance for the need to do something. What that 'something' is will normally become more clearly specified in the second stage, which is labelled **alternatives** and refers to the relevant repertoire of ways of framing the problem and terminates in a set of more specific decision options. An actor's scope for wriggle room is affected by the actor's ability to set forth one's own preferred options. Wriggle room is also affected by actors' access to knowledge of the relevant alternatives.

We explicate these two first stages in further detail now. Broadly speaking, in the EU's Community System[3] portion of the EU's decision-making system, the European Commission has the *de jure* right of initiative. However, as a non-member, Norway 'has' no commissioner, and lacks representation in the European Parliament, European Council, and Council of Ministers, all of which are relevant venues for taking decision-making initiatives.[4] This shows that Norway's ability to initiate new legislation is very limited indeed. Nevertheless, it is well-known that experts and administrative staff in the various institutions are important for policy-making; hence, presence in preparatory forums provides some access to decision-relevant knowledge. There is some scope for accessing decision-relevant knowledge of alternatives through Norway's representation in various expert groups in the European Commission. But this must be assessed in relation to the following: to what extent does this representation cover all relevant aspects of EU decision-making? The more encompassing this presence, one may assume the greater the Norwegian government's knowledge of the relevant alternatives in play in EU legislative proposals, also in terms of how proposals in different sectors might mutually impinge on each other. Here it is important to look at the effects of different facets of EU decision-making with an important distinction running between the Community System (the internal market and flanking areas for Norway regulated through the EEA Agreement) and the less legally regulated and formalised Union System (coordination of national economic policies through the European semester and foreign and security policy) on the other. Multiple questions arise from this partial access structure for Norway: to what extent does the Norwegian government actively utilise the channels of access it possesses in the EU system? Does the government instruct and prepare experts and administrators (and treat them as delegates), or are they operating as freewheeling experts with vague or no national instructions (trustees)? Where do experts' and officials' loyalties lie? Is there high turn-over of personnel so that officials have limited time for understanding the complex EU? These questions are addressed in Chapter 8.

With regard to the third, **decision-making** stage, Norway has no direct presence or influence on the forums formally making EU decisions: the European Commission, the (Union) Council, the European Parliament, and, not the least in recent years, the European Council. However, there are provisions under the EEA Agreement for some element of decision-shaping. This pertains to the institutional arrangements, notably the EEA Committee and the EEA Council. There is a right to consultation. A study of EEA-EFTA Comments between 1995 and end of 2019 showed that, out of the 242 comments from the EEA countries, close to 40 per cent of the three states' preferences were wholly attended to (Karlsen, 2020).

There is also a right of reservation in the EEA Agreement (Article 102),[5] which has never been acted upon.[6] The considerations governments make not to trigger it are quite instructive for the type of asymmetrical relationship the EEA Agreement constitutes.

The fourth stage is **implementation and transposition.** An important matter for wriggle room is the degree of flexibility that is available in the various EU provisions. Here, the distinction between EU regulations and directives is important since directives leave far more scope for local (for Norway as such as well as within different parts of Norway) adaptation than is the case with regulations. The scope for wriggle room in the affiliation is clearly affected by the form of legislation that predominates. One relevant question is if there is a clear trend in changing forms of legislation over time, and the overall tendency is towards regulations, which offer less scope for wriggle room.

The scope for wriggle room can also be discerned by looking at how much flexibility in implementation the EU accepts. There is little systematic information on the reality on the ground here, in other words how EU provisions are actually put into practice across policy areas in the 30-member large and heterogenous EEA area (27 EU members and three EEA-EFTA states) (Princen et al., 2022; Schimmelfennig et al., 2022). This also applies to the role and salience of European Administrative Networks (for an assessment, see Martinsen et al., 2022). Systematic information on how other states implement EU provisions can be a source of additional wriggle room insofar as it reveals that the EU allows for flexible implementation.

A further aspect of wriggle room pertains to the nature, scope, and impact of the Norwegian presence in the system of comitology committees, and in Commission expert committees, in other words how and to what extent Norway is able to shape EU legislation and in what policy areas that is foremostly available. As we will discuss in Chapter 8, such influence also depends on whether the government instructs its EU-posted officials or not.

The fifth stage is **feedback and learning.** This refers to the dynamic and circular process of decision-making in the sense that new decisions build upon former ones; often a new decision is meant to correct for inadequacies in a previous one. Learning then means that those making decisions have obtained relevant knowledge and feedback on the effects of previous decisions and laws. The scope for wriggle room is affected by the structure of such 'learning cycles'. The general assumption is that the less a country is involved in the four prior stages of decision-making, the less complete the learning cycle is likely to be, and the less likely it is for new decisions to correct for previous inadequacies.

Thus far we have discussed wriggle room in relation to the stages of EU decision-making to ascertain how much scope for influence there is in the formal affiliation. In addition to this, an EEA-EFTA state such as Norway can seek out other forms of influence such as lobbying. In this regard, the Norwegian Delegation in Brussels may play a key role. Norwegian regions and governments at the local level also have offices in Brussels that undertake information-seeking and lobbying activities (for an assessment and comparison of the activities of two Norwegian and Swedish regional offices, see Haugen, 2022).

There is also the question of how much need there is to wriggle in the first place? If the European Commission's proposals were aligned 100 per cent of the time with the ideal preferences of the democratic majority within Norway, there would be zero need to wriggle. Of course, that example is hugely improbable, but it does make the point that the need to wriggle could be quite low.

RE: b) Wriggle room in relation to existing legislation

We need to consider the scope for wriggle room in relation to existing legislation. This is a matter of living with the laws and regulations that were passed under a) wriggle room in relation to new legislation. Wriggle room here refers to the scope there is within existing legislative arrangements to undertake active learning (including lesson-gathering from other countries, members and non-members); actively seek out best practices; and be on the lookout for the scope of wriggle room that is available to other comparable cases and what their affiliation means. It is obvious that the wriggle room here is greater the more general and unspecific the legislation is.[7] Conversely, the more specific and tailored it is to specific cases, the less wriggle room there is. Fritz Scharpf (2009) also makes the important observation that EU legislation is difficult to reverse.

RE: c) Wriggle room and the issue of 'dynamic homogeneity'

The third step is to establish the implications that derive from the fact that several of the core affiliations are dynamic, especially the EEA. To what extent and how does what legal scholars refer to as 'dynamic homogeneity' affect or shape wriggle room?

Dynamic homogeneity entails that the operating conditions are as similar as possible across both pillars of the EEA (EU institutions and EEA-EFTA institutions).[8] This may, on the one hand, refer to the extent to which each single piece of legislation is adopted equally across the entire EEA. On the other, in a dynamically integrating European context, dynamic homogeneity is difficult to contain within the initial terms of the agreement that has been entered into (as has been the case with the EEA Agreement, see later). Dynamic homogeneity may thus foster spillover across issue-areas and expand the scope of EU legal regulation of third countries' affairs. It follows that the greater this scope for spillover across issue-areas, the less scope for wriggle room. That is particularly salient for those issue-areas that, for political reasons, were excluded from the initial EEA Agreement. This aspect of dynamic homogeneity has direct bearings on autonomy, because the more comprehensive the spillover across issue-areas, the greater the constraints on the third country's autonomous will and capacity.

For Norway, a case in point is agriculture, which is, formally speaking, outside the EEA Agreement. However, the development of special agreements in this area has, together with spillovers from other sectors (notably fishery, see Chapter 4; and climate policies, see Chapter 3) reduced the wriggle-rom for Norwegian authorities in this area too. A further instance is transportation policy, where EUs railway package 4 has caused debate on the autonomy of Norwegian railway policy (Aftenposten, 2021).

However, one caveat is needed: third-country governments (or government bodies and agents) may use the EU as a pretext for pursuing an ideologically charged (such as a particularly market-friendly) policy that need not be prescribed by the EU (Reegård, 2020). In this case, governments create the impression that dynamic homogeneity compels governments to pursue a certain line of action. This is an interesting case of Norwegian governments referring to lack of wriggle room in the EU affiliation in order to increase their autonomy in relation to domestic Norwegian actors and forces.

The case of dynamic homogeneity shows us how the dynamics of a legally integrating EU converts Norway's action-space within issue-areas from matters of autonomy to matters of wriggle room.

RE: d) Wriggle room in the context of agencification and administrative interweaving

The fourth step is to assess the implications of agencification, the growth and proliferation of independent expert bodies, and what that entails for wriggle room. The European Commission, often supported by a rapidly growing number of EU agencies, has been increasingly getting directly involved in how EU legislation is applied by member-state authorities, often by cooperating closely with national agencies (directorates and supervisory authorities), and often without consulting national ministries to an equivalent extent.

EU agencies are mainly involved in non-regulatory or quasi-regulatory activities, that is, activities that might have regulatory consequences, such as collecting information, analysing information and disseminating it, coordinating technical standards, and being involved in how member-state administrations practice EU legislation. However, some agencies have been entrusted with decision-making authority in single cases – for example, decisions vis-à-vis single stakeholders – such as the European Union Aviation Safety Agency (EASA).

One reason for this involvement across administrative levels is that the EU's executive branch of government does not have its own agencies at the national level. They compensate for that by establishing strong ties to already relatively independent national agencies, which thereby adopt a 'two-hatted' role relative to their own ministry on the one hand, and to the European Commission and the EU agencies on the other (Egeberg and Trondal, 2009). Consequently, national agencies become part of two administrations: both a national and a general EU administration. In an EEA context, the European Commission and EU agencies get involved in national application of the Union legislation and thereby challenge their wriggle room. One example is the EASA, which can decide whether an airplane should be certified to fly in European airspace. This authority is final, and national aviation authorities are subject to it.[9]

The establishment of EU agencies has mainly taken place during the last twenty years. Since 2008, the growth in the number of EU agencies has accelerated. However, their mandate is often limited to tasks related to information processing and documentation, as well as facilitation of network activities among national regulatory authorities within the same policy area. The establishment of EU agencies may be regarded as a compromise between functional needs for more regulatory capacity at the European level, and member states' reluctance to transfer power to the European Commission (Kelemen, 2002). These agencies have gradually developed a substantial administrative capacity, though still not nearly as large as that of the European Commission. We also see a steady increase in the number of EU agencies, that new agencies that are established are delegated greater formal decision-making power (in individual cases), and that such bodies are established in relatively important policy areas. To govern these agencies, management boards are established in which the composition is dominated by representatives for national authorities. Norway is represented in 31 such management boards. However, studies show that both the substantial size of the boards and the relatively low frequency of their meetings limit their capacity to govern. There also appears to be a tendency for national representatives on the boards to be poorly prepared and relatively little involved in the discussions (Busuioc and Groenleer, 2012). These are, however, not national representative's, since they tend to be the heads of the national agencies who work within the respective EU agencies' policy fields. These representatives are relatively shielded from national political steering, and thus they do not provide 'national' wriggle room for the EEA countries. In fact, studies show that the European Commission (which is also represented on the board) is the agency's most important partner in their daily work (Egeberg and Trondal, 2011).

In sum, therefore, EU agencies support the European Commission by providing additional executive power to the EU branch of executive government, and they do not provide substantive executive wriggle room for the national executive branch. They may, however, provide administrative, or executive, wriggle room for national agencies, by providing administrative networks across European states, offering first-hand expertise in different domains, opportunities for collaboration between agencies, and so on. EU agencies, in this respect, represent a mode of governing by networks more than a transformation of executive governance in Europe (Curtin and Dehousse, 2012). However, due to the *direct* relationships that many EU agencies have established vis-à-vis national agencies, such administrative ties may indeed challenge the 'national' wriggle room of national agencies and thus contribute to a circumvention of executive governance within the state (including closely affiliated non-members such as Norway). EU agencies represent administrative wriggle room in their own right at the European level, but they also directly affect administrative, or executive, wriggle room within the state.

RE: e) Wriggle room in relation to sanctioning and compliance mechanisms

When considering wriggle room, it is important to have a clear sense of the mechanisms the EU has available for monitoring and sanctioning behaviour. With regard to the EEA Agreement, the main instruments are the EFTA Court (2023) and the EFTA Surveillance Authority (ESA, 2023). In this connection, it is important, when assessing wriggle room, to establish i) whether these bodies have the same or less bite than similar EU monitoring bodies;[10] ii) what monitoring philosophies such bodies adopt;[11] and iii) whether their rulings exhibit any clear pattern, for instance, in terms of leaning primarily towards the EU or towards the EEA-EFTA country in question.

The EU also monitors compliance. The EU's Single Market Scoreboard reveals that the transposition deficit in the three EEA-EFTA countries is not higher than the EU member state average; in Norway's case at 0.4, it is considerably lower (European Commission, 2020).

EU agreements may have certain compliance elements built into them. Consider, for instance, the so-called guillotine clause in the Schengen agreement.[12] Successive Norwegian governments have proven very reluctant to activate the reservation clause in the EEA Agreement.

Under this heading of sanctioning and compliance, we also need to consider the scope for shirking, bypassing, or undermining legislation and regulations. These phenomena raise a question of where to draw the distinction between what we have referred to as wriggle room, on the one hand, and autonomy, more broadly speaking, on the other. As a rule of thumb, we may say that, insofar as the agreement leaves scope for such action, we may talk about wriggle room, especially if there is no explicit intent on the part of the third country to shirk or undermine or bypass legislation and regulations. If, however, there is a deliberate intent, we are no longer talking about wriggle room but autonomy, because it reflects a clear will and interest.

An interesting case in this connection is when a state simply abides by a national rule despite the presence of an EU-imported one. A case in point is the so-called 'NAV social benefits scandal', which centred on the question of whether welfare unemployment recipients in Norway were allowed to travel outside of Norway, and the rights and benefits of temporary workers (export of social benefits and unequal pay and other conditions) (see also Chapter 7 and Chapter 8). Pavone and Stiansen (2021) state that this was a deliberate Norwegian choice and hence would not figure under our heading of wriggle room. At the same time, it is interesting to note that it was not the EU that picked up on this but the National Insurance Court in

32 Autonomy and wriggle room

Norway, which is an independent appellate body under the Ministry of Labour in issues of social security and pensions (Pavone and Stiansen, 2021). The scope for wriggle room is therefore not simply determined at the EU level by EU bodies but by the extent to which national bodies are tailored to ensure EU compliance. This matter has been frequently discussed in relation to the ESA (is it more Catholic than the Pope?).[13]

In a similar manner, a state can shirk EU rules by formulating new national rules despite the presence of EU-imported ones. Further, we need to pay attention to the scope for containing compliance.[14] A large implementation deficit is testimony either to shirking or containing compliance. In this sense, de facto wriggle room relates to the EU's ability to monitor and sanction behaviour. In practice, the weaker the EU's ability to monitor and sanction behaviour, the greater the scope for third country autonomy. Having said that, it is important to underline – especially with regard to the broader issue of autonomy – that in matters of shared competence, an EEA-EFTA state, like an EU member state, is only constrained from not legislating where the EU has not already made law in a contrary way. In spite of its wide scope, EU law is often simply silent on a particular matter.

RE: f) Wriggle room for third countries in between EU and UK agreements

The sixth step is to compare the Norway-EU and Norway-UK affiliations on the issue of wriggle room. The relevant issues are: How similar and different are these affiliations? What is the scope for cross-pressures? How rule-bound and predictable are they? Are there differences in Norway's wriggle room within each with bearings on Norway's overall wriggle room?

One possibility is that the EU and UK decide outstanding or ongoing TCA matters first (there is also ambiguity and openness associated with the TCA, as pointed out in Chapter 1). Norway will then find itself in the difficult position of having to decide after the other two on anything to do with its TCA-like agreement with the UK. The battery example mentioned in Chapter 3 is a case in point.[15] But there are plenty of reasons to expect things to be the other way round. Precisely because of the EEA, many things that come up in the TCA with the UK may be matters that Norway and the EU have discussed first.

RE: g) Wriggle room under conditions of exiting from a system of legally binding cooperation

Wriggle room is not only relevant with regard to the circumstances under which states operate under an agreed-upon legally regulated framework such as for the EEA-EFTA states the EEA Agreement. Chapter 9 shows the relevance of this in the UK's process of exiting from the EU. Once the UK decided to leave the EU, the EU activated and specified a range of procedures for how this was to be undertaken. That amplified by the special circumstances of Northern Ireland effectively set the framework for the UK's exit from the EU and, to a large extent, also the terms under which the UK would reassociate with the EU after it had formally exited.

RE: h) The EU-external dimension of wriggle room

The eighth and final step is to consider Norway's external wriggle room. With regard to the EU-external dimension of wriggle room, a prominent argument against Norwegian EU membership has been that Norway has more international leverage and more room of manoeuvre in its relations to the world outside the EU, which is of obvious relevance to the 'global Britain' debate and the aspiration of many Brexiters to create a global Britain rather than a narrowly 'Europeanised' UK.

Formally speaking, the EEA-EFTA countries, as opposed to EU member states, are allowed to form trade and other agreements with countries outside of the EU (see Chapter 5). In that sense, Norway's EU affiliation provides more wriggle room than is the case for EU member states.

The question of whether this element of wriggle room translates into a greater scope of autonomy overall became particularly relevant when Norway took up a temporary seat in the UN Security Council. What implications, if any, does this have for wriggle room? Another interesting issue pertains to the EFTA-Mercosur agreement that has sparked criticism. While EU member states have been more vocal in opposing signing of the EU-Mercosur agreement (due to deforestation of the Amazon), the public debate regarding these issues in the EFTA countries have been almost non-existent, and national parliaments have refrained from interfering with the negotiations. We will examine what reasons the actors give for their different stances with a view to establish if this has bearings on the issue of wriggle room, as part of a broader assessment of what implications for autonomy the fact that the EFTA countries can sign their own trade agreements may have. In a similar manner, we will discuss how Norway's current relations with China show that the wriggle room to negotiate is present; however, Norway's autonomy of will depends in large part on its European counterparts moving ahead first. The same applies to what Norway, being a major international aid donor, with a strong and distinct development identity, tells us about wriggle room. While Norway enjoys autonomy of will to set their own agenda, their autonomy of action is constrained by European counterparts in multilateral fora, when their position differs from that of the EU.

To sum up thus far, the earlier section has unpacked a set of relevant dimensions to help us clarify what is meant by wriggle room in an EU–third country context. We have shown that it is useful to single out a subtheme of autonomy to discuss under the heading of wriggle room. At the same time, it is also clear that there are grey zones between what we lump under the heading of wriggle room and what we consider under the broader heading of autonomy. This problem is amplified by the fact that EU integration is dynamic. This has bearings on the analysis in the sense that we also need to consider such issues as **temporality**: the speed of EU-driven policy processes; the sequence of initiatives and their deadlines (tight/fixed versus loose/non-fixed; short-term versus long-term); the **size or scope** of EU-driven policy initiatives (these can be scaled from small to large and comprehensive initiatives); **sector-specific versus broad cross-sectoral** policy initiatives; and **stability versus instability** (we already mentioned rule-shirking/undermining, and when that happens on the part of any one actor it spills over on the triangular relationship Norway-EU-UK).

These factors show that the legal relationship is dynamic; hence, the issue of wriggle room must also be considered as having a dynamic element to it, and that, in turn, raises questions about the relationship between wriggle room and autonomy, broadly speaking. That is particularly so when we consider changes in the basic framework of rules, such as broader EU-driven reform processes and, in particular, large-scale EU treaty changes. Then the very legal framework that sets the terms for secondary legislation and the scope and application of Norway's EU affiliation changes, as was, for instance, the case with the many rounds of EU enlargements and the many EU treaty changes. Schengen is a case in point. It was initially an agreement forged outside the EU treaties, but through successive treaty changes, much of the substance of the initial agreement has become part of the *EU acquis*. In a similar manner, successive EU enlargements have fundamentally changed the dynamics of the EU's single market, for Norway, perhaps, especially through greatly heightened internal EEA migration. The point is that significant changes in the legal framework guiding EU–third country relations do not only affect the scope for wriggle room but also shape the conditions guiding autonomy.

Autonomy broadly conceived

This book defines autonomy as will and capacity, or as having choices and an ability to will choices. Our focus on autonomy draws on several sources. First is the literature on state autonomy; second is the literature on individual autonomy; and third is the EU's recent preoccupation with strategic autonomy (Council of the EU, 2016).[16] Chapter 7 is explicitly dedicated to individual autonomy and unpacks that. The remainder of the chapters focus on forms of state autonomy. We therefore focus on the notion of state autonomy in this chapter.

Autonomy as will or the pursuit of own goals

As already stated, this book's focus is on autonomy under conditions of complex interstate interdependence. That is different from the state autonomy literature that emerged in the 1980s, which was focused on state-internal matters, that is, the degree to which the state can carry through its goals in relation to society (Skocpol 1985;

Nordlinger, 1981). Nevertheless, as we show, there are important insights from this body of literature that are of relevance for understanding Norway's and the UK's autonomy in relation to the EU. Earlier studies have pointed to how the interaction between state-societal and inter-governmental dynamics have given direction to and shaped outcomes.[17]

In the following section, we start by reverting to the mainstream state-society dynamics and then move to third country–EU or, more specifically, Norway-EU relations. With regard to autonomy, the general understanding pertains to a state's or collective's will and ability to stake out its own course. This is most explicitly stated in the literature on state autonomy. As Skocpol (1985, p. 9) has noted, 'States conceived as organisations claiming control over territories and people may formulate and pursue goals that are not simply reflective of the demands or interests of social groups, classes, or society. . . . Unless such independent goal formulation occurs, there is little need to talk about states as important actors.' Still, autonomy does not necessarily translate into independence from societal actors. Eric Nordlinger (1981) formulates his state-centred model on six propositions:

a) Among the panoply of state preferences many converge with, many are compatible with, and many diverge from societal preferences.
b) When state and societal preferences do not diverge, public officials invariably translate their own preferences into authoritative actions, and their preferences have at least as much explanatory importance as societal preferences.
c) When state and societal preferences do not diverge, public officials periodically capitalise upon their autonomy-enhancing capacities and opportunities to reinforce societal convergence, deference, and indifference so as to forestall the emergence of preferences that diverge from the state's.
d) When state and societal preferences diverge, public officials periodically capitalise upon their autonomy-enhancing capacities and opportunities to bring about a shift in societal preferences and/or the alignment of societal resources in order to make for nondivergent preferences, and they then translate their own preferences into authoritative actions.
e) When state and societal preferences diverge, public officials periodically capitalize upon their autonomy-enhancing capacities and opportunities to free themselves from societal constraints, and they then translate their own preferences into authoritative actions.
f) When state and societal preferences diverge, public officials periodically rely on the inherent powers of the state to translate their preferences into authoritative actions.

As we see from earlier, the state autonomy literature is focused on state-internal matters, notably on the extent to which the state is able to carry through its goals in relation to society. That of course is different from a state's relations to other states. As noted earlier, the core insights from the state autonomy literature can be translated to the context of third country–EU relations. This type of analogical thinking has two advantages. For one, it provides us with a set of ready-made analytical distinctions of relevance for assessing the nature and degree of third-country autonomy in relation to the EU. For two, it provides us with a reminder of the important internal dynamics within third countries. This book's emphasis is on the first point, but the state autonomy literature's focus on state-society relations is also useful here. State autonomy as presented here sheds new light on (external) EU–third country and (internal) third country state-society relations and dynamics. The latter adds a distinct twist to the line of reasoning propounded in the state autonomy literature in the sense that, for a third country, whether the state is aligned with its domestic society has autonomy implications for its EU relations. In general, we may assume that the more aligned the state is with its domestic society, the more autonomy it can wield. This is different from Putnam's (1988) two-level dynamics where state-society conflict or misalignment can be a bargaining chip for a state in its bargaining with other states. For our book we may posit that the less scope a tightly affiliated non-member state has for bargaining with other states and international organisations over the rules of the game, the more important for its overall autonomy and wriggle room will be how that state is internally aligned with society. Such internal alignment is assured through i) active mobilisation of society to cohere with the state's position (presupposes a clearly articulated set of state goals in the first place); ii) active compensation of losers or dissatisfied members to ensure maximum state-society alignment; or iii) gag rules and other mechanisms for removing as much as possible of the EU issue or imprint (an uncertain and volatile form of alignment).

Autonomy is also related to the extent to which there are built-in societal constraints on the state's goal formulation and pursuit of its self-chosen actions. One such obvious constraint in Norway is the referendum requirement, which is now understood as a constitutional convention (even if it is not a formal requirement for dealing with the EU issue). How much of a constraint this is on the state is important to clarify.

Capabilities/capacities

Applied to EU third countries, autonomy then pertains to the country's will and ability to broadly shape society regardless of the constraints embedded in the EU affiliation. That includes ability to counter or counteract what the third country perceives to be negative effects of Europeanisation, in other words, the manner in which the EU and the EU's member states contribute to transform Norway's political, cultural, and socio-economic landscape in directions that Norwegians are not comfortable with.

If we take a step back and consult the public administration and public management literature on autonomy, we find a general concern with agency, a sense of actorness, and the ability to act in a coherent fashion and with a measure of independence. '[A]utonomy is about discretion, or the extent to which [an organisation] can decide itself about matters that it considers important' (Verhoest et al., 2010, pp. 18–19). Lipsky (1980, p. 19) claimed that autonomy is driven by actors' conspicuous desire for maximising their own autonomy. By contrast, it may be argued that autonomy is institutionally contingent. An institutional approach assumes that organisational capacity-building supplies governmental institutions with leverage to act autonomously (Trondal and Peters, 2013). This idea departs from the assumption that institutions mobilise biases in public policy because they supply cognitive and normative shortcuts and categories that simplify and guide decision-makers' behaviour (Schattschneider, 1975; Simon, 1965).

The notion of autonomous action thus presupposes the existence of autonomous institutional resources and capabilities. One necessary, although not sufficient, factor in building political order is the establishment of common institutions, including permanent executive institutions, legislative chambers, and judicial bodies serving the common interest (Trondal and Peters, 2013). These capacities provide actors with resources for problem-solving, management and coordination, administrative leadership, engagement with its environment, and accountability relationships (Joaquin and Greitens, 2022). The rise of a common political order through institutional capacity-building is seen as one key ingredient of state formation (Bartolini, 2005). Yet, if one focuses on the formation of autonomy and wriggle room in a European context, as we do in this book, what matters is the extent to which national actors in practice enjoy autonomy and wriggle room from key components of the EU system, *not* whether they are autonomous and enjoy wriggle room in general. If one focuses on such questions within the context of EU membership, what matters is the extent to which member-state governmental institutions are able to make individual decisions within the constraints of their EU affiliation. Such autonomy may be driven by mechanisms other than pure calculus. Arguably, institutions of the member-state may provide states with the ability to act more or less autonomously vis-à-vis the EU.

Following this line of argument, a Weberian model of the state would assume that government institutions possess internal capacities to shape their staff through mechanisms such as socialisation (behavioural internalisation through established cultures), discipline (behavioural adaptation through incentive systems) and control (behavioural adaptation through hierarchical control and supervision) (Page, 1992; Weber, 1983). These mechanisms ensure that governing institutions perform their tasks relatively independently from outside pressure but within boundaries set by the legal authority and (political) leadership of which they serve (Weber, 1924). The latter point is, however, pushing the definition closer to our concept of wriggle room, which is also suggestive of the complex relationships that may emerge between wriggle room and autonomy, as already noted. Nevertheless, causal emphasis is put on the internal institutional structures of the system more than on the actors themselves. A Weberian model provides a picture of governing institutions as creator of 'organisational man' (Simon, 1965) and as a stabilising element in politics more broadly (Olsen, 2010). According to this model, autonomy is shaped by the institutions that embed actors and governing processes. It is thus the institutional rules established in a political order that regulate, constitute, and bias the decision-making behaviour of actors, ultimately enhancing autonomy and wriggle room. Decision-makers live with a constant overload of potential and inconsistent information that may be attended to at decision situations. Institutional rules guide the behaviour of decision-makers due to the computational limitations and the need for selective search. Actors must also address time-inconsistency problems. They can more credibly bind themselves to solutions that can only work across time.

Institutions provide collective order out of cognitive disorders by creating local rationalities among the members (March and Shapira, 1992). Institutions are systematic devices for simplifying, classifying, routinising, directing, and sequencing information towards particular decision situations (Schattschneider, 1975, p. 58), and for solving i) collective action problems and ii) coordinating problems by encouraging convergence around salient solutions (Schelling, 1960). These can be other ways in which institutions can be autonomy-enhancing by creating choices and not just constraining them.

Autonomy and wriggle room are shaped by institutions as 'collections of structures, rules and standard operating procedures that have a partly autonomous role in political life' (March and Olsen, 2006, p. 4). Autonomy in particular, as perceived by decision-makers, is thus arguably conditioned – both constrained and enabled – by institutional rules and routines.

This political-institutional-administrative conception of autonomy translates to different degrees to the state's role in the economy, in culture, and in science and knowledge production. We will, in the following, unpack autonomy with explicit reference to this. Before doing so, it should be noted that in the EU context, the issue of autonomy has taken on a distinct hue, with bearings on the relationship between autonomy and independence. EU member states accept constraints on formal sovereignty and give up independence when joining the EU as member states. The institutional arrangement at the EU level has independent action capacity and hence has a measure of autonomy. But in contrast to a federal state, the EU level is far more constrained, contained, and controlled by the member states than would be the case in a federal state. This takes place through a very pronounced EU member state participation in joint EU institutions (Lindseth, 2010), especially the intergovernmental ones. For EU member states, this arrangement can be autonomy-enhancing, insofar as the arrangement enables member states to pursue their interest and reach goals that they would not have been able to do on their own, and insofar as each member state has veto.[18] This shows that for EU member states, there is a significant difference between autonomy and independence.

A critically important question is: can legally regulated cooperation that locks state actors in and constrains who else they can sign agreements with still be compatible with autonomy? If, as noted, such legal ties enable states to realise core interests that they would not have been able to do without these ties – and if these legal ties reduce vulnerability – then such legal ties and arrangements are compatible with autonomy. How much and in what sense requires further scrutiny and will depend on the specific circumstances. From this we can thus say that EU member states voluntarily submit to EU rules and regulations and open themselves up to each other; hence, they agree to delimit independence. EU cooperation can produce 'participation-enhanced autonomy' insofar as they are able to agree on a common course of action that is aligned with their core interests, and through the increase in action capability that the cooperation provides.[19]

For non-members, the issue of autonomy typically takes on a much more conventional shape, namely as a matter of regaining or retaining control within the context of a legally regulated (albeit highly asymmetrical) relationship. However, there are instances of direct participation-enhanced autonomy even for non-member states. Norway's decision to collaborate with the EU on reaching the Paris climate targets were largely due to the possibilities this would give Norway in buying emissions cuts in the EU and to bind the targets to the EU to ensure implementation (see Chapter 3 on climate and energy).

Dimensions of autonomy

Following from this brief excursus, we may envisage at least five dimensions of autonomy.

Political and institutional autonomy refer to the will and ability of the elected political leadership to stake out its own chosen course of action to shape society and the world around it. Will can refer to how a government sees its main interest as directly associated with a political program and staked-out course of action with or without being motivated by a distinct political ideology. The scope for political autonomy is profoundly affected by the presence or absence of internal conflict and division, over ideas, values, and appropriate direction for action. Ceteris paribus, the more internally riven a country, the more it will struggle to forge a coherent will (Jacobsen, 1964; Birkeland and Trondal, 2022). Further, autonomy, as underlined earlier, hinges, to a large extent, on the availability of adequate political and administrative competence to handle complex problems, coordinate policies, and sustain a strategic orientation to the outside world. Further still, autonomy hinges on the state's ability to direct society's development under conditions of complex interdependence. In this context, it matters how the government shapes and conveys knowledge of the EU affiliation to the population. Here, somewhat ironically, a high level of government autonomy in the sense of not being socially constrained may be counterproductive in that it widens the gap between a government quite EU-entangled on the one hand and a population largely out of step with what goes on in relation to the EU. This is an issue with the EEA Agreement and Norway's other EU affiliations, all of which are quite executive- and jurist-dominated. Autonomy through opportunities to participate in policy-shaping gives the Norway model a technocratic bias. Those most likely to get to take part in policy-shaping are experts and officials (Fossum, 2023).

The implication is that we need to include a temporal dimension to autonomy and distinguish between short-term and long-term autonomy: in the Norwegian context, short-term autonomy entails little societal involvement; long-term autonomy is only ensured insofar as state and society are aligned. For that the government must make special effort to reach into society to ensure that the population is kept up to date with its position on and the unfolding of European developments, challenges, and opportunities.

Legal autonomy refers to the will and ability to formulate the legal rules that guide state and societal conduct. As noted earlier, this takes on a distinct shape when it comes to legally binding affiliations with other states or polities such as the EU. Such agreements entail constraints on legal autonomy. We have suggested that a useful approach to establishing how constraining such affiliations are will benefit from introducing a distinct notion of wriggle room. At the same time, it is clear that we cannot confine legal autonomy to wriggle room for two reasons. One is the scope a third country such as Norway has for autonomous legal action outside the EU affiliation; the other is that the scope for legal *autonomy* is profoundly affected by major changes to the rules of the game, such as through EU treaty changes or large-scale enlargement.

Economic autonomy refers to the will and ability to pursue a self-chosen line of economic development and conduct. On will, there is the question of whether a third country propounds a distinct socio-economic model with ideological overtones and whether that is coherent with the EU's or not. The greater the divergence, the easier it is to assess the third country's level of autonomy, that is, whether it is capable of sustaining such divergence under the conditions of Europeanisation or not. For Norway, the question is relevant because it refers to whether it is possible to maintain traits of the Nordic model in a Europeanised context. Nordic model proponents assert that the Nordic region shares a set of values that are closely associated with social democracy and that are sustained by historically entrenched political and socio-economic factors. These relate to societal corporatism and tripartism (structured employer-employee-state cooperation and concertation). Norwegian EU critics argue that the EU propounds a neoliberal economic stance, which is incompatible with core traits of the Nordic model. Finally, economic autonomy is associated with a third country's ability to make up for negative effects of the EU (external) affiliation by, for instance, compensating losers of Europeanisation (social benefits, compensation schemes for businesses losing out). Inability to compensate is generally associated with lack of capacity or a straitjacket affiliation; both of which are reflective of a low degree of autonomy. This last point is closely related to the state's ability to direct society and its development.

Cultural autonomy refers to the will and ability to pursue a self-chosen cultural trajectory. We may here also differentiate between states with regard to whether they harbour an autonomy-seeking political culture or not. Further, some states have political cultures that are more conducive to autonomy than others. One such issue is trust. This dimension includes both the vertical dimension of citizens' trust in government and the horizontal dimension as trust among citizens and within society. Why is a high level of trust autonomy-enhancing? It is because trust provides social cohesion and enhances action capacity. It furnishes the government with a 'legitimacy buffer' that it can rely on when needed.

Epistemic/knowledge/expertise-based autonomy refers to the society's reservoir or repertoire of relevant knowledge and expertise which is essential for diagnosing and acting upon problems. That includes knowledge of those aspects of any given EU affiliation that will limit the scope for wriggle room and autonomy. Knowledge of Norway's overall situation vis-à-vis the EU, including the neighbours' situation; the European 'system' and European developments (within the multilevel EU configuration); and its global location. Included in this is academia's competence and training of personnel, such as being up to date on European developments, challenges, and opportunities.

This conceptual unpacking provides a set of proxies of relevance to our analysis of autonomy. Yet, our conceptual exercise is far from exhaustive. Autonomy relies on a whole host of other factors, not the least the extent to which the world is rule-based and predictable versus volatile and quite inattentive to rules and norms. A useful approach here is to consider **turbulence and the distinct effects of temporality**. We may distinguish between patterns of dynamic vs. static resilience (Ansell and Trondal, 2018), and more specifically between the pace of governing, in which we might envisage a state ridden by two parallel tempos. Here are some preliminary reflections that we will revisit in later chapters: The first is high-tempo governance during crises, in which the autonomy of actors might be reduced due to merely keeping track of events when the tempo is high and the time for decision-making is low. The second is slow-tempo governance during everyday processes, in which more government actors more easily stay involved in decision-making processes and thus preserve some degree of autonomy. The challenge for government institutions might be to act quickly when needed and slow when needed, and make sure that high-tempo governance, featured by improvisation and ad hoc solutions, does not intrude into domains driven by slow-tempo governance based on rules and routines. An autonomy challenge is likely to come about if high speed governance is omnipresent in situations calling for slow-tempo governance. Yet, high speed governance is generally also likely to challenge the autonomy of actors that are not invited into the governing machine room.

Conclusion

This chapter provides core elements of the book's analytical framework. The main purpose of this analytical framework was to increase our understanding of autonomy under conditions of complex interdependence. This book zooms in on one particular form of legally regulated complex interdependence, which marks the

EU's relations with such third countries as Norway and the UK. We introduced the notion of wriggle room to understand how much autonomy states can sustain under various forms of legally binding interstate and supranational collaboration.

Building on this distinction, we can assert that the state's overall autonomy can be discerned through establishing how much autonomy it has given up through entering a system of legally binding international collaboration; the scope for wriggle room that is available in such a legally binding collaboration; how or to what extent such legally binding international collaboration improves on the state's ability to pursue its goals; and the state's residual autonomy in terms of will and capacity.

The chapter proceeded to unpack wriggle room, along eight different dimensions: new legislation from the EU; existing legislation; 'dynamic homogeneity'; agencification and administrative interweaving; sanctioning and compliance mechanisms; differences between the Norway-EU and the Norway-UK formal affiliations; wriggle room under conditions of exiting from a system of legally binding cooperation and the EU-external dimension of wriggle room. These dimensions will inform the analyses in Chapters 3 through 6.

The final part of the chapter proceeded to further unpack autonomy. This took inspiration from the state autonomy literature that emerged in the 1980s, which understood autonomy as a state or collective's will and ability to stake out its own course. This body of literature was, as we have noted, primarily focused on state-internal matters, or the state's ability to carry through its goals in relation to society. This chapter has shown that the insights that this body of literature produced are useful for the analysis of autonomy under conditions of complex interdependence. The chapter's unpacking of autonomy distinguished between will and capacity/capability, a distinction that we will develop further in Chapter 8. In addition, it distinguished the following forms of autonomy: political and institutional; legal; economic; cultural; and epistemic or expertise-based autonomy.

This rendition of autonomy highlights the role of the state as actor (and structure). That does not, however, exhaust the meaning of autonomy that is addressed in this book. We also, in Chapter 7, introduce a conception of individual autonomy and show the relevance of such a different vantage point. A systematic analysis of the relationship between state and individual autonomy is beyond the scope of this book but is an important task that requires future attention.

The dimensions of autonomy – especially legal – overlap with how we have defined wriggle room. That is inevitable and poses challenges for analytical clarity. At the same time, overlaps and grey zones are productive in the sense that probing them further in depth provides a better understanding of the phenomena under study.

Notes

1 We could refer to that as 'wriggle room plus'.
2 Such a distinction is analytically useful but may be difficult to detect in practice.

Autonomy and wriggle room   43

3   Fabbrini (2015, 2019) and Bátora and Fossum (2020) distinguish between the EU's Community and Union Systems. The distinction relates back to the Maastricht pillar structure where the Community System refers to the supranational arrangements constituting and operating the EU's internal market and flanking areas; the Union System refers to the more intergovernmental arrangements guiding tax, fiscal, and large parts of foreign and security policy.
4   The European Commission's formal initiative role does not imply that it de facto operates autonomously at the level of the initiative.
5   Agreement on the European Economic Area (1994). For a legal assessment, see Arnesen et al. (2018, pp. 803–819).
6   The centre-left Stoltenberg government (2005–2013) agreed after pressure from the Trade Union Confederation (LO) to use it in relation to the third postal directive. The change in government in 2013 meant that the possibility to invoke the reservation was not acted upon.
7   These are themes that reverberate through the large body of literature on differentiated integration. See, for instance, Andersen and Sitter (2006); Bellamy (2019); Boasson et al. (2022); Dyson and Sepos (2010); Eriksen (2018); Fossum (2015, 2019); Kölliker (2006); Leruth et al. (2022); Leuffen et al. (2022); Piris (2012); Schimmelfennig and Winzen (2020); Stubb (1996); and Warleigh-Lack (2015).
8   See Arnesen et al. (2018).
9   For an overview of this agency, see (EASA, 2023).
10 The EFTA Court has less bite than the CJEU.
11 Analysts have, for instance, discussed whether ESA is 'more catholic than the pope'. See Graver and Sverdrup (2002).
12 Schengen Agreement Article 8 is described as a guillotine clause (NOU 2012:2, Chapter 22.2.3).
13 Graver and Sverdrup (2002).
14 For an excellent assessment, see Conant (2002).
15 In one of the interviews, the question was raised whether Norway should have followed the negotiations between the UK and the EU more closely. Could it have changed the output?
16 The EU's usage of this term is similar to ours in the sense that it includes cooperation with others when that enhances one's strategic autonomy (Romanyshyn, 2021).
17 Consider Fossum's (1997) analysis of the Canadian state's ability to control multinational oil companies (MNCs) during the oil crises in the 1970s. He shows that state-society dynamics (state-MNCs) were subverted by jurisdictional struggles within the state pitting the federal government against oil producing provinces and oil-consuming and oil-producing provinces against each other. Simeon (1972) pointed to an important Canada-EU parallel here in that federal-provincial relations bear resemblance to the type of interstate diplomacy that we find in the realm of international relations. The upshot is that it is useful to consider state autonomy in relation to two sets of dynamics: state-society and interstate ones. If anything, the EU–third country analogy is even more telling than the EU member state one, given that at the heart of the Canadian struggle was the issue of Quebec secession. The issue of sovereignty-association was at the heart of the jurisdictional struggle.
18 Though sometimes they may have to give up their vetoes to make various choices. Then autonomy depends more on periodic reviews of politics through, for example, the multi-annual financial frameworks and ultimate powers to withdraw from situations of self-bind.
19 The scope for issue linkage can enhance autonomy insofar as an actor agrees to compromise on areas of strength in return for support in areas where the actor is weak or vulnerable. This applies for EU members because they have to take into consideration the future; for non-members it is very difficult to obtain similar benefits.

References

Aftenposten (2021) *Regjeringen på kollisjonskurs med SV og Rødt om jernbanepakken*. Available at: www.aftenposten.no/norge/politikk/i/lVlgM9/regjeringen-paa-kollisjonskurs-med-sv-og-roedt-om-jernbanepakken (Accessed 24 January 2023).

Agreement on the European Economic Area (1994) *Official Journal of the European Communities*, L 1/3, 3 January.

Andersen, S. S. and Sitter, N. (2006) 'Differentiated Integration: What Is It and How Much Can the EU Accommodate?', *European Integration*, 28(4): 313–330.

Ansell, C. and Trondal, J. (2018) 'Governing Turbulence. An Organisational-Institutional Agenda', *Perspectives on Public Management and Governance*, 1(1): 43–57.

Arnesen, F., Fredriksen, H. H., Graver, H. P., Mestad, O. and Vedder, C. (2018) *Agreement on the European Economic Area – A Commentary*, Baden-Baden, Germany: Nomos.

Bartolini, S. (2005) *Restructuring Europe*, Oxford: Oxford University Press.

Bátora, J. and Fossum, J. E. (eds) (2020) *Towards a Segmented European Political Order*, London: Routledge.

Bellamy, R. (2019) *A Republican Europe of States*, Cambridge: Cambridge University Press.

Birkeland, T. and Trondal, J. (2022) 'The Rift Between Executive Contraction and Executive Detraction: The Case of European Commission Battery Policy-Making', *Journal of European Public Policy*. https://doi.org/10.1080/13501763.2022.2118356.

Boasson, E. L., Leiren, M. D. and Wettestad, J. (2022) 'Differentiated Integration in EU Climate Policy', in Leruth, B., Gänzle, S. and Trondal, J. (eds) *The Routledge Handbook of Differentiation in the European Union*, London: Routledge, pp. 340–354.

Busuioc, M. and Groenleer, M. (2012) 'Wielders of Supranational Power? The Administrative Behaviour of the Heads of European Union Agencies', in Busuioc, M., Groenleer, M. and Trondal, J. (eds) *The Agency Phenomenon in the European Union*, Manchester: Manchester University Press.

Conant, L. (2002) *Justice Contained – Law and Politics in the European Union*, Ithaca: Cornell University Press.

Council of the EU (2016) *Outcome of Proceedings 14 November 2016*. Available at: www.consilium.europa.eu/media/22459/eugs-conclusions-st14149en16.pdf (Accessed 24 January 2023).

Curtin, D. and Dehousse, R. (2012) 'European Union Agencies: Tipping the Balance?', in Busuioc, M., Groenleer, M. and Trondal, J. (eds) *The Agency Phenomenon in the European Union*, Manchester: Manchester University Press.

Dyson, K. and Sepos, A. (eds) (2010) *Which Europe? The Politics of Differentiated Integration*, Basingstoke: Palgrave Macmillan.

EASA (2023) *Your Safety Is Our Mission*. Available at: www.easa.europa.eu/en (Accessed 24 January 2023).

EFTA Court (2023) *EFTA Court*. Available at: https://eftacourt.int (Accessed 24 January 2023).

EFTA Surveillance Authority (2023) *EFTA Surveillance Authority*. Available at: www.eftasurv.int (Accessed 24 January 2023).

Egeberg, M. and Trondal, J. (2009) 'National Agencies in the European Administrative Space: Government Driven, Commission Driven, or Networked?', *Public Administration*, 87(4): 779–790.

Egeberg, M. and Trondal, J. (2011) 'EU-level Agencies: New Executive Centre Formation or Vehicles for National Control?', *Journal of European Public Policy*, 18(6): 868–887.

Eriksen, E. O. (2018) 'Political Differentiation and the Problem of Dominance: Segmentation and Hegemony', *European Journal of Political Research*, 57(4): 989–1008.

European Commission (2020) *Single Market Scoreboard* [online]. Available at: https://ec.europa.eu/internal_market/scoreboard/performance_by_governance_tool/transposition/index_en.htm#changes-transposition-deficit (Accessed 8 February 2022).
Evans, P., Rueschemeyer, D. and Skocpol, T. (eds) (1985) *Bringing the State Back In*, Cambridge: Cambridge University Press.
Fabbrini, S. (2015) *Which European Union? Europe After the Euro Crisis*, Cambridge: Cambridge University Press.
Fabbrini, S. (2019) *Europe's Future – Decoupling and Reforming*, Cambridge: Cambridge University Press.
Fossum, J. E. (1997) *Oil, the State and Federalism*, Toronto: Toronto University Press.
Fossum, J. E. (2015) 'Democracy and Differentiation in Europe', *Journal of European Public Policy*, 22(6): 799–815.
Fossum, J. E. (2019) 'Europe's Triangular Challenge: Differentiation, Dominance and Democracy', *EU3D Research Papers*, 1/2019. Available at: https://papers.ssrn.com/sol3/Papers.cfm?abstract_id=3505864 (Accessed 13 July 2021).
Fossum, J. E. (2023) 'The Political Future of the European Economic Area', in Butler, G. (ed) *Research Handbook on EEA Internal Market Law*, Cheltenham: Edward Elgar (forthcoming).
Graver, H. P. and Sverdrup, U. (2002) 'ESA – mer katolsk enn paven?', *ARENA Working Paper Series*, 11/2002, ARENA Centre for European Studies: University of Oslo.
Haugen, M. C. (2022) 'Regional Presence in the EU – A Qualitative Study of Regional Offices' Activity in Brussels', *EU3D Report* 8/22, ARENA Centre for European Studies: University of Oslo.
Jacobsen, K. D. (1964) *Teknisk hjelp og politisk struktur*, Oslo: Universitetsforlaget.
Joaquin, M. E. and Greitens, T. J. (2022) *American Administrative Capacity. Decline, Decay, and Resilience*, Cham: Springer.
Karlsen, O. J. (2020) *Decision-Shaping from the Outside: Measuring and Explaining the Degree of Preference Attainment in the EEA EFTA Comments* (Master's thesis). University of Bergen, Norway.
Kelemen, D. (2002) 'The Politics of "Eurocratic" Structure and the New European Agencies', *West European Politics*, 25(4): 93–118.
Kölliker, A. (2006) *Flexibility and European Unification: The Logic of Differentiated Integration*, Lanham, MD: Rowman and Littlefield.
Leruth, B., Gänzle, S. and Trondal, J. (eds) (2022) *The Routledge Handbook of Differentiation in the European Union*, London: Routledge.
Leuffen, D., Rittberger, B. and Schimmelfennig, F. (2022) *Integration and Differentiation in the European Union: Theory and Policies*, Basingstoke: Palgrave Macmillan.
Lindseth, P. L. (2010) *Power and Legitimacy. Reconciling Europe and the Nation-State*, Oxford: Oxford University Press.
Lipsky, M. (1980) *Street-Level Bureaucracy*, New York: Russel Sage Foundation.
March, J. G. and Olsen, J. P. (2006) 'Elaborating the "New Institutionalism"', in Rhodes, R. A. W., Binder, S. A. and Rockman, B. A. (eds) *The Oxford Handbook of Political Institutions*, Oxford: Oxford University Press.
March, J. G. and Shapira, Z. (1992) 'Behavioral Decision Making Theory and Organisational Decision Theory', in Zey, M. (ed) *Decision Making*, Newbury Park: SAGE.
Martinsen, D., Mastenbroek, E., Schrama, R. and Soares, A. C. (2022) 'European Administrative Networks and Differentiated Implementation', *EU3D Research Paper*, 30/2022, ARENA Centre for European Studies: University of Oslo.

Nordlinger, E. A. (1981) *On the Autonomy of the Democratic State*, Harvard: Harvard University Press.

NOU 2012:2 (2012) 'Utenfor og innenfor – Norges avtaler med EU' ['Outside and Inside: Norway's Agreements with the European Union'] [online], *Norwegian Ministry of Foreign Affairs*. Available at: www.regjeringen.no/no/dokumenter/nou-2012-2/id669368/ (Accessed 17 January 2022).

Olsen, J. P. (2010) *Governing Through Institutional Building*, Oxford: Oxford University Press.

Page, E. C. (1992) *Political Authority and Bureaucratic Power*, New York: Harvester Wheatsheaf.

Pavone, T. and Stiansen, Ø. (2021) 'The Shadow Effect of Courts: Judicial Review and the Politics of Preemptive Reform', *American Political Science Review*, 116(1): 322–336.

Piris, J.-C. (2012) *The Future of Europe: Towards a Two-Speed EU?*, Cambridge: Cambridge University Press.

Princen, S., Schimmelfennig, F., Sczepanski, R., Smekal, H. and Zbiral, R. (2022) 'Differentiated Integration and Flexible Implementation', *EUI RSC 2022/17*, Robert Schuman Centre for Advanced Studies.

Putnam, R. D. (1988) 'Diplomacy and Domestic Politics: The Logic of Two-Level Games', *International Organisation*, 42(3): 427–460.

Reegård, S. (2020) 'Stort og smått; rødt og blått – Eksempler på hvordan en regjering tilpasser seg internasjonaliseringens utfordringer', in Veggeland, N. (ed) *Den Solbergske staten*, Oslo: Sandnes Forlag

Romanyshyn, I. (2021) 'EU Strategic Autonomy: Unpacking the "Essentially Contested Concept"', *Encompass*. Available at: https://encompass-europe.com/comment/eu-strategic-autonomy-unpacking-the-essentially-contested-concept (Accessed 24 January 2023).

Scharpf, F. (2009) 'Legitimacy in the Multilevel European Polity', *European Political Science Review*, 1(2): 173–204.

Schattschneider, E. E. (1975) *The Semisovereign People*, Fort Worth: Harcourt Brace Jovanovich College Publishers.

Schelling, T. (1960) *The Strategy of Conflict*, Cambridge MA: Harvard University Press.

Schimmelfennig, F., Leuffen, D. and de Vries, C. (2022) 'Differentiated Integration in the European Union: Institutional Effects, Public Opinion, and Alternative Flexibility Arrangements', *European Union Politics*, 24(1): 1–18.

Schimmelfennig, F. and Winzen, T. (2020) *Ever Looser Union? Differentiated European Integration*, Oxford: Oxford University Press.

Simeon, R. (1972) *Federal-Provincial Diplomacy: The Making of Recent Policy in Canada*, Toronto: University of Toronto Press.

Simon, H. A. (1965) *Administrative Behavior*, New York: The Free Press.

Skocpol, T. (1985) 'Bringing the State Back In: Current Research', in Evans, P., Rueschemeyer, D. and Skocpol, T. (eds) *Bringing the State Back In*, Cambridge: Cambridge University Press.

Stubb, A. C. G. (1996) 'A Categorization of Differentiated Integration', *Journal of Common Market Studies*, 34(3): 283–295.

Trondal, J. and Peters, B. G. (2013) 'The Rise of European Administrative Space. Lessons Learned', *Journal of European Public Policy*, 20(2): 295–307.

Verhoest, K., Roness, P. G., Verschuere, B., Rubecksen, K. and MacCarthaigh, M. (2010) *Autonomy and Control of State Agencies*, Houndmills: Palgrave Macmillan.

Warleigh-Lack, A. (2015) 'Differentiated Integration in the European Union: Towards a Comparative Regionalism Perspective', *Journal of European Public Policy*, 22(6): 871–887.

Weber, M. (1924) 'Legitimate Authority and Bureaucracy', in Pugh, D. S. (ed) (1990) *Organisation Theory: Selected Readings*, 3rd ed., London: Penguin Books.

Weber, M. (1983) *On Capitalism, Bureaucracy and Religion*, Glasgow: Harper Collins Publishers.

3
POST-BREXIT CLIMATE AND ENERGY POLICY IN THE EU, UK, AND NORWAY

A new trilateral relationship?

Introduction

The EU has long taken the role as an international leader on climate change, with ambitious climate and energy goals in place since 2008 (Wurzel and Connelly, 2011). With its European Green Deal (EGD), the EU has arguably introduced the world's most ambitious and encompassing climate strategy (Oberthür and Dupont, 2021). Within Europe, both the UK and Norway label themselves as climate leaders (e.g., Rayner and Jordan, 2017; Kern et al., 2014; Boasson and Lahn, 2017; Farstad, 2019), though they have taken radically different approaches towards the EU. Whereas Norway has decided to cooperate more closely with the EU on climate policy, participating in key parts of the EGD, the UK has extricated itself post-Brexit. What characterises and explains these different paths, and what are the implications of the new relationships for the countries' ability to stake out their own course and make choices within climate and energy policy?

These questions are important as both Norway and the UK have decided to be outside of the EU to protect areas of national interest such as fisheries and agriculture (see Chapter 4) in the case of Norway or to 'take back control' and regain sovereignty in the case of the UK. However, given the asymmetry of size and power, the EU is arguably a hegemon. It is therefore pertinent to ask how these countries' autonomy (defined as their wish to stake out their own course and direction) and wriggle room (defined as their capability within the trilateral framework to make choices) are affected post-Brexit within climate and energy policy. Although a growing body of literature has assessed the evolving bilateral relationship between the UK and the EU (e.g. Burns et al., 2019; Moore and Jordan, 2021; Rayner et al., 2021) and Norway and the EU (Eriksen and Fossum,

2014; Jevnaker, 2016; Farstad et al., 2021; Boasson, 2021; Farstad, 2022), no research has examined the post-Brexit bilateral relationship between the UK and Norway or the new trilateral relationship between these countries and the EU when it comes to energy and climate policy. Given the importance of North Sea energy cooperation for multiple European countries' energy supply and decarbonisation – made only more pertinent in light of the war in Ukraine – and given that the UK is Norway's single largest trade partner and a major importer of Norwegian oil and gas, this is a serious omission. Moreover, including insights on how these changing relationships are accepted by domestic actors in Norway and the UK helps shed light on opportunities and barriers for the low carbon transition.

As such, it is relevant to characterise the post-Brexit European political order when it comes to climate and energy policy. We do this through extensive document analysis (covering academic research, grey literature, consultation responses, policy papers, agreements including the TCA (2021) and the FTA (2021), and media coverage) and eight semi-structured interviews with key actors within climate and energy policy based in Norway, the UK, and Brussels. These include energy industry representatives, civil servants engaged in the post-Brexit trade negotiations, environmental non-governmental organisation (ENGO) representatives, and a former UK Cabinet minister. Interviews were conducted during the first half of 2022. Our analysis is also complemented by findings from a policy roundtable and a stakeholder workshop, both conducted in the autumn of 2021. The policy roundtable and workshop operated under Chatham House Rules and consisted primarily of Norwegian stakeholders, though a limited number of stakeholders from an EU and UK perspective were also included (see Annex I for details).

The chapter is structured as follows. The first and second sections analyse the divergent EU relationships sought post-Brexit by the UK and Norway respectively, and the implications for energy and climate policy. The third section analyses the relationship between UK and Norway, before the fourth section analyses the trilateral relationship between the UK, Norway, and the EU. The fifth section discusses the findings before concluding. We argue that, in light of Brexit disruptions, the new political order is surprisingly stable. While the UK has increased its autonomy and wriggle room, those of Norway are becoming more limited. All parties share a common interest in continuing cooperation on energy and climate change, all desire to be climate leaders and have managed to find workable solutions, although there is less efficiency for all parties post-Brexit. There is, however, a real concern related to 'zombie legislation' in the UK and a growing concern about instability in Norway related to public opinion on interconnectors and how they are perceived to be linked to rising electricity prices, unpopular seizure of nature for wind power purposes, and EU governance. Moreover, instability concerns have also grown in the UK related to the rapid shifts in government and ministers' agendas following Liz Truss and Rishi Sunak's succession of Boris Johnson in 2022.

The UK-EU relationship and implications for climate and energy policy post-Brexit

Although Britain was labelled the 'Dirty Man of Europe' in the 1970s, EU membership gradually transformed the UK into an environmental leader (Burns, 2020). The UK has a history of committing itself to environmental protection and sustainable development, which became a guiding principle for the Conservative Party in the 1990s, providing it did not hinder economic growth (Leiren and Takle, 2022; Ross, 2012). Running into the early 2000s, the emphasis was on market liberalisation as a way of delivering affordable and reliable energy to citizens, with the UK also shaping several waves of energy liberalisation by the EU (Watson, 2021). In 2008, the UK was the first country in the world to introduce a Climate Change Act (CCA), contributing to its reputation as a climate leader (Averchenkova et al., 2020). The CCA was underpinned by a high level of public concern for climate change and strong cross-party consensus at the time (Carter and Childs, 2017). Following the passing of the CCA and the global financial crisis, however, climate change descended the political agenda again and was affected by several austerity measures in the 2010s, such as the zero carbon homes scheme being scrapped and the government selling off the Green Investment Bank (Carter and Clements, 2015). The UK has nonetheless been able to meet its international climate commitments, largely due to the replacement of coal in the electricity sector (Carbon Brief, 2019). Renewables such as wind and solar now generate around a third of UK electricity, an achievement that has also been spurred on by the EU's 2009 Renewable Energy Directive targets (Watson, 2021; Rayner et al., 2021). More recently, the UK became one of the first countries to legislate a net zero target under the May government in 2019, which was followed by Johnson's Ten Point Plan for a Green Industrial Revolution in 2020. The latter includes goals and additional funding for initiatives such as the development of offshore wind, hydrogen, nuclear energy, and carbon capture and storage (CCS).

Given the UK's green credentials, it was therefore surprising that climate change did not feature more prominently in debates running up to the 2016 EU referendum. Since then, however, these topics have received significant attention. There has been widespread concern, especially amongst the environmental movement, that Brexit will weaken environmental standards and safeguards as EU regulations no longer apply and recourse to EU institutions has disappeared (Burns et al., 2019; Gravey et al., 2016; Jordan et al., 2020). These concerns amplified under the Truss government with the tabling of the Brexit Freedoms Bill, which seeks to introduce a 'sunset clause' on all EU-derived legislation, most of which relates to the environment. Given the devolved nature of the issues, Brexit also poses a significant governance challenge for the UK (Burns et al., 2018; Reid, 2017). Consecutive Conservative governments have been keen to assuage such fears, bringing forward a wide-ranging Environment Bill in 2021 and an Office for Environmental Protection (OEP) to replace EU safeguards. However, reservations remain about the prospect of 'zombie legislation' (i.e., legislation that is not enforced) (Burns et al., 2018) and the independence of the OEP (Moore and Jordan, 2021). Moreover, despite the Trade and Cooperation Agreement (TCA) between the UK and the EU including a non-regression clause, meaning protections should not be reduced below those existing at the end of the transition period, this clause has received criticism for only applying to the weakening of protections as they impact on trade and investment. Any impact on other areas of protection, for example importing goods that do not meet certain standards or more general environmental protections, are not covered. Furthermore, oral evidence provided to House of Commons Committee on the Future Relationship with the European Union highlighted that it is difficult to identify the point at which a dispute could be triggered under this clause, and that the potential fallout from regression is more severe than other countries' trade agreements with the EU (House of Commons, 2021). Critics have also pointed out that UK policy measures still fail to close the gap to meet the UK's existing carbon budgets and are insufficient to meet the net zero target (see Tobin, 2021). Concerns have also been raised about the climate credentials of the Truss and, subsequently, Sunak governments, as energy crisis plans and financial turmoil in the wake of Truss' mini-budget pushed climate action down on the political agenda (see e.g., Paterson, 2022; ENDS Report, 2022).

Despite the UK government seeking to allay concerns of policy regression and divergence post-Brexit, they have nonetheless decided to extricate the UK from the single energy market, the EU's Emissions Trading Scheme (ETS), and the EU Environment Agency, despite these being open to non-EU members. These structures and institutions are key policy tools for the green energy transition; thus, a key question is why the government made these decisions and what the implications will be for climate and energy policy.

Despite the Brexit disruptions to UK climate and energy policy, and in comparison to other policy areas such as the discussions over the Northern Ireland Protocol, there has been a surprisingly stable cooperative relationship with the EU. Blondeel et al. (2022, p. 2) note that 'the impact of Brexit on new electricity interconnector capacity has not been as significant as some commentators feared, albeit three cable projects have been suspended and existing links are being used less efficiently due to default trade rules'. Stakeholders and interviewees also emphasise surprising stability despite the UK extricating itself from key EU climate and energy initiatives. As highlighted by a British energy sector representative:

We were very pleased with the energy chapter in the TCA because it is actually one of the areas of the TCA that provides the basis for a decent strong relationship going forwards, I would argue, probably compared to any of the other sectors.

(Interview 1)

Similarly, the UK ETS has worked far better than critics expected. A British ENGO representative pointed out that critics likely underestimated the size and stability of the UK market compared to other schemes such as that of California (Interview 5). Several reasons for the lack of disruption to climate and energy policy and cooperation have been highlighted.

Firstly, the UK's Climate Change Act and its commitments under the Paris Agreement have ensured continued commitment on climate change. The UK's desire to be a climate leader has not changed significantly post-Brexit, demonstrated by its hosting COP26 in Glasgow in 2021. Moreover, having similarly ambitious targets as the EU, at least for the time being, has ensured convergence of policy. As a British energy industry representative put it: 'If you look at the macro approach on climate, there is just no difference (...) we have exactly the same strategic long-term interests as the EU and we are legally bound to those' (Interview 1).

Secondly, climate change has been an area where the government has been able and keen to demonstrate a 'Brexit success' (Interview 5). Similarly, energy cooperation has not been significantly disrupted as

> energy and climate are not really 'Global Britain' issues. You do not trade electricity on an intercontinental basis, you trade it on an intracontinental basis. Gas is slightly different, and oil obviously, but those are both global commodities. Electricity is a very specific regional issue.
>
> *(Interview 1)*

This has been important for a country which imports 50 per cent of its gas and a smaller amount of its electricity (Office for National Statistics, 2022). The UK's export of crude oil is about the same as its import.

The regional dimension is significant, as interviewees describe being 'connected by interconnectors'. The reality of shared physical infrastructure and the need for cooperation to drive decarbonisation and ensure energy security has prevented large-scale disruption to energy policy. This is particularly the case in the North Sea, where electricity cables connect multiple European countries such as the UK, Norway, Germany, the Netherlands, and Belgium. As a large part of the North Sea is British territory, 'there is a widespread acknowledgement that certainly in the North Sea you cannot do it without the Brits' (Interview 1). There is also a need for coordinated maritime spatial planning across borders to reduce the number of landing points, as large pieces of infrastructure are unpopular with local populations (Interview 1). On a political level, interviewees highlight that although the relationship between the UK and the EU has been, and remains, fractious, this does not extend to individual countries or commercial relationships, thereby rendering North Sea energy cooperation smoother.

A further reason for the relative stability post-Brexit is that the energy industry and ENGOs ferociously lobbied policymakers, and particularly civil servants in the Department for Business, Energy and Industrial Strategy (BEIS), about the importance of maintaining good energy cooperation, with interviewees reporting that the importance of avoiding unnecessary disruption was 'well understood' by policymakers (Interview 1, Interview 3, Interview 5). As such, there has been a strong recognition from both the UK and the EU of the need for continued and strong cooperation on energy and climate. As pointed out by a British energy industry representative, this need was understood on 'almost an emotional level. If the UK and Europe, with all of those shared targets and shared interests, cannot cooperate on energy and climate, what can we cooperate on?' (Interview 1).

However, although the cooperative relationship on climate and energy has remained surprisingly stable post-Brexit, the new relationship is certainly not without its challenges. The administrative burden pre- and post-Brexit, the loss of trade, and increase in costs are well documented (e.g., Blondeel et al., 2022). This administrative burden is likely to increase with new EGD measures such as the Carbon Border Adjustment Mechanism (CBAM) (Lowe, 2021). A British energy industry representative admitted that, despite surprisingly smooth cooperation, there had still been a 'massive reduction in the legal framework [for cooperation]', also noting worse access to skilled workers and supply chain constraints (Interview 1). A representative from an EU ENGO also pointed out that as the UK remained in certain EU schemes and programmes for a few more years, the full extent of Brexit impacts on climate and energy policy was not yet possible to assess (Interview 6). Moreover, in light of the war in Ukraine, the EU and the UK have taken different approaches to the energy crisis, with the UK not being subject to the proposals in the EU's 'REPowerEU'-plan.

Likewise, although the British energy industry representative noted earlier their pleasure with the energy section of the TCA, this enthusiasm was not echoed by all the interviewees. ENGO representatives noted that, although the relationship to the EU was better on climate and energy than other policy areas, cooperation had undoubtedly become more difficult post-Brexit due to the government's emphasis on 'red lines' and 'clean breaks' (Interview 3, Interview 5). The situation had not been helped by Boris Johnson's emphasis on domestic politics and 'getting Brexit done' as quickly as possible, marking a break with former Prime Minister Theresa May's attempts at fine-tuning and improving the final trade agreement. Likewise, discussions around the 'sunset clause' in the Brexit Freedoms Bill under the Truss and Sunak governments have not alleviated the situation. A British ENGO representative called the TCA a 'paradox', noting that on the one hand the TCA was a more comprehensive agreement than seen elsewhere, whilst on the other hand 'it is actually pretty unambitious in terms of doing anything interesting, bespoke or radical . . . indicative of the close relationship between the UK and the EU. . . . [It is a] missed opportunity' (Interview 3). Due to the politicised and polarised debate, the same informant argued it had been difficult for UK-based ENGOs to present their asks for the TCA due to the 'optics' when having sister groups in Brussels. They also pointed out the irony of Brexit supposedly being about cutting red tape when the TCA had created new advisory groups and increased the administrative burden for trade (Interview 3).

Lastly, referring to the governance challenge mentioned earlier (Reid, 2017), a British ENGO representative argued that although Brexit was about 'taking back control', it is still unclear where that control is transferred to –

> [Does power go] to the government or to Parliament? And within the UK government, does it go to central government, regulators or arms-length bodies? And then [where does it go] within the four nations of the UK? All of that is unresolved and this is six years later.
>
> *(Interview 3)*

A related point was raised by a former Cabinet minister, who pointed out that the UK's power and scope to influence EU policy was reduced post-Brexit:

> Practically there is little difference in energy and climate policy, but that's very much seen from the outside. From the inside we are no longer having those crucial and continuous negotiations and discussions. . . . We were a real force for good, pushing the agenda. Now we come in at the end – not at the initial stages or in the middle, just at the end.
>
> *(Interview 8)*

The Norway-EU relationship and implications for climate and energy policy post-Brexit

Norway has the reputation of being a climate leader (Eckersley, 2016; Boasson and Lahn, 2017). It was among the world's first countries to set a unilateral climate mitigation target in 1989 (Hovden and Lindseth, 2004), which came into being through Norway's follow-up of the Brundtland Commission's report 'Our Common Future', which had been released two years prior. A carbon tax was introduced as early as in 1991, and an emissions trading scheme (ETS) was introduced in 2005 (this was incorporated into the EU ETS in 2008). Over time, Norway has gradually increased its climate mitigation target, from its initial goal of stabilising emissions at 1989 levels by 2000, to more recently updating its Nationally Determined Contribution (NDC) under the Paris Agreement to at least 55 per cent compared to 1990 levels by 2030 (UNCC, 2022). Norwegian climate policy has also been underpinned by strong cross-party consensus and Climate Settlements (*Klimaforlik*) signed by six out of seven parties in the Storting (Norwegian Parliament) (Farstad, 2019).

However, despite its ambitious goals and cross-party consensus, Norway has only reduced its domestic greenhouse gas (GHG) emissions by 4.7 per cent between 1990 and 2021 (SSB, 2022) – primarily because of a booming petroleum sector, but also because Norwegian electricity supply is essentially already decarbonised due to the prominence of hydropower (Boasson and Jevnaker, 2019). As such, Norwegian climate policy has been dominated by a logic of cost-efficiency, leading to emission reductions abroad (Ćetković and Skjærseth, 2019). The country has always met its mitigation targets at the international level, though this has largely been achieved by purchasing UN-approved credits generated by projects under the Clean Development Mechanism under the Kyoto Protocol (Tellmann, 2012) and the EU ETS. Eckersley (2016, p. 191) points out that Norwegian politicians have applied various rhetorical ploys to 'manage and minimise the tensions between Norway's role as an ambitious climate leader and its economic role as a major petroleum and gas producer', for example by promoting CCS (Boasson, 2015; Roettereng, 2016) or seeking international cooperation on climate issues within the EU (Boasson, 2015; Jevnaker, 2016; Christensen, 2018) and the UN (Boasson and Lahn, 2017).

Norway has been a member of the EEA since 1992, meaning it is part of the single market, though it has exemptions for certain areas such as fisheries and agriculture, and it is not part of the Customs Union. Norway's EEA membership means it largely has to follow the EU's environmental and energy *acquis* (the collection of laws and regulations). As mentioned, Norway merged its ETS with the EU in 2008. It also cooperates with the EU on energy laws such as parts of the Clean Energy Package. In 2019, Norway also entered into an agreement with the EU to cooperate on reaching their climate goals. Norway chose to join the EU's Effort-Sharing Regulation (ESR) (which covers emissions from sectors such as road transport, agriculture, buildings, and waste) and the Land Use, Land Use Change and Forestry (LULUCF) Regulation. The ESR sets an overall emission reduction target for ESR sectors in the participating countries and awards them annual emissions budgets based on this target, although there is an opportunity to buy emission allocations from EU countries. Christensen (2018) argues that Norway's decision to join the ESR was largely due to this possibility to buy emission cuts abroad, also in sectors that were not part of the ETS. At the time, key politicians also argued that it was important to bind the Norwegian climate targets to the EU to ensure implementation (Farstad et al., 2022, p. 7).

As a non-EU member, Norway has the largest scope to influence EU policies 'upstream', that is, when proposals are being discussed, through expert group participation and through 'corridor diplomacy' (NOU 2012:2; also pointed out in Interview 2 and Interview 6). Hofmann et al. (2019) point to Norway's access and structural power, arguing that Norway is a 'shaper' of EU energy policy, with influence occasionally even surpassing that of smaller EU member states. However, Gullberg (2015) points out that although Norwegian interest groups have access to the European Commission to influence EU legislation, they still mainly lobby the Norwegian government, rendering their lobbying strategies insufficient to compensate for lack of representation in EU institutions. Others (e.g., Farstad et al., 2021) have pointed out that businesses nonetheless take a more active approach to EU legislation than the Parliament. Several interviewees argued that EU policy receives far too little attention in Parliament and in the Norwegian media (Interview 2, Interview 6, policy dialogue). Although EU policy is slowly but surely gaining more attention as the Norwegian public realises that the EGD and the war in Ukraine will have significant implications for Norwegian climate and energy policy (Farstad, 2022, p. 16), Norway's position as partly 'inside' and partly 'outside' the EU nonetheless leads to democratic challenges (NOU 2012:2; Eriksen and Fossum, 2014). This is particularly the case in the energy area, where Norway's situation is different to other EU countries. Norway has a tradition of strong state participation (Austvik and Claes, 2011) and an almost fully renewable power sector with an electricity surplus and being a net exporter of electricity. These conditions make the Norwegian interests align with EU interests to a lesser extent than in many other sectors (Gullberg, 2015) and makes it politically harder to defend investments in interconnectors and wind power, given the negative externalities of such projects (Leiren et al., 2020). Gullberg (2015) argues that this lack of alignment makes the Norwegian democratic challenge in the energy sector more severe.

These challenges are compounded by the EGD and the war in Ukraine. The speed at which the von der Leyen Commission is pushing through its green agenda and regulating energy markets under its 'REPowerEU' plan makes it difficult for Norway to influence outcomes through their traditional channels. Moreover, the cross-sectoral nature of the EGD makes it tricky for the country to unpack which parts of the EGD are EEA-relevant, and to protect areas of national competency (such as agriculture) which become entangled by being covered by various parts of the EGD (Farstad et al., 2021). Norway's current ESR target is 40 per cent compared to 1990 levels by 2030, which is likely to increase to 50 per cent in light of the EU's 'Fit for 55' package (Farstad et al., 2021). By joining the ESR, the EU has therefore increased its control over Norwegian climate policy. For example, transport and agricultural policy have not previously been affected by EU climate policy to any great extent. Furthermore, the ESR is enforced through annual reporting requirements and reviews, and the EFTA Surveillance Authority (ESA) can demand new action plans or increased emissions cuts if Norway fails to meet requirements, yet it is unclear whether ESA can impose penalties (Frisvold, 2019). Moreover, the energy situation in Europe in light of the war in Ukraine has reduced Norway's electricity surplus and increased costs for consumers, making energy exports and energy cooperation with the EU less popular.

Furthermore, a Norwegian energy industry representative pointed out that Norway's scope to carve out exemptions from EU policy has become increasingly constrained, particularly post-Brexit, and 'due to the Commission's conflicts with Switzerland and because of Brexit, Norway increasingly finds itself in a third country position than before' (Interview 2). A pertinent example is how batteries produced in Norway and exported to the UK via the EU will face an additional customs duty post-Brexit, due to the rules around country origin in the TCA, which defines Norway as a third country. This risk is compounded by Norway being slow to implement EU regulations (Interview 2). There is a considerable delay in implementation related to the EEA Agreement, as the process for transposing EU laws into the EEA Agreement begins when EU laws have been completed (Jevnaker,

2019). One example is the third energy package, which established the Agency for the Cooperation of Energy Regulators (ACER) and caused large opposition in Norway due to concerns that ACER would encroach on sovereignty, by making decisions related to licenses and interconnectors. This debate occurred 10 years later in Norway than in the EU.

The UK-Norway relationship and implications for climate and energy policy post-Brexit

Norwegian and British climate and energy policies are interrelated, and in some areas interdependent. The UK and Norway have often had similar views on EU climate and energy governance. Both countries liberalised their power sector early, they are connected through electricity and gas infrastructure, both have favoured a cost-efficient climate policy, and emissions trading has been the cornerstone in both countries' climate policies. Hence, when the UK left the EU, there were concerns in Norway about the loss of an ally inside the EU with similar positions on market liberalisation within energy (Interview 2, Interview 6). Norway has indeed lost the presence of an ally in the EU institutions (Interview 6, policy dialogue). Moreover, while representatives of Norwegian businesses and the government are present in Brussels, the UK is no longer there (Interview 1) and 'we [Norwegians] cannot bring Brits along with us to meetings with the [European] Commission' (Interview 2). The market liberalisation approach to EU energy policies remained unchanged immediately post-Brexit. The French presidency has been heavily involved in improving the energy market, for example (Interview 2). However, the war in Ukraine, high energy prices, and discussions about energy security have brought about a significant punctuation to this approach, with the European Commission working on a revision of the energy market and having revised the state aid rules for climate, environmental protection and energy, making the market-orientation less strict (European Commission, 2022; Interview 2).

There were also concerns about trade of electricity, as the most efficient trading across UK electricity interconnectors can only take place if the UK is part of the trading mechanisms that couples together the EU's electricity markets (Dutton, 2019). A UK opt-out of the trading mechanism would affect the ability to deliver on climate targets, as electricity interconnectors are of key importance for decarbonisation, and Norway and the UK are linked through the world's longest subsea interconnector, the North Sea Link. Although Norway is an important crude oil supplier to the UK and typically the UK's largest gas supplier (Office for National Statistics, 2022), oil and gas trading were of less concern as they are a different kind of commodity and not in the same way dependent on trading solutions as electricity is (Interview 7; SSB, 2019). Brexit decoupled the UK's auctions from the trading mechanism; hence, for the North Sea Link, the two infrastructure operators for electricity, National Grid in the UK and Statnett in Norway, had to develop their own trading solution, which is less efficient than the mechanism in the EU electricity market but more efficient than the new solution between the UK and the EU (Interview 2; Interview 7). Strong regulatory certainty characterised the initial phase of the North Sea Link project (the investment decision was made in 2015), but Brexit created considerable doubts and demanded considerable resources for collaboration from both sides.

In addition to agreements between the system operators, the Agreement on cross-border trade in electricity and cooperation on electricity interconnection (signed in September 2021) was important for ensuring cooperation in this area. There was a need for a regulatory framework, as Brexit meant that there was otherwise no structure regulating the relationship between the British and Norwegian authorities. Hence, the Agreement created a sense of safety, clear frameworks, was quite concrete, and drew on the TCA between the UK and the EU as a benchmark in terms of wording (Interview 7). The key aim was to facilitate efficient electricity trading, which the UK was particularly keen on achieving. However, the interviewees agreed that EU membership (i.e., market integration) was preferable (Interview 7, policy dialogue). One British energy industry representative highlighted, 'They [the Norwegians] want a stable regulatory framework that replaces the one that we [the UK] just ripped up' (Interview 1).

The cross-country electricity trade agreement was an addition to the Free-Trade Agreement (FTA). The two negotiations went on simultaneously (beginning in August 2020 and ending in June 2021) and under considerable time pressure, but the cross-country electricity trade agreement was only between the UK and Norway, while Norway also acted as a spokesperson for Iceland and Liechtenstein in the case of the FTA (Prime Minister's Office, 2021). The chapter in the FTA on trade and sustainable development (Chapter 13) is of particular relevance for the area of climate and energy policy. The EFTA countries desired an agreement that was as similar to the EEA Agreement as possible and would be at least as good as the TCA (Prop. 210 S (2020–2021), p. 15). The Norwegian agreement was unsuccessful on the issue of non-regression, however. While the EU can sanction the UK if it does not maintain levels of environmental protection, Norway cannot do so. Having repeatedly claimed that it will not regress its environmental standards after Brexit, accepting non-regression had been difficult for the UK in the UK-EU negotiations (Jordan et al., 2020). To achieve similar non-regression formulations in the FTA would have required Norway to give further concessions in other politically vital sectors like agriculture (Interview 4).

The countries' communication with the outside world in their press releases highlight discrepancies between them on climate policy. While it was important for Norway to convey that the agreement with the United Kingdom was good for the climate,[1] for Britain it was more important to show that the country retained sovereignty and maintained its right to make ambitious climate policy.[2] The UK government wanted to express that it has room to manoeuvre and that this room was achieved because of Brexit. This is also highlighted in the UK's impact assessment of the Agreement (Department for International Trade, 2021b, p. 20): 'Nothing in the Agreement prevents the United Kingdom from continuing to uphold its high environmental standards nor to implement policy in support of our climate change objectives'. The UK emphasised that it would not bind itself to international climate goals through a trade agreement. A consequence was that the UK pushed for a rather lukewarm formulation of environmental protection (Interview 4). While Norway wanted to use a more binding language (e.g., 'the Parties commit to'), the UK wanted weaker formulations (e.g., 'the Parties recognise the importance of achieving the ultimate objective of' the Paris Agreement). This discussion underscores the leaked government document drawn up by officials in the Department for International Trade, stating that Britain should prioritise economic growth over environmental protections in trade deals – although the government denied considering the advice (Sky News, 2021). The parties eventually agreed on the weaker formulations (Article 13.22), which will probably make a legal challenge more difficult (Interview 4). Time pressures also played a role in giving in to the weaker formulation.

Climate and energy policy post-Brexit in the trilateral relationship

Stakeholders and interviewees highlight that Europe has moved from a situation with regulatory stability and alignment pre-Brexit to a more complex and uncertain situation post-Brexit. The uncertainties pertain more to the implementation of policy rather than goals or the political relationship, however, especially since the trade agreements (TCA, FTA, and the cross-border electricity trade agreement) have ensured relative stability. As pointed out by a Brussel-based ENGO representative: 'The discussion has moved on. It's no longer about the goal or the timeline, it's about how we get there – there's broad support for net zero' (Interview 6). Mutual interests and similarly ambitious climate goals have secured a decent cooperative relationship and relative policy convergence on climate and energy post-Brexit. The uncertainties nonetheless entail an increased administrative burden, for example in following policy developments in the respective jurisdictions, operating in the different countries, and maintaining trade (Interview 2, Interview 7, policy dialogue). Likewise, a former Cabinet minister pointed out that, with the UK outside of the EU, the UK was no longer there to 'keep the commonality between countries, which is so important in this issue area' (Interview 8).

The new trade relationships have implications across the different jurisdictions. For example, the extent to which the UK aligns its laws and regulations to retain access to the internal energy market post-Brexit has been important for Norway, as the consequences of Brexit for Norway is dependent on the nature of the EU-UK relationship. This is seen clearly in the battery example, which was briefly mentioned in Chapter 2, but there are also barriers for Norway in the case of North Sea cooperation, where an extensive offshore wind development is foreseen. Several EU members (e.g., Denmark, Germany, the Netherlands, and Belgium) have ambitious plans for offshore wind development, as highlighted at high-level meetings in

Denmark in May and August 2022 on development of offshore renewable energy in the North Sea and the Baltic Sea respectively. The UK and Norway were (as the only non-EU members) not invited. However, the UK has signed bilateral agreements with several EU countries, opening up for hybrid interconnectors. In contrast, Norway is moving more slowly due to popular opposition to interconnectors and disagreement about them within government.

It is interesting to note that interviewees point to popular opposition to interconnectors, particularly in Norway, as a greater challenge to North Sea energy cooperation than Brexit. As described by a British energy industry representative, 'For me, the bigger risks [to energy cooperation] are domestic opinion in Norway' (Interview 1). In contrast to the UK where interconnectors have received relatively limited media attention (Interview 1, Interview 5), interconnectors have been of significant public interest in Norway (Hermansen and Bang, 2022). As noted by a Norwegian energy industry representative, 'We get a vast amount more conflict in Norway [on this issue] than in our neighbouring countries' (Interview 2). Norway is not the only country struggling with popular opposition to energy policy, however. A former Cabinet minister argued that the biggest challenge for climate and energy policy post-Brexit was faced by every nation, namely right-wing populists deriding the costs of the net zero goal. They also noted that 'the EU doing this [developing climate and energy policy] together is really helpful', whereas UK politicians would increasingly have to develop and defend policies by themselves (Interview 8).

Likewise, some argue that, although energy cooperation continues to be a policy priority for all parties in the triangular relationship (EU-UK-Norway), there has been an increasing 'nationalism' within energy politics post-Brexit, for example the UK emphasising that supply chains should be British, or the EU emphasising less dependence on foreign supply chains in its EGD. A Brussel-based ENGO representative argued that the UK's increased nationalism in this area was 'infecting other countries' (Interview 6). For a small yet open economy like Norway, such a trend can be problematic (stakeholder workshop Annex I). Despite the challenges a more nationalist approach to energy would pose for Norway, the debate over energy exports and hostility to interconnectors reveals an increasingly nationalist trend also here.

The war in Ukraine has certainly also influenced the triangular energy and climate relationship. As mentioned, the European Commission is rethinking its regulation of the energy market and state aid guidelines, but more broadly the war has reaffirmed the need for energy cooperation and development of renewables (Interview 1, Interview 2, Interview 6). As a British energy industry representative put it:

> Putting it bluntly, I think there have been some people in the UK who had forgotten who our allies are, and actually the events of the last week [referring to the outbreak of war in Ukraine] just reiterate the fact that we are on the same side.
>
> *(Interview 1)*

A representative from a Brussels-based ENGO asked whether Norway would become more popular as an energy exporter in light of the conflict, or whether the drive to phase Europe off gas could 'burn the gas bridge' (Interview 6). Likewise, a Norwegian energy industry representative pointed out that Norway is a dependable exporter of gas, but that the country should be wary of its position in future given the drive around renewables and offshore wind as the solution to dependence on Russian gas (Interview 2). Indeed, while the EU's initial reaction to the war in Ukraine was to buy more gas from other countries than Russia (such as Norway), the REPowerEU plan emphasises a rapid expansion of renewable energy. The war might also dampen domestic resistance in Norway towards interconnectors, as solidarity with Ukraine and Europe increases, although so far there is little indication of this happening. There is, however, a risk that Norway is falling outside the 'exceptional institutional strengthening' and 'solidarity' occurring in the EU following the COVID-19 pandemic and in light of the war in Ukraine: 'Norway needs to be careful not to become further marginalised as an energy actor' (Interview 2). Indeed, as Norway is benefitting extensively from the high gas prices in light of the war, it is being increasingly criticised for not reducing prices or sharing profits. Even so, reducing dependency on Russian gas might temporarily give Norway considerable negotiating power, given the increased dependence on Norway as a reliable gas exporter.

Discussion

The chapter shows how Norway meets the climate crisis through ever-closer bonds with the EU, whereas the UK has seen major punctuations in its EU relationship, pulling out of key initiatives. In Norway's case, their closer EU relationship achieves increased flexibility in terms of how they reach their target and harmonisation beneficial for trade, at the expense of democratic legitimacy. The country's autonomy, that is, its wish to stake out its own course and create a direction for society, is becoming increasingly constrained by the speed and cross-sectoral nature of the EGD. In line with this, Norway's wriggle room, that is, its capability to act within the EEA framework, is, in certain respects, more limited as a consequence of the new trilateral relationship (e.g., the mentioned battery example). The decision to cooperate with the EU in reaching climate targets also narrows Norway's wriggle room. As the country has bound their climate policy to the EU, it risks actions from the EU (ESA and the European Commission) if it does not adhere to the rules.

Moreover, although the climate agreement with the EU affords more flexibility to Norway overall in terms of how it achieves its climate targets (e.g., through purchasing emissions allowances through the ESR in addition to the ETS), any changes to accounting rules and flexibility suggested in the European Commission's 'Fit for 55' package and in the future will affect how Norway can achieve its climate goals (if Norway decides to maintain the agreement). Moreover, the country's ability to influence the EU relationship and EU policy through traditional channels becomes increasingly tricky due to the EGD and having lost the UK as an insider. The war in Ukraine and the drive around the European Commission's REPowerEU plan could have different consequences for Norway. In the short run, Norway plays an important role in terms of being the largest gas exporter to the EU; however, in the long run Norway might play a weaker role in influencing EU energy policy, if the country continues to rely on the petroleum sector in future. In the Norwegian case, the democratic challenge of EEA membership – with its lack of representation in EU institutions – is intensified by the great importance of energy policy and by the different interests of Norway (a large energy exporter) and the EU (a large energy importer). However, a shared interest in solving the climate crisis with the EU might make Norway's interests in the energy sector more in line with EU interests, albeit public opinion might also create a backlash. Finally, it is worth noting that Brexit not only changes the autonomy and wriggle room of non-members versus the EU (as the EU is arguably a hegemon), but it also alters the autonomy and wriggle room between non-members, as the UK is a larger and more powerful country than Norway.

The UK has chosen a different path to Norway – sacrificing the benefits of cooperation and the risks of 'zombie legislation' for increased autonomy. In issue-areas that are repatriated from the EU, the UK has shifted from a situation where non-compliance is enforced by the European Court of Justice (ECJ) and the European Commission with the threat of significant fines, to a UK governance system where enforcement is not as independent or efficient. This situation may have implications for the implementation of climate and policy, as, while on the face of it, policy remains the same, removing the European governance structures means running the risk of 'zombie legislation'. As such, this situation has increased the autonomy and wriggle room of the UK, but only to a certain extent. For example, non-regression in the TCA includes possibilities of the EU to sanction the UK on matters of environmental protection. Moreover, the UK can no longer influence the agenda of the EU and its member states to the same extent and lacks Norway's non-member experiences of 'corridor diplomacy'. Being a 'divorced' partner and not an EEA member, the UK also has less possibilities to influence policies at the technical level. Increased autonomy also comes at the cost of less efficiency in electricity trading, which the UK is dependent on to achieve its electrification and climate goals. Moreover, the question of 'where does power return to' post-Brexit is a pertinent one. The governance challenge of dividing and wielding power via the government, parliament, arms-length bodies, and the devolved nations is unlikely to be solved in the near term, with contention likely to remain. Although power conflicts between the devolved nations, and between Westminster and Scotland in particular, can potentially lead to a 'race to the top' in terms of energy and climate policy, with no restrictions on downward divergence in the UK Internal Market Bill. There are also significant risks that Westminster can erode policy ambitions over time, especially in its drive for new trade agreements, or, in a worst-case scenario, lead to a 'race to the bottom'. For the devolved nations, therefore, Brexit has been a significant infringement on their autonomy.

This analysis of the climate and energy sectors suggests that, where the UK continues to have similar aspirations as the EU and Norway, the political order remains relatively stable. The triangular relationship post-Brexit in the areas of climate change and energy has been surprisingly stable and cooperative despite the significant punctuations in the UK's relationships with the EU and Norway post-Brexit, and particularly in comparison to other policy areas. Being connected by interconnectors and the physical reality of shared infrastructure, as well as sharing the ambition of being climate change leaders, has worked like political glue, though the challenges of the new regime should not be underestimated. Brexit has led to increased administrative burdens and impacts to trade and moves towards increased nationalism (though the war in Ukraine might change this).

Conclusion

Despite significant similarities, the UK and Norway have selected different approaches as to how they cooperate with the EU on climate and energy issues. Whereas the UK has extricated itself from key EU climate and energy initiatives, Norway cooperates increasingly closer with the EU. In this chapter we have characterised and explained these diverging paths and assessed their implications for the post-Brexit relationships (both bilateral and trilateral) and climate and energy policy. Both Norway and the UK have decided to be outside of the EU to protect areas of national interest or regain autonomy. The UK has indeed become more autonomous post-Brexit, but not as much as it wants to convey. In contrast, Norway's path is characterised by decreasing autonomy, although with the benefits of increased flexibility in reaching its climate targets. Within climate and energy policies the interests of the UK, Norway and the EU are, at least for the time being, coherent. Physical infrastructure, similar climate ambitions, and the three parties wanting to cooperate on these issues have ensured relatively smooth cooperation, at least in comparison to other policy areas. However, Brexit has increased hurdles and administrative costs. Moreover, while the impacts of the COVID-19 pandemic continue to be felt across European economies, and the war in Ukraine introduces new challenges in the form of increasing power prices, there is a need to follow the developments of the trilateral relationship ahead during turbulent times.

Notes

1 '[T]here are a number of commitments relating to climate change, the environment and labour rights, as well as general commitments supporting the green transition. The goal is to enhance awareness and increase acceptance of the need to ensure that trade contributes to sustainable development' (The Office of the Prime Minister, 2021).
2 'The agreement strongly supports the UK's ambitions as a global leader on climate and environmental protection. It preserves the UK's right to regulate to reach our Net Zero

target, promotes trade and investment to grow the low carbon economy, and addresses numerous issues related to environmental protection, including biodiversity, forestry and sustainable fisheries' (Department for International Trade, 2021a).

References

Austvik, O. G. and Claes, D. H. (2011) *EØS-avtalen og norsk energipolitikk*, Oslo: Europautredningen.

Averchenkova, A., Fankhauser, S. and Finnegan, J. (2020) 'The Impact of Strategic Climate Legislation: Evidence from Expert Interviews on the UK Climate Change Act', *Climate Policy*, 21(2): 251–263.

Blondeel, M., Froggatt, A. and Kuzemko, C. (2022) 'Brexit and Decarbonisation, One Year On: Friction, Fish and Fine Tuning', *UK Energy Research Centre Briefing Paper*. https://doi.org/10.5286/ukerc.edc.000952.

Boasson, E. L. (2015) *National Climate Policy. A Multi-Field Approach*, Abingdon: Routledge.

Boasson, E. L. (2021) 'Norway: Certificate Supporters Turning Opponents', in Boasson, E. L., Leiren, M. D. and Wettestad, J. (eds) *Comparative Renewables Policy. Political, Organisational and European Fields*, New York: Routledge, pp. 193–216.

Boasson, E. L. and Jevnaker, T. (2019) 'Energy Governance in Norway: Too Much of a Good Thing?', in Knodt, M. and Kemmerzell, J. (eds) *Handbook of Energy Governance in Europe*, Cham: Springer, pp. 1–25.

Boasson, E. L. and Lahn, B. (2017) 'Norway: A Dissonant Cognitive Leader?', in Wurzel, R. K. W., Connely, J. and Liefferink, D. (eds) *The European Union in International Climate Change Politics: Still Taking a Lead?*, London: Routledge.

Burns, C. (2020) 'Brexit's Implications for Environmental Policy', *UK in a Changing Europe*. Available at: https://ukandeu.ac.uk/long-read-pdf/?postid=39648 (Accessed 25 January 2023).

Burns, C., Carter, N., Cowell, R., Eckersley, P., Farstad, F., Gravey, V., Jordan, A, Moore, B. and Reid, C. (2018) 'Environmental Policy in a Devolved United Kingdom: Challenges and Opportunities after Brexit', *UK in a Changing Europe Policy Brief*. Available at: www.brexitenvironment.co.uk/wp-content/uploads/2018/10/BrexitEnvUKReport.pdf (Accessed 25 February 2023).

Burns, C., Gravey, V., Jordan, A. and Zito, A. (2019) 'De-Europeanising or Disengaging? EU Environmental Policy and Brexit', *Environmental Politics*, 28(2): 271–292.

Carbon Brief (2019) *Analysis: Why the UK's CO2 Emissions Have Fallen 38% Since 1990*. Available at: www.carbonbrief.org/analysis-why-the-uks-co2-emissions-have-fallen-38-since-1990 (Accessed 25 February 2023).

Carter, N. and Childs, M. (2017) 'Friends of the Earth as a Policy Entrepreneur: "The Big Ask" Campaign for a UK Climate Change Act', *Environmental Politics*, 27(6): 994–1013.

Carter, N. and Clements, B. (2015) 'From "Greenest Government Ever" to "Get Rid of All the Green Crap": David Cameron, the Conservatives and the Environment', *British Politics*, 10: 204–225.

Ćetković, S. and Skjærseth, J. B. (2019) 'Creative 735 and Disruptive Elements in Norway's Climate Policy Mix: The Small-State Perspective', *Environmental Politics*, 26: 1039–1060.

Christensen, L. (2018) 'Norges Klimamål for 2030', *Norsk Statsvitenskapelig Tidsskrift*, 34(2–3): 113–133.

Coates, S. (2021) 'UK Trade Deals Should Prioritise Economic Growth Over Environmental Protections – Leaked Govt Document', *Sky News*, 14 October. Available at: https://news.

sky.com/story/uk-trade-deals-should-prioritise-economic-growth-over-environmental-protections-leaked-govt-document-12433808 (Accessed 25 February 2023).

Department for International Trade (2021a) *United Kingdom Signs Free-Trade Deal with Norway, Iceland and Liechtenstein*. Available at: www.gov.uk/government/news/united-kingdom-signs-free-trade-deal-with-norway-iceland-and-liechtenstein (Accessed 25 February 2023).

Department for International Trade (2021b) 'Free-trade Agreement between the United Kingdom and Norway, Iceland, and Liechtenstein', *Impact Assessment*. Available at: https://assets.publishing.service.gov.uk/government/uploads/system/uploads/attachment_data/file/1002867/UK-Norway-Iceland-and-Liechtenstein-Impact-Assessment-final.pdf (Accessed 25 February 2023).

Dutton, J. (2019) 'UK-EU Electricity Interconnection: The UK's Low Carbon Future and Regional Cooperation After Brexit', *E3G Briefing Paper*. Available at: https://www.e3g.org/publications/uk-eu-electricity-interconnection-low-carbon-future-and-brexit/ (Accessed 26 July 2023).

Eckersley, R. (2016) 'National Identities, International Roles, and the Legitimation of Climate Leadership: Germany and Norway compared', *Environmental Politics*, 25(1): 180–201.

ENDS Europe (2022) *How Green is Rishi Sunak?*. Available at: www.endsreport.com/article/1802990/green-rishi-sunak?bulletin=the-saturday-report&utm_medium=EMAIL&utm_campaign=eNews%20Bulletin&utm_source=20221029&utm_content=ENDS%20Report%20The%20Saturday%20Report%20(13)::&email_hash= (Accessed 25 February 2023).

Eriksen, E. O. and Fossum, J. E. (2014) *Det norske paradoks. Om Norges forhold til Den europeiske union*, Oslo: Universitetsforlaget.

European Commission (2022) *State Aid: Commission Amends the Temporary Crisis Framework*. Available at: https://ec.europa.eu/commission/presscorner/detail/en/ip_22_4622 (Accessed 25 February 2023).

Farstad, F. M. (2019) 'Does Size Matter? Comparing the Party Politics of Climate Change in Australia and Norway', *Environmental Politics*, 28: 997–1016.

Farstad, F. M. (2022) 'EUs grønne giv: Status etter sommeren 2022 og mulige implikasjoner for Norge', *CICERO Report 2022: 09*. Available at: www.platonklima.no/wp-content/uploads/2022/09/EUs-gronne-giv-09_2022.pdf (Accessed 25 February 2023).

Farstad, F. M., Hermansen, E. A. T., Grasbekk, B. S., Brudevoll, K. and van Oort, B. (2022) 'Explaining Radical Policy Change: Norwegian Climate Policy and the Ban on Cultivating Peatlands', *Global Environmental Change*, 74: 1–10.

Farstad, F. M., Hermansen, E. A. T., Leiren, M. D., Wettestad, J., Gulbrandsen, L. H., Søgaard, G., Øistad, K., Fridstrøm, K., Knapskog, M. and Uteng, T. P. (2021) 'Klar for 55? EUs nye klimaregelverk og betydningen for Norge', *CICERO Report 2021:07*. Available at: www.platonklima.no/wp-content/uploads/2021/12/Klar-for-55_EUs-nye-klima-regelverk-og-betydningen-for-Norge.pdf (Accessed 25 February 2023).

Frisvold, P. (2019) *EUs klimasanksjoner i det blå? Energi og klima*. Available at: https://energiogklima.no/meninger-og-analyse/debatt/eus-klimasanksjoner-i-det-bla/ (Accessed 25 February 2023).

FTA; Free-trade Agreement (2021) *Free Trade Agreement between Iceland, the Principality of Liechtenstein and the Kingdom of Norway and the United Kingdom of Great Britain and Northern Ireland*. Available at: https://assets.publishing.service.gov.uk/government/uploads/system/uploads/attachment_data/file/1003335/Free_trade_agreement_between_UK-Northern_Ireland_and_Liechtenstein__Iceland_and_Norway_volume_1.pdf (Accessed 25 February 2023).

Gravey, V., Jordan, A. and Burns, C. (2016) 'Environmental Policy after Brexit: Mind the Governance Gap', *UK in a Changing Europe Commentary*. Available at: http://ukandeu.ac.uk/environmental-policy-after-brexit-mind-the-governance-gap/ (Accessed 25 February 2023).

Gullberg, A. T. (2015) 'Lobbying in Oslo or in Brussels? The Case of a European Economic Area Country', *Journal of European Public Policy*, 22(10): 1531–1550.

Hermansen, E. A. T. and Bang, G. (2022) 'A "Green Battery" with Limited Interconnector Capacity? Conflicting Interests in Norwegian Interconnector Politics', *Working Paper*. Oslo: CICERO.

Hofmann, B., Jevnaker, T. and Thaler, P. (2019) 'Following, Challenging, or Shaping: Can Third Countries Influence EU Energy Policy?', *Politics and Governance*, 7(1): 152–164.

House of Commons (2021) 'Committee on the Future Relationship with the European Union', *Oral Evidence: Progress of the Negotiations on the UK's Future Relationship with the EU, HC 203*. Available at: https://committees.parliament.uk/oralevidence/1465/pdf/ (Accessed 25 February 2023).

Hovden, E. and Lindseth, G. (2004) 'Discourses in Norwegian Climate Policy: National Action or Thinking Globally?', *Political Studies*, 52(1): 63–81.

Jevnaker, T. (2016) 'Implementation in Norway', in Skjærseth, J. B., Eikeland, P. O., Gulbrandsen, L. H. and Jevnaker, T. (eds) *Linking EU Climate and Energy Policies: Decision-making, Implementation and Reform*, Cheltenham: Edward Elgar Publishing.

Jevnaker, T. (2019) 'ACER i perspektiv. EUs energipolitikk og behovet for en god norsk debatt', *FNI Report 4*. Oslo: Fritjof Nansen Institute.

Jordan, A., Gravey, V., Moore, B. and Reid, C. (2020) "EU-UK Trade Relations: Why Environmental Policy Regression Will Undermine the Level Playing Field and What the UK Can Do to Limit It', *Research Paper on the Level Playing Field*. Available at: https://cdn.friendsoftheearth.uk/sites/default/files/downloads/Regression%20report%202020.pdf (Accessed 25 February 2023).

Kern, F., Smith, A., Shaw, C., Raven, R. and Verhees, B. (2014) 'From Laggard to Leader: Explaining Offshore Wind Developments in the UK', *Energy Policy*, 69: 635–646.

Leiren, M. D., Aakre, S., Linnerud, K., Julsrud, T. E., Di Nucci, R. and Krug, M. (2020) 'Community Acceptance of Wind Energy Developments: Experience from Wind Energy Scarce Regions in Europe', *Sustainability*, 12(5): 1–22.

Leiren, M. D. and Takle, M. (2022) 'The United Kingdom: A Merging Climate and Sustainability Agenda', in Schøyen, M.-A., Hvinden, B. and Leiren, M. D. (eds) *Towards Sustainable Welfare States in Europe. Social Policy and Climate Change*, Cheltenham: Edward Elgar Publishing.

Lowe, S. (2021) 'CBAM: What Might an EU Carbon-Border Adjustment Mechanism for the UK?', *UK in a Changing Europe Commentary*. Available at: https://ukandeu.ac.uk/eu-cbam-uk/ (Accessed 25 February 2023).

Moore, B. and Jordan, A. (2021) 'Climate Policy', in *UK Regulation after Brexit*, UK in a Changing Europe. Available at: https://ukandeu.ac.uk/wp-content/uploads/2021/02/UK-regulation-after-Brexit.pdf (Accessed 25 February 2023).

NOU 2012:12 (2012) *Utenfor og innenfor. Norges avtaler med EU*, Oslo: Utenriksdepartementet.

Oberthür, S. and Dupont, C. (2021) 'The European Union's International Climate Leadership: Towards a Grand Climate Strategy?', *Journal of European Public Policy*, 28(7): 1095–1114.

Office for National Statistics (2022) *Trends in UK Imports and Exports of Fuels*. Available at: www.ons.gov.uk/economy/nationalaccounts/balanceofpayments/articles/trendsinukimportsandexportsoffuels/2022-06-29#:~:text=This%20European%20demand%20for%20gas,of%20exports%20in%20April%202022 (Accessed 25 February 2023).

The Office of the Prime Minister (2021) *Historic Free-Trade Agreement with the UK*. Available at: www.regjeringen.no/en/historical-archive/solbergs-government/Ministries/smk/Press-releases/2021/historic-free-trade-agreement-with-the-uk/id2857147/ (Accessed 25 February 2023).

Paterson, M. (2022) 'What Liz Truss's Government Means for Climate Action', *The Conversation*. Available at: https://theconversation.com/what-liz-trusss-government-means-for-climate-action-190280 (Accessed 25 February 2023).

Prime Minister's Office (2021) *Inngår historisk frihandelsavtale med Storbritannia*. Available at: www.regjeringen.no/no/dokumentarkiv/regjeringen-solberg/aktuelt-regjeringen-solberg/smk/pressemeldinger/2021/inngar-historisk-frihandelsavtale-med-storbritannia/id2857147/ (Accessed 25 February 2023).

Prop. 210 S (2020–2021) *Samtykke til inngåelse av frihandelsavtale mellom Island, Liechtenstein, Norge og Storbritannia*, Oslo: Utenriksdepartementet. Available at: https://www.regjeringen.no/contentassets/3022d0715d85448a9cccb1de4049fa9e/no/pdfs/prp202020210210000dddpdfs.pdf (Accessed 27 July 2023).

Rayner, T. and Jordan, A. (2017) 'The United Kingdom: A record of leadership under threat?', in Wurzel, R. K. W., Connely, J. and Liefferink, D. (eds) *The European Union in International Climate Change Politics: Still Taking a Lead?* London: Routledge, pp. 173–188.

Rayner, T., Leiren, M. D. and Inderberg, T. H. J. (2021) 'The United Kingdom. From Market-led Policy Towards Technology Steering', in Boasson, E. L., Leiren, M. D. and Wettestad, J. (eds) *Comparative Renewables Policy: Political, Organisational and European Fields*, New York: Routledge, pp. 103–125.

Reid, C. (2017) 'Brexit and the Devolution Dynamics', *Environmental Law Review*, 19(1): 3–5.

Roettereng, J.-K. S. (2016) 'How the Global and National Levels Interrelate in Climate Policy-Making: Foreign Policy Analysis and the Case of Carbon Capture Storage in Norway's Foreign Policy', *Energy Policy*, 97: 475–484.

Ross, A. (2012) *Sustainable Development Law in the UK. From Rhetoric To Reality?*, New York: Earthscan.

Statistics Norway (SSB) (2019) *Brexit: Norges Handel Med Storbritannia*. Available at: www.ssb.no/utenriksokonomi/artikler-og-publikasjoner/norges-handel-med-storbritannia-for-brexit (Accessed 25 February 2023).

Statistics Norway (SSB) (2022) *Emissions to Air*. Available at: www.ssb.no/natur-og-miljo/forurensning-og-klima/statistikk/utslipp-til-luft (Accessed 25 February 2023).

TCA. (2021) 'Trade and Cooperation Agreement Between the European Union and the European Atomic Energy Community, of the One Part, and the United Kingdom of Great Britain and Northern Ireland, of the Other Part', *Official Journal of the European Union*, 30 April, L, 149: 10–2539.

Tellmann, S. M. (2012) 'The Constrained Influence of Discourses: The Case of Norwegian Climate Policy', *Environmental Politics*, 21(5): 734–752.

Tobin, P. (2021) 'Climate Change', in *Brexit and Beyond*. UK in a Changing Europe Report. Available at: https://ukandeu.ac.uk/wp-content/uploads/2021/01/Brexit-and-Beyond-report-compressed.pdf (Accessed 25 February 2023).

UNCC (2022) *Norway First NDC* (Second updated submission). Available at: Norway First NDC (Second updated submission) | UNFCCC (Accessed 10 February 2023).

Watson, J. (2021) 'Energy', in *Brexit and Beyond*. UK in a Changing Europe Report. Available at: https://ukandeu.ac.uk/wp-content/uploads/2021/01/Brexit-and-Beyond-report-compressed.pdf (Accessed 25 February 2023).

Wurzel, R. K.W and Connelly, J. (eds) (2011) *The European Union as a Leader in International Climate Change Politics*, Oxford: Routledge.

ANNEX I

Interviewees

Interviewees

1. Energy industry representative in the UK, Teams, 1 March 2022
2. Energy industry representative in Norway, Teams, 8 March 2022
3. Environmental organisation representative in the UK, Teams, 9 March 2022
4. Civil servant, the Norwegian Ministry of Trade, Industries and Fisheries, Oslo, 11 March 2022
5. Environmental organisation representative in the UK, Teams, 16 March 2022
6. Environmental organisation representative in Brussels, Teams, 17 March 2022
7. Two civil servants, the Norwegian Ministry of Petroleum and Energy, Oslo, 23 March 2022
8. Former Cabinet minister, Teams, 23 March 2022

Stakeholder workshop, teams, 29 October 2021

Representatives from: Academia, the Norwegian Ministry of Climate and Environment, Norwegian Ministry of Foreign Affairs, Norwegian Environment Agency, Norwegian Agriculture Agency, the Norwegian Agency for Local Governments ('Kommunalbanken'), the Norwegian Board of Technology, Statkraft, Statnett, Bellona, Sabima, Confederation of Norwegian Enterprise, Norwegian Shipowners' Association, Norwegian Forest Owners Association, Norwegian Farmers Union.

Policy dialogue, Oslo, 01 December 2021

Representatives from: Academia, two representatives of the Mission of Norway to the EU, two representatives from the energy industry, one environmental organisation.

4
FISHERIES, AQUACULTURE, AND AGRICULTURE

Autonomy and wriggle room in primary industry policies

Introduction

Primary industries, here understood as fisheries, aquaculture, and agriculture, are, to varying degrees, influenced by Norway's EEA affiliation. Although Norway is outside the EU's Common Fisheries Policy (CFP), fisheries and aquaculture form part of a sector that 'can *really* be said to be outside and inside the EU at the same time' (NOU 2012:2, p. 666; Laurantzon and Arnesen, 2020). Fisheries are mostly outside, while tariff-free trade in seafood is closely connected to the EEA grant which finances regional development in the EU. Agriculture, for its part, is outside the Common Agriculture Policy (CAP), and Norway is free to design its own agricultural policy instruments such as support schemes, market regulations, and tariff system. However, there is an article in the EEA Agreement that covers trade in some agricultural products (Article 19) and a protocol that covers some trade in processed food (Protocol 3) (NOU 2012:2, p. 657). Furthermore, the value chains of primary industries have, since 1998, been subject to all EU regulations for sanitary and phytosanitary measures, often referred to as SPS rules (NOU 2012:2, p. 645).

In this chapter, our point of departure is to explain how two industries, whose interests were important for why Norway voted no to membership in the EU in 1972, have become so closely affiliated with the EU's legal order. We ask: what is Norwegian authorities' autonomy and wriggle room in primary industry policies outside and inside the EEA framework? We will be unpacking the autonomy and wriggle room within each sector. However, since there are several issue linkages and spillovers between different primary industry policies, we also need to explore the importance of the connection between them. Furthermore, we ask what are the Norwegian lessons for the UK post-Brexit? And what are the implications of different legal EU affiliations for the relations between Norway and the UK after Brexit? The discussion of the last question is limited to fisheries and trade in goods from the primary industries.

Drawing on the theoretical concept of the book in Chapter 2, with autonomy we refer to will and ability to pursue what one takes to be one's own (authentic) interest. This may or may not be under conditions of independence. It follows that a state may be reliant on others and yet still pursue an autonomous interest and course of action. The issue is how much space or scope the relationship provides for that. Furthermore, wriggle room is a subcategory of autonomy and refers in this book to the action space that a third country has within the context of its legally regulated EU affiliation agreements. In this context, it is also important to take multilateral agreements into account, like the United Nations Convention on the Law of the Sea (UNCLOS) for fisheries, the WTO-agreement for agriculture, and the SPS agreement in the WTO. These agreements may underpin national autonomy and wriggle room outside the EU's legal order.

The chapter proceeds in the following manner.[1] The next part provides an overview over the UNCLOS framework. Part 3 reviews the EUs Common Fisheries Policy (CFP). Part 4 reviews how primary industries in the UK has been influenced by membership in the CFP and the CAP. Furthermore, we assess how the Withdrawal Agreement and the Trade and Cooperation Agreement (TCA) have influenced primary industries in the UK. The main emphasis is on fisheries, but we also discuss agriculture and trade. Part 5 discusses Norway's EU relations in primary industries. This part covers fisheries, aquaculture, market access for seafood,[2] fisheries and the EEA grant, agriculture, and the incorporation of the EU's SPS framework in the EEA Agreement. Part 6 analyses the EU-UK-Norway relations after Brexit. The final part summaries the observations and draw conclusions regarding autonomy and wriggle room.

The multilateral framework for fisheries

International maritime law forms the basis for the coastal states' autonomy since its basic principle is that states have sovereign control over natural resources within their territorial waters. Historically, this was limited to three nautical miles from the shore, but as early as the 1940s, several coastal states started to extend their territorial waters beyond that limit. In response to this, the United Nations initiated a process that, in 1982, led to the signing of the United Nation Convention on the Law of the Sea (UNCLOS) (Foss, 2011, p. 7). The convention was formally implemented from 1994. However, Norway, the EU, and other countries projected this outcome when they established their 200 miles Exclusive Economic Zones (EEZ) as early as in 1977 (Bjørndal and Munro, 2020, p. 267).

The UNCLOS agreement meant that the territorial waters of coastal states expanded to 12 nautical miles, and their rights over all natural resources expanded to 200 miles from the shore (Foss, 2011, p. 7). Thus, each costal state can, in principle, regulate what fishers can catch (types of fish and shellfish, broadly speaking); how much they can catch (quotas); and where they can catch it by setting the terms of access (Phillipson and Symes, 2018, p. 170). However, there are also obligations for coastal states. First, fish stocks are a vulnerable natural recourse that needs to be managed sustainably over time. Since many commercially viable fish stocks are shared by two or more countries, or they migrate between different EEZs, there are requirements for joint management of them (Bjørndal and Munro, 2020, p. 268). This is regulated by a supplementary agreement to the UNCLOS – the UN Fish Stock Agreement from 1995. The agreement imposes costal states and states who operate fishing vessels on the open sea to take part in regional cooperation on the management for migrating fish stocks. These Regional Fisheries Management Organisations (RFMOs) provide advice on how to manage fish stocks, and they provide a platform for policy coordination (Meld St. 8, 2021–2022, p. 16).

One final point is that the UNCLOS agreement requires that management of fish stocks is guided by scientific advice. It is the International Council for the Exploration of the Sea (ICES) which guides authorities on both sides of the North Atlantic. ICES was established in 1902 and has 20 member states. Its main responsibility is to provide scientific knowledge about marine ecosystems. ICES has an advisory committee (ACOM) which provides yearly advice on how much fish can be fished, also known as Maximum Sustainable Yield (MSY) in the Northeast Atlantic (Meld St. 8, 2021–2022, pp. 19–20). These recommendations are of crucial importance when coastal states negotiate yearly quotas for shared fish stocks, also known as Total Allowed Catch (TAC) (Foss, 2011, p. 9). These are all factors that influence the autonomy of coastal states in fisheries matters, and we will return to their implications later in the chapter.

The Common Fisheries Policy of the EU

It was the Treaty of Rome that established the legal basis for a Common Fisheries Policy (CFP). However, since fishing was a small industry in the six original member states, fisheries became part of the Commissions agricultural responsibilities (Lado, 2016, p. 28). The CFP was developed gradually during the 1970s and 1980s. The Commission established an independent Directorate General for Fisheries in 1976 (Holden, 1996). Today, the CFP consists of four pillars: a structural policy, a common organisation of the market (both implemented in 1970), an external fisheries policy (implemented in 1976), and a policy for conservation and management of fish stocks (implemented in 1983). It is normal to refer to 1983 as the foundation year of the CFP (Symes, 1997, p. 137).

It is possible to describe the evolution of the CFP as a series of reforms and geographical expansions with consequences for member states' autonomy and wriggle room. An important decision with implications for future member states' wriggle room came in 1970 when the EU decided to 'establish the principle of free access to each other waters as an acquis that new Member States would have to accept' (Lado, 2016, p. 45). Since the decision was made just before the membership negotiations started with Denmark, Ireland, Norway, and the UK in 1971, 'it caused bitterness among the applicants' (Holden, 1996, p. 19). The new members were able to negotiate a 10-year derogation from the equal access principle for their territorial waters of 12 miles (Churchill, 2022, p. 12). However, as members, they had to accept that the European Commission oversaw the management of their fisheries (Lado, 2016, p. 45).

An important factor in the development of the EU's common fisheries policy was the expansion of the Union's EEZ to 200 miles in 1977. This enlargement meant that the European Commission became responsible for the management of resources in large areas with considerable fish stocks. It took member states six years of negotiations to find solutions to the challenges that arose when the areas of responsibility were expanded (Holden, 1996; Conceição-Heldt, 2006). The outcome from these negotiations has constituted the framework for the EU's fisheries policy since then.

Firstly, the CFP established that all member states were allowed to keep some wriggle room within a 12-mile limit of their territorial waters. Inside six miles they received the right to only grant access to their own vessels, but in a zone stretching from six to 12 miles they should allow the continuation of access by vessels from other member states if the fishing activity was based on existing practice (Lado, 2016, pp. 53–54). Second, it implemented the Total Allowable Catch (TAC) system. This entails that each member state is allocated a national fishing quota based upon the total available resources for each species. Furthermore, the distribution of resources is based on 'relative stability principle', which combines three elements – past catches, preferential treatment for regions particularly dependent on fishing, and a compensation for loss of caches resulting from the exclusion of EU vessels following from the extension of fisheries jurisdiction to 200 miles (Churchill, 2022, p. 14). This implies that 'the individual member state could expect its fishing industry to retain its position relative to other member states' (Symes, 1997, p. 143). The CFP has been reviewed and modified in 1992, 2002, and 2012/2013, but 'its basic features . . . have remained unchanged' (Churchill, 2022, p. 14).

The CFP is an exclusive competence for the EU, and the legislation to manage fishery resources generally take the form of regulations. Up until the implementation of the Lisbon Treaty in 2008, these regulations were decided by the Council of Ministers. The Treaty of Lisbon formally enshrined fisheries conservation policy as 'one of the five only exclusive competences of the Union and the application of co-decision between the Council and the European Parliament as the ordinary legislative procedure of the CFP' (Lado, 2016, p. 29). There is an important exception from this procedure: the adoption of annual quotas is an exclusive prerogative of the Council of Ministers. The result of this is a system in which the final quotas for the following year have been negotiated at a ministerial meeting in December. 'Horse trading' is an expression that has been used about this system (Lado, 2016, p. 386). Symes describes this final decision-making as 'a purely political process, in which national self-interest and undeclared social objectives are the dominant influence' (Symes, 1997, p. 146). The result has been that the European Commission has adopted far higher fishing quotas than the MSY recommended by ICES. This practice has weakened the efficiency and sustainability of the CFP, and thus its legitimacy (Holden, 1996; Lado, 2016).

Even though the European Commission is responsible for the CFP, the member states have considerable wriggle room in the implementation of CFP policy. First, the allocation of national quotas among the fishermen of each member state is an exclusive national competence (Lado, 2016, p. 388). This means that each member can apply its own socio-economic model for management of domestic fisheries. Thus, they can decide who has the right to catch fish, distinguishing between regions or types of vessels, they can involve producer organisations, or they can decide that allocation is up to market forces (ibid.). Second, the European Commission have no rights or tools that can supervise national implementation of CFP decisions, and each member state is therefore free to establish its own control regime. This wriggle room, in turn, has meant that there are differences and, more importantly, varying and weak enforcement of the CFP regulations. Over the years, the lack of enforcement has had several negative consequences, including the introduction of lower TACs to compensate for previous poor enforcement. And, in the end, poor enforcement creates an impression of lack of a level playing field, which does not encourage enforcement in member states (Lado, 2016, p. 279).

UK-EU relations in primary industries before and after Brexit

Brexit means that the UK starts an existence outside the EU. We will start this section by unpacking the wriggle room the UK had in fisheries before Brexit and continue by evaluating autonomy and wriggle room in fisheries, agriculture, and trade in primary industries in the TCA.

The EU-UK relationship in fisheries

Fisheries has been one of the most controversial issues in the EU-UK relations throughout the entire Brexit process. It was a central issue for both the leave and the remain campaigns before the referendum in 2016, it was important in the negotiations of the Withdrawal Agreement, and it was a major stumbling block in the TCA negotiations (Stewart et al., 2022, pp. 3–4). However, it is possible to trace British dissatisfaction with the CFP all the way back to the 1972 membership agreement. Then, the 'UK fishing interests were allegedly sacrificed in achieving a more favourable settlement of the UK's accession to the European Community' (Phillipson and Symes, 2018, p. 169). The expansion of the EU's EEZ in 1977 gave the British fishing industry further arguments against the CFP. The European Commission's original proposal from 1976 recommended an unrestricted application of the equal access principle and common management of fish resources in the whole EEZ. The UK and Ireland had originally opposed this proposal, not least 'because their waters are rich in resources, and therefore there was no necessity for their fishing vessels to enter the waters of other Member States' (Da Conceição-Heldt, 2006, p. 288).

The UK and Ireland had originally demanded an exclusive economic zone of 50 miles within the EU's zone, and since 60 per cent of the EU's catch was taken in the UK EEZ, the UK demanded the same percentage of the EU's allocation of fish stocks (Da Conceição-Heldt, 2006, p. 289). Again, the outcome of the negotiations was influenced by the fact that the British authorities sought to achieve results in other areas than increased fishing quotas. In the end, the UK accepted a 31 per cent share of the total EU TAC and agreed to the conservation and management policy proposed by the Commission in exchange for a rebate on the British contribution to the EU budget (Da Conceição-Heldt, 2006, p. 291). A long-term effect of the agreement came from the introduction of the relative stability principle, which blocked British fishers' opportunity to obtain a larger share of quotas in the future.

A third source of dissatisfaction with the CFP can be linked to how UK authorities have implemented its fisheries policy. As mentioned previously, member states enjoy a certain level of wriggle room in that regard. Different British governments practiced a liberal investment policy from 1980 onwards, which allowed fishers from other European countries to buy British fishing vessels and their quotas (Lequesne, 2000, p. 783). This so-called *quota hopping* increased resentment and mobilised political action illustrating some wriggle room. After pressure from the government, the UK was allowed to implement several policy adjustments in 1999 to mitigate negative consequences for UK fishing communities. These included requirements on landing of catch, employment of local crew, and purchases of goods and services in UK coastal areas. Thus, the owners must provide sufficient benefit to populations dependent on fisheries and related industries (Lequesne, 2000, p. 789). Since it would be economically costly to buy back the quotas, a considerable share of English entitlements is still in foreign hands (Phillipson and Symes, 2018, p. 170).

The general resentment towards the functioning of the CFP has been a recurring phenomenon in the UK debate. Phillipson and Symes (2018, p. 171) argues that the 'systemic rigidities go a long way to explain UK fishing interests' deep hostility towards the CFP (and thus to EU membership)'. Slow pace of fundamental reform is one issue they mention, but also the rigidity of the relative stability principle. Churchill (2022, pp. 14–15) argues that it is this principle together with the equal access principle that 'have proved very unpopular with the UK fishing industry and may UK politicians', since they 'are seen as the reason for why vessels from EU member states have taken what many in the UK have regarded as a disproportionate proportion of the catch in UK waters in recent years'.

Nevertheless, the UK has exploited its wriggle room in the development of a national fisheries administration. The devolution of competence in fisheries policy to the Scottish, Welsh, and Northern Irish legislatures in 1998 is an important example of this (Lennan et al., 2022, p. 76). In England, the responsibilities for managing fisheries were delegated to the Marine Management Organisation and 10 Inshore Fisheries and Conservation Authorities. However, 'prior to Brexit, much of the enforcement activity by the competent authorities within the UK was ensuring compliance with the CFP' (Rosello et al., 2022, p. 92). Thus, given the opposition to many aspects of the CFP, it is understandable that 'take back control' had strong support in coastal communities in the UK (Phillipson and Symes, 2018; Stewart et al., 2022).

Brexit and fisheries

The previous discussion illustrates that the fishing industry has some political significance for the UK. However, what is striking is how small it is measured in economic terms. In 2018, 31,000 people were employed in the sector. Of these, 12,000 were professional fishers. The industry, which consists of fishing, aquaculture, and fish processing, contributes £1.4 billion, or 0.12 per cent of GDP annually (Fernández et al., 2022, p. 2). Furthermore, the UK imports more fish than it exports, but it has a surplus in trade with the EU, due to the fact that the UK exports around 80 per cent of its catch (ibid., pp. 3–5). The EU numbers are not easy to compare with the UK numbers, since the EU industry includes parts of the EEZ not influenced by Brexit. However, the fishing industry constitutes a small part of the EU economy (ibid., p. 7). What was important in connection with Brexit was that 41 per cent of the EU catch is fished in the UK sector, mostly by fishers from Denmark, France, and Spain. This was a lot compared to the UK fishers who fished 13 per cent of its quotas in the EU EEZ. This seems to have influenced the UK position prior to the negotiations:

> Fishing, at least in the UK public's imagination, appears to be a largely romanticised image of itself as an island nation rather than a currently accurate statistical fact. This, in conjunction with the fact that UK waters are a major source of fish for EU vessels, appeared to have given confidence to UK government negotiators that they had the upper hand when finalising the Trade and Cooperation Agreement (TCA) with their EU counterparts.
> *(Fernández et al., 2022, p. 7)*

In this section we will present the key issues in the negotiations of the two agreements and assess the autonomy and wriggle room for the UK in fisheries and trade in seafood post-Brexit.

The Withdrawal Agreement

The initial UK ambition was to get separate agreements on fisheries and trade. The desired goal in fisheries, as stated in a 2018 White Paper, was annual quota negotiations rather than a long-term agreement. 'In these it wished to secure a much larger share of the fish stocks than under the CFP' (Serdy, 2022, p. 32). The ambition in trade was stated in the notification letter, from March 2017, where Prime Minister Theresa May made it clear that 'the United Kingdom does not seek membership of the single market'. Instead, the ambition was 'a bold and ambitious Free Trade Agreement' with 'greater scope and ambition than any such agreement'. Furthermore, 'we believe it is necessary to agree the terms of our future partnership alongside our withdrawal' (May, 2017).

However, it soon became clear that the EU didn't share these ambitions. This can be illustrated by the European Council response from April 2017. Here the Union stated that 'an agreement on the future of the relationship between the Union and the United Kingdom as such can only be concluded once the United Kingdom has become a third country' (Council of the European Union, 2017, p. 4). By this the EU clearly sought to limit the UK's newly acquired autonomy in the forthcoming negotiations, since it always could threaten to set the free-trade agreement itself aside if they did not get their own demands passed.

As we know, the EU and the UK needed two negotiation rounds to conclude a Withdrawal Agreement. This was mostly due to the UK Parliament's refusal to approve Theresa May's agreement from November 2018 due to concern over the Northern Ireland protocol. Boris Johnson took over as prime minister in July 2019, and a revised Withdrawal Agreement and Political Declaration was signed in October that year. This again meant that there was very little time to finalise the negotiations of a free-trade agreement before the UK left the EU's single market at the end of 2020.

The Political Declaration contains some elements that points to the next round of the negotiations. First, the ambition was to minimise trade barriers, including mutual acceptance of SPS rules, but 'the Parties will retain their autonomy and the ability to regulate economic activity according to the level of protection each deem appropriate' (political declaration setting out the framework for the future relationship between the European Union and the United Kingdom, 2019, p. 6). Secondly and more directly related to the fishing sector, it is emphasised that 'within the context of the overall partnership the Parties should establish a new fisheries agreement on, inter alia, access to waters and quota shares' (ibid., 2019, p. 14). These negotiations should have been concluded by 1 July 2020, but 'negotiations became so protracted that it proved impossible to conclude the separate fisheries agreement' (Churchill, 2022, p. 18).

The Trade and Cooperation Agreement

The parties had opposing interest in the TCA negotiations, and fisheries became one of the most contested issues in the negotiations, especially in the final phase (Barnier, 2021; Fernández et al., 2022). The EU wanted to maintain cooperation on conservation, management, and regulation. More controversial, seen from a UK position, was that the EU stated that 'the provisions on fisheries should build on existing reciprocal access conditions, quota shares and the traditional activity of the Union fleet' (European Commission, 2020, p. 25). The UK had a clear ambition for change in the distribution of quotas. In short, the UK suggested to implement the same system that the EU and Norway has in their agreement: annual negotiations would cover the allocation of TACs between the parties, based on the principle of zonal attachment (Churchill, 2022, p. 18).

The UK government wanted to use the opportunity to 'take back control' over its fisheries. To achieve this, the British position was to try to isolate fisheries from other negotiation areas. However, the EU's negotiators put strong emphasis on the interests of the Union's own fishing communities. They argued that they had historical rights within the UK's EEZ. Furthermore, national governments in France and Germany had given salience to interest of their own fishing communities, and similar support came from Belgium, Denmark, Ireland, the Netherlands, and Spain (Barnier, 2021). However, the EU's strongest card was that the UK needed a free-trade agreement. Thus, the EU's point of departure was to see fisheries as part of a larger agenda where the goal was a levelled playing field between the EU and the UK.

Fisheries was important right up to the end of the negotiations; indeed at one point these issues threatened the entire agreement, because 'a bad deal would be definitive for European fishermen, whereas a no deal would not be' (Barnier, 2021, p. 396). A compromise was found in the final discussions between the president of the European Commission, Ursula von der Leyen, and UK Prime Minister Boris Johnson the day before the Trade and Cooperation Agreement (TCA) was signed on December 24, 2020. This was just in time for the deadline for the UK leaving the single market.

There are several paragraphs that are related to fisheries. First, the TCA 'provides that in principle the EU and UK each has regulatory autonomy for the management of the fish stocks found in its waters' (Churchill, 2022, p. 18). However, this autonomy is subjected to several wide-ranging constrains in the TCA. Among them was objectives and principles of fisheries management; the joint management of many stocks; and the access of EU vessels to UK waters (ibid., p. 20). It is possible to divide the outcome into three parts.

The first outcome is the fisheries agreement. The UK government declared that 'the Agreement firmly and explicitly recognises UK sovereignty over our fishing waters and puts us in a position to rebuild our fishing fleet and increases quotas in the next few years' (UK Government, 2020, p. 6). Although the EU had to give up 25 per cent of the quotas EU fishers had before Brexit, they kept considerable fishing quotas and rights in British waters. The fisheries agreement has a duration of five years, but the EU has introduced a 'mirror clause' which implied that if the British would like to exclude EU fishers in 2027, the EU would cut electricity interconnectivity for the UK valued at the same value as the fishing quotas (Barnier, 2021, p. 395). Some observers, cited by Wachowiak and Zuleeg (2022, p. 148), have already identified a potential for politicisation and 'future friction, which could lead to the collapse of (parts of) the current arrangements'.

The second outcome is to be found in the trade framework. The TCA contains provisions on tariff and quota free trade in fish and seafood between the EU and the UK which are of mutual benefits for both parties. The UK is the first country who has achieved this in a free-trade agreement with the EU, and in principle it gives more market access for seafood than Norway has for its exports. However, there is a caveat here, because the UK has decided that it will not subordinate itself to EU regulations, and that means technical barriers to trade.

Thus, the third outcome is potential technical barriers to trade. The UK's summary of the TAC states that 'this agreement includes an SPS Chapter which ensures that the UK and the EU can maintain fully independent SPS rules' (UK Government, 2020, p. 9). However, since the UK wanted to stay outside the single market, British seafood must comply with the EU's SPS framework, and this must be documented for each trailer with seafood crossing the border (Churchill, 2022, p. 29). This implies a bureaucracy in the form of documents who are checked at the border. Initially, it helps that the UK still has the same rules as the EU, but if or when they are changed, this would have large consequences for all food exports. As argued by Churchill: 'There is little doubt that overall, the UK fishing industry is worse off after Brexit, very much contrary to what it had been led to expect by the UK government' (Churchill, 2022, p. 30). This question is, as we shall see, also relevant for trade in agricultural products.

Agriculture and Brexit

It is not within the framework of this chapter to give a full review of EU-UK relations in agriculture. However, it is worth noting that it seems to have been more supported for Brexit among farmers than in the general population (Sheingate and Greer, 2021, p. 549). Sheingate and Greer find that 'frustrations with the Common Agricultural Policy' was an important factor behind UK farmers voting no in the Brexit referendum. They also identify 'broader political concerns about sovereignty and the impact of immigration in rural areas' as significant factors behind this attitude. Furthermore, they also argue that leave groups promised that there would be 'plenty of money' for agricultural support after Brexit probably did not hurt the support for Brexit among farmers.

Agriculture and food processing are also influenced by the TCA. In this regard, it is important to emphasise that this is a huge industry in the UK. In 2019, agriculture had nearly half a million employed and contributed £10 billion to the gross domestic product. The whole agri-food sector is worth £113 billion to the UK economy and employs just under four million people (Petetin and Dobbs, 2022, p. 1). That year, 64 per cent of UK food consumption originated from national production. Imports valued at £47.9 covered the rest, with 70 per cent coming from the EU. The UK also exports agri-food products, and the value was £23.6 billion in 2019, of which 60 per cent was to the EU (ibid., p. 5). The fact that the UK has decided to leave the EU's SPS framework will influence trade in agri-food from the UK to the EU, and from the EU to the UK.

Petetin and Dobbs (2022, p. 192) argues that the TCA is the first free-trade agreement 'in the world that re-erects barriers to trade between parties rather than creating greater trade liberalisation'. Many of these barriers are rules that limit free movement of food between the EU and the UK. Petetin and Dobbs distinguish between different types of effects. First, to qualify for tariff-free trade, processed food need to fulfil rules of origin requirements, which is especially difficult for this type of products, 'which may contain ingredients from all around the globe' (Petetin and Dobbs, 2022, p. 193). This can have positive effects since it is an incentive for increased use of locally produced inputs. However, it will also mean more paperwork and cheeks to verify the origins of products (Petetin and Dobbs, 2022, p. 194). Second, the TCA reinstates customs formalities and multiple administrative burdens on the border, which means that trade with the EU is not as financially and economically advantageous as when the UK was an EU member (Petetin and Dobbs, 2022, p. 195). However, the UK will have regulatory autonomy to make its own rules. The price of this autonomy is paid by EU and UK exporters, and indirectly by EU and UK consumers who now pay more for food than before the UK left the single market.

Norway-EU relations in primary industries

The membership agreement from 1972 is a crucial point of departure for understanding why and how Norway has sought to pursue autonomous fishery and agricultural policies outside the EU. Membership would have meant full integration in the emerging CFP and the well-established CAP. When the agreement was presented to the Norwegian electorate in a referendum, a majority voted no. The two primary industries – agriculture and fisheries – received significant political attention prior to the vote. The no-campaign emphasised their importance to Norwegian economy and society, especially the industries' contribution to maintaining a decentralised population pattern, which was and remains an important political objective in Norway. Thus, it is reasonable to argue that the no-majority was partly built on the electorate's wish to protect Norwegian sovereignty over its fishery resources and independent management of its primary industries. However, this did not mean that Norway could keep its autonomy in these policy areas when it developed closer links with the EU through the EEA Agreement. We will unpack this in the following paragraphs.

EU-Norway relations in fisheries

As we have seen, in 1972 the EU demanded that fisheries came under the management of the European Commission and the introduction of access for EU fishers inside Norway's 12 miles of territorial waters.[3] Although the candidate countries were able to negotiate a decade-long derogation from the latter element, the overall outcome was perceived by the Norwegian fishing industry to be too negative for them to accept (Frøland, 2015, p. 149). The fact that membership would have provided tariff-free market access for all Norwegian seafood received less attention. In general, the EU had quite high tariffs on seafood (on average 12 per cent), with the exception of fresh salmon where it was only two per cent due to a concession the EU had given the United States in a negotiation round in the GATT (Melchior, 2020c, p. 185).

For Norway, the alternative to membership was a free-trade agreement with the EU, and this was signed in 1973. The agreement excluded tariff reductions for fish and seafood since these products where 'classified as agricultural products' by the EU (St.prp. nr. 126, 1972–73, p. 34). Nevertheless, Norway asked for better market access for its seafood exports during the negotiations. The solution was a formal exchange of letters from the same year committing Norway to give market access for certain agricultural products (most notably wine) in exchange for tariff reductions in some seafood categories (Foss, 2011, pp. 14–15).

The follow-up of the International Law of the Sea became the most important fisheries policy issue between Norway and the EU in the second half of the 1970s. Both parties sought to expand their control over natural resources when they established their 200-mile EEZ in 1977. One consequence was that areas where fishing was traditionally carried out by vessels from both the EU and Norway now became part of one of the parties' EEZ. There was thus a need for new rules and regulations regarding access and quotas. However, since Norwegian resources were and are more plentiful, especially in the north, Norway had the upper hand when it came to the distribution of access rights and quotas. Especially for cod in the North Atlantic and the Barents Sea, which was a valuable resource for fishers from several EU member states, including the UK. Although Norway could have excluded EU fishers from its territorial waters in the Barents Sea, the Norwegian government decided for political and practical reasons to implement a seven-year transition period. This agreement also meant that Norwegian fishers got permission to fish some of their quotas within the EU's EEZ (Foss, 2011, p. 8).

The system for regulating the relationship between the EU and Norway was developed based on the UNCLOS framework described previously in the chapter. Negotiations began immediately after the expansion of territorial waters, and in 1980 Norway and the EU signed the 'Agreement on fishing', which resulted in the implementation of a new administrative regime for the management of their joint resources. The agreement institutionalised the TAC principle. The parties also agreed on how the joint stocks should be distributed. The solution they came up with was to divide the stocks in the North Sea according to a principle of zonal attachment and based on certain criteria (fishing area, spawning area, and rearing area). This gave each party a share of a particular stock. By doing this they accommodated rights, historical traditions, and national preferences for certain species. In 1992, the parties amended the agreement to increase cooperation and exchange of quotas (Foss, 2011, p. 9).

Furthermore, they agreed on the principles for how to negotiate the yearly 'Agreed Minutes' for quotas. First, the agreement includes all fishing of the seven commercially important species that is shared between Norway and the EU in the

North Sea, the Norwegian fisheries west of the British Isles and off Greenland, and EU fisheries in the Norwegian part of the Barents Sea. Second, the agreement facilitates extensive cooperation on fisheries management between the two parties. This is done through the annual quota negotiations where both parties are obliged to follow 'the best scientific advice available' (Foss, 2011, p. 11).

Therefore, a well-functioning system for negotiating fishing quotas has existed between Norway and the EU since 1980. There is relatively little national wriggle room in the negotiations since the system is based on principles and guidelines from the UNCLOS framework and the provisions laid down in the agreement between the EU and Norway. However, they do not always agree on the interpretation of the scientific advice, and this can be a source of conflict between the parties. The system is highly institutionalised, and the Norwegian Directorate of Fisheries cooperates extensively with European agencies, both at national and EU level. Market access for seafood, however, is not covered by this agreement.

At the same time, it is important to emphasise that Norway has autonomy outside the CFP. First, Norway has separate agreements with Russia, Faroe Islands, Iceland, and Greenland regulating quotas and mutual access to national EEZs (Meld. St. 8, 2021–2022, p. 35). Second, domestically, fishing is managed in accordance with national priorities in areas like the distribution of quotas between different types of vessels and regions, and it can implement its own environmental standards. The Ministry of Fisheries interacts with representatives from interest groups through several boards and committees (Mikalsen and Jentoft, 2003, p. 400). This is basically 'a public-private partnership where policy is the outcome of consultations and negotiations' (Jentoft and Mikalsen, 2014, p. 1). Quotas and regulatory issues are the most important topics. All control is conducted by the by the Directorate of Fisheries and enforced by the Coast Guard (Meld. St. 8, 2021–2022, p. 25). The autonomy Norway has over its fisheries resources is therefore much larger than the wriggle room EU member states have in implementing the CFP.

The EEA Agreement and fisheries

Originally, and as a consequence of a Norwegian wish for continued autonomy, fisheries were left out of the agenda for the EEA negotiations. Nevertheless, Norway wanted tariff-free access for all its export of seafood to the EU market. The reasoning was that since there was free trade in seafood within both EFTA and EU, this should also apply to the new European Economic Area (Rye, 2015, p. 164). The European Commission met this proposal with a counterclaim where the EU demanded quotas in exchange for market access. Spain and Portugal, in particular, were pushing for this since their fishermen had lost the opportunity to catch fish when Norway expanded its territorial waters in 1977. Norway, however, was initially not prepared to give EU fishers substantial increases in quotas in return for better market access. However, the proposal from the EU made quotas and market access a topic in the negotiations.

The parties were never able to negotiate a full-fledged agreement on market access and quotas. However, they agreed on a package deal that gave Norwegian exporters considerable tariff reductions and EU fishers some new quotas in Norwegian waters. This solution was based on an issue linkage between trade and quotas established after Spain and Portugal joined the EU in 1986 (Melchior, 2020b, p. 51). It is estimated that two-thirds of the reductions in tariffs Norway has obtained from the EU since 1980 is a result of the EEA Agreement (Melchior, 2020a, p. 31). These are mainly for white fish, while the EU received an extra quota for Arctic cod of 11.000 tonnes (Melchior, 2020b, p. 53). It is Protocol 9 in the EEA Agreement which regulates tariffs for fish and seafood. It also covers regulatory issues concerning anti-dumping, state aid, competition, and rules for sale of fish (St.prp. nr. 100, 1991–92, p. 135). The increased fishing quotas was formalised through an exchange of letters under the fisheries agreement of 1980 (Melchior, 2020b, p. 53).

Another difficult question in the negotiations was that the European Commission demanded that fisheries should be covered by the provision on free movement of capital (St.prp. nr. 100, 1991–92, p. 135). Norway wanted to exempt the fishing industry from this provision, more specifically the right of foreigners to buy Norwegian fishing vessels. The fear was that foreign fishing enterprises would buy Norwegian vessels and thus get the right to fish in Norwegian waters, what is known as quota hopping in the UK. This was easier for the EU to accept since their own provisions on relative stability in the allocation of fishing quotas enabled Member States to prioritise national and local ownership (Maurseth and Medin, 2020, p. 238). The compromise was that Norway could limit foreign ownership to 40 per cent of each vessel (Melchior, 2020b, p. 56).

A final topic in the fisheries negotiations was based on an idea of a separate EFTA development fund originally proposed by Spain and Portugal. The European Commission was sceptical, because they considered that EFTA representation in the management of such a fund would threaten the autonomy of the Community. However, EFTA suggested a fund as part of a comprehensive agreement in the fisheries negotiations (Rye, 2015, pp. 168–169). This issue linkage was not formalised, but the idea that EFTA should contribute money to development in the poor regions of the EU gradually gained traction in the negotiations. In the end, the EEA Agreement led to the establishment of a loan and grant scheme for development in poor areas of the Union which was to last from 1994 to 1998 (St.prp. nr. 100, 1991–92, p. 44).

Aquaculture: marked access, tariffs, and anti-dumping

As mentioned earlier, Protocol 9 of the EEA Agreement covers many of the regulatory issues related to the seafood industry, but it does not incorporate EU law in the area of fisheries into the agreement and subsequently into Norwegian law (St. prp. nr. 100, 1991–92, p. 137). Therefore, the protocol does not cover all questions related to state aid and competition, and it is still possible for the EU to implement anti-dumping and anti-subsidy measures against Norwegian seafood (Prop. 160 S,

2009–2010, p. 6). It is mostly the aquaculture industry, or more precisely the export of farmed salmon, which has been affected.

Aquaculture, and especially the fish farms producing large quantities of salmon, is a relatively new industry in Norway. The industry's economic importance has grown strongly since the 1970s. In 1992, when the EEA Agreement was signed, Norway exported 62,000 tons of farmed salmon to the EU. The export volume had increased to 461,000 tons in 2010 (NOU 2012:2, p. 67), and more than 1.1 million tons in 2021 (Directorate of Fisheries, 2022, p. 22). This has shifted the Norwegian interest somewhat from fish quotas to market access for seafood. The EU has occasionally tried to exploit a potential conflict of interests between fishers and fish farmers and offered better market access in exchange for fishing quotas. Internally, fishers have rejected this, but the fish farmers have been more positive. In the end, Norwegian governments have sided with the fishers (Hersoug, 2014, p. 296).

The growth in exports from this industry has also led to conflicts between Norway and the EU. This is mainly because the production increase in Norwegian aquaculture has challenged a growing industry in the EU. The production costs are generally lower in Norway, and the EU is bound by its two per cent tariff rate. So, at times when prices have been pushed down in the European market, this has triggered accusations that Norwegian salmon, due to subsidies, is sold at prices below production costs. The EU introduced minimum prices several times in the 1990s, and in 2006 it imposed a definitive anti-dumping duty on farmed salmon imported from Norway (Farsund and Langhelle, 2015). Previously, Norway had tried to accommodate the EU, but this time it brought the case to the Dispute Settlement Mechanism of the World Trade Organization in 2007. Norway won a partial victory, and the EU removed its anti-dumping measures (Farsund, 2014, p. 166). However, the underlying conflict was not resolved, and there is a potential for it to return to the agenda again (NOU 2012:2, p. 676), which illustrates the limited wriggle room for Norway outside the single market. As we shall see later in this chapter, it is the growth of exports from this industry that led to Norway joining the EU's SPS framework.

Market access and the EEA grant

There has been considerable development when it comes to tariff reductions for Norwegian seafood since the signing of the EEA Agreement in 1992. When Finland, Sweden, and Austria became EU members in 1995, Norway received 35 relatively small but permanent tariff-free quotas for seafood in the whole EU market. The quotas were based on trade in the previous three years. Norwegian authorities had argued that according to WTO rules, Norway was entitled to compensation for the loss of tariff-free access for seafood in these markets. The EU contested this argument but accepted the aforementioned quotas (Melchior, 2020b, p. 61).

The question of what rights Norway had regarding compensation when former free-trade partners became members of the EU came up again in connection with the EU's planned eastern enlargements in the early 2000s. Most of the 11 countries that became members during that decade had tariff-free quotas for seafood in their free-trade agreements with EFTA. Norway demanded compensation through permanent tariff-free quotas in the EU, which this time was also contested by the EU. Norwegian scholars agree with the EU's reading of the WTO rules that there is no legal requirement for compensation (Laurantzon and Arnesen, 2020, pp. 108–109). The solution was a more political compromise illustrating wriggle room; Norway received some tariff-free quotas while the EU received approval for their demand that they were temporary (until 2009).

The eastward expansion had other implications for the seafood trade framework. As mentioned earlier, EFTA established a temporary regional development fund for poor regions in the EU. In 1998, at the request of the EU, the scheme was continued until 2003. In a new extension (until 2009) the scheme was further expanded as a result of the Union accepting new members from central and eastern Europe. It was a new negotiation round in 2009 that led to a close link between the negotiations on EEA funds and market access for seafood (Prop. 160 S, 2009–2010, p. 1). Even though the Norwegian government assessed that Norway was not legally obliged to continue funding regional development in the EU, it was open to continue to make a 'reasonable' Norwegian contribution to programs and countries which Norway should be involved in selecting. Furthermore, Norway 'made it clear during the negotiations that a continuation of Norwegian funding to the EU was depended on a satisfactory solution for market access for fish' (Prop. 160 S, 2009–2010, p. 3).

The two agreements were negotiated in parallel, and the two parties achieved results in their priority areas, the EU in grants and Norway in market access. Both agreements had a time frame of April 30, 2014. By now, Norway had 52 tariff free quotas, and it had committed to pay 349 million euro yearly to regional development in the EU. A new round of negotiations was started in January 2014, and the final agreements were signed in May 2016 (Prop. 119 S, 2015–2016, p. 5). The main principles remained unchanged, but there were adjustments made in both agreements. For example, the duration was extended to seven years, which increased the predictability for Norwegian exporters. However, Norway did not get the desired tariff reductions for processed seafood because this was perceived by the EU as a threat to its own industry (ibid., p. 17). The two interconnected agreements are still temporary, and Norway and the EU began a new round of negotiations in the summer of 2022. In her latest briefing to Parliament, Foreign Minister Anniken Huitfeldt stated that the negotiations in both areas are 'difficult' and 'it will take time to reach an agreement' (Norwegian Ministry of Foreign Affairs, 2022), illustrating that the wriggle room is limited for both parties.

Autonomy and wriggle room in agriculture

The EEA Agreement does not include the EU's agricultural policy (CAP) nor free movement of agricultural goods (NOU 2012:2, p. 657). An important reason for that is that Norway, the EU, the USA, and Switzerland are among the rich countries who, in the whole post-war period, have treated agriculture as a special industry. In the literature, this has been defined as *agricultural exceptionalism*, which is a set of policy ideas that assumes that agriculture is a unique economic sector with special market and production conditions that deserves special treatment in terms of government intervention because it contributes to national goals (Coleman et al., 1997; Skogstad, 1998). Securing income for farmers is at the core of exceptionalist policies. This requires different types of policy instruments since it is observed that market mechanisms do not function properly in the agricultural sector. Both oversupply and crop failure are recurring phenomena, resulting in unstable farm incomes (Langhelle et al., 2014, p. 6).

Farmers are, in general, a well-organised interest group with considerable political influence, which in Norway is expressed through annual negotiations on income opportunities in the industry (Farsund, 2014). In addition, Norwegian agriculture operates under unfavourable climatic and topographical conditions, and therefore this industry receives far more economic support than agricultural industries in other countries, including the EU. This has had, and will continue to have, implications for Norway's EU affiliation. One reason is that farmers and other rural voters fear that membership in the EU, and implicitly the CAP, would mean that a large part of domestic food production would be replaced by cheaper imports from Europe. There was and is cross-party support for Norway being able to pursue an independent agricultural policy (Rommetvedt and Veggeland, 2019).

The autonomy gained by Norway's non-member status after the 1972 referendum allowed for further development of its exceptionalist policies. A Parliament decision from 1975 expressed an ambition to equalise income in agriculture with income in industry within six years. This resulted in a sharp increase in financial support for agriculture. The policy involved direct support to farmers so that they could increase production, and national prices were administratively decided to be far above prices in Europe. Thus, the success of this policy was highly dependent on import restrictions. Farm incomes did indeed increase, but overproduction was an unintended and costly effect of this policy (Farsund and Veggeland, 2016).

Importantly, it was the Uruguay round of the GATT which resulted in the WTO agreement that reduced some of the autonomy the Norwegian government had enjoyed in this area. The WTO agreement meant that all trade restrictions were converted to tariffs, support programs promoting increased production were to be curtailed, but programs supporting so-called no-trade concerns, including environmental programs, were still allowed. The tariffication of import restrictions also meant obligations to introduce small tariff-free quotas for some agricultural products. To secure trade in food, the WTO agreement incorporated its own SPS framework. The SPS agreement includes measures to protect human, animal, and plant life or health. The reason for incorporating binding rules and disciplines in the WTO is to prevent members from using SPS measures to create arbitrary or unjustifiable discrimination or disguise barriers to trade (Petetin and Dobbs, 2022, p. 58).

The Uruguay-round negotiations were started at the end of the 1980s when EFTA and EU discussed closer economic integration. The GATT mandate made it clear that a global agreement would entail significant challenges for Norwegian agriculture. It is therefore not difficult to understand that Norway did not want to include agriculture in the EEA negotiations. This was also the result, and trade in agricultural product is, in general, not a part of the EEA Agreement (St.prp. nr. 100, 1991–92, p. 119). However, there was a paradox recognised by the EU's negotiators: Norway needed better market access for its growing production of seafood. This is the background for why the EU explored the possibility to link market access for Norwegian seafood to market access for European agriculture in the EEA negotiations. The EU offered Norway tariff-free access for all seafood export in exchange for tariff-free access for their agricultural products in Norway. However, Norway refused to make this issue linkage in the negotiations (Farsund and Langhelle, 2015, p. 115). Trade in agricultural products is instead covered by Protocol 3 and Article 19 in the EEA Agreement.

Protocol 3 covers trade in certain types of processed food, and this was originally a part of the 1973 free-trade agreement between Norway and the EU. The intention was to increase competition between industrial companies. Therefore, commodities may be given tariff compensation to level the playing field between companies operating under different domestic price regimes. There is no formal procedure for re-negotiating Protocol 3, but the EU has been pushing for more market access in this area (Farsund, 2014, p. 165), but Norway has exploited the wriggle room in the agreement when it has refused this demand.

Article 19 is more ambitious than Protocol 3, since it states that the aim is a gradual liberalisation of agricultural trade through negotiations every second year. In principle there are no limits, but the Article states that trade should be mutually beneficial and in line with the parties' agricultural policies (St.prp. nr. 100, 1991–92, p. 121). This has given Norwegian authorities some wriggle room in the three negotiation rounds which have been carried out since the implementation of the EEA Agreement in 1994. The first round of negotiations was carried out from 1995 to 1997, but the agreement was initially rejected by EU member states who alleged that Norway had not given enough concessions to the EU. A final agreement was reached in 2002, and even though the agreement resulted in market access for both parties, it is EU exporters (and Norwegian consumers) that benefitted the most from it (Veggeland, 2016, p. 11). The quotas have been expanded further through two rounds of negotiations, in 2006–2010 and 2014–2017 respectively (Prop. 115 S, 2016–2017, pp. 1–2).

Norwegian governments have been under considerable pressure from domestic agricultural interests in these negotiations, and different governments have been very reluctant to negotiate in accordance with the wording of Article 19 – 'gradual liberalisation' and 'every second year'. This illustrates that there is wriggle room in this part of the agreement. Furthermore, Norway has refused to link Article 19 negotiations to its quest for free trade in seafood. This was on the agenda when several member states blocked the first Article 19 agreement in the late 1990s, but in recent years the two areas have been handled separately (Veggeland, 2016, p. 11). This is in line with a position Norway pursues in all trade negotiations, whether it concerns GATT/WTO, EFTA, the EFTA free-trade agreements or in relations with the EU. Norwegian authorities have, to a very large extent, sought to protect the defensive agricultural interest (Farsund, 2014, 2021; Frøland, 2015). According to Frøland, who has analysed Norwegian trade policymaking in the period from 1945 to 1995, there are only two exceptions from this 'rule'. These are the membership agreements signed in 1972 and 1994 (Frøland, 2015), since they would have had major influence on agriculture in Norway.

Norway joins the EU's framework for sanitary and phytosanitary measures

The EEA Agreement originally contained only parts of the EU's SPS rules. The EU's regulatory framework was established to facilitate cross-border trade without this leading to the spread of infectious diseases threatening animal, human, and plant health. The regulations were closely connected to the CAP and the CFP. The EFTA quest for exceptions were partly justified by a desire to retain border controls as a means of preventing the spread of animal diseases (NOU 2012:2, p. 646). In the final agreement, Norway won approval for exceptions from EU regulations covering plant and animal health, and it was also allowed to keep border control for animals and animal products. The downside from a Norwegian perspective was that Norway was perceived as a third country, and exports were subject to border control when Norwegian goods entered the EU (Veggeland, 2016, p. 4).

It was in many ways agricultural interests who had asked for these exceptions from the EU's SPS framework. However, it was the seafood industry that reported problems right from the start. Bureaucratic procedures and subsequent delays at the EU's borders led to increased time consumption, loss of quality, and waste. Norwegian seafood exporters demanded a harmonisation of rules and the elimination of border control to counter negative economic consequences. Nevertheless, key parts of the veterinary community and the agricultural organisations wished to retain border control to safeguard public and animal health in Norway. Two successive governments considered the issue, and eventually the export interests won out, and in 1997 Norway and the EU started to negotiate an extension of the EEA Agreement which would mean the implementation of the whole EU acquis in the agreement (Veggeland, 2016, p. 7).

In 1998, an amendment to the EEA Agreement resulted in Norway implementing the whole EU acquis on hygiene and veterinary rules (NOU 2012:2, pp. 646–647). The rules cover food production and food safety and includes provisions on hygiene, labelling, use of additives, documentation, border control, technical trade requirements, and rules for supervision and control of slaughterhouses and businesses. Thus, the whole value change, from farms and fish farms to slaughterhouses, food industry, grocery chain and restaurants, is now integrated in the EU's SPS framework. It is estimated that currently 40 per cent of all EU acquis incorporated in Norwegian law is in this area. Furthermore, the amendment meant an end to border controls and further that Norway's border would become the EU's outer border for veterinarian controls (NOU 2012:2, p. 646).

Compliance with the regulations is the responsibility of the Norwegian Food Safety Authority. However, ESA is also directly supervising how the rules are followed in practice. Annual controls are carried out, and ESA supervises both the authorities and businesses in all parts of the food sector. However, there is also some wriggle rooms in the form of national regulations. The Norwegian Food and Safety Authority estimates that 10 per cent of the rules in this area are national (NOU 2012:2, p. 651).

The incorporation of the whole SPS acquis at the request of seafood exporters has major consequences for agricultural-based food production. Still, common rules here have less consequences than market opening and do not prevent Norway from pursuing an independent agricultural policy. The reason is that most of the EU law on food has, according to the Norwegian Food Safety Authority, been 'unproblematic' for Norway, because they do not see 'principle disagreements between Norway and the EU in this area'. These are technical regulations that Norway would have an interest in implementing anyway, and many of the recommendations are from international organisations which Norway used in national legislation even before the implementation of the EEA Agreement (NOU 2012:2, p. 652).

Furthermore, the veterinarian agreement gives Norway access to all relevant committees and work groups under the Commission (ibid., p. 649). The Norwegian Food Safety Authority participates in six standing groups under DG SANCO, and approximately 80 different expert groups. Norway participates as an equal partner with member states and contributes with considerable expertise, especially on fish disease (ibid., p. 651). Thus, Norway has wriggle room when it actively participates in rule development within the EU framework, rather than passively implementing rules developed to take care of the interests of EU members (Elvestad and Veggeland, 2020, p. 148). However, when the political decisions are made, Norway is not at the table. With this amendment, Norway relinquished some of its autonomy in matters that concerned SPS issues to improve market access for its large and growing seafood exports.

EU-Norway-UK relations in primary industries after Brexit

So far, the discussions in this chapter have shown that Brexit will have substantial consequences for the relationship between the EU and the UK in the areas of agriculture, fisheries, and trade in products from primary industries. In this part, we will briefly discuss the consequences of Brexit for relations between the EU,

Norway, and the UK in fisheries, and then the relationship between Norway and the UK in fisheries and trade in seafood and agricultural products.

The relationship in fisheries

The TCA has no direct consequences for the relationship between the EU and Norway in fisheries. However, as mentioned earlier in the chapter, the UNCLOS agreements requires that countries who share commercially exploitable fish resources must jointly manage them sustainably. This is the background for why the EU, Norway, and the UK started to negotiate a tripartite framework agreement in early 2021, but already in March, the parties signed an agreement on jointly managed fisheries stocks in the North Sea for 2021. This agreement states that important instruments such as 'arrangements for access, quota transfer and other conditions for fishing in the respective zones of fisheries jurisdiction, may be regulated by bilateral arrangements' (EU, Norway, UK, 2021a, p. 1). A similar agreement for 2022 was signed in December 2021, and now it was said that a framework agreement 'which will be the basis for their future cooperation to ensure the long-term conservation and sustainable use of fisheries resources in the North Sea should be finalised during 2022' (EU, Norway, UK, 2021b, p. 1). When the parties signed a new one-year agreement for 2023 in December 2022, it stated that 'the parties took note of the progress made in consulting on a trilateral framework agreement', and they 'confirmed their ambition that that agreement should enter into force in good time before the annual consultations for 2024' (EU, Norway, UK, 2022, p. 1).

The three mentioned agreements cover the management of six fish stocks shared by the parties. However, they do not provide specific information on the issues that make it difficult for the parties to conclude a permanent framework agreement. But, since the EU and Norway have jointly managed their fisheries since 1980, it seems reasonable to argue that it is the UK's recently achieved autonomy over its own EEZ that is of importance. An observation that supports this argument is found in the bilateral fisheries relationship between Norway and the UK. A framework agreement covering exchange of quotas and mutual access to their EEZs was signed in September 2020 (Prop. 37 S, 2020–2021). Nevertheless, it was impossible for the parties to agree on mutual access and exchange of quotas for 2021. Brexit was, from a Norwegian perspective, an important explanation in this regard. The government stated that 'it is better not to sign an agreement if we do not return to the situation as it was before Brexit' (Ministry of Trade, Industry and Fisheries, 2021).

The situation was somewhat better in December of 2021, when a bilateral agreement for 2022 was signed by the parties. The agreement covers some mutual zonal access, small exchanges of quotas, and cooperation on control and enforcement (Norway, UK, 2021, pp. 1–2). The agreement for 2023 was signed in November 2022, but this contains no substantial changes from the previous year (Norway, UK, 2022, pp. 1–2). Still, the relationship is not the same as before Brexit, and

Norwegian authorities are under increasing pressure from the fishing industry who wants to have more access to the British EEZ to optimise their catches of mackerel in particular. The current situation means that Norwegian trawlers need to catch their quotas earlier in the year, which have consequences for costs, quality, and even the sustainability of these fisheries (NRK, 2022). Seen from a Norwegian perspective, it seems that the UK is testing its autonomy post-Brexit.

The free-trade agreement between Norway and the UK after Brexit

The conclusion of the TCA opened for free-trade negotiations between EFTA and the UK which would also cover trade in seafood and agricultural products. Because of the EEA Agreement, Iceland, Lichtenstein, and Norway needed to negotiate a joint agreement with the UK, while Switzerland could negotiate its own free-trade agreement with the UK. A general description of Norwegian autonomy and wriggle-rom in trade policymaking is found in Chapter 5, including an analysis of the free-trade agreement with the UK. In this section we focus on consequences for primary industries. An important point of departure was that the parties had limited time available for the negotiations. The free-trade negotiations started in the summer of 2020, and after intense negotiations, an agreement was reached in June 2021. The free-trade agreement was presented to the Norwegian Parliament in a proposition (Prop. 210 S, 2020–2021).

If, as argued by Petetin and Dobbs (2022) and others, the TCA represents the first free-trade agreement to increase trade barriers between the signing parties, the EFTA-UK agreement may be viewed as the second. Unlike the TCA, this agreement does not mean tariff- and quota- free trade in agricultural products and seafood. However, this was achieved for other industrial goods. This is in line with the EFTA position. The free-trade agreement offers more market access for Norwegian seafood exports than the EEA Agreement. However, there are only limited improvements seen from an exporter's perspective who had hoped for full tariff-free marked access. This can partly be explained by the deal in agriculture, where the UK only gained limited tariff-free quotas in areas where Norway already had established tariff-free quotas for the EU (Prop. 210 S, 2020–2021, pp. 15–16). Media reports suggests that this had been a controversial topic in the Norwegian government during the negotiations where the interest of agriculture was defended by the Christian Peoples Party while the interests of seafood exporters were supported by the Conservatives and the Liberals (Dagens Næringsliv, 2021). In the end, it seems that the traditional Norwegian position was upheld, and the defensive agriculture interest was prioritised higher than the offensive interest of the seafood sector.

The most consequential part of the agreement is the part that covers the SPS issue. In this area Norway had to take its affiliation with the EU system into consideration. As we have seen, Norway and the other EFTA states have little wiggle-room here, while the UK has the autonomy to make its own rules. Thus, trade in seafood is to be conducted under SPS rules provided by the WTO agreement (Prop. 210 S, 2020–2021, p. 29). This implies increased bureaucratisation of seafood trade between Norway and the UK, since there would be more documents to be handled at the border.

Conclusion

In this chapter we have examined the autonomy and wriggle room that exists in Norwegian primary industry policies outside and inside Norway's formal EU affiliation. Our first observation is that Norway has managed to keep some autonomy in agriculture and fisheries. Norway has retained control over its fishery resources, and the rules in the UNCLOS agreement have been crucial in that regard. Norway has also kept agricultural policymaking outside all agreements with the EU, and it is still able to design its own support schemes, market regulations, and tariff system. Our second observation is that over time there has been difficulties maintaining autonomy in all aspects of these policy areas. In some instances, Norway has given up its autonomy voluntary, while in other cases it is a result of pressure from the EU. The implementation of the whole SPS framework in the EEA Agreement is an example of a voluntary relinquishment of autonomy, since this was a consequence of Norwegian seafood export needing easier border crossing into the EU. Still, Norway has gained some wriggle room when it comes to the development of SPS rules both domestically and in the EU. The EEA grant may be viewed as a more involuntary example since it is indirectly a payment for tariff-free export quotas for seafood. In this latter example, Norway could have 'paid' with fishing quotas or tariff-free import quotas for food from the EU's agricultural industries, illustrating that there is autonomy for taking domestic concerns into consideration.

For the UK, membership in the EU meant relinquishment of autonomy to the EU institutions. However, we have observed that the UK has enjoyed considerable wriggle room in its primary industry policies as a member of the EU. This wriggle room was available in decision-making, implementation, feedback, and learning. However, fishermen and farmers have wanted more autonomy, and these industries' demand for control over resources and policies was among the reasons why many voted for Brexit. The Trade and Cooperation Agreement answered several of the complaints raised by primary industries but created new ones. In fisheries, the UK gained some of the autonomy Norway enjoys through the provision of the UNCLOS agreement. However, the quota shares are smaller since the EU has rights within the UK's EEZ. In agriculture, farmers are no longer bounded by European rules, and the four nations of the UK can now implement their own devolved policies.

The TCA gives both parties tariff- and quota-free market access for goods, including all types of food products. This is an important difference from the Norwegian situation in the EEA. The biggest challenge, however, lies in the fact that the TCA gives the UK autonomy to make its own rules in the SPS area. Furthermore, being outside both the Customs Union and the single market means that UK exporters need to document the origin of all exports of agri-food and seafood products. This implies technical barriers to trade through costly border checks between the UK and the EU. Even without tariffs, border checks hamper transport and increase prices for consumers. Seen from the perspective of UK's food exporters, it is a challenge that the UK has left the EU's Customs Union, single market, and SPS framework. However, seen from the UK government's perspective, it makes sense, since the goal was that the UK should be able to make its own rules outside the EU, that is, the whole idea is to 'take back control'. This situation can be reinforced if, or when, the UK starts to implement its own rules, for example in connection with a free-trade agreement with the United States.

Notes

1 The analysis draws on previous research on Norwegian agriculture and fisheries policy, official documents from Norway, the EU and the UK, news sources, and secondary literature.
2 Understood here as raw fish, processed fish, mussels, and crustaceans.
3 Norway had unilaterally expanded its territorial waters to 12 miles in 1961 (Frøland, 2015, p. 151).

References

Barnier, M. (2021) *My Secret Brexit Diary*, Cambridge: Polity Press.
Bjørndal, T. and Munro, G. T. (2020) 'Brexit og framtidig fiskeriforvaltning i Europa', in Melchior, A. and Nilssen, F. (eds) *Sjømatnæringen og Europa: EØS og alternativene*, Oslo: Universitetsforlaget, pp. 264–291.
Churchill, R. (2022) 'Fisheries Management in United Kingdom Waters after Brexit', in Fernández, J. E., Johansson, T. M., Skinner, J. A. and Lennan, M. (eds) *Fisheries and the Law in Europe: Regulation After Brexit*, London: Routledge, pp. 11–31.
Coleman, W. D., Skogstad, G. and Atkinson, M. M. (1997) 'Paradigm Shifts and Policy Networks: Cumulative Change in Agriculture', *Journal of Public Policy*, 16(3): 273–301.
Council of the European Union (2017) *Draft Guidelines Following the United Kingdom's Notification Under Article 50 TEU*, 31 March, Brussels: European Council.
Da Conceição-Heldt, E. (2006) 'Taking Actors' Preferences and the Institutional Setting Seriously: The EU Common Fisheries Policy', *Journal of Public Policy*, 26(3): 279–299.
Dagens Næringsliv (2021) 'Splittelse om handelsavtale – kan falle i fisk', *Dagens Næringsliv*, 7 May.
Directorate of Fisheries (2022) *Nøkkeltall for norsk havbruksnæring 2021*, Bergen: Fiskeridirektoratet. Available at: www.fiskeridir.no/Akvakultur/Tall-og-analyse/Statistiske-publikasjoner/Noekkeltall-for-norsk-havbruksnaering (Accessed 10 February 2023).
Elvestad, C. and Veggeland, F. (2020) 'Sjømateksport og veterinær grensekontroll', in Melchior, A. and Nilssen, F. (eds) *Sjømatnæringen og Europa: EØS og alternativene*, Oslo: Universitetsforlaget, pp. 120–153.
EU, Norway, UK (2021a) *Agreed Record of Fisheries Consultations Between the European Union, Norway, and the United Kingdom for 2021*, 16 March. Available at: www.gov.uk/government/publications/fisheries-cod-haddock-saithe-whiting-plaice-and-herring-management-in-the-north-sea (Accessed 10 February 2023).

EU, Norway, UK (2021b). *Agreed Record of Fisheries Consultations Between the European Union, Norway, and the United Kingdom for 2022*, 10 December. Available at: www.gov.uk/government/publications/fisheries-cod-haddock-saithe-whiting-plaice-and-herring-management-in-the-north-sea (Accessed 10 February 2023).

EU, Norway, UK (2022) *Agreed Record of Fisheries Consultations Between the European Union, Norway, and the United Kingdom for 2023*, 9 December. Available at: www.gov.uk/government/publications/fisheries-cod-haddock-saithe-whiting-plaice-and-herring-management-in-the-north-sea (Accessed 10 February 2023).

European Commission (2020) *Concluding Discussion Authorising the Opening of Negotiations for a New Partnership with the United Kingdom of Great Britain and Northern Ireland. COM (2020) 25 Final*, Brussels: European Commission.

Farsund, A. A. (2014) 'Norway – Agricultural Exceptionalism and Quest for Free Trade', in Langhelle, O. (ed) *International Trade Negotiations and Domestic Politics*, London: Routledge, pp. 148–173.

Farsund, A. A. (2021) 'Politicization Strategies in Domestic Trade Policy Making: Comparing Agriculture and Seafood Sectors in Norway', *Journal of Comparative Policy Analysis: Research and Practice*, 23(5–6): 576–591.

Farsund, A. A. and Langhelle, O. (2015) 'Nasjonal politikk og internasjonale forhandlinger. Norsk handelspolitikk etter 1995', in Sverdrup, U. and Melchior, A. (eds) *Interessekonflikter i norsk handelspolitikk*, Oslo: Universitetsforlaget, pp. 105–129.

Farsund, A. A. and Veggeland, F. (2016) 'Historiske veivalg i jordbrukspolitikken', in Mittenzwei, K., Hegrenes, A. and Prestegard, S. S. (eds) *Norsk jordbruks- og matpolitikk: handlingsrom i endring*, Bergen: Fagbokforlaget, pp. 23–40.

Fernández, J. E., Johansson, T. M., Skinner, J. A. and Lennan, M. (eds) (2022) *Fisheries and the Law in Europe: Regulation After Brexit*, London: Routledge.

Foss, T. (2011) *Analyse av Norges avtaler og samarbeid med EU på fiskeriområdet*, Europautredningen report nr. 4, Oslo: Europautredningen.

Frøland, H. O. (2015) 'Fisk versus landbruk i norske handelsforhandlinger, 1947–1994', in Sverdrup, U. and Melchior, A. (eds) *Interessekonflikter i norsk handelspolitikk*, Oslo: Universitetsforlaget, pp. 130–154.

Hersoug, B. (2014) 'Oppdrett på børs: Boom and bust', in Hovland, E. (ed) *Over den leiken ville han rå: Norsk havbruksnærings historie, Bind 5 i Norsk fiskeri- og kysthistorie*, Bergen: Fagbokforlaget, pp. 279–314.

Holden, M. (1996) *The Common Fisheries Policy: Origin, Evaluation, and Future*, Oxford: Blackwell.

Huitfeldt, A. (2022) *Redegjørelse om viktige EU og EØS spørsmål 17.november*, Oslo: Norwegian Ministry of Foreign Affairs, 17 November. Available at: www.regjeringen.no/no/aktuelt/utgreiing_europa/id2947378/.

Jentoft, S. and Mikalsen, K. H. (2014) 'Do National Resources Have to be Centrally Managed? Vested Interests and Institutional Reform in Norwegian Fisheries Governance', *Maritime Studies*, 13(5): 1–16.

Korsvoll, A. S. and Larsen, S. (2022) 'Fiskarar skildrar Brexit-kaos på havet', *NRK*, 27 November. Available at: www.nrk.no/vestland/kappfiske-og-kaos-_-men-a-lande-ei-fiskeavtale-kan-ta-fleire-ar-1.16188189 (Accessed 25 January 2023).

Lado, E. P. (2016) *The Common Fisheries Policy. The Quest for Sustainability*, London: Wiley Blackwell.

Langhelle, O., Farsund, A. A. and Rommetvedt, H. (2014) 'The Global Trade Agenda', in Langhelle, O. (ed) *International Trade Negotiations and Domestic Politics*, Oxford: Routledge, pp. 23–48.

Laurantzon, M. A. B. and Arnesen, F. (2020) 'Rettslige konsekvenser for norsk sjømatnæring ved bortfall av EØS-avtalen', in Melchior, A. and Nilssen, F. (eds) *Sjømatnæringen og Europa: EØS og alternativene*, Oslo: Universitetsforlaget, pp. 83–119.

Lennan, M., Fernández, J. E. and Johansson, T. M. (2022) 'The Fisheries Act 2020 and Devolution', in Fernández, J. E., Johansson, T. M., Skinner, J. A. and Lennan, M. (eds) *Fisheries and the Law in Europe: Regulation After Brexit*, London: Routledge, pp. 68–80.

Lequesne, C. (2000) 'Quota Hopping: The Common Fisheries Policy Between States and Markets', *Journal of Common Market Studies*, 38(5): 779–793.

Maurseth, P. B. and Medin, H. (2020) 'Utenlandsinvesteringer i sjømatnæringen og norsk tilknytning til EU', in Melchior, A. and Nilssen, F. (2020) *Sjømatnæringen og Europa: EØS og alternativene*, Oslo: Universitetsforlaget, pp. 232–263.

May, T. (2017) *Prime Minister's Letter to Donald Tusk Triggering Article 50. 29 March 2017*, London: UK Government. Available at: www.gov.uk/government/publications/prime-ministers-letter-to-donald-tusk-triggering-article-50 (Accessed 10 February 2023).

Melchior, A. (2020a) 'Sjømatnæringen og Europa: EU-medlemskap, EØS eller NOREXIT?', in Melchior, A. and Nilssen, F. (eds) *Sjømatnæringen og Europa: EØS og alternativene*, Oslo: Universitetsforlaget, pp. 13–42.

Melchior, A. (2020b) 'Norges handelsforhandlinger med EU gjennom 50 år: Sakskoblinger og forhandlingsmakt', in Melchior, A. and Nilssen, F. (eds) *Sjømatnæringen og Europa: EØS og alternativene*, Oslo: Universitetsforlaget, pp. 43–82.

Melchior, A. (2020c) 'fiskebrevet til EØS: Betydningen av toll på norsk eksport til EU', in Melchior, A. and Nilssen, F. (eds) *Sjømatnæringen og Europa: EØS og alternativene*, Oslo: Universitetsforlaget, pp. 180–212.

Meld. St. 8 (2021–2022) *Noregs fiskeriavtalar for 2022 og fisket etter avtalane i 2020 og 2021*, Oslo: Ministry of Trade, Industry and Fisheries.

Mikalsen, K. H. and Jentoft, S. (2003) 'Limits to Participation? On the History, Structure and Reform of Norwegian Fisheries Management', *Marine Policy*, 27(5): 397–407.

Ministry of Trade, Industry and Fisheries (2021) 'Norge og Storbritannia avslutter fiskeriforhandlinger', *NTB Kommunikasjon*, 30 April. Available at: https://kommunikasjon.ntb.no/pressemelding/norge-og-storbritannia-avslutter-fiskeriforhandlinger?publisherId=14943704&releaseId=17906734.

Norway, UK (2021) *Agreed Record of Fisheries Consultations Between the United Kingdom and Norway for 2022*, 21 December. Available at: www.regjeringen.no/contentassets/8e674a19756e44518c4641287b28e4db/uk-norge-avtale.pdf (Accessed 10 February 2023).

Norway, UK (2022) *Agreed Record of Fisheries Consultations Between the United Kingdom and Norway for 2023*, 24 November. Available at: www.gov.scot/publications/united-kingdom-and-norway-fisheries-consultations-agreed-record-for-2023/documents/ (Accessed 10 February 2023).

NOU 2012:2 (2012) 'Utenfor og innenfor – Norges avtaler med EU' ['Outside and Inside: Norway's Agreements with the European Union'] [online], *Norwegian Ministry of Foreign Affairs*. Available at: www.regjeringen.no/no/dokumenter/nou-2012-2/id669368/ (Accessed 17 January 2022).

Petetin, L. and Dobbs, M. (2022) *Brexit and Agriculture*, London: Routledge.

Phillipson, J. and Symes, D. (2018) 'A Sea of Trouble: Brexit and the Fisheries Question', *Marine Policy*, 90: 168–173.

Political Declaration Setting Out the Framework for the Future Relationship Between the European Union and the United Kingdom (2019) *Official Journal of the European Union*, C 384 I/178, 12 November.

Prop. 37 S (2020–2021) *Samtykke til inngåelse av rammeavtale om fiskeri mellom Norge og Storbritannia av 30. september 2020*, Oslo: Ministry of Foreign Affairs.

Prop. 115 S (2016–2017) *Samtykke til inngåelse av avtale med Den europeiske union (EU) om utvidet handel med landbruksvarer etter EØS-avtalens artikkel 19*, Oslo: Ministry of Foreign Affairs.

Prop. 119 S (2015–2016) *Samtykke til ratifikasjon av avtale mellom EØS/EFTA-statene og EU om en EØS-finansieringsordning 2014–2021 og tilleggsprotokoll til frihandelsavtalen mellom Norge og Det europeiske økonomiske fellesskapet om handel med fisk, alle av 3. mai 2016*, Oslo: Ministry of Foreign Affairs.

Prop. 160 S (2009–2010) *Samtykke til ratifikasjon av avtale mellom EØS/EFTA-statene og EU om en EØS-finansieringsordning 2009–2014 og tilleggsprotokoll til frihandelsavtalen mellom Norge og Det europeiske økonomiske fellesskapet om handel med fisk, alle av 28. juli 2010*, Oslo: Ministry of Foreign Affairs.

Prop. 210 S (2020–2021) *Samtykke til inngåelse av frihandelsavtale mellom Island, Liechtenstein, Norge og Storbritannia*, Oslo: Ministry of Foreign Affairs.

Rommetvedt, H. and Veggeland, F. (2019) 'Parliamentary Government and Corporatism at the Crossroads: Principals and Agents in Norwegian Agricultural Policy-making', *Government and Opposition*, 54(4): 661–685.

Rosello, M., Lennan, M., Fernández, J. E. and Johansson, T. M. (2022) 'Fisheries Enforcement Post-Brexit', in Fernández, J. E., Johansson, T. M., Skinner, J. A. and Lennan, M. (eds) *Fisheries and the Law in Europe. Regulation After Brexit*, London: Routledge, pp. 81–97.

Rye, L. (2015) 'Sakskoblinger i EØS-forhandlingene (1990–91)', in Sverdrup, U. and Melchior, A. (eds) *Interessekonflikter i norsk handelspolitikk*, Oslo: Universitetsforlaget, pp. 155–181.

Serdy, A. (2022) 'The Fisheries Provision of the Trade and Cooperation Agreement: An Analytical Conspectus', in Fernández, J. E., Johansson, T. M., Skinner, J. A. and Lennan, M. (eds) *Fisheries and the Law in Europe. Regulation After Brexit*, London: Routledge, pp. 32–54.

Sheingate, A. and Greer, A. (2021) 'Populism, Politicization and Policy Change in US and UK Agro-food Policies', *Journal of Comparative Policy Analysis: Research and Practice*, 23(5–6): 544–560.

Skogstad, G. (1998) 'Ideas, Paradigms, and Institutions: Agricultural Exceptionalism in the European Union and the United States', *Governance*, 11(4): 463–490.

Stewart, B. D., Williams, C., Barnes, R., Walmsley, S. F., and Carpenter, G. (2022) 'The Brexit Deal and UK Fisheries – Has Reality Matched the Rhetoric?', *Maritime Studies*, 21: 1–17.

St.prp. nr. 100 (1991–92) *Om samtykke til ratifikasjon av Avtale om Det Europeiske Økonomiske Samarbeidsområdet (EØS)*, Oslo: Stortinget.

St.prp. nr. 126 (1972–73) *Om samtykke til ratifikasjon av Avtale mellom Norge og Det Europeiske Økonomiske Fellesskap og Avtale mellom Norge og medlemsstatene i Det Europeiske Kull- og Stålfellesskap og Det Europeiske Kull og Stålfellesskap*, Oslo: Stortinget. Available at: www.stortinget.no/no/Saker-og-publikasjoner/Stortingsforhandlinger/Saksside/?pid=1970-1981&mtid=109&vt=b&did=DIVL117440.

Symes, D. (1997) 'The European Community's Common Fisheries Policy', *Ocean & Coastal Management*, 35(2–3): 137–155.

UK Government (2020) *UK-EU Trade and Cooperation Agreement – Summary*, London: UK Government. Available at: https://assets.publishing.service.gov.uk/government/

uploads/system/uploads/attachment_data/file/962125/TCA_SUMMARY_PDF_V1-.
pdf.
Veggeland, F. (2016) 'Internasjonale bindinger og interessekamp: Norges tilpasning til EU på mat- og landbruksfeltet', *Internasjonal Politikk*, 74(1): 1–23.
Wachowiak, J. and Zuleeg, F. (2022) 'Brexit and the Trade and Cooperation Agreement; Implications for Internal and External EU Differentiation', *International Spectator*, 57(1): 142–159.

5
GLOBAL TRADE AND DEVELOPMENT

The challenge of translating legal wriggle room into autonomy

Introduction

This chapter discusses Norway and Britain's wriggle room and autonomy in the policy areas of global trade and development, often referred to as 'external policies'. These realms are closely tied to foreign policy but also differ in important ways when it comes to the wriggle room and autonomy non-members enjoy in relation to the EU. First, global trade and development have been important features of Norway and Britain's international roles. Norway, as a non-member, seeks to protect its agricultural and seafood sectors in trade and promotes itself as a humanitarian superpower supported by a strong development policy. Britain, on their side, has been a norm-setter in international development over many years. Second, a prominent argument against EU membership both in Norway and in Britain has been that, as an outsider, you have more room for manoeuvre in relation to the world outside the EU. Indeed, a prime justification for Brexit was Britain's ambition to regain its status as a global power in the world. Hence, these policy areas are important examples of Norway and Britain's alleged independence from the EU and relevant empirical areas to investigate these countries' ability to stake out their own course in global affairs, and thus warrant further investigation.

Then what opportunities and constraints exist for non-members in a post-Brexit European political order? In this chapter we will focus on what we, in Chapter 2, defined as the EU-external dimension of wriggle room, in other words to what extent non-members are constrained from forming agreements with other states, independently of the EU. As such, we focus on Norway and Britain's trade and development agreements with third states, although the trade and cooperation agreements between Norway, Iceland and the UK, and UK and the EU influence their wriggle room to conclude global agreement and will thus be touched upon in the analysis.

DOI: 10.4324/9781003246961-5

98 Global trade and development

At first sight, non-members enjoy a larger legal space to stake out their own course in the realms of trade and development than what EU members have. In trade, the EU has exclusive competence, something that means that it is the EU and not the member states that legislates on matters of global trade and enters into international trade agreements with third countries. Thus, formally, there are no legal or institutional constraints on non-members' wriggle room to negotiate agreements with third states. Yet, the EU, with its market size and acting as a bloc negotiator, shapes important aspects of global trade, thereby setting constraints for non-members (Bradford, 2020). In the realm of development, the EU has so-called shared competences, where member states and EU institutions develop legislation alongside each other, thereby leaving an even larger formal wriggle room for both members and non-members to stake out their own course. Yet, in a similar vein as in trade, other multilateral fora, notably the Development Assistance Committee (DAC) of the Organisation for Economic Cooperation and Development (OECD), plays an important role in regulating global standards in key areas of development. The EU enjoys full membership status in DAC, and EU membership is increasingly functioning as a straitjacket for member states which find common solutions and compromises at the EU level and take these already-agreed-upon compromises to the DAC (Verschaeve and Orbie, 2016, 2017). Hence, also for non-EU members, the EU-dominated DAC limits their room for manoeuvre.

There are many types of constraints in a rule-bound international order. Globalisation and power and norm structures in the international system affects non-members and EU-members in their trade and development policies. For instance, as we saw in Chapter 3, the Paris Agreement and the sustainable development goals set global standards in sustainable development and environmental policies that European countries have committed to follow. The growing role of China under President Xi in international affairs, including its Belt and Road Initiative which promotes China's economic development and inter-regional connectivity, is an example of how international power dynamics affect the wriggle room and autonomy of European states. In this book we look at the constraints non-members experience from their relationship with the EU. While these might be interconnected with wider global factors and structures, the book focuses on the EU-specific constraints that reduces non-members' wriggle room and autonomy and seeks to tease out the specific effects of non-members' relationship to the EU on their autonomy.

This chapter[1] proceeds by exploring what wriggle room and autonomy Norway and Britain enjoy in the policy areas of global trade and development vis-à-vis the EU. While there is substantial formal wriggle room, at first sight, we shall see that their autonomy is constrained in important ways by the EU setting the standards as a bloc negotiator. For Britain, this results in a paradox. The wish for showcasing autonomous will-formation has been more important than their capacity to act autonomously. Britain's newly gained wriggle room in trade has mainly been used to secure the same trade benefits as they enjoyed under EU membership. Whereas Britain has had willingness to negotiate trade agreements with new partners, these negotiations have proved more difficult than anticipated, something which indicates that Britain has over-evaluated its position in the post-2020 global trade order. We see a similar paradox for Norway's relationship with the EU. Although Norway has maintained and used substantial wriggle room in global trade and development by acting alone and in alliance with the EFTA states and some like-minded EU member states, Norway's capacity to act autonomously is constrained by the EU's actions on the global stage. In addition, Brexit led to a shake-up in the power balance between non-members as Britain significantly outweighs other non-EU countries in terms of the size of its economy, international influence, and status vis-à-vis the Union. We will return to this at the end of the chapter. But first we will discuss how and why the EU constrains respectively Norway's and Britain's wriggle room and autonomy in their trade and development policies.

Norway: quasi-member or autonomous global actor?

Norway, a country that is often labelled a quasi-member of the EU due to its close externally integration through the EEA Agreement, has a population with significant Eurosceptic attitudes. While Norwegian Euroscepticism is often explained by pointing to interests in the agrarian sector, a strong periphery including aversion to power concentration, and Norway's historic struggle for sovereignty and self-rule, Norway's identity as an independent and different foreign policy actor also plays an important role. Central to this identity is Norwegian scepticism towards the EU as a project of economic growth and Norway as an alternative humanitarian and solidary actor. The EU's obsession with growth has historically been conceived of as a barrier to equality, sustainability, and solidarity for the world's poor. During the 1972 and 1994 EU debates in Norway, the EU's trade policies were, by many, viewed as discriminatory, because it limits members to make bilateral and pro-poor trade agreements with developing countries. Hence, many Norwegian voters believed that Norway's solidarity with the developing world is better exercised outside of the EU (Skinner, 2012, pp. 432–433). Although, as we saw in Chapter 3, the EU has more recently been leading by example in progressive sustainability and environmental policies, it remains unclear whether this has led to a change in Eurosceptic attitudes in Norway.

In line with these Eurosceptic attitudes, Norway has used its wriggle room as a non-member to wield an autonomous approach to both development and global trade. There is both a substantial and symbolic importance connected to these two policy areas in terms of showcasing Norwegian autonomy from the EU. Substantially, Norway has been able to exercise an autonomous approach to global trade, protecting its agricultural sector to a larger extent than EU member states and avoiding participation in the EU's controversial Economic Partnership Agreements (EPAs) with former colonies in Africa, Caribbean, and the Pacific. According to the Norwegian lobby organisation 'No to the EU', Norway's status as a non-member, has allowed it to find a solidaric alternative to the EU's neo-colonial trade approach

(Nei til EU, 2021). While many would question whether Norway's trade policy is more solidaristic than that of the EU, the statement illustrates the symbolic importance of being an autonomous outsider, with the possibility to adopt a different approach than the EU towards developing countries.

So to what extent has Norway been able to exercise its autonomy in global trade and development? In Chapter 2 we defined wriggle room narrowly, entailing the scope of influence non-members have in the context of legal affiliations with the EU. We distinguished between *internal wriggle room*, which denotes Norway's ability to affect EU decisions with respect to its own EU affiliation, and *external wriggle room*, which pertains to Norway's ability to form agreement with states outside the EU. In this chapter we focus on the EU-external dimension of non-members' wriggle room. Further, we understand wriggle room as a subcategory of autonomy. Autonomy is defined more broadly as 'a country's will and ability to broadly shape society regardless of the constraints embedded in the EU affiliation'. We differentiated between two defining traits of autonomy, namely will-formation (agenda-setting) and capacity (implementation). Given the EU's exclusive competence on trade and shared competence in development, we expect that Norway's formal wriggle room and will-formation are large in both the realms of trade and development, but that processes of interweaving and interdependence with the EU constrains Norway's capacity to act autonomously.

Norway and the EU in global trade

Agricultural exceptionalism

As we write in Chapter 4, the status of agriculture in Norwegian trade is exceptional. The Norwegian economy is generally open to trade, with imports amounting to 33 per cent of GDP and exports to 26.5 per cent of GDP in 2020 (World Bank Data, 2022a). A large part of Norwegian exports come from oil and gas (60 per cent in 2021) (Statistics Norway, 2022). The exception is trade in agriculture which is heavily protected with high tariffs, something that is often denoted as 'agricultural exceptionalism' (Farsund, 2014). The wish for protection of Norwegian agriculture and national control over fish stocks, in other words, sovereignty on trade in agriculture and fisheries both with European countries and the world, was a central argument for the no-votes to EU membership in 1972 and 1994. The concern for protecting national agriculture is something Norway shares with the other EFTA states and results in EFTA free-trade agreements being rather narrow. Norway also shares with the other EFTA states the characteristic of being small and rich countries while they have different expansive interests in trade, something that often works well for them to achieve package deals.

Since trade is not an exclusive competence for EFTA, the EFTA states, including Norway, are free to conclude free-trade agreements (FTAs) either as a group or bilaterally. EFTA has sought to broaden and deepen trade relations with third countries and parties and has so far concluded 29 agreements covering 40 countries and territories outside the EU. As a result, third counties' trade volume with EFTA states increased from 284,510 million EUR in 2002 to 532,977 million EUR in 2020 (EFTA Trade Statistics, 2022). The EFTA FTAs range from non-members in Europe (Balkan states, Ukraine, and Turkey) across the Americas (Canada, Central American states, Chile, Colombia, Mexico, Ecuador, and Peru), Africa and the Middle East (the South African Customs Union (SACU), the Gulf Cooperation Council, Egypt, Jordan, Israel, Palestine Authority, Lebanon, Morocco, and Tunisia), and Asia-Pacific (Hong-Kong, Indonesia, Korea, Philippines, and Singapore). These agreements are evidence of how non-members enjoy legal wriggle room in relation to existing EU legislation. Yet this does not automatically lead to space for autonomously staking out its own course. Rather, the EU might still be constraining non-members' autonomy by being a powerful bloc negotiator.

Parallelism and coherence with the EU

While Norway enjoys wriggle room to stake out its own trade agreements with third states, its autonomy is constrained in important ways. We see this, inter alia, through how parallelism with the EU has become one of the central characteristics of Norway's trade policy. Norway and EFTA states have chosen to act in parallel with initiatives taken by the EU (Farsund, 2014, p. 167). Although we have witnessed some relaxation in this principle since 1995, parallelism with the EU's approach is still an important feature of EFTA's global trade. A prime example is the parallel negotiations of an EU-Mercosur[2] and an EFTA-Mercosur agreement. The choice to mirror the EU's initiative with an EFTA-Mercosur agreement has certain consequences for Norway and EFTA's autonomy versus the EU. When trade agreements are negotiated in parallel, it is natural to compare the concessions and gains made in the respective deals. Given the size of the EU's market and that it operates as a trade bloc, it is difficult for the 'little brother' EFTA to gain any further concessions from partners than what the EU gains. Though, this parallelism also gives the EFTA states certain advantages, for instance the possibility to consult the EU on important questions and, thereby, the ability to request the same concessions as the EU gains in their negotiations.

Unlike in the EU, EFTA membership does not require Norway to harmonise their free-trade policy with the other EFTA members; hence, their wriggle room is large than for EU member states which can only influence via common EU negotiations. When EFTA states negotiate as a bloc, all members must agree on the negotiation mandate and parameters in each negotiation. In this way, EFTA members remain free to decide whether it wants to negotiate as an EFTA member or whether it would rather negotiate by its own. This has led to a differentiated global trade systems where some EFTA trade deals are complemented by bilateral FTAs between individual EFTA states and third countries.

One example is the UK free-trade agreement with Norway, Iceland, and Lichtenstein that was negotiated following Brexit and came into effect 1 December

2021 (see also Chapter 4). The agreement allows the entry of high-skilled British professionals to enter Norway, Iceland, and Liechtenstein for business purposes, and includes elements on digital trade, that is, electronic documents, contracts, and signatures, that goes beyond what the EU has. Regarding free trade of goods, the agreement was presented in Norway as an important possibility for the seafood market as Great Britain is the largest market for Norwegian exports after the EU. While some gains were achieved compared to the EEA Agreement, for instance duty-free access for peeled shrimps and whitefish, Norwegian authorities have recognised that the Norway-UK agreement falls short of the benefits Norway had when Britain was part of the EEA Agreement (Norwegian Government, 2021). It thus illustrates the wriggle room in between the EU and UK agreements is relevant (see Chapter 2), with Brexit causing negative consequences for Norwegian access to the British market. Britain, on their side, gained reduced tariffs for 26 agri-food products, including British cheese, to the Norwegian market. Although it has been symbolically important for Britain to showcase their autonomy in trade, British authorities have recognised that replicating, as far as possible, pre-Brexit trade agreements has been the main task for Britain after Brexit (Department for International Trade, 2020).

Examples of bilateral agreements have also occurred. Iceland was the first EFTA country to conclude an FTA with China in 2014. The negotiations were launched in 2007. Switzerland followed and concluded an agreement later in 2014. Norway has also embarked on the path to conclude a free-trade agreement with China and launched negotiations in 2008. These processes exemplify that these states enjoy some autonomy vis-à-vis the EU, although the EU followed and started their own negotiations in 2012. There were several rounds of negotiations between Norway and China in 2008, but the negotiations came to a halt in 2010 after the Nobel Peace Prize Committee awarded Chinese dissident Liu Xiaobo its price in 2010. The free-trade negotiations re-emerged on the agenda after Norway signed a normalisation agreement with China in 2016, and the negotiations have continued since. An FTA with China would save 8 per cent import duty on Norwegian salmon and thereby strengthen Norway vis-à-vis Chile who is Norway's main competitor in the salmon market. In 2020 Norway seemed to move ahead on its negotiations with China, and there were forces within the conservative government that pushed for signing an agreement. In September 2020, Thorbjørn Røe Isaksen, the Norwegian industry minister stated that he was hoping that a free-trade agreement with China would be signed by the end of the year (Reuters, 2020). Yet the negotiations faced criticism from human rights activists, NGOs, and politicians alike. A letter sent by a coalition of four advocacy groups in September 2020 called for a halt to the negotiations. Their main argument is that trading with authoritarian states help legitimise and strengthen them and thereby also undermine democracy both in China and in Norway (Allen-Ebrahimian, 2021). Also in the run-up to the Chinese Olympics in 2022, there was intensified criticism. The Norwegian Green Party has, for instance, called for a halt to the negotiations and for the foreign minister to stay home from the Olympics (Haugan and Husøy, 2022). With the change of Norwegian government in 2021, negotiations are now frozen. Prime Minister Jonas Gahr Støre reported to have put a stop to the negotiations, among other things, due to a close dialogue with the EU:

> It is important to have a close dialogue with the EU when it comes to trade relations, in particular with a country as China. The EU has their own process which has now been halted by the European Parliament and with regards to our own process there is no movement at the moment.
> *(Støre, 2022 – authors' translation)*

The EU-China investment agreement concluded in 2021 was frozen by the European Parliament in May 2022, due, among other things, to the human rights situation in China.

Differentiated politicisation in the EU-Mercosur and the EFTA-Mercosur trade agreements

The Norway-China FTA negotiations are not the only ones that are criticised. The EFTA-Mercosur FTA has received critique for the lack of binding sustainability safeguards from Norwegian NGOs. Greenpeace (2022), for instance, says that it is irresponsible to reward a Brazilian government with a trade deal that puts the global fight against climate change in danger, threatens indigenous peoples' way of life, and undermines Norway's billion-krone international climate and forest initiative. The EFTA-Mercosur FTA was negotiated in parallel with the EU-Mercosur agreement. Although a declaration of cooperation was signed already in 2000, the negotiations between EFTA and Mercosur did not properly start until 2017. One of the reasons why the negotiations were relatively quick was Argentinian president Mauricio Macri's personal prioritisation of the EU and EFTA-Mercosur negotiations. Macri was keen to reach agreements with the EU and EFTA to ease the pressure from international creditors as Argentina was facing an increasingly severe economic recession (Nolte and Neto, 2021).[3] Macri's ambitions succeeded, and Mercosur reached an agreement first with the EU in June 2019 and later with EFTA in August the same year. However, since 2019 the EU and the EFTA states have not moved ahead on the preparations to sign the agreement. This is due to a substantial increase in deforestation in the Amazon and the Bolsonaro government making several national reforms that have severely weakened government agencies and NGOs that work to reduce deforestation and to secure the rights of indigenous peoples in the Amazon.

Since 2019 this has created a political environment where it would be difficult for the EU and the EFTA states to move ahead with the signing and ratification of their agreements with Mercosur. Yet, while there has been a comprehensive debate in EU member states' parliaments and the EU parliament, there has been less debate within the EFTA countries. In Norway, criticism has mainly come from environmental NGOs. On behalf of Norwegian authorities, successive ministers for Trade and Industry have repeatedly stated that the EFTA-Mercosur agreement contains sufficient sustainability safeguards. They also emphasise that the political discussion that has emerged in the EU regarding Brazil and deforestation clearly impacts the Norwegian government's capacity to act:

> This agreement is in line with Norway's policies in other areas than trade, such as rainforests, so there is nothing that indicates that the government will not suggest a ratification. . . . But as the process in the EU shows, there might be a huge discussion about this. What happens in the EU, for example, clearly have consequences for the discussion in Norway.
>
> *(Isaksen, 2019 – authors' translation)*

> In our assessment we will look at the ongoing discussion between the EU Commission and Mercosur regarding deforestation and indigenous peoples' rights, something that will be of importance for signing and ratifying the EU's free-trade agreement with Mercosur. Norway will together with the other EFTA countries follow the EU's initiative closely, says Nybø.
>
> *(NTB, 2021 – authors' translation)*

In EU member states, on the other hand, the issue has been politicised and widely debated among parliamentarians, decision-makers and NGOs. Several EU member states have demanded a strengthening of the sustainable development chapters including enforcement mechanisms to be added in an annex to the agreement. The possibility of an 'additional instrument' containing sustainability safeguards to be added to the agreement is currently being developed by DG Trade.[4]

The EU has launched the idea to not reopen the negotiations of the agreement but to rather ask for some additional commitments in an annex or side agreement. Although it is still unclear what this entails more concretely, the EFTA countries have communicated to Mercosur that they will shadow this process closely, and they are considering asking for something similar.[5]

EU member states have been vocal in signalling that a ratification of the agreement is off the table, as long as the deforestation levels remain high in Brazil. French and Dutch governments published a non-paper in May 2020 calling for stronger sustainability chapters in all trade agreements (Kingdom of the Netherlands, 2020). After France, the Netherlands, Ireland, Belgium, Luxembourg, Austria, and Germany removed their support to the agreement, the European Parliament passed a resolution on October 7, 2020, stating that 'the EU-Mercosur agreement cannot be ratified as it stands' (European Parliament, 2020). Within EFTA, we have not witnessed the same level of politicisation among political bodies. Thus, it is not Norway's wriggle room that is constrained but rather the interweaving with the political context of the EU that limits their will-formation with the South American trade giant.

With the October 2022 election of Luiz Inácio 'Lula' da Silva in Brazil, the EU and EFTA states again eye hope to move ahead on their agreements with Mercosur. Lula signalled during the election campaign that he would bring deforestation in the Amazon to zero. He also enjoys strong political ties with EFTA and EU diplomats and European heads of state. The Commission has been keen to speed up the ratification of the agreement. One option they are considering is to isolate trade aspects in a separate agreement, something that would bypass member state parliaments and only having to pass by the European Parliament and the Council of the EU by a qualified majority.[6] The wider political context is also of essence. Russia's war on Ukraine has created a stronger political will among EU member states to seek alliances with like-minded partners around the world. The Mercosur countries appear as increasingly relevant partners and allies for the EU and EFTA.

On the one hand, then, one could say that Norway has a quite large autonomy with regards to Mercosur, in that it can negotiate an agreement that is more designed to meet Norway and the EFTA countries' national interests. For instance, The EFTA-Mercosur agreement will go further in liberalising trade in industry goods, while agricultural products will have higher barriers than in the EU agreement.[7] This is in line with Norway's agricultural exceptionalism policy. But, on the other hand, the EFTA countries won't be able to negotiate a radically different agreement than the EU's. Mercosur was cautious in giving the EFTA states concessions on top of what they had given to the EU, because then the EU would demand the same.

> The central questions in the EFTA Mercosur agreement are not bound by the EEA agreement. With the exception of Sanitary and Phyto Sanitary (SPS) measure and technical Barriers to trade (TBT) we are free to do what we want. But, since we are part of Europe, many will compare our results to those that the EU gains – so we see a political binding to the EU – it will be difficult for us to gain support for a result that is not equally good as the one the EU gains with Mercosur.[8]

Furthermore, given the high levels of deforestation in Brazil, it would be difficult for EFTA to sign and ratify their agreement with Mercosur without agreeing on new safeguards and without the EU choosing to move ahead on their agreement. For Norwegian policymakers, the EU context is important in this regard:

> In the EU there is a recognition that if one is to move ahead with ratification in all EU countries and the EU parliament, a change in Brazil's tropical forest policy must occur. real commitments from Mercosur and commitments that lead to real changes on the ground is necessary. . . . Also, in Norway we need to see a change on the ground in Brazil before we can move ahead with this agreement.[9]

Hence, while we see that Norway and the other EFTA states' wriggle room is quite large, their autonomy is constrained by the interweaving and interdependence

Norway experiences with the EU. The political interweaving with Europe plays a more important role than the formal affiliations with the EU.

The EU regulates global markets

Also multilaterally, the EU is a trade giant that shapes non-members' wriggle room in multilateral trade negotiations. The EU has, since its inception, played a central role in multilateral trade negotiations and presented itself as a champion of the multilateral trade system (Meunier and Nicolaïdis, 2017; Young and Peterson, 2014). Due to the share size of its market and the fact that the EU has exclusive competences on trade, it can regulate global markets by setting common standards. EU-style regulations are thus becoming common also in third states (Bradford, 2020). In the World Trade Organization, the EU is a significant actor due to its size. Smaller economies must abide by the approval of new provisions by larger countries or big coalitions of countries. When WTO member states, led by a proposal by the EU and Brazil, decided to eliminate export subsidies for agricultural products in 2015, Norway's ministry of Foreign Affairs had no choice but to look for domestic support for the decision, although it would have long-term negative effects for domestic agricultural production (Farsund, 2021, p. 589)

To sum up, Norway's status as a non-member has provided significant wriggle room in the realm of global trade. Norway has concluded free-trade agreements together with the EFTA member states that it would not have been able to do as an EU member. Yet there are also constraints. These constraints do not emanate from the lack of wriggle room, but rather from how Norway is interweaved in a European context. It is theoretically possible but, in practice, impossible for Norway to act in a radically different way than its European counterpart. The EU is seen as an ambitious climate actor, and Norwegian politicians are not ready to do less. Both the reluctance to move ahead on the deal with Mercosur and Norway's acceptance of the elimination of export subsidies on agricultural products in the WTO exemplifies this.

Norway and the EU in development: humanitarian superpower ambitions

The Nordics as preferred partners in development

Also in the realm of development, Norway has chosen to use its wriggle room as a non-member to exercise an autonomous development policy. There are several reasons for this choice. Rather than looking to the EU, Norway has chosen to coordinate and cooperate with its 'like-minded partners', also known as the Nordic Plus countries (the Nordics, the Netherlands, the UK, and Ireland) in development (Saltnes, 2022).[10] They have relied on close informal cooperation since the group was founded in 1998 at the Utstein monastery in Norway, by the then development minister Hilde Frafjord Johnson and her fellow development minister colleagues, all from social democratic parties from Germany (Heidemarie Wieczorek-Zeul), the Netherlands (Eveline Herfkens), and the UK (Clare Short) (Michalopoulos, 2020).

The Nordic Plus countries relies on a common set of values and goals in their approach to development. Central to their approach is to maintain a rights-based approach to development, encourage partner country ownership, focus on the poorest countries, and show solidarity with the global south. These values result in a common focus on maintaining a high level of development aid (at least 0.7 per cent of their budgets – several members also reach 1 per cent), a focus on Africa, multilateralism, and a UN-led world order, and seeking to contribute to the strategies and goals of the partner countries (Saltnes, 2022). Their cooperation is informal but strong and varies in degree depending on the projects and initiatives in question.

> With the Nordic plus countries, the history and the trust between the countries are so strong and the common interest in keeping up such a community and dialogue that there has been no need to formalise this coordination. . . . They are a much more natural partner for us to coordinate with than the EU.[11]

Hence, while Norway cooperates closely with some EU member states on development policies, coordination with EU institutions and the EU's common development has been a low priority in the Norwegian foreign service.

A strong development identity

Second, Norway has a strong identity as a humanitarian development actor. And, in Norway, the self-conception as a nation of peace and that of being a strong development actor are tied together (Leira et al., 2007). One Norwegian policymaker put it like this: 'The Norwegian development identity is very strong globally. Our identity is that of a humanitarian superpower'.[12] This identity has exacerbated Norway's cautiousness to coordinate with the EU in new development initiatives. A recent example is illustrative: in April 2020 the EU and its member states put together a financial package to support partner countries in addressing the pandemic and its consequences, an initiative known as 'Team Europe'. While Norway has been interested in monitoring Team Europe, it has been cautious about participating because they want to maintain their own approach and identity: 'Is it Europe or is it the EU, what can we gain from joining this initiative? We have had reservations. . . . This is because our development identity is so strong'.[13] Hence, Norway has limited interest in being associated with the EU in the realm of development. Rather, it prefers to limit cooperation with the EU as such and maintain cooperation with its like-minded European states.

While Norway's humanitarian superpower ambitions have led it to be cautious about coordinating with the EU, the size and power of the EU still constrains Norway's autonomy. We see this primarily in multilateral fora. For instance, in the negotiations in the OECD-DAC, the EU plays an important role. The Development Assistance Committee of the OECD has the task to define and monitor global development principles and standards on behalf of its members, the world's largest Western donors (Australia, Austria, Belgium, Canada, Denmark, the EU, Finland, France, Germany, Greece, Ireland, Italy, Japan, South Korea, Luxembourg, the Netherlands, New Zealand, Norway, Portugal, Spain, Sweden, Switzerland, the UK, and the US). Out of 24 members, 15 are from the EU, including the EU delegation which is a member of its own. The importance of DAC can be illustrated by its track record in fostering some of the most important aid principles in the last decades, including the Paris Declaration of Aid Effectiveness (2005), which included the coining of the ownership, alignment, and harmonisation principles, and its power in defining what its members can report as Official Development Assistance (ODA) (Verschaeve and Takacs, 2013). Although consultations in the DAC have a deliberative character, the size and coordination of the EU and its member states matter. The EU delegation to the OECD and EU member states that are DAC members meet monthly and consult and coordinate before all DAC meetings. There are also regular meetings with non-DAC EU members to keep them involved. The result is that harmonisation occurs continuously between EU member states' development policies and agreements, and compromises are often found before they meet in DAC (Verschaeve and Orbie, 2016, 2017).

Negative consequences of Europeanisation

A typical example of how non-EU members' autonomy is constrained is how the norm *policy coherence for development* has gained traction in non-EU organisations because of the EU's agenda-setting power. Policy coherence for development (PCD), a 'flagship' in EU external relations (Carbone, 2017), is a norm that encourages actors to prioritise development objectives in policies (other than development) that are likely to have an impact on developing countries. DAC conducted a strategic reflection exercise in 2007 where it sought to evaluate its role, structure, function, and composition in an, at the time, moving aid-landscape. During the exercise, the EU suggested to set up a task force on PCD to make sure PCD became an essential DAC norm in the future. Yet non-EU DAC members (including Australia, Canada, Japan, Norway, Switzerland, US) opposed the task force because they did not see PCD as an essential norm for DAC's future work. However, the EU and its member states had already adopted common policies on PCD, and it formed an integral part of the EU development policy, and therefore they were determined to make it integral also to DAC's work. The non-EU members eventually gave in and agreed to the task force on policy coherence which the EU had proposed. They came to the realisation that it would be impossible to convince the large group of EU members to change their position (Verschaeve and Orbie, 2017).

The earlier example is illustrative of how not only prior coordination or EU compromises are important but also how EU integration leads to harmonisation of values that is essential to how the EU and its member states operate in multilateral settings. Thus, while the member states are free to pursue their own development polices, the EU no longer works only as a bilateral donor alongside the member states but also operates as a coordinator of its members' development policies (Carbone, 2017). The result is that non-members' autonomy is constrained. Their will-formation remains intact; however, their autonomous capacity of action, when their position differs from that of the EU, becomes difficult to exercise. This is what we, in Chapter 2, refer to as negative effects of Europeanisation. The nuances are important here. In the example about policy coherence for development, described earlier, Norway was not opposed to the norm itself. But what the example illustrates is that while Norway and other non-members did not want the PCD norm to take centre stage in the DAC in the same way as the EU and its member states wanted it prioritised. Yet the non-members were unable to present convincing arguments as to why the PCD norm should not be prioritised and ended up not being able to stake out the course they wanted in DAC.

But increased cooperation in the development-migration nexus

One exception from Norway's hesitancy to collaborate with the EU is the EU Emergency Trust Fund for Africa (EUTF), where Norway has been a regular contributor and part of the fund's board since it was established in 2015. The purpose of this fund is to aid in combating root causes of migration and, in that way, contribute to halt migration inflows to the European continent. The fund has developed from a more traditional development initiative to include elements of security policy, such as border control and anti-smuggling initiatives. On the one hand, this closer cooperation with the EU has been a positive experience for Norway, in eyes of the foreign service, because it required little responsibility and concrete outcomes. It was simply a pay-in option which led to little extra work for Norway.[14] This experience could lead to a stronger willingness by Norway to participate in EU initiatives that are open to non-members (other trust funds, for example). Norway, contrary to the UK, is a donor that channels a large part of its development cooperation through multilateral institutions and would therefore, in principle, be interested in channelling its aid via European institutions, as we see in the example of the EUTF. But, on the other hand, Norway's strong development identity is likely to limit future cooperation with the EU. Cooperation is possible where there are strong overlapping interests, such as in the case of migration, yet these instances have so far been marginal.

To sum up, the EU is not a major player in Norway's development policy. While the like-minded European member states are important partners for Norway, EU institutions are not. Yet this does not mean that the EU is not an irrelevant actor for Norway. The EU and its member states are an important voice in the international fora where the multilateral development norms and principles are debated and decided upon. Hence, while Norway's institutional and legal wriggle room is large, their capacity to act is constrained by the EU in the OECD-DAC.

We now turn to discuss the relationship between Britain and the EU in the realms of global trade and development. As a major actor in both realms, a close partner for Norway in development issues and the second biggest market for Norwegian exporters (after the EU), Brexit has implications for the triangular relationship between Norway, Britain, and the EU that we will explore further later.

Britain: regaining autonomy?

Regaining sovereignty and autonomy were presented by the Brexiteers as the main gains for Britain during the Brexit campaign. The leave campaign promised that Brexit would allow Britain to 'take back control' over its borders, laws, money, and trade rules, among other things. The expectation was that increased wriggle room through Brexit would also give Britain its desired autonomy to stake out its own course in world affairs. Yet the latter does not necessarily follow from the former. In a similar vein as Norway, Britain is now faced with the challenges of living under the shadow of EU hegemony. Given the asymmetry in power and global influence between Norway and the UK, one might assume that British autonomy might be less affected by EU hegemony than Norway. Yet, the realms of global trade and development, as we shall see, are illustrative of the how increased legal wriggle room does not necessarily lead to a similar increase in autonomy. The British authorities' wish for showing their *autonomy in terms of will-formation* to stake out their own direction has been more important than their capacity to exercise autonomous actions. Hence, the policy areas of global trade and development provide lessons for the UK from Norway's EU experience.

Britain and the EU in global trade

High ambitions

When exiting the Union, Britain significantly increased its wriggle room in global trade. When exiting all the EU's global trade agreements, as of January 2021, Britain was free to pursue its own free-trade agreements, just as Norway and the EFTA states. Regaining sovereignty in trade has figured as a significant justification for Brexit.[15] Brexiteers promised a renewed role for Britain. The promises were ambitious: 'Global Britain is leading the world as a force of good', Dominic Raab (2019) wrote in the *Telegraph* in September 2019. Furthermore, Boris Johnson in his Global Britain speech stated:

> It is our historic post-Brexit function to be the leading agitators for free-trade ... seizing the moment to campaign for openness and open markets across the globe beginning with some of those dynamic commonwealth economies that are already queuing up to do free-trade deals.
>
> *(Johnson, 2019)*

In their White Paper on Brexit, the Department for Exiting the European Union (DEEU, 2017) stated:

> By leaving the EU we will have the opportunity to strike free-trade agreements with countries around the world. We will be champions of free-trade driving forward liberalisation bilaterally, as well as in wider groupings, and we will continue to support the international rules-based system.

Also, when it came to the question of whether Britain should be part of the Customs Union or not after Brexit, global trade was a key argument for the Conservative government. Trade minister Liam Fox stated in a speech in February (2018) that 'we need the ability to exercise a fully independent trade policy'. According to Fox (2018), remaining in the Customs Union would not only limit Britain's 'ability to reach new trade agreements with the world's fastest-growing economies' but it would also limit 'new ways for the world's poorest nations to trade their way out of poverty'.

Securing trade benefits lost with Brexit

Yet, Britain's role as a global trade power after Brexit has been far from as transformative and autonomous as was promised. While a repeated argument during the Brexit campaign was that Brexit would allow the UK government to exercise their 'sovereignty' – what we in this book define as autonomy – this has not been a key feature of Global Britain's trade policy. Rather, what we have seen is a Britain that has tried to punch above its weight, and failed, and a Britain that has used its newly gained wriggle room only to replicate EU trade agreements with third countries.

To take the latter first. Post-Brexit, Britain has negotiated so-called roll-over deals with countries and territories that EU has free-trade agreements with. At the time of Brexit, the EU had 41 FTA covering over 75 countries and territories around the world. Without the conclusion of roll-over deals with former colonies and other countries, these countries would lose their preferential access to the UK market, and the UK would pay increased tariffs and be subject to more paperwork for imports of goods, as they would trade on WTO terms (Price, 2018). Britain has, as of 7 February 2022, negotiated 36 roll-over agreements with 67 countries and territories. Hence, far from using the newly gained wriggle room to 'drive forward liberalisation' (DEEU, 2017), Britain has replicated the EU's approach to secure the same trade benefits it enjoyed under EU membership. Rather than creating new benefits, the focus has been renegotiating the benefits they had under EU membership. Those countries that have not concluded an agreement with Britain will trade under the newly established UK's Generalised Scheme of Preferences which, to a large extent, mirrors the EU's GSP. Least developed countries will quote free access and nil rates of import duty to the UK on all goods except arms and ammunition, mirroring the EU's Everything but Arms agreement (EBA).

While the Brexiteers promised to take back control over Britain's trade policy, what we have seen in practice is a Britain that has used its newly gained wriggle room to copy-paste the EU's agreements and secure the benefits it lost when exiting the Union. While in theory there are possibilities for Britain to gain new and more tailor-made concessions from negotiating bilateral agreements with its partners in the Commonwealth, in practice we see that it is a challenge for individual countries to gain concessions that are better than what is granted to the EU.

Trying to punch above its weight

Second, it may seem like Brexiteers have over-evaluated Britain's power in the post 2020 global trade order. A ministry for international trade was formed just a month after the Brexit referendum, and there has not been a lack of ambition. PM Theresa May (2017) stated in a speech in January 2017 that

> countries including China, Brazil, and the Gulf States have already expressed their interest in striking trade deals with us. We have started discussions on future trade ties with countries like Australia, New Zealand, and India. And President-Elect Trump has said Britain is not 'at the back of the queue' for a trade deal with the United States, the world's biggest economy, but front of the line.

And Britain looked first to the US. In the aftermath of Brexit, a free-trade agreement with the US has been at the forefront of Britain's trade agenda. The British government reportedly even considered to apply to join the newly agreed US-Mexico-Canada free-trade agreement which replaced the 1994 North American Free Trade Agreement (NAFTA) (*Financial Times*, 2021). Yet, despite the negotiating efforts of the conservative governments, the US-UK trade talks quickly became difficult, and a UK-US free-trade agreement now seems far away from becoming a reality. The Johnson government seems to have been more concerned about showcasing their independence than serve as an agitator for free trade (Heron and Siles-Brügge, 2021).

Also, the Commonwealth figured prominently in the Conservative government's promises for a powerful Global Britain after Brexit. Trade links with African Commonwealth nations were central to this ambition, which has been reported to be described by Whitehall officials as 'Empire 2.0' (Coates, 2017). Liam Fox, the British trade secretary, and his colleagues aim to pursue a more liberal trade agenda with the Commonwealth and escape what they see as EU protectionism and internal struggles. Yet African nations have shown significant resistance to trade liberalisation with the EU in the Economic Partnership Agreement negotiations over the last 15 years, something that suggests that the British liberal trade agenda will not be welcomed in the African Commonwealth nations (Murray-Evans, 2016).

Similarly, negotiations of a trade agreement with India were launched with fanfare in January 2022 with the aim of concluding negotiations by the end of the year, but critics point to many obstacles before an agreement can be reached. For instance, India wants relaxed immigration rules for Indian workers, and the conservative British government might find this difficult to swallow as many of their voters are sceptical of loosening visa rules (Gamble, 2018; Wilkinson, 2022). Hence, the assumption of Britain again being a significant world trade power seems to have been based on unrealistic expectations and a self-understanding deeply entrenched in its colonial roots.

Despite these developments, Britain has gained some successes in global trade post-Brexit, showing that the wriggle room they have obtained by exiting the EU exists, at least to a certain extent. A free-trade agreement was signed with Japan in October 2020, which was the first that differed from an existing EU deal. Although the conservative government has presented the deal as a 'landmark moment' showing what Britain is capable of as an 'independent trading nation' (British Embassy Tokyo, 2020), the deal is similar to the EU-Japan deal, with additional elements in the areas of digital, data, and financial services (House of Commons, 2020). In addition to Japan, Britain has looked to the Asia-Pacific more broadly. In addition, a free-trade agreement was signed with Australia in December 2021 and is awaiting ratification. Yet critics fear that Britain's agricultural concessions in the UK-Australia deal will undercut UK farmers and lower animal welfare and environmental standards (Independent, 2022), illustrating the trade-off the UK faces when negotiating alone. Hence, when pursuing agreements with partners that the EU does not have an agreement with, Britain has been forced to make significant concessions to be able to strike agreements.

Summing up, the UK's push towards the Asia-Pacific and the fact that several other trade agreements have been signed indicates that non-members enjoy wriggle room to seek an independent trade approach with third states. This wriggle room has, however, not translated into Britain being an autonomous trade actor, but rather showed that Britain post-Brexit experiences constraints on its autonomy by the global trade order in general and the EU's trade power in particular. What we have seen in practice is a Britain that has tried to punch above its weight and met resistance from trading partners. Britain's neoliberal trading agenda is not necessarily what third states want. This illustrates that also, when operating as a single actor in global trade, Britain faces constraints on its autonomy. These constraints might even be bigger than what they faced under EU membership (Gamble, 2018). Britain has, post-Brexit, in large part, been forced to focus on securing the same benefits it enjoyed under EU membership.

During the Brexit campaigns, it was not only trade policy that was in focus for the Brexiteers. Also Britain's autonomous development policy was central to the campaigns envisioning of a stronger and autonomous Global Britain. We now turn to an analysis the paradox of how Britain could move from a strong and distinct UK development policy during EU membership to a diminished and normalized UK development policy post-Brexit.

UK and the EU in development

From autonomous actor within the EU . . .

UK has, until Brexit, been seen as a highly influential actor in international development, a normative leader and one of the top contributors to global aid both in absolute terms and in percentage of gross national income (Lightfoot et al., 2017). For the UK, development assistance has been a realm where it had to balance its own policy goals and priorities with the increasing role of the EU commission as a federator of the EU member states development policies. The EU has, since the early 2000s, released several common development statements which sets out common goals for the EU's and the member states development policies. One the one hand, the UK has supported the EU. For instance, the UK, together with like-minded EU member states, supported the EU commissions proposal to set common targets for aid spending and the subsequent proposals to increase these from 0.4 to 0.5 to 0.7 (Carbone, 2007). The UK first met the 0.7 per cent spending target in 2013 (World Bank data, 2022b), and in 2015 it introduced a national legislation that codified that it is the 'duty of the Secretary of State to ensure that the target for official development assistance to amount to 0,7%' (UK Government, 2015). The 0.7 per cent spending target was also included in the UN's Millennium Development Goals and in OECD-DAC.

But the UK has also been a fierce critic of the EU's development policy and acted autonomously by keeping a close political relationship to UK aid beneficiaries and by distancing itself symbolically and politically from the EU development policy. For instance, prominent UK secretary of state for international development Clare Short (2000) criticised the Commission in an op-ed in the in the *Financial Times* in June 2000: 'the Commission is the worst development agency in the world. The poor quality and reputation of its aid brings Europe into disrepute'. She followed up with threats of re-nationalising aid if the European Commission did not improve two years later (Short, 2002). Also, in the UK Parliament, there has been recurrent concern for the efficiency and legitimacy of the EU's common development policy. For instance, in the European Standing Committee, Mark Simmonds (Conservatives) responds to the Parliamentary Undersecretary of State for International Development Gareth Thomas in the following way:

> [We] wish to see British taxpayers' money used effectively and efficiently for the maximum impact in the shortest possible time. If that means that funds should be transferred through highly efficient DFID structures rather than relatively inefficient EU ones, we should not be put at fault for pointing that out.
>
> *(House of Commons, 2007)*

These observations suggest that there has been a lack of trust in the EU's ability to deliver the same quality of aid as what could be done nationally. This has led to recurrent scepticism of EU projects and the wish to maintain a strong national department for international development (DFID).

One example of the UK exercising its autonomy was when the European Commission proposed an initiative that sought to enhance coordination among the member states' donor practices. The Commission proposed geographical and sectoral concentration of aid monies to avoid that recipient countries would have to report to many different donors, and instead limit presence to two or three donors. But a group of like-minded countries, with the UK in the lead, voiced reluctance to let the EU interfere with their choice of partner countries and sectors within these countries. Especially the UK wanted to be able to work in several different sectors in countries where they had already established cooperation. This led the UK to oppose the European Commission's proposal and veto it until it got a footnote included which allowed it to work in more than the proposed number of sectors (Saltnes, 2019). This example shows that the UK has managed to exercise its autonomy within the EU and has managed to shape the EU's development policy in a manner which suits their interests, values, and preferences.

Then, while the UK has been part of a gradual coordination of EU member states' development policies, it has also been a sceptic and a rebel. It has managed to secure solutions where the UK maintains autonomy to decide on its collaboration with recipients and not being straightjacketed by the European Commission. Thus, the need for an increased wriggle room and autonomy did not seem imminent before Brexit, although such arguments were recurrently used by politicians and proponents of Brexit.

. . . to 'normalisation' after Brexit

Paradoxically, the role as a norm-setter and vanguard in development issues, which the UK managed to exercise while being a member of the Union, has slowly vanished in parallel with the decision to exit the Union. Several reforms attest to this.

On the one hand, we have seen a turn towards a more interest-driven UK development policy and rhetoric about how to increase the benefits for UK citizens. For instance, Britain's new development strategy was released on 16 May 2022 by the newly created Foreign, Commonwealth and Development Office (FCDO). In the new strategy, development is framed as a key foreign policy tool to be used to tackle an increasing geopolitical world. The policy is designed to meet recipients needs but at the same time do more to promote the UK's own foreign policy objectives, such as global trade and investment partnerships. One major shift will be done to achieve these goals, and that is a reduction in funding for multilateral development agencies such as the United Nations from approximately 40 to 25 per cent (by 2025) (FCDO, 2022). Furthermore, shortly after Brexit, the highly respected, at least among its European counterparts, Department for International Development (DFID) was incorporated into the Foreign Office. The inclusion of DFID into the foreign ministry was preceded by an overall cut in the spending target of 0.7 per cent (Loft and Brien, 2022). In November 2020 the then UK Chancellor Rishi Sunak announced that the UK would not meet its target of spending 0.7 per cent of gross national income on official development assistance (ODA) due to the consequences of the COVID-19 pandemic on the British economy. Sunak promised that the target will be reversed by 2024/2025, and that it will remain at 0.5 per cent for the next three years. Hence, we also witness a substantial lowering of ambition with regards to the UK's development policy.

Another example is Britain's choice to use aid to control migration to the UK. Britain signed in April 2022 an agreement with Rwanda for them to host illegal migrants and asylum seekers arriving in the UK while their applications are processed. While this deal was presented by the UK's home secretary Priti Patel (Patel, 2022) as a possibility *presented by Brexit*, we observe that EU member states have also made similar migration deals with the African country (e.g., Denmark). Thus, rather than being an opportunity presented by Brexit, it showcases the wriggle room both EU and non-EU member states enjoy in this realm.

Boris Johnson's promise to make sure the UK aid budget would do more to advance Britain's political and commercial interests, at first sight, seems to be effectively happening. While this, to some extent, illustrates Britain's autonomy, these reforms mirror similar reforms both in the EU and within EU member states. For instance, the 2021 reform of the EU's aid architecture, the transition from DG Devco to DG International Partnerships, and the launch of Team Europe can be interpreted in line with a wish to increase visibility of the EU's actions and increase opportunities for responding to short-term challenges (Keijzer et al., 2021). Already in the EU's 2016 global strategy, a similar tendency was visible: 'Development policy also needs to become more flexible and aligned with our strategic priorities' (EEAS, 2016, p. 11). According to Bergmann et al. (2019), this is evidence of a turn from an autonomous development policy to a normalisation or 'return to form' where development policy facilitates the EU's external action. Hence, the British aid reforms should be seen in the context of the wider reform processes in Europe and understood as a step to bring development policy in line with its foreign policy, rather than compensating for negative consequences of Europeanisation. As we saw in the case of trade, the showcasing of autonomy has been more important than exercising a policy that is autonomous to the EU. This has led analysts to conclude that 'the UK's standing as a self-declared 'development superpower' has taken a serious knock' (Sheriff, 2021).

New development financing mechanism in the EU

As we pointed out in Chapter 2, significant changes in the legal framework guiding the EU shape third states' wriggle room and the conditions guiding autonomy (wriggle room in relation to new EU legislation). In the realm of development, we have witnessed a major legal reform over the last years that has consequences for non-members wriggle room to coordinate their policies with the EU. A particular trait of the EU's aid architecture has been its prioritisation of former colonies in the Africa, Caribbean, and Pacific, and the commitment to provide these countries with financial aid through the intergovernmental European Development Fund (EDF). The UK was a top contributor to the EDF, thereby channelling a large part of their aid budget through EU institutions. With Brexit, one option would be for the UK to negotiate the opportunity to continue to channel their aid monies through EU institutions, to avoid the bureaucratic burden of financing former colonies through their own aid institutions (Price, 2018). To keep up their financial development commitment, the UK would need to up their bureaucratic and operational capacity nationally and in beneficiary countries or negotiate a deal with the EU where they could continue to distribute their finances through EU institutions.

However, recent developments in the EU have made this opt-in scenario difficult. The EU's new budget includes a new financial instrument for external funding, NDICI – the Neighbourhood, Development, and International Cooperation Instrument (also known as Global Europe Instrument). This instrument integrates all extra-budgetary instruments into the EU's budget. The European Development Fund (EDF), the intergovernmental budget with contributions from the member states financing programmes with the Africa, Caribbean, and Pacific group of states, is thus now part of the EU's budget. Since the EDF had its own legal and institutional basis, it could have been preserved as a pan-European development fund. The UK accounted for 15 per cent of the most recent EDF (Olivie and Perez, 2017), but with NDICI, the possibility of an opt-in for non-EU members is not possible. If the EDF was preserved, it would 'keep the doors open to the UK' and leave the EU-ACP relationship untouched, if the UK would stay on as a signatory to Cotonou and the new post-Cotonou agreement (Price, 2018). However, this option is now no longer on the table. Paradoxically, the UK was one of the proponents of the budgetisation of the EDF, an option that was already on the table in 2013, something that now makes it more difficult for the UK to contribute to finance their former colonies via the EU's channels.

In sum, the UK has, since Brexit, taken steps to lower its ambitions in the realm of development and to use its development policy as a tool for promoting and securing British interests abroad. Yet this change has not happened because of Brexit, but rather in the context of a wider change in the international donor community's aid rhetoric. Similar reforms are seen within EU member states and in the EU's development statements. Thus, Britain has been more concerned about showcasing their *autonomous will-formation* for domestic voters than to make use of their status as a non-EU member to strengthen its normative leadership among Western donor states. The observations earlier also show that when your wriggle room is constrained, by being an EU member, it does not mean that members' room for exercising autonomy is inexistent. The UK, pre-Brexit, and other like-minded states' ability to shape the EU's development policy testifies to this.

Conclusion

In this chapter we have seen that the legal wriggle room Norway enjoys as a non-member and what Britain has gained through Brexit does not lead automatically to the possibility of exercising an autonomous trade and development policy. While Norway enjoys wriggle room to embark on bilateral or EFTA-led trade agreements with third states, their autonomy is constrained by living in the shadow of the EU. Trade negotiations often occur in parallel with the EU, and due to the political interweaving with the European continent, it is practically impossible for Norway to move ahead on trade deals with third states if the EU decides to halt, as the negotiations with Mercosur illustrates. The UK after Brexit has been faced with a similar non-member conundrum. While some new bilateral trade agreements have been achieved, the UK is still faced primarily with the task of securing the trade benefits they lost by Brexit. British authorities have spent significant efforts on showcasing their autonomy, namely the possibility of staking out their own course, but in practice their capacity to act autonomously is constrained. Although the legal wriggle room for non-members is significant in the realms of trade and development, the EU dominates non-members in multilateral institutions due to their share size and normative leadership. This finding has implications for the triangular relationship between Norway, Britain, and the EU.

With Brexit, Britain has reshuffled the balance between members and non-members on the European continent and contributed to a more complex reality of externally differentiated integration with the EU. While Norway and Britain have a history of working closely together and coordinating their policies (with other like-minded countries) in the realm of development, the recent U-turn in Britain's development policy leaves little room for finding a common non-EU basis for cooperation and, by that, influencing the wider trends and normative agendas in European development discourse. It seems the normative consensus that informed the aid effectiveness agenda, of which both Britain and Norway were proponents, has lost its consensus. In addition, Brexit significantly reshuffles non-members' power in the realm of trade. Norway, the largest and most powerful EEA-EFTA state, will now have to compete with a much bigger market and political actor, namely Britain, in global trade negotiations. Britain remains Norway's most important trading partner, after the EU itself, and although a trade agreement has been reached, Norway has recognized that it had better trading conditions with Britain through the EEA Agreement than with non-EU agreement between Norway, Iceland, and Britain. The torturous Brexit negotiations illustrate that, rather than being an ally outside the Union, Brexit might serve to further complicate non-members' relationship with and autonomy from the EU.

A practical example of how such trilateral Norway-UK-EU dynamics occur is the fragmentation of requirements for rules of origin when seeking preferential treatment for trade in goods. Norwegian exports to Europe are now regulated not only by the EEA Agreement but also the TCA between the UK and the EU, and Norway and Iceland's trade agreement with the UK. The requirements for rules of origin are not harmonised in these three agreements, complicating the situation for exporters who seek to claim preferential treatment. While all EEA states and several Mediterranean states such as Turkey, Western Balkans, Georgia, and Ukraine have harmonised their rule of origin requirements (the so-called PEM convention), these are not fully harmonised with the TCA, and thereby also affect the Norwegian export of goods which have origin or have been packaged in an EEA country.

The global context is also relevant for non-members' de facto ability to stake out their own course and cooperate with the Union when this is seen as in their interest. China's increasing influence in international affairs and Russia's aggressive war on Ukraine has led Western leaders to look for new allies. Within this geopolitical context, autonomy is no longer what is at the top of Western leaders' agenda, but rather seeking and compromising with like-minded states to bandwagon against authoritarian states' non-liberal agendas. Within this context, Latin America proves to be a region of interest to the West. With Bolsonaro out of the equation in Brazil, the EU is looking to save the EU-Mercosur agreement from a political death and work towards closer political cooperation through trade. As we will explore further in in the next chapter, the current uncertain geopolitical environment means that larger states and polities' foreign policies, to a larger extent, will determine the political directions in international relations. Although Britain relies on a self-understanding as a significant and autonomous power in global affairs, they might have to rely on the EU to a larger extent than what Brexiteers had envisaged. For Norway, the EU is already a significant partner and determinant of foreign policy decisions, something that is not likely to change in any foreseeable future.

Notes

1 The analysis draws on document analysis of EU, British, and Norwegian official documents, policymakers' statements in the press, four semi-structured interviews with Norwegian and EU policymakers conducted in February, March, and November 2022, NGO reports and statements, and secondary literature.
2 Mercosur is the Spanish abbreviation for El Mercado Comum del Sur (Mercosul in Portuguese), a free-trade bloc formed by Brazil, Argentina, Uruguay, and Paraguay in 1991.
3 Interview with a representative from the Trade, Industry and Fisheries Ministry, 21.2.22.
4 Interview with EEAS representative, 16.11.22.
5 Interview with a representative from the Trade, Industry and Fisheries Ministry, 21.2.22.
6 Interview with an EEAS representative, 16.11.22.
7 Interview with two representatives from the Trade, Industry and Fisheries Ministry, 21.2.22.
8 Interview with a representative from the Trade, Industry and Fisheries Ministry, 21.2.22, authors' translation.
9 Interview with a representative from the Trade, Industry and Fisheries Ministry, 21.2.22, authors' translation.
10 Interview with a representative from the Ministry of Foreign Affairs, 20.01.22.
11 Interview with a representative from the Ministry of Foreign Affairs, 20.01.22.
12 Interview with a representative from the Ministry of Foreign Affairs, 20.01.22.
13 Interview with a representative from the Ministry of Foreign Affairs, 20.01.22.
14 Interview with a representative from the Ministry of Foreign Affairs, 20.01.22.
15 While trade policy was not a significant part of the referendum campaign, it became a significant justification for Brexit after the referendum, with PM May launching a new department for international trade a month after the referendum and frequently used in the conservative governments' speeches (Heron and Siles-Brügge, 2021, p. 733).

References

Allen-Ebrahimian, B. (2021) *Norway's Youth Parties Call for End to China Free-Trade Talks*. Available at: www.axios.com/2021/02/10/norways-youth-parties-call-for-end-to-china-free-trade-talks (Accessed 25 January 2023).

Bergmann, J., Delputte, S., Keijzer, N. and Verschaeve, J. (2019) 'The Evolution of the EU's Development Policy: Turning Full Circle', *European Foreign Affairs Review*, 24(4): 533–554.

Bradford, A. (2020) *The Brussels Effect. How the European Union Rules the World*, Oxford: Oxford University Press.

British Embassy Tokyo (2020) *UK and Japan Signs Free-Trade Agreement*. Available at: www.gov.uk/government/news/uk-and-japan-sign-free-trade-agreement (Accessed 25 January 2023).

Carbone, M. (2007). *The European Union and international development*. London and New York: Routledge.

Carbone, M. (2017) 'Make Europe Happen on the Ground? Enabling and Constraining Factors for European Union Aid Coordination in Africa', *Development Policy Review*, 35(4): 531–548.

Coates, S. (2017) 'Ministers Aim to Build "Empire 2.0." with African Commonwealth', *The Times*, 6 March. Available at: www.thetimes.co.uk/article/ministers-aim-to-build-empire-2-0-with-african-commonwealth-after-brexit-v9bs6f6z9 (Accessed 25 January 2023).

Cockburn, H. (2022) 'UK Farmers Must Compete with "Cruel and Unsustainable" Farming Practices Due to Australia Trade Deal', *Independent*, 30 March. Available at: www.independent.co.uk/climate-change/news/uk-farmers-trade-deal-australia-b2046471.html (Accessed 25 January 2023).

DEEU (2017) *The United Kingdom's Exit from, and New Partnership with, the European Union*, London: Department for Exiting the European Union. Available at: www.gov.uk/government/publications/the-united-kingdoms-exit-from-and-new-partnership-with-the-european-union-white-paper/the-united-kingdoms-exit-from-and-new-partnership-with-the-european-union – 2#contents (Accessed 25 January 2023).

Department for International Trade (2020) *Continuing the UK's Trade Relationship with Iceland and the Kingdom of Norway*, London: Department of International Trade. Available at: https://assets.publishing.service.gov.uk/government/uploads/system/uploads/attachment_data/file/945225/ccs1220699560-trade-iceland-norway-parl-report-accessible.pdf#page=6 (Accessed 25 January 2023).

EEAS (2016) *A Global Strategy for the European Union's Foreign and Security Policy. Shared Vision, Common Action: A Stronger Europe*, Brussels European External Action Service.

EFTA Trade Statistics (2022) *Trade between EFTA and the World*. Available at: https://trade.efta.int/#/country-graph/EFTA/WORLD/2020/HS2 (Accessed 25 January 2023).

European Parliament (2020) *Implementation of the Common Commercial Policy*. Available at: www.europarl.europa.eu/doceo/document/TA-9-2020-0252_EN.html (Accessed 25 January 2023).

Farsund, A. A. (2014) 'Norway: Agricultural Exeptionalism and the Quest for Free Trade', in Langhelle, O. (ed) *International Trade Negotiations and Domestic Politics. The Intermestic Politics of Trade Liberalisation*, London: Routledge, pp. 148–173.

Farsund, A. A. (2021) 'Politicization Strategies in Domestic Trade Policy Making: Comparing Agriculture and Seafood Sectors in Norway', *Journal of Comparative Policy Analysis: Research and Practice*, 23(5–6): 576–591.

FCDO (2022) *The UK Government's Strategy for International Development. May 2022*, London: Foreign, Commonwealth and Development Office. Available at: https://assets.publishing.service.gov.uk/government/uploads/system/uploads/attachment_data/

file/1075328/uk-governments-strategy-international-development.pdf (Accessed 25 January 2023).

Financial Times. (2021) UK pins hope on joining US-Mexico-Canada trade pact. 22 September 2021. Available at: https://www.ft.com/content/b519921f-8d14-4948-9afa-f2340b0d25db

Fox, L. (2018) *Britain's Trading Future (Speech) Bloomberg HQ*, 27 February. Available at: www.gov.uk/government/speeches/britains-trading-future (Accessed 25 January 2023).

Gamble, A. (2018) 'Taking Back Control: The Political Implications of Brexit', *Journal of European Public Policy*, 25(8): 1215–1232.

Greenpeace (2022) 'Derfor er handelsavtalen med Brasil dårlig nytt for Amazonas', *Greenpeace*, 24 November. Available at: www.greenpeace.org/norway/nyheter/skog-og-landbruk/derfor-er-handelsavtalen-med-brasil-darlig-nytt-for-amazonas/ (Accessed 25 January 2023).

Haugan, B. and Husøy, E. (2022) 'MDG krever at Norge stanser handelsavtale og ber Huitfeldt bli hjemme fra vinter-OL', *Verdens Gang*, 18 January. Available at: www.vg.no/nyheter/innenriks/i/BjnrJ0/mdg-krever-at-norge-stanser-handelsavtale-og-ber-huitfeldt-bli-hjemme-fra-vinter-ol (Accessed 25 January 2023).

Heron, T. and Siles-Brügge, G. (2021) 'UK-US Trade Relations and "Global Britain"', *The Political Quarterly*, 94(4): 732–736.

House of Commons (2007) 'EU Development Policy', *Debate in the European Standing Committee*, 8 May. Available at: https://publications.parliament.uk/pa/cm200607/cmgeneral/euro/070508/70508s01.htm (Accessed 9 February 2023).

House of Commons (2020) *UK-Japan Comprehensive Economic Partnership Agreement. Second Report of 2019–21* (HC 914), London: House of Commons.

Isaksen, T. R. (2019) *Møte i Europautvalget mandag 21 oktober*. Available at: www.stortinget.no/no/Saker-og-publikasjoner/Publikasjoner/Referater/Europautvalget/2019-2020/refe-201920-10-21/?m=1 (Accessed 25 January 2023).

Johnson, B. (2019) 'Global Britain: UK Foreign Policy in the Era of Brexit', *Transcript*. Available at: www.chathamhouse.org/sites/default/files/events/special/2016-12-02-Boris-Johnson.pdf (Accessed 25 January 2023).

Keijzer, N., Burni, A., Erforth, B., & Friesen, I. (2021). *The rise of the Team Europe approach in EU development cooperation: Assessing a moving target: Vol. Discussion paper 22/2021*. Bonn: German Development Institute.

Kingdom of the Netherlands (2020) *Non-Paper from the Netherlands and France on Trade, Social Economic Effects and Sustainable Development*, May 8. Available at: www.permanentrepresentations.nl/documents/publications/2020/05/08/non-paper-from-nl-and-fr-on-trade-social-economic-effects-and-sustainable-development (Accessed 25 January 2023).

Leira, H., Borchgrevink, A., Græger, N., Melchior, A., Stamnes, E. and Øverland, I. (2007) *Norske Selvbilder Og Norsk Utenrikspolitikk*, Oslo: Norsk Utenrikspolitisk Institutt NUPI.

Lightfoot, S., Mawdsley, E. and Szent-Iványi, B. (2017) 'Brexit and UK International Development Policy', *Political Quarterly*, 88(3): 517–524.

Loft, P. and Brien, P. (2022) *The 0.7 % Aid Target*, 25 March, House of Commons Library. Available at: https://researchbriefings.files.parliament.uk/documents/SN03714/SN03714.pdf (Accessed 25 January 2023).

May, T. (2017) *The Government's Negotiating Objectives for Exiting the EU*. PM Speech, 17 January. Available at: www.gov.uk/government/speeches/the-governments-negotiating-objectives-for-exiting-the-eu-pm-speech (Accessed 25 January 2023).

Meunier, S. and Nicolaïdis, K. (2017) 'The European Union as a Trade Power', in Hill, C., Smith, M. and Vanhoonacker, S. (eds) *International Relations and the European Union*, Oxford: Oxford University Press, pp. 209–234.

Michalopoulos, C. (2020) *Ending Global Poverty. Four Women's Global Conspiracy*, Oxford: Oxford University Press.

Murray-Evans, P. (2016) 'Myths of Commonwealth Betrayal: UK – Africa Trade Before and After Brexit', *The Round Table*, 105(5): 489–498. https://doi.org/10.1080/00358533.2016.1233760.

Nei til EU (2021) *Solidaritet*. Available at: https://neitileu.no/kampanjer/4-grunner/solidaritet (Accessed 25 January 2023).

Nolte, D. and Neto, C. C. R. (2021) 'Mercosur and the EU: The False Mirror', *Lua Nova: Revista de Cultura e Politica*, 112(January–April 2021): 87–122. https://doi.org/10.1590/0102-087122/112.

Norwegian Government (2021) *Nå kan næringslivet ta i bruk handelsavtalen med Storbritannia*. Available at: www.regjeringen.no/no/aktuelt/na-kan-naringslivet-ta-i-bruk-frihandelsavtalen-med-storbritannia/id2890358/ (Accessed 25 January 2023).

NTB (2021) 'Regnskogfondet skuffet over nordmenns likgyldighet til stans av frihandelsavtalen med Brasil', *NTB*, 11 February. Available at: https://enerwe.no/brasil-klima-ntb/regnskogfondet-skuffet-over-nordmenns-likegyldighet-til-stans-av-frihandelsavtalen-med-brasil/396564 (Accessed 25 January 2023).

Olivie, I. and Perez, A. (2017) 'Possible Impacts of Brexit on EU Development and Humanitarian Policies', *European Parliament*. Available at: www.europarl.europa.eu/RegData/etudes/STUD/2017/578042/EXPO_STU(2017)578042_EN.pdf (Accessed 25 January 2023).

Patel, P. (2022) *Oral Statement on Rwanda*, London: Home Office.

Price, S. (2018) 'Brexit and the UK-Africa Caribbean and Pacific Aid Relationship', *Global Policy*, 9(3): 420–428.

Raab, D. (2019) 'Global Britain is a Force of Good in the World', *The Telegraph*, 21 September. Available at: www.telegraph.co.uk/politics/2019/09/21/global-britain-leading-world-force-good/?WT.mc_id=tmgoff_psc_conversion-subscription_core_10/05_EGW-13_ppc_politics_dsa&gclid=Cj0KCQiAkNiMBhCxARIsAIDDKNX_a0IhjcvvND3Iz4VTBv7OlgGxbSmD-6S0So2ULCivFhcL7FSZGO0aAo3zEALw_wcB (Accessed 25 January 2023).

Reuters (2020) 'Norway Hopes for China Free-Trade Deal in 2020, Minister Says', *Reuters*, 8 January. Available at: www.reuters.com/article/us-norway-china-trade/norway-hopes-for-china-free-trade-deal-in-2020-industry-minister-says-idUSKBN1Z71FP (Accessed 25 January 2023).

Saltnes, J. D. (2019) 'Resistance to EU Integration? Norm Collision in the Coordination of Development Aid', *Journal of European Integration*, 41(4): 525–541. https://doi.org/10.1080/07036337.2018.1533007.

Saltnes, J. D. (2022) *The European Union and Global Development: A Rights-based Approach?*, Routledge Studies on the European Union and Global Order, Abingdon: Routledge.

Sheriff, A. (2021) *Brexit and Development Cooperation. A Major Connection Problem*. Available at: https://ecdpm.org/talking-points/brexit-development-cooperation-major-connection-problem/ (Accessed 25 January 2023).

Short, C. (2000) 'Aid that Doesn't Help', *Financial Times*, 23 June.

Short, C. (2002) 'Reform of EU Aid Programme is Overdue', *The Guardian*, 19 July.

Skinner, M. S. (2012) 'Norwegian Euroscepticism: Values, Identity, or Interest', *JCMS: Journal of Common Market Studies*, 50(3): 422–440.

Statistics Norway (2022) *Oil and Energy*. Available at: www.ssb.no/energi-og-industri/faktaside/olje-og-energi (Accessed 25 January 2023).

Støre, J. G. (2022) 'Halvårlig oppsummerende pressekonferanse', *Regjeringen*, 23 June. Available at: www.regjeringen.no/no/aktuelt/halvarlig-oppsummerende-pressekonferanse/id2920534/ (Accessed 25 January 2023).

UK Government (2015) *International Development (Official Development Assistance Target) Act 2015*. Available at: www.legislation.gov.uk/ukpga/2015/12/contents/enacted (Accessed 25 January 2023).

Verschaeve, J. and Orbie, J. (2016) 'Once a Member, Always a Member? Assessing the Importance of Time in the Relationship Between the European Union and the Development Assistance Committee', *Cambridge Review of International Affairs*, 29(2): 512–527.

Verschaeve, J. and Orbie, J. (2017) 'Ignoring the Elephant in the Room? Assessing the Impact of the European Union on the Development Assistance Committee's Role in International Development', *Development Policy Review*, 36(1): 44–58.

Verschaeve, J. and Takacs, T. (2013) 'The He EU's International Identity: The Curious Case of the OECD', in D'ewaele, H. and Kuipers, J. (eds) *The European Union's Global Identity: Views from the Global Arena*, Leiden: Martinus Nijhoff Publishers.

Wilkinson, T. (2022) 'Boris Johnson Wants a Trade Deal with India. But Will the UK Accept Loser Immigration Rules?', *The Wire*, 24 January 2022. Available at: https://thewire.in/trade/india-uk-trade-deal-immigration (Accessed 25 January 2023).

World Bank Data (2022a) *Imports (% of GDP) Norway*. Available at: https://data.worldbank.org/indicator/NE.IMP.GNFS.ZS?end=2020&locations=NO&start=2000&view=chart (Accessed 25 January 2023).

World Bank Data (2022b) *Net ODA Provided (% of GDP) UK*. Available at: https://data.worldbank.org/indicator/DC.ODA.TOTL.GN.ZS?locations=GB&view=chart (Accessed 25 January 2023).

Young, A. and Peterson, J. (2014) *Parochial Global Europe. 21st Century Trade Politics*, Oxford: Oxford University Press.

6
FLEXIBLE ASSOCIATION IN FOREIGN, SECURITY, AND DEFENCE POLICY

A case of gradually diminishing autonomy?

Introduction

As a third country, Norway is a close partner to the EU in foreign, security, and defence policy. The EU's most recent strategic document – the Strategic Compass from 2022 – reaffirmed this fact (European Union, 2022). In it the EU highlighted its desire to deepen its constructive relations with Norway, a country it describes as its most closely associated partner. This is so particularly due to the EEA Agreement, but the Norwegian relationship with the EU is governed also by a range of other agreements, several of which lay the foundations for foreign, security, and defence cooperation. The general assumption in Norway has been that the comprehensive EEA Agreement has opened avenues for cooperation also in areas not covered by the agreement. Seen in this light, the EEA Agreement has had a 'spin-off' effect into the area of foreign, security, and defence cooperation (Svendsen and Rieker, 2019).

To evaluate the autonomy and wriggle room that third countries have in EU foreign, security, and defence cooperation, we address a range of questions. First, what does Norway's close cooperation with the EU in foreign, security, and defence policy look like in practice? In the Norwegian case, the expansion of cooperation has been organic and incremental, but not without limitations. Second, what wriggle room and autonomy does Norway have in foreign and security policy? Third, we will consider the UK's developing relations with the EU in this area and evaluate the UK's autonomy as a non-member. This also allows us to compare the Norway-EU and UK-EU relationships. The EU's Strategic Compass document simply states that the union remains open to a broad and ambitious security and defence engagement with the UK, but the current affiliation is much thinner than that. Finally, what factors will decide how cooperation with non-EU members in foreign, security, and defence will develop in the future?

It is crucial to take note of the fact that Norway's affiliation with the EU in foreign, security, and defence policy, for the most part, is *not* part of the EEA Agreement. Rather, it is a dynamic area of cooperation in which the parties have entered into several agreements over time. As EU member states have retained an extensive amount of formal sovereignty in foreign, security, and defence, we can also expect this to remain a largely flexible area in which third countries like Norway and the UK can enter into agreements on important topics and in vital areas. Thus, this field is a differentiated area of cooperation governed largely by an intergovernmental logic, meaning that cooperating non-members should enjoy a high degree of autonomy (the will and ability to pursue self-chosen goals) and wriggle room (as a third country's action space within the context of its legally regulated EU affiliation). Yet in practice we will argue and show that even in the foreign, security, and defence domain, which is characterised by relatively low levels of formal integration, autonomy is contested and largely dependent on (often self-perceived) power asymmetries.

Norway's long-standing third-country status and the UK's recently negotiated relationship into the same category look quite different. In the Norway case, we have seen cooperation develop through a gradual expansion of agreements and alignment. With the UK during and after the Brexit process, quite the opposite has happened. So far, no agreements have been reached in the domain, and uncertainties over what relationship the UK wants with the EU – and partly vice versa – in foreign, security, and defence remains ever-present, several years after the 2016 referendum that sealed the fate of the UK's EU membership at large. The UK is indeed also the first ex-member of the EU. At the same time, the cataclysmic Russian invasion of Ukraine in February 2022 could contribute to a redrawing of the European security architecture, including the extent to which the EU and UK are willing and able to cooperate on foreign, security, and defence policies.

The remainder of the chapter is organised as follows. First, we define what we mean by foreign, security, and defence policy and present Norway's formal relationship to the EU in this area. Second, we discuss Norway's de facto relationship to the EU in foreign, security, and defence policies by putting the conceptual apparatus of this book to use. Here we discuss Norway's *wriggle room* and what Norway's relationship to the EU after the Russian invasion in Ukraine implies for our understanding of its broader *autonomy* in relation to the EU. As we will see, although Norway has much formal foreign, security, and defence wriggle room, its autonomy is less certain: while often arguing that Norway aligns with the EU since their interests and values overlap, the Ukraine war illustrates how Norway follows the EU more or less automatically, often without explicit decision-making processes, suggesting that it sets out its own course. Third, we touch upon the Brexit process, indicating how the ground was (ill-) prepared for future EU-UK cooperation on foreign, security, and defence issues in and through the process. Finally, we conclude with a brief consideration of how the Norway model in foreign, security, and defence can be useful or not for the UK's association with the EU in this area. Recent developments in the EU's approach to foreign, security, and defence policy as well as the Russian war of aggression in Ukraine will play their part in the emerging European order in this area.

Norway's foreign, security, and defence relationship with the EU

In this section we present the current relationship that Norway has with the EU in foreign, security, and defence policy. First, however, we shall define EU foreign, security, and defence policies as policies and actions decided within the framework of the EU's Common Foreign and Security Policy (CFSP). The CFSP contains all agreed foreign policies that do not fall under the policy category of external relations. Most importantly, the CFSP includes the CSDP (i.e., civilian and military operations and common security strategies), common EU diplomacy and sanctions, and common policies and positions in a variety of intergovernmental organisations where the Commission does not speak on behalf of the EU due to its common market competences. Formally, EU foreign and security policies continue to be 'subject to specific rules and procedures', where the member states decide by unanimity in the Council and special CFSP institutions (Consolidated version of the Treaty on European Union, 2012, Art. 24.1(2)). The European Commission does *not* have monopoly of initiative, and the Council does *not* share decision-making powers with the Parliament.

Due to the EU treaty's overall aim of 'consistency between the different areas of its external action and between these and its other policies' (Art. 21), the Council and the European Commission, assisted by the High Representative of the Union for Foreign Affairs and Security Policy (HR), 'shall cooperate to that effect' (Art. 21), except in security and defence. The European Commission and the HR may thus also 'submit joint proposals to the Council' in areas other than the CSDP (Art. 22). The way that foreign, security, and defence policies are set up in the EU thus makes it an interesting case to study the wriggle room and autonomy of third countries, as it is an area characterised by few legal constraints and possibilities for flexible solutions, such as Permanent Structured Cooperation (PESCO), also for member states. It is therefore crucial to note that the amount of supranational regulation in the otherwise highly regulated EU is limited in foreign, security, and defence policy.

In general, Norway and the EU have a close relationship in foreign, security, and defence policies, and from the Norwegian point of view, that is explained by common values and interests (Norwegian Government, 2021). In declaratory terms, there is hardly friction at all. An important point to reiterate in the context of a differentiated and flexible area of cooperation was made in a government commissioned report on Norway's relations with the EU in 2012, namely that this area is governed mostly by politics, not law (NOU 2012:2, p. 724). Considering how the EU and UK failed to include any meaningful provisions on foreign, security, and defence policy in their Trade and Partnership Agreement (TCA), it is worth noting that the Norwegian affiliation with the EU shows how foreign, security, and defence policy cooperation can be built outside of the main framework for cooperation in general. Yet there is general agreement in Norway that the EEA Agreement and willingness to cooperate over time without conflict and friction spills over to other areas, such as foreign, security, and defence policy (Hillion, 2019). As such, Norway is a subservient state under EU hegemonic leadership in Europe, and that arguably increases Norwegian wriggle room in foreign and security policy writ large. A recent example of this form of legitimisation was Norway's inclusion in the EU's vaccination scheme in the COVID-19 pandemic, and the oft-stated argument that Norway would not be able to obtain the necessary number of vaccines on its own. At the same time, studies have found that there is a general understanding among practitioners that the full potential of Norway-EU relations in foreign, security, and defence policy has not been realised (Græger and Haugevik, 2022). Research has also shown how Norwegian officials find it frustrating that the EU is restrictive in terms of including Norway in an early phase in its initiatives under the CFSP (Svendsen, 2022).

As already mentioned, Norway-EU relations in foreign, security, and defence are based on flexibility and ad hoc arrangements. Still, a number of institutionalised practices govern the relationship. As part of the EEA Agreement, there are biannual dialogues on questions concerning foreign policy. The foreign minister meets its colleague from the country holding the EU presidency at least once every six months, and the prime minister does the same with its counterpart whenever a new presidency takes over. Also, the Norwegian foreign minister meets with the High Representative of the EU for Foreign Affairs and Security Policy (HRVP). In addition to this, Norwegian officials, on a frequent basis, take part in expert-level meetings with the European External Action Service (EEAS). There are yearly meetings in the Middle East, Balkan, OSSE, Russia/Central Asia, and Africa, as well as biannual high-level consultations with EEAS. Norway also takes part in programs that aim to reduce mutual vulnerabilities and increase resilience: Horizon Europe, Galileo, Copernicus, Digital, Cise, and the EU civil protection mechanism.

Furthermore, Norway frequently adopts the EU's declarations and sanctions, as well as statements in international organisations. In fact, adopting the sanctions packages decided by EU member states is the main rule, and there is no better example than the response to the Russian invasion of Ukraine. As the EU moved relatively swiftly to implement its most hard-hitting package of economic sanctions ever, the Norwegian government waited for the decision and, with few exceptions, immediately adopted the same sanctions after the EU had decided. This persisted as the war continued, and the EU's sanctioning regime intensified (Norwegian Government, 2022a).[1]

There is a Norway-EU agreement that opens for Norwegian participation in civil and military crisis management operations, such as was the case when Norway contributed to the anti-piracy operation Atalanta (EUNAVFOR) off the coast of Somalia. In the case of Atalanta, Norway even chose to contribute to EU's operation instead of to the NATO operation that was operating in the same area (Riddervold, 2016). Norway has also, on two occasions, provided troops to the EU's Battlegroups and has, since 2006, been an associate member to the European Defence Agency (EDA).

Starting with the publication of a new Global Strategy in the summer of 2016, the EU has taken several steps towards strengthening its common security and defence policy (European Union, 2016). There is also a literature connecting this development to Brexit. On the one hand, it has been discussed whether Brexit weakens European/EU defence, and on the other, questions have been raised about the effect that Brexit itself has had for the new push from the EU as the UK was considered a hindrance for further development of CSDP (see Svendsen and Adler-Nissen, 2019 for an overview). Notably, Norway has been keen to take part in these recent initiatives. First, Norway took part in the European Defence Industrial Development Programme (EDIDP), the preparatory program for the European Defence Fund (EDF). Norway joined EDF in 2021, and Norway's inclusion in the fund was done within the framework of the EEA Agreement, meaning that the EEA Agreement for the period 2021–2027 included defence industrial cooperation with the EU. Curiously, the EU-friendly conservative Norwegian government did not initially set aside the necessary funding for EDF membership in its budget proposal for 2021, but after some limited public debate and a likely internal process to fill that blank spot in the national budget, funding for EDF was eventually included (see Friis, 2020). Despite the bureaucratic process that eventually led to Norway's participation in EDF, there was hardly any domestic debate about whether Norway should join in or not.

Furthermore, the EU in 2017 activated PESCO, a possibility within the Lisbon Treaty for willing and capable states to go forward on defence integration without unanimity. Twenty-five member states eventually joined the initiative as only Denmark (which had an opt-out from defence), Malta (claiming neutrality), and the UK (as it was leaving the EU anyways) did not. Importantly, PESCO opened for project-by-project involvement of third countries, and together with Canada and the US, Norway was invited to join in on a project called Military Mobility, a project to simplify transportation of troops and military equipment across Europe. This project also had a clear NATO dimension to it, as it aimed to contribute to the European deterrent and collective defence. As of 2022, PESCO will also include the UK, which is the first instance of rebuilding EU-UK relations in foreign, security, and defence policy after Brexit (see UK Parliament, 2022).

Any international cooperation needs to have some degree of legitimacy in the domestic context. Norway's foreign, security, and defence cooperation with the EU has in fact not been subject to much debate, and thus the incremental development of the relations have not been hampered by domestic politicisation (Svendsen, 2022; NOU 2012:2). Despite some debate over Norway's contribution to the EU's Battlegroups in the mid-2000s, this area has been dealt with largely within the state bureaucracy. In the UK, things, of course, look very different. The fear of, and domestic spin about, a potential EU army in the making provided a salient argument for the leave campaign in the run up to the 2016 membership referendum. With regards to domestic legitimacy, the discussion of wriggle room and autonomy that we have in this book certainly would fit more in an analysis of the epistemic and political community in Norway, whereas there is in the UK a more deeply situated scepticism towards the EU ambitions in foreign, security, and defence policy both in the public and in Westminster, that is, processes around foreign, security, and defence cooperation with the EU is more likely to be a public spectacle in the UK than in Norway.

The narrative presented thus far, however, mainly tells the story of an incrementally developing and progressing Norway-EU relationship in foreign, security, and defence policy. Partly, this is due to the shared interests and oft-corresponding foreign policy identities of European states. At the same time, there are certainly those in Norway that would have liked to see an even closer and more structured relationship. That, however, remains difficult so long as Norway remains a non-member; there are, after all, also limits to how willing the EU is to include third states in foreign, security, and defence policies, and, as with the wider Brexit process, the most fruitful associations happen within formalised structures. Yet the argued benefit of not formalising structures from a political point of view is the potential for retaining autonomy and wriggle room, at least in cases where Norway-EU cooperation is not desired. The track record shows that this is rarely the case. Moreover, as we will show in the next section, formal wriggle room does not automatically imply autonomy in the sense of having the will and being able to pursue one's own course.

Norway's wriggle room in EU foreign, security, and defence

The section earlier described the agreements and relationship Norway has with the EU in foreign, security, and defence policies. But how much does this restrict Norway's autonomy and wriggle room in relation to the EU in this domain? What is its actual ability to conduct foreign policy independently of the EU? To tease this out, we operationalise and apply the framework developed in Chapter 2. The framework includes the concept of wriggle room as a distinct form of autonomy and sets out an approach for applying these concepts in studies of EU-Norway relations across policy areas but herein related to foreign, security, and defence policy.

As already mentioned, a third country's *autonomy* vis-à-vis the EU refers to its ability to stake out its own course regardless of constraints embedded in the EU affiliation, that is, the way the EU and the EU's member states contribute to transform Norway's political, cultural, and socio-economic landscape in directions that Norwegians are not comfortable with. A key part of this is also whether Norwegian decision-making institutions can make independent decisions within the constraints that follow from Norway's EU affiliation. This definition is particularly helpful for understanding Norway's foreign, security, and defence policy relationship to the EU because it allows us to not only consider the formal restrictions that come with Norway's affiliation but also the institutional and behavioural consequences of Norway's long-term relations to the EU.

As we know from the Europeanisation literature, common norms and routines also affect the extent to which a country like Norway acts autonomously in various policy domains, including in foreign policy (Gross, 2009; see also Olsen, 2002). The extent to which Norwegian civil servants and decision-makers become socialized into the EU's ways of doing things, establish close informal networks of cooperation with EU officials and other member states, and establish habits for coordination and even duplication may, for example, affect Norwegian decision-making processes and outcomes. And thus, the extent to which Norway de facto acts independently of the EU or not in the foreign policy domain. Another aspect the concept allows us to appreciate is whether close cooperation and coordination with the EU may in fact be characterised as autonomous, even if it, at the outset, might seem the opposite: if following the EU is seen to be in Norway's interest, one can argue that Norway's policy is an autonomous choice.

To allow for a more systematic teasing out of Norway's autonomy from the EU, the concept of wriggle room is helpful as a subcategory of autonomy. In Chapter 2 we developed a stepwise framework that can be applied in empirical studies of third countries, such as Norway's, relations to the EU. Wriggle room is defined as a third country's action space within the context of its legally regulated EU affiliation, emphasis on the rules, and arrangements governing these. Empirically, it refers to Norway's ability to operate within the constraints of its EU and UK legally regulated affiliations, at all stages. When exploring this, we distinguish between the internal and external dimension of Norway's wriggle room vis-à-vis the EU: while the *internal dimension* refers to Norway's de facto ability to affect EU decision-making in the domain, the *external dimension* refers to the extent to which Norway's relations to the EU limits its abilities to act independently.

The **first step** is to consider Norway's wriggle room in CFSP decision-making processes. Chapter 2 distinguishes different ways in which Norway putatively may inform the different stages of EU decision-making processes. The first two stages are *initiative* and *alternatives* and refer to the ability to put preferred policy options on the EU agenda, that is, Norway's ability to suggest and affect the content of new EU policies or actions (that it wants to join). While Norway can affect new EU regulations within EEA policy areas through working groups and the like, there are no such formal avenues of influence on CFSP decision-making processes. Norway might, however, influence agenda-setting through more informal modes of influence, for example linked to persuasion through diplomatic practices or by cooperating with certain member states who put forward shared preferences. Fossum (2015) has, for example, showed how Norway often seeks to influence EU decision-making by cooperating with the other Nordic EU member states, which is something it may also do in the CFSP.

Regarding the third phase, *decision-making*, Norway does not have any formal avenues of influence. Formal participation in CFSP is limited to regular consultation meetings, mostly including other third countries. Like in phase two, it can, however, influence decision-making indirectly, which is further discussed later. The fourth stage refers to *implementation*, where we expect that Norway, if joining a common policy or action, such as a sanctions package or a civilian and military mission, will basically have the same wriggle room as other EU member states: in the CFSP, the member states and associated states mainly implement decisions through their national foreign policy tools, rather than through implementing common directives or regulations. In general, one would thus expect more wriggle room in implementing foreign, security, and defence policies than in areas falling under the EEA Agreement, where common law is to be implemented through national legislation. Lastly, *feedback and learning* refer to the ability to learn from previous processes and thereby gain more wriggle room in the four other stages in future decision-making processes. This necessarily depends on Norway's ability to influence decision-making in the first place, but one could imagine situations where Norway seeks to influence agenda-setting and fails, learns from this experience, and changes its approach the next time there is a foreign policy issue it wants to place on the EU's agenda.

The **second step** is to explore the *scope* for wriggle room in relation to existing EU legislation, which, as mentioned earlier, will be different in CFSP compared to other policy areas. After all, CFSP is very much ad hoc and driven by events: the EU does not agree common directives and regulations in this domain. Instead, common actions and policies are agreed in the Council, often in response to events, such as when agreeing on sanctions, a military mission, or a common position in ongoing international negotiations on a new treaty. The more general and unspecific a common regulation is, the greater the wriggle room. Similarly, the fewer options the EU has in order to sanction Norway, the more wriggle room. At the outset, due to the limited number of legal obligations and few or no established sanctioning mechanisms, then, Norway has considerable wriggle room in the foreign and security domain compared to in EEA and Schengen-related issues.

However, **third,** and as discussed in Chapter 2, due to the issue of 'dynamic homogeneity', it is increasingly difficult to distinguish CFSP from other policy areas. For one, the European Commission has succeeded in linking procurement and other industrial defence aspects to inner market regulations, with relevance also for Norway. There is also increasingly more spillover to and from other policy areas. An increasing number of CFSP actions and policies are cross-sectoral or have a non-security dimension. Examples include the EU's strategic documents, such as the EU's Maritime Security Strategy, the Arctic Strategy, or the Space Strategy. All of these are decided within the CFSP but also contain policies that fall under or are related to other policy areas – some of which are also EEA relevant. There are, hence, often spillovers from one area to the other, affecting Norway's wriggle room vis-à-vis the EU also in foreign, security, and defence policy. In general, the greater the scope for spillover, the more Norway's formal and de facto wriggle room is reduced. Thus, even in the perhaps least formally integrated of all policy areas in the EU and where Norway has the most formal wriggle room, spillover reduces Norway's de facto wriggle room. This spillover may also go the other way, due to the securitisation of policy areas that would not normally be dealt with within the foreign and security policy realm. Examples are health, migration, and climate and energy policies. In some of these areas, Norway is legally bound by EU legislation due to EEA or Schengen agreements; in others they are not. However, as regulations increasingly spill over from one area to the area of foreign, security, and defence, the lines between foreign and security on the one hand and other policy areas on the other become increasingly blurred and may reduce Norway's de facto wriggle room also in the area of foreign, security, and defence policy. In this regard, the broader EU ambition for *open strategic autonomy* limits the small and relatively vulnerable wriggle room that Norway has enjoyed as a non-member (see Molthof et al., 2021). In sum, it is increasingly challenging to distinguish Norway's wriggle room in the CFSP from other policy areas.

In a **fourth step**, the wriggle room framework sets out to compare Norway-EU foreign, security, and defence relations to EU-UK relations in the domain. As already mentioned, the EU and the UK had not agreed any formal agreements linked to the CFSP. And it cannot be reiterated enough that foreign, security, and defence is very limited in terms of formal integration but is a flexible domain with room for improvisation and ad hoc solutions. There are many overlapping inter-linkages not only between the EU and the UK but also between Norway, the EU, and the UK also in the area of foreign, security, and defence policies. Thus, on a general basis, we posit that the ties in the EU-Norway-UK axis are many and close.

Finally, the **fifth step** in exploring Norway's wriggle room in its relations to the EU is the external dimension of the relationship. This pertains to the extent to which Norway can enter into international treaties and agreements independently of the EU. Formally, Norway is indeed legally allowed to enter into any bilateral or multilateral agreement it desires, so long as it is not in breach of its obligations under the EEA or Schengen agreements. In other areas, Norway is formally free to do as it pleases, unless bilateral agreements, for example, on participation in missions and operations suggest otherwise (but these agreements will be agreed for each mission, and Norway can thus formally consider various interests before deciding to operate under EU command). In practice, however, we know that Norway almost always aligns with the EU in international and multilateral forums, for example in negotiations on new treaties or when presenting declarations, for example in the UN (NOU 2012:2): Norway either tries to get access to EU internal coordination meetings, or it waits for the EU member states to reach common positions before joining the common EU stance. The exception is linked to conflicts where Norway acts as a mediator: to appear neutral in such cases, Norway tends not to sign up to common EU declarations, for example condemning one of the parties to a conflict (NOU 2012:2). This would of course be much more difficult had Norway been a full EU member, suggesting that non-membership in some instances allows Norway to act independently of the EU.

Whereas the wriggle room in relation to other policies such as declarations and sanctions appears limited – and, as we will discuss later, even may be shrinking in a complex and increasingly uncertain environment – it should be stated that Norway does have substantial wriggle room in defence. Although the EU has developed several security and defence tools, deterrence and territorial defence is mainly dealt with in NATO, where Norway is a member. As a NATO member, Norway's core interests in defence are safeguarded in and through that very organisation. This is arguably enabled by the EU's member states themselves, as most of them are also members of NATO, often prioritising NATO structures over EU ones when push comes to shove.

At the same time, today's security threats are complex, transnational, and often hybrid in nature. Issues such as energy security, food security, cyber security, protection of critical infrastructure, or the weaponisation of migration all have direct consequences for national security. Therefore, most states' defence systems also have a very strong civilian component that aim to be interoperable with the military defence system, which is what the Nordic states refer to as a 'total defence system'. And although NATO (read the US) remains Europe's main security guarantee, most other aspects of security and defence are dealt with by the EU, not by NATO. The Ukraine war serves to exemplify this. In this conflict, NATO's deterrence capacities have proved strong: even as the allies have increased their support to Ukraine, they have not been met with countermeasures from Russia directed at any of the NATO members. NATO also conducts training of Ukrainian soldiers and have stationed more troops along Russia's border. But all other aspects linked to this hybrid war is dealt with by the EU, which, as a political organisation, has many more tools at its disposal than a pure military defence alliance like NATO. EU sanctions limit Russia's access to key technological military components and access to its central bank assets. The EU deals with energy and food security. The EU has launched a military training mission of Ukrainian soldiers, member states cooperate on cyber security, and it provides direct financial support for military equipment to Ukraine, something that cannot be done through the NATO budget. This just to mention a few examples.

Already before the war, European states, scholars, and other observers were discussing how to develop a new security architecture in Europe, where the EU and NATO find some sort of division of labour in European defence. Also, the US has been, and continues to be, pushing Europe to take up a bigger responsibility for its own security, including in the EU. The situation that will be a reality once the US returns to its focus on Asia and China, perhaps under a president that is less interested in European security, is that more of the burden of defending Europe falls on Europe. Hence, although Norway has wriggle room in territorial defence, other aspects of its defence is more linked to the EU, where it, as a non-member, has much less influence than in NATO.

In sum, discussing the different aspects of *wriggle room*, we see that Norway has much formal but limited de facto wriggle room vis-à-vis the EU. On the one hand, there is much formal scope for independent action, although the opportunity is seldomly used in practice, with conflict resolution processes and core defence issues linked to NATO being the main exceptions. On the other hand, Norway has few direct avenues of influence over EU decision-making processes. Other policy areas increasingly spill over to foreign policy – and the other way around – making foreign policy increasingly difficult to distinguish from EEA- and Schengen-related areas. Finally, Norway tends to align with EU in almost everything it does in its foreign policy, especially in declaratory politics.

Not so autonomous after all?

What, then, does the preceding discussion imply for our understanding of Norway's broader autonomy in relation to the EU? Under the complex interdependence that this book takes as a starting point, the concepts of wriggle room and autonomy can help in evaluating interstate relationships not only in terms of dependence and independence but in terms of the extent to which states can stake out their desired paths from within the set of legal affiliations that they have with others. As discussed earlier, autonomy refers to a third country's ability to conduct its preferred foreign policies independently of the EU, that is, the extent to which it has clear preferences and decides on how to best reach them through independent decision-making processes. It is, of course, difficult to measure whether Norway's preferences are formed by the EU. What we can discuss, however, is i) the level of overlap between the EU's and Norway's foreign policy preferences and ii) the extent to which Norway decides on its foreign policies through established decision-making procedures or more or less automatically adopts the policies agreed to by the EU member states. By automatically, we mean without formal deliberative processes within ministries or in the wider foreign and security policy debates. Of course, decisions must often be reached quickly in many security- and defence-related situations. If, however, there is evidence to suggest that Norway perceives a strong alignment with the EU to further its own interests and values, and there are decision-making processes preceding such decisions, a close connection between the two may suggest a high level of autonomy even if this, at the outset, may seem like a low level of Norwegian independence of the EU.

The 2012 government commissioned report (NOU 2012:2) argues that this is indeed often the case. Rather than tracing alignment to lack of autonomy on the Norwegian side in its relationship with the EU, it emphasises that most of the time there is alignment of interests and identities that drive the common positions and the 'EU following' of Norway. Since that report was published, however, we have seen not only that EU foreign policy is increasingly driven by crises and geopolitical events but also that the EU reaches agreements on actions and policies more and more quickly (Riddervold et al., 2021). Given the very nature of crises, often requiring quick responses, and the fact that the EU seems increasingly competent in taking such decisions, there is potentially less room for Norway to influence EU decision-making processes and actions.

Also here, Norway's cooperation and alignment with the EU in response to the Russian full-scale invasion of Ukraine serves to illustrate this argument. An obvious example is how Norwegian Prime Minister Jonas Gahr Støre guaranteed that Norway would adopt EU's sanctions – before the EU had decided on what they would be (ABC Nyheter, 2022). It is possible to argue that Norway's steadfast following of the EU's policies in relation to the war in Ukraine suggests that Norway's foreign policy autonomy is quite limited in relation to the EU: being a small country close to Russia, Norway did not appear to have much choice other than to follow its bigger partners, the US and the EU, in response to Russian aggression. One may, as discussed earlier, argue that EU policies are in line with Norway's interests and in accordance with its foreign policy values and, hence, that its decision to follow the EU has been an autonomous choice. To the extent that this is true, the same actions could thus be interpreted as indicating a high level of autonomy. However, in the case of Ukraine, there is not much evidence to suggest that Norway actually did many calculations on the extent to which EU policies were in line with Norwegian interests. Instead, with few exceptions, the government openly said it would follow EU policies, also before the EU member states had agreed on what policies to conduct. Hence, rather than suggesting that Norway has much autonomy, the Ukraine war suggests that Norway's autonomy is decreasing in an uncertain geopolitical environment in which larger states and polities increasingly appear to dictate the political directions to be taken. Consequently, despite the legal freedom in foreign and security policy, the more the EU takes up a central role in the European security architecture – across traditional sectors – the less de facto autonomy will be left for Norway.

Foreign, security, and defence in the Brexit process

Having discussed Norway's wriggle room and autonomy in EU foreign, security, and defence policy, we now turn to the recent history of EU-UK relations, as the UK gradually moved from a member to a non-member of the EU. When then Prime Minister Theresa May presented her 12 priorities for the UK's negotiations with the EU at Lancaster House in January 2017, foreign, security, and defence cooperation was considered an important area for future EU-UK relations, but after years of negotiations and a relationship turning more and more sour, PM Boris Johnson effectively killed the prospects for any formal and binding security cooperation in February 2020, when publishing his government's negotiation mandate for the future EU-UK relationship (UK Government, 2017, 2020). In short, the parties ended up failing to include any meaningful provisions on foreign, security, and defence in the Trade and Cooperation Agreement (Whitman, 2020).

Yet, even as late as in the Political Declaration that was annexed to the Withdrawal Agreement that was the basis on which the UK left the EU in January 2020, visions for close cooperation were prevalent. Also, the document clearly reflected the ability to design flexible solutions in this area, for instance in how it stated that 'The Parties should design flexible and scalable cooperation that would ensure that the United Kingdom can combine efforts with the Union to the greatest effect, including in times of crisis or when serious incidents occur'. Furthermore, it asked for several mechanisms to be introduced to develop a close relationship: 'To this end, the future relationship should provide for appropriate dialogue, consultation, coordination, exchange of information and cooperation mechanisms. It should also allow for secondment of experts where appropriate and in the Parties' mutual interest' (European Union, 2020). Even though these would be loose types of coordination, the outcome of the Brexit process meant a situation where there were no formal limitations to the UK's autonomy and wriggle room in relation to the EU in foreign, security, and defence policies.

Indeed, things increasingly went sour in the overall Brexit negotiations, and we must assume that this spilled over into the ability to formally agree any provisions on foreign, security, and defence policy. Also, as the Brexit in the first place was about re-establishing 'sovereignty' for the UK, this area of high politics was particularly sensitive to politicisation. One month after the UK formally left the EU, Boris Johnson's government published its negotiation approach, effectively taking foreign, security, and defence policy out of the equation. Early in the document it was emphasised that 'many policy areas – for example foreign policy . . . are for the UK Government to determine, within a framework of broader friendly dialogue and cooperation between the UK and the EU: they do not require an institutionalised relationship' (UK Government, 2020, p. 4). Of course, as the parties only had months to negotiate a free-trade agreement, making priorities was necessary. Time was, to put it carefully, scarce. However, still, observers that had, since the early days of the Brexit process, envisioned – and partly expected – that some form of foreign, security, and, potentially, defence cooperation would be possible, were slightly surprised that it was taken off the table entirely. At the same time, some of the practical cooperation envisioned by the UK had taken place, for instance in a coordinated sanctions regime together with the US and Canada on Belarus.

It is certainly not irrelevant that the Brexit process turned out to be exceptionally tortuous. Obviously, the severe domestic problems on finding a ratifiable solution in the UK impeded on the ability to come out with the kind of deep and close partnership some were hoping for and that could span all areas. Instead, the negotiators had only a few months to agree on a TCA that only minimally avoided a so-called hard Brexit. Perhaps even more noteworthy with regards to the flexible area of foreign, security, and defence policy, the emergence of distrust and increasingly bitter relations between the parties might have impeded on the ability to develop any meaningful cooperation also in the medium and long term as the Brexit dust settled. Frankly, some observers might also argue that the UK was and remains uninterested in more than a minimal relationship, considering, for instance, how it decided to go ahead with the AUKUS deal with Australia and the US, which created a serious rift in already-damaged UK/NATO-French/EU relations. The inclusion of the UK into the EU's PESCO project on military mobility might contribute to re-balance some of the tensions following Brexit.

Born with Brexit was also a vision of 'Global Britain', brought into life by Theresa May's government. Subject to widespread mockery, the actual content of the slogan and what it would mean was quite difficult to grapple with, partly due to how it was so uncertain what the UK wanted with Brexit in the first place. There is, however, some logic to the vision for 'Global Britain' and the UK's reluctance to include cooperation with the EU in it. The UK chose to leave the EU. Thus, as it was exiting, it needed to find new meaning to its role in the world and its international relationships. Including close cooperation with the EU on foreign, security, and defence policy could be read as admitting the limitations inherent in Brexit in the first place. Taking into consideration also the strong UK scepticism against any prospects of an EU army (which was a central focus of the leave campaign) and the country's imperial legacy, the hitherto limits to post-Brexit EU-UK cooperation on foreign, security, and defence policy becomes less puzzling. Indeed, as part of this the UK's strategy document – Global Britain in a Competitive Age – makes little notice of the EU but launches a range of priorities around the world (UK Government, 2021). As part of this, the UK has also increased its interest in the High North and the Arctic, including seeking to strengthen its bilateral ties with Norway. All in all, the *independence* that the UK sought with Brexit clearly came to fruition in foreign, security, and defence. The UK sought *independence* from the EU, and it was no pretty diplomatic and political process as it tore apart from it. But a consequence is that the UK remained autonomous to act according to its own will in foreign, security, and defence policy, with no real need to wriggle around any EU-determined limitations and structures.

Conclusion

In this chapter we have studied autonomy and wriggle room in foreign, security, and defence policy. Importantly, third-country association with the EU in foreign, security, and defence policy is not driven by treaties and lengthy negotiations of formal relationships but continue to be shaped by practical cooperation and compromises. Thus, it is quite possible for both Norway and the UK to cooperate closely with the EU on foreign, security, and defence policy should they desire to do so. This even though they have a very different historical trajectories in this field. Also, they can cooperate with the EU without ceding their ability to determine their own political, economic, social, and cultural development. In other words, there are limited legal constraints in the mix here.

On the one hand, cooperation in foreign, security, and defence should be quite simple between like-minded European states. Both due to the current security situation in and around Europe and the wider world, as well as because cooperation does not really take ceding national sovereignty to a supranational organisation. Indeed, the Norwegian experience shows that it is possible to develop a foreign, security, and defence relationship that is flexible, allows for a substantial amount of wriggle room, and retains formal autonomy. Yet what over time has become an under-the-radar and wide-ranging patchwork of cooperation between Norway and the EU in which Norwegian autonomy seems to be shrinking, the UK case became hostage to the Brexit process and a real thorn in the side on both sides of the

English Channel. As the Brexit dust gradually settles, the wider security situation, the EU's development as a foreign, security, and defence actor, and domestic appetite are all factors that will determine how third countries like Norway and the UK will cooperate with the EU in foreign, security, and defence policy. The inclusion of the UK in PESCO adds to the empirical track record in this regard. In relation to this, it is significant to also consider what we find to be gradually diminishing Norwegian autonomy due to a changing geopolitical context and the spillover across a range of policy areas to the domain of foreign, security, and defence policy.

Despite the failed attempt to include foreign, security, and defence policy in the formal Brexit process, the UK is not cut off from the European security order. Yet it chose not to build a strong foreign, security, and defence relationship with the EU. The Norway model, which is based on a typical EU approach to third countries, may prove illustrative for the UK in the longer term. For Norwegian officials, the main problem associated with a close non-member relationship with the EU in this area is that it is not always possible to get as close to processes as possible. Yet at the same time Norway is free to opt in or out across the whole spectrum of EU initiatives, ranging from declarations and sanctions to crisis management operations. If the UK would choose to engage more actively at some point, the Norwegian experience is testament to how that is possible without having to compromise on some of the core values that drove the Brexit process in the UK, yet that would have to be consolidated in the domestic debate. Both at home and in relation to power symmetries, Norway and the UK are quite different cases of EU partners in this regard.

In the European foreign, security, and defence architecture, NATO is the prime territorial defence institution, and the EU has been increasing its efforts to support NATO and carve out its own contribution. Due to the complexities of current security threats and imaginaries, the EU is building a framework that cut across traditional policy areas. This emerging and complex architecture both provides some wriggle room and ability for states to retain autonomy but, as we have seen, potentially contributes to limit it.

Note

1 There was one sanction, however, that Norway did not sign fully up to, namely restrictive measures against Russian fishing vessels in Norwegian ports (Norwegian Government, 2022b).

References

ABC Nyheter (2022) *Store varsler norsk støtte til EU-sanksjoner*. Available at: www.abc-nyheter.no/nyheter/norge/2022/02/22/195827386/store-varsler-norsk-stotte-til-eu-sanksjoner (Accessed 25 January 2023).

Consolidated version of the Treaty on European Union (2012) *Official Journal of the European Union*, C 326/13, 26 October. Available at: https://eur-lex.europa.eu/resource.html?uri=cellar:2bf140bf-a3f8-4ab2-b506-fd71826e6da6.0023.02/DOC_1&format=PDF (Accessed 10 February 2023).

European Union (2016) *Shared Vision, Common Action: A Stronger Europe. A Global Strategy for the European Union's Foreign and Security Policy*. Available at: www.eeas.europa.eu/sites/default/files/eugs_review_web_0.pdf (Accessed 25 January 2023).

European Union (2020) *Political Declaration Setting Out the Framework for the Future Relationship between the European Union and the United Kingdom*. Available at: https://eur-lex.europa.eu/legal-content/EN/TXT/?qid=1592316528275&uri=CELEX%3A12019W/DCL%2801%29 (Accessed 25 January 2023).

European Union (2022) *A Strategic Compass for Security and Defence*. Available at: www.eeas.europa.eu/sites/default/files/documents/strategic_compass_en3_web.pdf (Accessed 25 January 2023).

Fossum, J. E. (2015) 'Representation under Hegemony? On Norway's relationship to the EU', in Eriksen, E. O. and Fossum, J. E. (eds) *The European Union's Non-Members*, London: Routledge.

Friis, K. (2020) 'Hvorfor sier regjeringen nei til forsvarsfondet?', *Dagens Næringsliv*, 12 October. Available at: www.dn.no/innlegg/nato/eu/forsvarsdepartementet/innlegg-hvor-for-sier-regjeringen-nei-til-forsvarsfondet/2-1-890211 (Accessed 25 January 2023).

Græger, N. and Haugevik, K. M. (2022) 'Differentiated Integration and EU Outsiders: A Norwegian View', *EUIDEA Policy Paper*. Available at: https://nupi.brage.unit.no/nupi-xmlui/handle/11250/2985498 (Accessed 25 January 2023).

Gross, E. (2009) *The Europeanization of National Foreign Policy: Continuity and Change in European Crisis Management*, London: Palgrave MacMillan.

Hillion, C. (2019) 'Norway and the Changing Common Foreign and Security Policy of the European Union', *NUPI Report* 1/2019: 1–34. https://www.nupi.no/en/publications/cristin-pub/norway-and-the-changing-common-foreign-and-security-policy-of-the-european-union

Molthof, L., Zandee, D. and Cretti, G. (2021) 'Unpacking Open Strategic Autonomy. From Concept to Practice', *Clingendael Report*. Available at: www.clingendael.org/sites/default/files/2021-11/Unpacking_open_strategic_autonomy.pdf (Accessed 25 January 2023).

Norwegian Government (2021) *Utenriks- og sikkerhetspolitisk samarbeid*. Available at: www.regjeringen.no/no/tema/europapolitikk/tema-norge-eu/utenriks-sikkerhetspolitisk-samarbeid/id684931/ (Accessed 25 January 2023).

Norwegian Government (2022a) *Ny runde med sanksjoner innført mot Russland*. Available at: www.regjeringen.no/no/aktuelt/flere-sanksjoner-mot-russland/id2925555/ (Accessed 25 January 2023).

Norwegian Government (2022b) *Vedr. russiske fiskefartøy*. Available at: www.regjeringen.no/no/aktuelt/dep/ud/brev_ud/svar_ud/2022/svar_fiskefartoy/id2946719/ (Accessed 25 January 2023).

NOU 2012:2 (2012) *Utenfor og innenfor. Norges avtaler med EU*, Oslo: Norwegian Ministry of Foreign Affairs.

Olsen, J. P. (2002) 'The Many Faces of Europeanization', *Journal of Common Market Studies*, 40(5): 921–952.

Riddervold, M. (2016) 'Et spørsmål om legitimitet. Hvorfor Norge valgte EU foran NATO i kampen mot somaliske pirater', *Norsk Statsvitenskapelig Tidsskrift*, 32(4): 363–282.

Riddervold, M., Trondal, J. and Newsome, A. (2021) *Palgrave Handbook of EU Crises*, Houndmills: Palgrave Macmillan.

Svendsen, Ø. (2022) *The Politics of Third Countries in EU Security and Defence: Norway, Brexit and Beyond*, Houndmills: Palgrave Macmillan.

Svendsen, Ø. and Adler-Nissen, R. (2019) 'Differentiated (Dis)integration in Practice: The Diplomacy of Brexit and the "Low" Politics of "High" Politics', *Journal of Common Market Studies*, 57(6): 1419–1430.

Svendsen, Ø. and Rieker, P. (2019) 'Spin-off av EØS? Norge og europeisk utenriks-, sikkerhets-og forsvarssamarbeid', *Internasjonal Politikk*, 77(4): 378–387.

UK Government (2017) *The Government's Negotiating Objectives for Exiting the EU*. PM Speech. Available at: www.gov.uk/government/speeches/the-governments-negotiating-objectives-for-exiting-the-eu-pm-speech (Accessed 25 January 2023).

UK Government (2020) *The Future Relationship with the EU. The UK's Approach to Neogitations*. Available at: https://assets.publishing.service.gov.uk/government/uploads/system/uploads/attachment_data/file/868874/The_Future_Relationship_with_the_EU.pdf (Accessed 25 January 2023).

UK Government (2021) *Global Britain in a Competitive Age: The Integrated Review of Security, Defence, Development and Foreign Policy*. Available at: www.gov.uk/government/publications/global-britain-in-a-competitive-age-the-integrated-review-of-security-defence-development-and-foreign-policy (Accessed 25 January 2023).

UK Parliament (2022) *EU Permanent Structured Cooperation (PESCO): A Future Role for UK Defence?* Available at: https://commonslibrary.parliament.uk/research-briefings/cbp-9058/ (Accessed 25 January 2023).

Whitman, R. G. (2020) 'Missing in Action: The EU-UK Foreign, Security and Defence Policy Relationship After Brexit', *European View*, 19(2): 222–229.

7
CITIZENSHIP, MIGRATION, AND MOBILITY

Introduction

The EU has instituted EU citizenship as a form of *transnational* citizenship that is distinct and unprecedented among international organisations in the rights and obligations it confers on citizens. In the European optic, there is no clear-cut distinction between national and EU citizenship. The two are inter-weaved, with legal, political, social, economic, and cultural ramifications. This is very much at the core of this book's topic. What are institutional and political inter-linkages in Europe's multilevel political space, and how do changes in this institutional configuration – Brexit being an ultimate form of such transformation – affect the autonomy and wriggle room of domestic institutions?

Citizenship is at the very core of political order (see Kratochwil, 1994). It confers on individuals a rights-based membership of the political community *within* the borders of a state. EU citizenship, on the other hand, is at the core premised on *mobility across* those very state borders. The development of citizenship in the EU links, therefore, rights, mobility, and migration. As the EU and the EEA are rights-based legal orders, changes to individual rights systems, citizenship institutions, and migration policies will provide strong proof of the overall transformative effects on national political institutions.

We define citizenship as full membership in a political community (see also Menéndez and Olsen, 2020). Based on this definition, the chapter operationalises citizenship as a status of rights (*private autonomy*) and political participation (*public autonomy*) (Habermas, 1996). This means that we can chart different consequences for national citizenship institutions and practice in terms of different types of rights as well as political participation. This conception of citizenship as conditioned on different types of autonomy diverges somewhat from the more general concept of autonomy applied in this book. While

DOI: 10.4324/9781003246961-7

the book, on a whole, discusses the issue of state autonomy and wriggle room, this chapter starts out from citizenship as *individual* autonomy. Still, the citizenship practice related to the private and public autonomy of citizens is indirectly related to state autonomy under complex interdependence as this book argues marks states involved with Europeanisation processes. When the chapter relates to state autonomy and wriggle room, this will be addressed explicitly.

This is key, as the citizens of non-EU states of the EEA Agreement have rights which are akin to those of EU citizens. The rights of free movement are foremost in the EEA register of rights. In other words: non-EU citizens from an EEA country such as Norway have extensive rights as *second country nationals* in the EU states. There is also reciprocity here: EU citizens hold the same set of rights in the EEA states. This is the case as the rights-based EU political order sought to 'abolish the disabilities of alienage' as Preuss (1998, p. 145) so succinctly put it, through principles of free movement and non-discrimination. EU citizenship was constructed around such principles (see e.g., Maas, 2007; Olsen, 2008; Wiener, 1998) creating a form of internal and privileged migration and membership status for member state nationals (Menéndez and Olsen, 2020). As such, there is a clear connection between the issues of EU citizenship and migration, also for non-member states with different affiliations to the EU, as is the case with Norway and the UK. Through Brexit, UK citizens lost their rights as EU citizens, thus making them migrants in a more classical sense, than that of intra-EU migration through the exercise of EU citizenship rights. Indeed, migration and mobile European citizens were at the forefront of the Brexit debate leading up to the referendum. It can be argued that curtailing migration was one of the main objectives of Brexit. It follows from this that Brexit has deep implications for citizens' rights and transnational citizenship. UK citizens lost their EU citizenship, and EU citizens' status in the UK has changed post-Brexit.

We trace the status of citizenship rights and migration issues of Norway and the UK as two different non-member states. First, the chapter addresses citizenship in what we call 'EU transnational'. The definition of citizenship as private and public autonomy in a constitutional democratic sense is followed by a general introduction to main citizenship developments in the EU. In so doing, we also explain what EEA citizenship entails, the basic principles it is based on, and its place in the larger citizenship 'architecture', leading to what may be called *depoliticisation* of citizenship. This lines up with Chapter 8's account of how the Norwegian political system has depoliticised the EU affiliation issue.

The chapter does not look at specific cases, but rather charts the status of citizenship after Europeanisation: how autonomous are Norwegian citizens? And what is the upshot of this peculiar status of differentiated citizenship in European integration for citizenship and post-Brexit UK citizenship? Further, the chapter addresses the migration policies of Norway and the UK, with special emphasis on how these link up with the EU migration system. This is of special interest, as mobility and migration are at the very heart of the European integration project. Moreover, both intra- and extra-EU migration were central issues in the debates on Brexit.

EU transnational: citizenship, mobility, migration

Citizenship defined

We will, in this subsection, provide a conceptual starting point for our analysis. Citizenship is a form of membership, a rights status, modes of participation, and an identity marker. In this book, we define citizenship as full membership in a political community. At first sight, this definition is centred on the individual citizen: her membership, rights, duties, and identity. Still, citizenship also harbours a collective component in that decisions on the different citizenship dimensions are made by political and legal institutions with constitutional powers. The *political community* of the definition is exactly that, defined by the constitutional practice and constitutive borders of the polity, as well as boundaries that determine who are on the inside of the community and who are on the outside. This inclusion/exclusion dimension of citizenship was first addressed by T. H. Marshall (1950) who highlighted how democratic citizenship developed through the gradual inclusion of ever more individuals and groups in society through first civil, then political, and, finally, social rights.

The individual/collective nexus of citizenship has been at the core of debate on citizenship and constitutional rule since Aristotle's discussion in *Politics* (Aristotle, 1992) on how to decide on who the 'citizen' is and how to organise the state through a constitution. One of the most important points of *Politics* was that the rights and duties of the members of the polity is reflected in constitutional rules and practice. This trickled down to the idea of a popular basis for the constitution in the age of democratic revolutions. The idea was that 'we, the people' came together in a community to create a constitutional order based on equal rights and duties for all citizens (Ackerman, 1991). In other words, as a community, the citizens grant *each other* rights to regulate their common affairs through the constitution (Habermas, 1996, p. 82).

This constitutional basis of democratic citizenship provides us with an operationalisation of citizenship as consisting of two forms of autonomy: private and public. The two conceptualises different aspects to the system of rights and citizenship. *Private* autonomy is the basic status of rights that protects individual freedom through civil, social, and economic rights. Yet rights are not only protections for the individual integrity of the citizen. There is also a political dimension, which transcends the 'atomistic' tendencies that follow from only focusing on the private (Habermas, 1996, p. 88). *Public autonomy* enables political action, individually and in collective action with other citizens in the democratic community. This rights status builds on political rights and coexists with civil, social, and economic rights in legitimating the democratic institution (Habermas, 1996, p. 88).

This conceptualisation highlights how citizenship grants citizens the capability to be part of society and the democratic community, which is constituted by the basic rules of the polity through the democratic constitution. The citizen can sign private contracts, has freedom of speech and organisation, welfare rights, and the ability to hold political representatives *accountable* for their actions. Since the aim of this chapter is to make sense of citizenship developments, in legal and political terms, we therefore focus on three interrelated aspects. The first is changes to *individual rights and duties*, through law-making or court decisions. The second is changes to citizenship *practice*, that is, the mix between different types of rights, as well as modes of citizen participation. The third is changes to the citizenship *institution* in terms of who grants which rights to whom.

Transnational citizenship in the EU and the EEA dimension

As we have seen in so far in this book, the EU is a construction that enmeshes the member states into a multilevel political and legal system, marked by different degrees of intergovernmental and supranational arrangements. Citizenship adds a dimension to this multilevel system, as European citizenship is *transnational*. It is multilevel in that it 'works' in practice, both on the member state level and on the European level. In citizenship terms, this is conceptualised here as transnational, meaning that, while it gives certain concrete rights linked to the EU, it is also based on national citizenship. It is, therefore, a form of rights status that is 'in between' different levels of policymaking and binding political decisions.

Moreover, EU citizens become transnational citizens when they utilise their rights of free movement. In other words, any discussion of EU, Europeanisation, and citizenship relates in some form to the idea and practice of free movement in political, economic, social, and legal terms. We can, then, preliminarily state that a definitional perspective on European citizenship as transnational highlights why analysing citizenship as private and public autonomy is fruitful. The strong onus on free movement and non-discrimination based on nationality points toward a focus, in the first instance, on civil rights – with, for instance, social rights to follow as 'knock-on' effects (Olsen, 2008).

This is clear when we account for the relationship between EU and EEA citizenship. EU citizenship has created what could be called a 'fundamental' status of the *second country national*. This status is premised on the *use* of free movement rights to travel across internal EU borders between the member states. It is a status linked to the act of moving, an act which is not different between EU and EEA citizens – or between EU and EEA states. In other words, EEA citizens, at the core, hold the same status as second-country nationals as EU citizens do. The main difference lies in political rights. In EU citizenship, these are enshrined in the Treaties as part of the catalogue of rights that follow from the status. These give EU citizens voting rights in European and local elections, leading to what Shaw (2007) has called 'the restructuring of political space'. What is important to notice for the purposes of our analyses of Norway and the UK 'in Europe' is that this transformation of the potential for political citizenship is out of reach for citizens of third countries. While Norway is closely affiliated with the EU and strongly Europeanised in numerous policy areas, it is *not* a political relationship understood as means to engage in collective action over public goods (see Menéndez and Olsen, 2020). In the case of the UK, this status has become rescinded due to Brexit. In terms of political citizenship, UK citizens lost their EU citizenship: they became *disenfranchised* as political citizens in the EU sense.

Migration policy and differentiated personal statuses

The EU is *premised* on migration. Free movement of workers and persons can be seen as the very core of the EU constitutional order (Olsen, 2012; see also Maas, 2007). Mobility across borders has been understood as a central policy when EU institutions and national leaders have crafted what is dubbed 'an ever-closer union'. As a fundamental element of the Treaties, it is further a main issue in the jurisprudence of the EU court. In addition, it is of importance to underline that the term 'migrant' must be qualified when used in EU terms. *Intra-EU* migration through the exercise of EU citizenship rights by member state citizens is a very different phenomenon from *extra-EU* migration of asylum seekers and refugees. Such third-country nationals can, moreover, also enter EU and member state territory through different schemes for labour migration.

EU migration policy developed from initial initiatives of the Trevi Group in the 1970s to common asylum policies embedded in the second pillar of 'justice and home affairs' after the Maastricht Treaty. This system gradually developed toward more supranationalism in decision-making, thus foregoing the long-standing idea that migration is an exclusive national prerogative. Both the Dublin and Schengen systems are constructed around a supranational logic of common norms and rules that all member states must adhere to. In this, the system of migration control from third countries also shares characteristics with that of intra-EU migration. Free movement and non-discrimination based on nationality are supranational and 'constitutional' principles of European integration. Member states are bound by the system of rights that these principles create as central elements of EU citizenship. In other words, their legal wriggle room is limited regarding this Europeanisation of migration. The UK's choice to exit the EU could, in this light, be understood as an act to restore autonomy over the political order, which, through European integration, had become enmeshed in a supranational decision-making system, with transnational citizenship rights. The slogan 'taking back control' implied, as it were, both increasing legal and political autonomy in policymaking and reframing the boundaries of the political community. The actual, physical border is back, both in practical terms and as a symbol of state sovereignty and the exercise of autonomy. Yet as we have argued throughout this book, the depth of European integration and the interdependence of its system of state/supranational relations is not easily amenable to such acts of exiting or rejecting full membership of the EU.

Citizenship and mobility in a non-member affiliated state: the case of Norway

EEA citizenship

How has EEA membership affected Norwegian citizenship in terms of individual rights and duties, citizenship practice, and institutional issues of membership? Moreover, what is the status of the Norwegian citizen as political citizen? As EEA members from 1994, Norway became part of the EU's internal market grounded on the principles of four freedoms and non-discrimination based on nationality. This not only secured market access for Norwegian businesses and products; Norwegians also gained new rights as EEA citizens. These rights are linked exactly to the principle of free movement of persons which forms the core right of EU citizenship. Free movement for citizens was originally based on the idea of creating a common labour market in Europe. In other words, it was first and foremost workers and 'market participants' that European citizens could utilise free movement. Citizens were, at the outset, not integrated as equal participants in a political community, but rather what Plender (1976, p. 39) has been called 'factors of production'.

Thus, the so-called 'market citizen' has been at the forefront (Everson, 1995). It is exactly as *market citizens* that Norwegian citizens have become integrated through the EEA Agreement. Through this, they have, without a doubt, increased their private autonomy as citizens, not the least given the possibility to cross borders in the pursuit of new life opportunities. This is not a trivial kind of development as the nation-state has traditionally been held to be the productive ground where individuals have their primary possibility to engage in concrete life projects. This is, of course, not unique to Norwegian citizens: they have, through a free-trade system such as the EEA, accessed rights that would otherwise only be available through full EU membership.

Political yet depoliticised

Europeanisation of citizenship has implications not only for market rights but also for *political* rights (Shaw, 2007). The link between the status of citizens and the territory of the state has been weakened. There is no longer a seamless, 'one-to-one' relationship between the access to membership and rights and territory. EU citizens have extensive rights in Norway through the EEA Agreement as well as voting rights in local elections. Depending on their own country's electoral laws, some EU citizens resident in Norway will also be able to vote in European Parliament elections. Paradoxically, an EU citizen with Norwegian residence can, then, have much more influence on EEA-relevant legislation than a Norwegian citizen who remains rooted to voting rights in national elections in Norway. Hence, despite *leaving* the EU to reside in Norway, an EU citizen can have a much stronger influence than her Norwegian co-residents on political processes with *direct* influence on Norwegian politics and society.

Yet, after two decades of EEA membership, Norwegians have, then, extended their civil and economic rights. Workers and students have considerably increased their private autonomy. Parallel to this expansion of Norwegians' private autonomy, Norway's relationship to the EU has become drastically transformed through the dynamic expansion of the EEA Agreement, as was highlighted in Chapter 1 of this book. This has the consequence of weaving Norwegian citizens much more strongly into the web of European decision-making some three decades since the EEA was negotiated in the beginning of the 1990s. The access to civil, economic, and, in part, social rights has not been equated by requisite political rights. This is, of course, natural as Norway is not member of the EU. Europeanisation of Norwegian citizenship follows from formal membership to international organisations and international agreements. This can be illustrated by the fact that implementation of supranational rights that do not directly relate to the EEA, for instance, has come about through making the European Convention on Human Rights to Norwegian law.[1]

Politically, however, EU-level decision-making has much bigger impact on Norwegian society and the autonomy of Norwegian citizens than international rights charters. Not only are Norwegian authorities and the democratic community outside formal decision-making channels in the Council of Ministers or the European Parliament. They have also been kept out of processes where other non-members have been included. One example is the Laeken constitutional process from 2001 to 2003. This process included all the accession states, while the EFTA states were on the outside although it would have far-reaching consequences also for the EEA. A European constitution was not realised, but much of its substance was re-enacted through the Lisbon Treaty. This last EU treaty has, for instance, increased the influence of national parliaments and made qualified majority voting a rule in policymaking.

Norwegian citizens have, in other words, not increased their public autonomy in the transnational political context post-EEA. This is exacerbated by the fact that as Norwegian governments are excluded from many decisions that affect Norway and its citizens, in the same period, the European Court of Justice (ECJ) has been especially active in interpreting the reach of basic EU principles and the rights of EU citizenship (see e.g., Kochenov, 2013; Lenaerts, 2015; Menéndez and Olsen, 2020). One concrete example is the development in the field of labour rights and workplace regulation, which have a direct influence on the rights of Norwegian citizens as market participants. As this status has been strengthened after closer integration with European market policies, it can be questioned whether such mobility rights will trump other rights. The ECJ verdicts in the Viking,[2] Laval,[3] and Rüffert[4] cases can be interpreted as a sign that free movement as a fundamental and baseline right of EU citizenship that trumps other rights will also have consequences in Norway. As such, the emphasis on free movement as a 'constitutional principle' leads to changes in Norwegian citizens' employee rights without their having had the chance to influence such profound developments politically.

In democratic terms, citizens of Norway are doubly on the sidelines under this kind of differentiated integration. They have rights but lack political and democratic influence. They are affected by political processes where they are not represented as well as by an intensified process of *juridification*. Yet there is no echo of the slogan from the American revolution about '*no taxation without representation*'[5] in public debates on citizens' relation to European processes: '*No implementation without participation*'.[6] This is especially important from the vantage point of citizenship as the concept of sovereignty in constitutional democracies seems to develop in the direction of 'co-determination' rather than 'self-determination' (Eriksen and Fossum, 2015). In other words: the increase in civil and economic rights has not been paralleled in the political side of citizenship. It can be argued that Norwegian citizens have less possibility to affect societal developments today than they had when the EEA Agreement was instituted.

Democracy, citizenship, and deep integration: whither wriggle room?

A democratic constitution as the Norwegian one is exactly based on the principle of the citizens as lawmakers that can hold their representatives *accountable* for their actions: 'Folket udøver den lovgivende Magt ved Storthinget'.[7] The citizens are, in this understanding of democracy, co-authors of their *own* laws. This is central to the idea of representative democracy and legislative politics. The Norwegian Parliament transposes relevant EU laws and policies as Norwegian law where applicable under the EEA. EU laws are first debated in the EEA Committee of the Parliament. Cases of specific importance must be approved by the Parliament in the plenary after § 26 of the Norwegian Constitution. Yet there is very little debate on these cases of law-making in the Parliament as well as in public debate. The Public Commission on relations with the EU documents that 287 cases were put to the Parliament between 1992 and 2011, of which 265 were decided by unanimity. Moreover, § 115 (§ 93 until 2014) of the Norwegian Constitution has only been used in one instance, that is, when Norway became EEA members. This requires three-fourths majority in the Parliament in cases of ceding sovereignty to international organisations.

The term 'fax democracy' has been used to illustrate how the system works. Policies that have gone through a complex legislative process in the EU are transposed virtually without debate in Norway. How can Norwegians, then, hold their representatives accountable for the policies that are implemented? Citizens are formally co-authors to their own laws but have been set aside in two main ways. Firstly, as Norway has no real representation in the process *prior* to the decision taken. Secondly, as there is a virtually automatic implementation through the Norwegian Parliament which seems to follow a logic of juridification rather than politics. When taking the European dimension as a starting point, democratic politics in Norway seems to have collapsed the representative dimension into a system of direct, non-political implementation of supranational legislation. To put it bluntly: the role as outsider is based on a logic of *formal* self-determination where co-determination is set aside due to a much stronger thrust of Europeanisation than what was foreseen in 1994. This is especially visible in terms of citizenship as public autonomy. This reconstruction of the constitutional backdrop for the exercise of active citizenship in a Europeanised Norway can be summarized as a tension between access and freedom. The principle of dynamic treaty development in the EEA links Norwegian democracy, politics, bureaucracy, and society to EU decision-making in a profound way. This has led to a development where the Norwegian citizen has become more of a *homo oeconomicus* and less than a *homo politicus* because of Europeanisation.

This highlights the issue of citizenship and wriggle room. In other policy areas, EU policies may involve more concrete possibilities for Norwegian decision-makers to make use of wriggle room to adapt these to Norwegian interests and societal circumstances. In this book, we show this, for instance, in security and defence policy, climate policy, as well as agriculture and fisheries. In the area of citizenship and individual rights, the stakes are clearly different. Firstly, as we have shown, the issue of autonomy relates not only to state capacity to act in a legal and political sense but also to the fact that democratic citizenship is premised on the dual promise of private and public autonomy. Secondly, rights that stem from EEA relevant legislation are often based on regulations where Norway, legally and politically, has little or no autonomy in their transposition into Norwegian law and their subsequent administrative implementation. In addition, the cornerstone of the EEA Agreement is derived from what some would call the EU's constitutional principles, those of free movement. Thus, there is little room for wriggling one's feet in the waters of autonomy for the Norwegian government.

It is interesting, then, that the recent, so-called NAV scandal exactly highlights the encounter between EU regulations and perceptions of wriggle room (see also Chapter 8). NAV, or the Norwegian Labour and Welfare Administration, had denied the portability of welfare payments within the EEA area. Recipients of such welfare payments who had nevertheless utilised free movement to travel to an EU or EEA country were found to have committed welfare fraud. Many were fined and some sentenced to prison time. Subsequent investigation (NOU 2020:9) highlighted how NAV officials had misinterpreted Regulation 883/2004[8] to the detriment of citizens' and permanent residents' rights. In other words, Norwegian authorities clearly have less wriggle room for interpretation and implementation of the individual rights that follow from the EEA Agreement.

Asylum policies, institutions, and practices in a European migration 'system'

The democratic issues of citizenship in the context of Norway's integration with Europe are further visible in the Europeanisation of legal frameworks, policy solutions, and individual rights in terms of migration. Norway's participation in the internal market has created a new concept of migration where there is a distinction between intra- and extra-EU migrants. And further, the 'economic migrant' is, then, increasingly equated with the status of holding EU citizenship or EEA citizenship (Olsen, 2021). In this sense, the economic citizenship of Norwegians as EEA citizens also provides them with such privileged status as 'economic migrants in the EU/EEA area'. This is a status that UK citizens were deprived of, in contrast, upon exiting the EU legal framework of free movement and individual rights.

Norway is part of the European asylum system after entering an association agreement to the Schengen Area in 1996 and operatively integrated from 2001. Equally important, Norway became part of the Dublin System in 2001, with the latest Dublin Regulation (the so-called Dublin III) transposed into Norwegian law from 2014. This Europeanisation of Norwegian migration policy has been supported by all governments since the mid-1990s, albeit with some dissenting voices, especially on the left. This was particularly the case when Norway made its first move of becoming Europeanised in this area with association and later membership in the Schengen Area. Some argued at the time that this would lead to Norway becoming part of a burgeoning 'Fortress Europe' where internal mobility was 'traded in' for stronger control on extra-European migration to European territory (Mathiesen, 2000).

As time has passed, the participation in the EU asylum system has become accepted and tolerated by most political parties and actors, yet with new criticism of free movement and diminished border control coming from, for instance, the Progress Party. Despite such criticism, there are no possibilities of imminent new coalitions that could end Norway's participation in the EU's asylum system. As we have seen in this book, the reason for this is that there is a deep cleavage in the Norwegian political system regarding extensive integration into the EU despite non-membership. Coalitions on both sides of the political spectrum are marked by this cleavage. This has led to a political stalemate in which the status quo is preferred over change, both in terms of Norway's membership status and strong participation as a non-member (Fossum, 2010).

In this sense, Norway is fully committed to the main principles of EU asylum law and politics as this has been developed since the Maastricht Treaty (1992). Foremost, this means that Norway adheres to the principle of 'first country of asylum' and is committed to returning asylum seekers to the European country where they were first registered for the handling of their asylum applications. It can be therefore said that Norway's migration policies as well as concept of the 'migrant' have become Europeanised in the last two decades (see NOU 2012:2). In this sense, its status as a non-EU state is, at the outset, not legally contested as Norway has committed to implementing EU asylum policies. This highlights Norway's status as a 'rule-taker' in relations with the EU (Fossum, 2022, p. 8). Indeed, in replying to the efforts of the EU, in the wake of the refugee crisis, to finally institute a Common European Asylum System (CEAS), the Norwegian government in 2016 maintained its intention to support this development. Of course, this leaves Norway dependent in legal terms, yet without due political influence in the policymaking of this legislation.

Citizenship, rights, and migration in the UK 'Brexit' state: taking stock and lessons from the EEA

Citizenship after Brexit

The notion 'ex-member' is now part of political, cultural, and academic commentary in the 'Eurosphere'. The UK parliament chose an exit from the EU which fell somewhere between a so-called 'hard' Brexit and a softer form akin to Norway's EEA solution. The long-term constitutional, institutional, political, and economic consequences of the UK's choice of a bilateral agreement with the EU which keeps them outside the single market and the Customs Union is, at the time of writing, unclear. Yet there are real existing examples of differentiated or partial forms of inclusion and membership in the institutions, policies, and principles of the EU, which grant us analytical purchase to discuss the effects on citizenship from the main principles and measures of the agreements between the UK and the EU. As we highlight in this book, the most prominent of these examples is the EEA Agreement.

The fate of citizenship rights for Britons as well as EU citizens residing in the UK was a thorny issue for the negotiations on exit from the EU (Mindus, 2017; Shaw, 2018). EU citizenship is a prime example of transnational integration in Europe. It has provided citizens of the member states with a special status of rights and residence in other member states and of a supranational polity. In the literature on citizenship and Brexit, it was asked whether such a status could be revoked, first for UK citizens and second for EU citizens with residence in the UK, and if so, what would be the correct procedure to do so (Mindus, 2017). Moreover, some form of rights allocation of this kind was held as a possible avenue for solving the conundrum of rights for UK citizens once the UK actually exited the EU (see e.g., Kostakopoulou, 2018; Mindus, 2017). Yet this did not emulate EEA citizenship as we know it, despite some political and academic calls for an EEA solution to post-Brexit rights, the Norway model (Fossum and Graver, 2018).

The impact on national citizenship and the rights of UK citizens and permanent residents from continuing EU member states became less one of 'privileged semi-citizenship' than what is the case for citizenship and rights under the EEA Agreement. The Withdrawal Agreement stipulates the rights of UK citizens in the EU and, reversely, of EU citizens in the UK. The policy settled in the agreement was to secure the rights to reside and work for UK and EU citizens (HM Government, 2020, p. 2). Yet this was not an unconditional right. It was a clause that focused on 'living persons' in the sense of those *already* residing on UK or EU territory. As a main rule, they had rights to retain residence in their host state, pending an application *within* the end of the transition period in mid-2020. In other words, the exercise of free movement for UK citizens had a clear *end date*. After this, UK citizens are *outsiders* in EU citizenship practice. They have become third-country nationals, that is, *de jure* extra-EU migrants.

Revoking citizenship by Brexit could be argued not to affect *national* citizenship. This is indeed true when we discuss citizenship within the confines of a national political community. Yet, if some form of rights attachment, especially regarding free movement, is desirable, how was this institutionalized? The UK chose to exit the EU, but interdependencies still matter. The relationship between the EU and the UK was not rescinded, rather continues under new legal and political obligations. In this light, traits of transnational citizenship could have been retained, akin to that of citizenship for the nationals of the EFTA member states in the EEA. Indeed, without freedom of movement, no EU citizenship in the transnational sense (Olsen, 2012). Kostakopoulou (2018) argues that Brexit opened the room for a 'special protected status of EU citizens' based on the template of post-colonial British nationality discourse. Shaw (2018) has highlighted how the veritable 'archipelago of contradictions' inherent in post-Brexit solutions to the issue of free movement could have led to creative solutions in the sphere of citizenship. What seems clear is that UK citizens did gain a form of special protected status, or what could be called privileged semi-citizenship, albeit *temporary*. The transition period opened for a special settled status for UK citizens, yet not as a basic status of rights, but rather as a *temporary* and *bureaucratic* measure before the terms of exiting the EU were formalised. In democratic polities, rights should be equal and not subject to arbitrary limits in terms of time constraints (Cohen, 2018, p. 142). The time limit of the transition period thus highlights how Brexit is an act of disenfranchising citizens, not only in terms of political rights but also in limiting rights already obtained by UK citizens as EU citizens. In other words, Brexit did mean *exit* in real terms for citizenship practice. In this sense, we would argue that the handling of residence rights as a temporary and transitional measure limits not only public autonomy but, crucially, also private autonomy in UK citizenship.

The Brexit referendum in 2016 was a highly politicised moment. The culmination of decades-long debates on the UK's affiliation with the European integration project was that a majority of the UK voters decided to leave the EU. In terms of citizenship, Brexit is interesting as it drove membership, rights, and identity into uncertainty (Mindus, 2017). EU citizenship has put such issues into question in the nation-state form of citizenship, as it has transnationalised rights, residence, and, to some extent, notions of identity (Olsen, 2012; see also Kostakopoulou, 2008). In this age of Europeanised and transnational citizenship, then, Brexit has reshuffled the cards, yet what are the implications in practice of dealing the deck anew? In the following, we address the issue of Brexit with citizenship and rights practices in the EEA as a contrasting, comparative background. Arguably, there are three main pillars of EEA citizenship: market-basis, free movement, residence rights, and depoliticisation. What is the lesson learned for post-Brexit UK, and what does this tell us about the citizenship/migration nexus of leaving an international organisation like the EU?

Depoliticisation

A first main feature of EEA citizenship is its inherent depoliticisation. EEA membership has empowered Norwegian citizens in their *private* capacity as economic and, in part, social rights holders. In terms of *public* autonomy, the political and democratic side to citizenship has become problematic. Democratic politics is no longer 'singular' in that it is confined to the nation-state. Decision-making in EU institutions affects societal conditions on the local, regional, national, and supranational level. EEA citizenship is a vivid example of this interdependence. It is a market membership which grants citizens mobility rights and economic rights yet requires the forfeiture of direct political rights. EEA-related issues encounter questions of public autonomy, yet are more implicit in parliamentary terms. As we have shown throughout this book, the national parliaments in the EEA countries cannot have a *direct* influence on EU decision-making. Yet the Norwegian parliament, as the highest representative institution of the country, also shies away from such influence *indirectly*. Debate on EEA-initiated legislation is not widespread, and much of it passes through without revision. The system is, in other words, akin to 'implementation without representation'.

Brexit was strongly politicised yet led to depoliticisation in the form of a formal exit from EU principles, laws, and institutions. In this sense, retaining some form of 'EEA-like' rights status could have been perceived as unproblematic from the vantage point of Brexit. After all, Brexit was about the 'high politics' of sovereignty and parliamentary democracy. Yet this, of course, hinges on a view of politics which overlooks that interdependent, cross-national, and multilevel decision-making is now the rule of modern politics. It is, then, an issue of perspective. In the 'sovereignty' camp, one will understand Brexit as an assertion of politics, as a re-politicisation of UK law and policymaking. In the 'interdependence' camp, it can be construed as politicisation in the Brexit moment but as a form of political loss in the longer run, as the UK clearly loses 'its place at the table'. Moreover, Brexit highlights how complex interdependence sets limits to how far any one democracy can materialise citizenship rights, obligations, and statuses independently of other democracies. And here there are not one, but two, counterfactuals to attempts by the Brexit state to define citizenship alone: not just the way the EU has added a transnational dimension to citizenship but also the slightly different way the EEA has done that.

What does this, then, mean for UK citizenship post-Brexit? Two things are worth highlighting. First, the politicisation of the Brexit moment led to depoliticisation in citizenship terms. UK citizens lost their EU citizenship and, followingly, their voting rights in European Parliament elections. Second, it has led to a differentiation of rights *within* the UK. UK citizens in Northern Ireland, with a claim to Irish citizenship, can assert this citizenship to invoke EU citizenship rights in given situations while continuing to reside in Northern Ireland with all rights that follow from residence and UK citizenship. Yet, since Irish election laws require residence in the Republic of Ireland for voting rights in all elections, Irish citizens resident in Northern Ireland do not enjoy EU election voting rights (De Mars et al., 2020). In other words, this differentiated status is complicated and not without barriers to the full enjoyment of EU citizenship.

Market basis

When the UK entered formalised European integration in 1973, the EU was a customs union and a budding project of 'internalising' European markets. Surely, there were political aspirations among member states as well as leading politicians and intellectuals. Yet the market was at the core of European integration, a core supported by most member states and political actors across the ideological spectrum. When the UK left the EU in 2019, it was from a Union which has expanded in all directions, geographically, politically, legally, and economically. The UK has, however, historically enjoyed opt-outs from several of these 'expansions' (Adler-Nissen, 2014). Most concretely, the UK has not participated fully in the internal border cooperation of the Schengen system, the Monetary Union, to some extent the Charter of Fundamental Rights, and secured flexible opt-out/opt-in from the area of freedom, security, and justice. Reticent of 'federal' overtures, theUK has stood on the sidelines of such forays in further integration.

The upshot is that the market core of the EEA Agreement and its effects would have fit quite well with citizenship after Brexit. It is a limited form of membership, stipulates certain confined rights, and would have given both UK citizens and companies market access for their goods and services. The Withdrawal Agreement, however, means a break with the principle of free movement, both in market and citizenship terms. Except for the transition period stipulated in the agreement, UK citizens are now *outsiders* in terms of citizenship rights derived from the legal status of EU membership, as UK businesses are outsiders in terms of market access.

The example of EEA citizenship highlights how this form of market membership has expanded the economic rights of Norwegian citizens, both in individual and collective terms. Without an EEA-type solution, Norway would have had to resort to some form of free-trade agreement based on a more static form of implementation, as has become the case for the UK in the Withdrawal Agreement. Market access would then have become more cumbersome and unstable, possibly with economic effects both for individuals and the larger economy. An EEA solution could have been a viable solution also for UK citizens. While there were many reasons for the Brexit vote, it seems that some form of regaining *political* decision-making powers was at the forefront of the arguments for Brexit. An agreement with the EU which returned sovereignty to the UK in formal terms, while retaining some form of market and economic rights, could then be acceptable for many so-called 'Brexiters'. It would revert the UK's European relations back to a form of relationship that is more akin to the basis for membership in 1973 than membership in an enlarged and deepened Union today. Indeed, there was some argument of this kind in the referendum debate where some form of market access was seen as a precondition for a workable solution post-Brexit (James and Quaglia, 2020). In choosing the bilateral solution of the Withdrawal Agreement, the UK regained formal sovereignty but remains tied to the complex interdependence of the European market economy. When viewed from the perspective of *national* citizenship, UK citizens have thus gained in public autonomy over their economic system but lost considerable private autonomy in terms of civil and social rights they previously enjoyed as EU citizens.

Free movement, residence rights, and new parameters of migration

The issue of borders, mobility, and free movement was at the heart of the referendum debates and was one of the most contentious items of the negotiations between the UK government and the EU. There are several reasons for this; a main one is clearly the principled, symbolic, and practical significance of free movement of persons in the politics of European integration. In principle, free movement of persons is a constitutive dogma of EU law and politics. European citizenship has been proclaimed by the European Court of Justice as a 'fundamental status' for European citizens.

Leaving the EU through Brexit meant to address the issue of territorial control, both in a physical and politico-legal sense. It relates to a claim to reclaim control of membership, as those 'who are already members, do the choosing' (Walzer, 1983, p. 32). This understanding of membership has become blurred with European citizenship. As we saw in the EEA context, the Europeanised form of 'mobile membership' and rights is in full effect. Rights to free movement is a key feature of cooperation between the EU and the three EFTA states. It is also frequently addressed in this way by the EFTA Surveillance Agency (ESA) and the EFTA Court. In other words, the principle of free movement has become 'constitutional' also for the EFTA states. An EEA without free movement of persons would be a very different agreement bent on free trade but without the citizen dimension.

This pre-choosing of the EU treaties in terms of who are members of the (economic) community and who are not was, then, a contentious issue in Brexit. The UK chose to exit without retaining free movement akin to that of EU and indeed EEA citizenship. To regain territorial control implies to forfeit free movement as a principle. Indeed, it could be argued that wriggle room was removed from the start by an understanding of the referendum result as ruling out any continuation of free movement. There is a reciprocity involved in this as the legitimate bestowing (or removal) of rights means that UK citizens lose their right to move within the legal and political community that previously granted them basic civil and economic rights to do so. The Withdrawal Agreement involved some form of agreement on mobility rights but precluded the 'dynamism' of an EEA solution. The rights of UK citizens to reside on EU territory (and, conversely, for EU citizens to reside on UK territory) was based on a principle of 'living persons'. This means that those citizens *already* resident at the end of the transition period retain the residence rights that followed from the exercise of free movement. Citizens with this status had the right to permanent residence after five years, yet with certain restrictions in terms of continued residence. In other words: after the transition period, UK citizens are now, in effect, third-country nationals on EU territory. In contrast, Norwegian citizens are second-country nationals with a much firmer status to utilise free movement. Conversely, EU citizens have lost requisite rights in the UK, thus forfeiting the ingenious aspect of an EEA solution from the standpoint of the EU as this secures the rights status of EU citizens. Moreover, it can potentially strengthen their position when the agreement is based on dynamic development, both in political and legal terms.

As we saw in Norway, as the main EFTA partner of the EEA, free movement has become part and parcel of citizenship practice, individually and collectively. There is some debate on the consequences of this system, especially from a labour economic perspective, yet its fundamental place in the EEA architecture is not questioned to any significant extent (see also Chapter 8). There is, however, a main difference between the UK and Norway in this regard. Norway had to accept the 'whole' package for the EEA to become a viable solution. It was also understood as an agreement that would be temporary if Norway became full members of the Union. The UK left the EU through a highly politicised moment. The concessions the UK made, then, were of a different character. Free movement and migration were at the core of Brexit discourse. While the issue of migration was muddled with deeper issues of extra-EU migration in the Brexit debates (Ammaturo, 2019), it is nevertheless clear that the European project of mobility was central to the notion of 'taking back control'.

For many, in the UK and beyond, free movement of persons is indeed a main symbol and marker of European integration. Soft Brexit with something akin to the EEA model of free movement of persons was, then, not acceptable in the eyes of many Brexiters. 'Unfettered' free movement would, in this sense, go completely against the politics and logic of Brexit in the first place. Yet this decision of not accommodating some form of mobility rights post-Brexit neatly highlights the distinction between public and private autonomy in citizenship. UK citizens may have gained in public autonomy in the sense of 'regaining' parliamentary sovereignty yet significantly lost in terms of private autonomy as they no longer hold the privilege of mobile EU citizens, as they are now third-country nationals.

Conclusion

We have shown in this chapter how the public and private autonomy of citizenship is not seamlessly linked to national citizenship. Through EEA citizenship, Norwegian citizens have gained in private autonomy as individuals in society and the marketplace, yet they have lost in terms of public autonomy. Democratic citizenship requires representation in decision-making which Norway lacks in terms of what legal terminology dryly dubs EEA-relevant legislation. In terms of citizenship, this puts further limits on legal autonomy, as the individual rights that follow from EEA membership are constitutionally grounded in EU treaties and non-negotiable in political terms. More concretely, this underlines the lack of political wriggle room in citizenship practice, for instance as the rules on mobility follow from free movement as a 'constitutional' principle of European integration, including the EEA Agreement.

As we have shown, the UK could have chosen the path of the Norway model post-Brexit. The choice not to do so has significant consequences for citizenship. UK citizens have become disenfranchised in Europe. In addition to this loss in political rights, they have lost civil rights and social rights that follow from EU citizenship. Yet this loss in private autonomy as EU citizens has happened at the same time as a claim to considerable gain in 'parliamentary sovereignty', which, however, is doubtful viewed from the prism of complex interdependence highlighted in this book.

This underlines that the form of affiliation chosen by a third country to the EU has significant effects for the rights of national citizens and the role of citizenship in the political community. In a complex and inter-dependent world with high degree of cross-border integration, with the EU as a 'vanguard', citizenship cannot be isolated as a 'purely internal' institution. It is always affected by political choices in terms of a state's international relations as well as by its affiliation with EU institutions in the European context. Norway and the UK are two non-EU states that have taken different paths, with different consequences for citizenship. How we conceptualise these differences will differ based on the understanding of what citizenship is as well as what European integration entails. Yet, the facts lay bare: In affiliation with the EU, non-member states will experience that a gain in autonomy in one may lead to a loss of autonomy in another. In terms of citizenship, this means that there is no uniform balancing between private and public autonomy.

Notes

1 (See menneskerettsloven, 1999) [Law on strengthening human rights in Norwegian jurisprudence].
2 Case C-438/05, *International Transport Workers' Federation and Finnish Seamen's Union v Viking Line ABP and OÜ Viking Line Eesti*.
3 Case C-341/05, *Laval un Partneri Ltd v Svenska Byggnadsarbetareförbundet, Svenska Byggnadsarbetareförbundets avdelning 1, Byggettan and Svenska Elektrikerförbundet*.
4 Case C-346/06, *Dirk Rüffert v Land Niedersachsen*.
5 The fight for US independence was, in part, based on the argument that citizens could not be taxed by London when the colonies had no representation in the Parliament.
6 One exception here are those political parties and organisations who favor the dissolution of the EEA Agreement and replacing it with some form of bilateral trade agreement with the EU.
7 The Norwegian Consitution, §49. Authors' English translation: 'The people exercises law-making through the Parliament'.
8 Regulation (EC) No 883/2004 of the European Parliament and of the Council of 29 April 2004 on the coordination of social security systems (Text with relevance for the EEA and for Switzerland), *OJ L 166, 30.4.2004*.

References

Ackerman, B. (1991) *We the People: Foundations*, Harvard: Harvard University Press.
Adler-Nissen, R. (2014) *Opting Out of the European Union. Diplomacy, Sovereignty and European Integration*, Cambridge: Cambridge University Press.
Ammaturo, F. R. (2019) 'Europe and Whiteness: Challenges to European Identity and European Citizenship in Light of Brexit and the "Refugees/Migrants Crisis"', *European Journal of Social Theory*, 22(4): 548–566.
Aristotle (1992) *The Politics*, translated by T. A. Sinclair, London: Penguin Books.
Cohen, E. (2018) *The Political Value of Time*, Cambridge: Cambridge University Press.
de Mars, S., Murray, C. R. G., O'Donoghue, A. and Warwick, B. (2020) 'Continuing EU Citizenship "Rights, Opportunities and Benefits" in Northern Ireland after Brexit', *Ireland Human Rights Commission and the Irish Human Rights and Equality Commission*. Available at: https://nihrc.org/publication/detail/continuing-eu-citizenship-rights-opportunities-and-benefits-in-northern-ireland-after-brexit (Accessed 9 February 2023).
Eriksen, E. O. and Fossum, J. E. (2015) 'Introduction: Asymmetry and the Problem of Dominance', in Eriksen, E. O. and Fossum, J. E. (eds) *The European Union's Non-Members. Independence Under Hegemony?*, London: Routledge.
Everson, M. (1995) 'The Legacy of the Market Citizen', in Shaw, J. and More, G. (eds) *New Legal Dynamics of European Union*, Oxford: Clarendon Press.
Fossum, J. E. (2010) 'Norway's European "Gag Rules"', *European Review*, 18(1): 73–92.
Fossum, J. E. (2022) 'The EU and Third Countries: Consequences for Democracy and the Political Order', *JCMS: Journal of Common Market Studies*: 1–17.
Fossum, J. E. and Graver, H. P. (2018) *Squaring the Circle on Brexit – Could the Norway Model Work?*, Bristol: Bristol University Press.
Habermas, J. (1996) *Between Facts and Norms: Contributions to a Discourse Theory of Law and Democracy*, Cambridge, MA: MIT Press.
HM Government (2020) 'Explainer for Part Two (Citizens' Rights) of the Agreement on the Withdrawal of the United Kingdom of Great Britain and Northern Ireland from the European Union', *HM Government*, 16 October. Available at: https://assets.publishing.service.gov.uk/government/uploads/system/uploads/attachment_data/file/927349/explainer-for-part-2-citizens-rights-of-agreement-on-withdrawal-uk-ni-from-eu.pdf (Accessed 25 January 2023).
James, S. and Quaglia, L. (2020) *The UK and Multi-Level Financial Regulation: From Post-Crisis Reform to Brexit*, Oxford: Oxford University Press.
Kochenov, D. (2013) 'The Essence of EU Citizenship Emerging from the Last Ten Years of Academic Debate: Beyond the Cherry Blossoms and the Moon?', *International and Comparative Law Quarterly*, 62(1): 97–136.
Kostakopoulou, D. (2008) *The Future Governance of Citizenship*, Cambridge: Cambridge University Press.
Kostakopoulou, D. (2018) 'Scala Civium: Citizenship Templates Post-Brexit and the European Union's Duty to Protect EU Citizens', *Journal of Common Market Studies*, 56(4): 854–869.
Kratochwil, F. (1994) 'Citizenship: On the Border of Order', *Alternatives*, 19(4): 485–506.
Lenaerts, K. (2015) 'EU Citizenship and the European Court of Justice's "Stone-by-Stone" Approach', *International Comparative Jurisprudence*, 1(1): 1–10.
Maas, W. (2007) *Creating European Citizens*, Lanham, MD: Rowman & Littlefield.
Marshall, T. H. (1950) *Citizenship and Social Class*, Cambridge: Cambridge University Press.

Mathiesen, T. (2000) *Siste ord er ikke sagt. Schengen og globaliseringen av kontroll*, Oslo: PAX.
Menéndez, A. J. and Olsen, E. D. H. (2020) *Challenging European Citizenship: Ideas and Realities in Contrast*, Houndmills: Palgrave Macmillan.
Menneskerettsloven (1999) *Lov om styrking av menneskerettighetenes stilling i norsk rett.* Available at: https://lovdata.no/dokument/NL/lov/1999-05-21-30.
Mindus, P. (2017) *European Citizenship after Brexit: Freedom of Movement and Rights of Residence*, Houndmills: Palgrave Macmillan.
NOU 2012:2 (2012) *Utenfor og innenfor: Norges avtaler med EU*, Oslo: Ministry of Foreign Affairs. Available at: www.regjeringen.no/contentassets/5d3982d042a2472eb1b20639c d8b2341/no/pdfs/nou201220120002000dddpdfs.pdf (Accessed 25 January 2023).
NOU 2020:9 (2020) *Blindsonen – Gransking av feilpraktiseringen av folketrygdlovens oppholdskrav ved reiser i EØS-området* [The Blind Zone: Investigation of the Malpractice over the National Insurance Law's Residence Demands for Travels Within the EEA Area], Oslo: Ministry of Labour and Social Inclusion & Ministry of Justice and Public Security. Available at: www.regjeringen.no/no/dokumenter/nou-2020-9/ id2723776/?ch=1 (Accessed 9 February 2023).
Olsen, E. D. H. (2008) 'The Origins of European Citizenship in the First Two Decades of European Integration', *Journal of European Public Policy*, 15(1): 40–56.
Olsen, E. D. H. (2012) *Transnational Citizenship in the European Union. Past, Present and Future*, London: Bloomsbury.
Olsen, E. D. H. (2021) 'Norway's Approach to Migration and Asylum as a Non-EU State: Out, But Still In', in Ceccorulli, M., Fassi, E. and Lucarelli, S. (eds) *The EU Migration System of Governance. Justice on the Move*, Houndmills: Palgrave Macmillan.
Plender, R. (1976) 'An Incipient form of European Citizenship', in Jacobs, F. G. (ed) *European Law and the Individual*, Amsterdam: North-Holland Publishing.
Preuss, U. (1998) 'Citizenship in the European Union: A Paradigm for Transnational Democracy?', in Archibugi, D., Held, D. and Köhler, M. (eds) *Re-Imagining Political Community*, Cambridge: Polity Press.
Shaw, J. (2007) *The Transformation of Citizenship in the European Union. Electoral Rights and the Restructuring of Political Space*, Cambridge: Cambridge University Press.
Shaw, J. (2018) 'Citizenship and Free Movement in a Changing EU: Navigating an Archipelago of Contradictions', in Martill, B. and Staiger, U. (eds) *Brexit and Beyond: Rethinking the Futures of Europe*, London: UCL Press.
Walzer, M. (1983) *Spheres of Justice: A Defense of Pluralism and Equality*, New York: Basic Books.
Wiener, A. (1998) *European Citizenship Practice. Building Institutions of a Non-State*, Boulder: Westview.

8
AUTONOMY UNDER COMPLEX INTERDEPENDENCE

The case of Norway and lessons for Brexit?

Introduction

This chapter is devoted to the broader issue of autonomy. We have defined autonomy as will and ability to pursue an own (or self-chosen) course and, thereafter, briefly unpacked it along political, institutional, legal, economic, cultural, and epistemic dimensions. Further, we have shown that it is useful to draw on the debate on state autonomy in the comparative politics literature but with an important proviso. While the comparative politics literature highlights the internal state-society dimension of autonomy, we highlight the circumstances of state autonomy under conditions of complex interdependence. From this vantage point, the internal state-society dimension refers explicitly to how this dynamic affects autonomy in interstate relations.

Chapters 3 through 7 have examined specific issue-areas and legal-institutional arrangements and analysed the relationship between autonomy and wriggle room. This chapter is more explicitly devoted to autonomy. Focusing on domestic politics and society and zooming in on the conditions for autonomous will and capacity, it complements the previous chapters' more explicit focus on wriggle room. The main contribution of the chapter is the uncovering of analytical dimensions and distinctions of relevance for further theorising and detailed empirical analysis. We assume that the highlighted dimensions are relevant for all instances of complex interdependence and add empirical illustrations to reflect the specifics of Norway as a case.

Autonomy under complex interdependence

The first part of the chapter focuses on the aspect of will as a critical condition for autonomy. That aspect can, in turn, be broken down into a commitment to pursue an own – self-chosen – course of action on the one hand and, on the other, that this

DOI: 10.4324/9781003246961-8

course is chosen to pursue a defined goal (an interest or set of values). Thus, one aspect is about how self-chosen the course of action really is. On that count, the more the course of action has been self-chosen, the greater the autonomy. Conversely, the more others determine, the lower the autonomy. The other aspect of autonomy is ability, which refers to value and interest realisation. There is little sense in staking out an own course if one is not also able to carry it out. As was underlined in Chapter 2, both will and ability can entail go-it-alone or collaboration with others.

An actor who commits to a self-chosen course of action may do so with little regard to alternative courses of action. That is typically the case with a zealot (dedicated to the pursuit of a given set of values or ideology). That is an extreme situation though. Most autonomy-oriented actors will be concerned with acquiring knowledge of the options that are available and will adjust the course of action when important changes take place and constraints occur. If not, there may be action opportunities 'out there' that are better aligned with one's basic interests than the course of action that one is currently pursuing. As long as we are *not* talking about zealots or deeply engaged ideological and value-oriented actors, autonomy of will ultimately hinges on knowledge of one's interest; a commitment to pursue that; knowledge of the options available, and power over relevant tools and resources to pursue these options. Hence, an important aspect of autonomy is to keep abreast with developments and identify and evaluate possible alternative courses of action.

As discussed in Chapter 1, at the face of it, autonomy's onus on a self-chosen course of action may appear to situate it very close to independence. Complex interdependence marks contemporary Europe, politically and institutionally. As a consequence, when we consider Norway's (and the UK's) situation under such complex interdependence, autonomy cannot be gauged simply with reference to the extent to which each state is independent of the EU. Autonomy is equally a matter of the government assessing to what extent it can recompense for the limits on influence that the EU affiliation imposes through the ability it has to co-decide issues with others in structured collaboration. Autonomy thus refers to two ways of handling externalities: staking out an independent course of action, or seeking binding collaboration with others to increase overall action capability and/or prevent others from instituting unwanted measures. We can expect EU member states to be able to juggle these two aspects of autonomy differently from affiliated non-members.

Methodologically speaking, it is difficult to establish autonomous will-formation with certainty, without getting into the heads of decision-makers. The approach we take for establishing will is more indirect, namely to consider what actors say and what they do based on the public record. This approach says less about how autonomous the decision to pursue a given course of action has been, but it does help to clarify to what extent there is an articulated position, whether that position is pursued, and whether it is consistent with or diverges from that of other actors.

Applied to Norway, the issue is first whether the government has *a clear stance* on what it intends to achieve in relation to the EU and towards the world outside the EU, whether that stance is based on a continuous assessment of the available options, and whether that stance informs its actions. It follows that the amount of wriggle room that is available to the government in its EU affiliation is closely related to the government's overall autonomy. In other words, the more a government is bent on ensuring its autonomy, the more concerned it should be with maximising its wriggle room. Conversely, of course, the less autonomy, the less wriggle room.

Second, we can expect that an autonomy-seeking actor will *actively consider the relevant range of options*, assess each of them with a view to establishing how much autonomy each provides, and remain in constant dialogue and cooperation with others to discern necessary information and lessons in a situation marked by dynamic changes. To what extent does the government embark on an ongoing search for the best option? This question includes inquiring whether changes in themselves spur exploration, for instance when there are changes in the EU affiliation, new forms of affiliation emerge that could serve as benchmarks, and the EU undergoes changes or mutations with bearings on Norway's EU affiliation.

Third, we need to consider autonomy with reference to *capacities and capabilities* for dealing with complex interdependence.[1] What type of capabilities – fiscal, administrative, legal, educational, and so forth – does the government possess to pursue its interests? We may distinguish between two broad sets of categories of capabilities. One is about the nature, scope, strength, and ready availability of fiscal clout and administrative competence; the other is about the ability to compensate 'losers' of Europeanisation to prevent legitimacy losses. An important distinction here pertains to the difference between constraints caused by Europeanisation and those caused by wider globalisation.

Fourth, autonomy is affected by *internal and external constraints* on the government. We focus here in particular on internal constraints and are interested in procedural obstacles to change as well as possible 'veto actors/players', in other words actors with the ability to block government action or who are capable of instructing the government to undertake a certain course of action.

Fifth, it is a question whether the government *operates relatively independently from society* or whether it and its EU position are firmly rooted in society. The former is, as noted earlier, about the conventional approach to state autonomy that we find in the comparative politics literature. In the context of our research agenda, which highlights a state's autonomy in the international realm, the implications of state-society relations for autonomy are less straightforward. Conventional wisdom holds that a government that is separated from society should, in general, have more leverage for independent goal formulation than would be the case with a state that is deeply embedded in society. However, such separation does not necessarily translate into action capability, as a government that is well entrenched or embedded in society can have ready access to resources and could enjoy social support and a high measure of social legitimacy, both of which could help facilitate action. Further, an EU affiliation that provides for an alert society capable of giving the government input on how best to manage its EU affiliation can help to empower the government. Conversely, a government faced with a recalcitrant society can use

Autonomy under complex interdependence **163**

that as a leverage in interstate negotiations. The implication is that we need to look more closely at how internal state-society dynamics affect the state's autonomy in the context of interstate relations.

Autonomy of will

In this section, we focus on autonomy of will in the Norwegian context, asking: is there an articulated autonomy of will regarding Norway's relationship to the European Union? The issue is relevant because the EU is a voluntary association of states, which also applies to all the EU's affiliations with associated non-members.[2] Each state is therefore in a position to develop its preferred stance on the EU.[3] There are, however, limits from the EU side, which became apparent in the Brexit process – with the UK seeking a bespoke agreement and the EU seeking to place the UK in an already-existing mode of affiliation (with an EEA-type agreement the EU's preferred choice, at least initially).[4]

Who would articulate an autonomous will? Is there anything resembling a unified will in a modern dynamic and pluralist state such as Norway? In any politically elected government, there are legitimate procedures for establishing what should be done from a wide range of different preferences. To what extent do such procedures ensure that such a will is internally generated under conditions of complex interdependence? For our purposes, that means internal to Norway, not necessarily internal to the state apparatus, as is the concern with autonomy in the comparative politics literature (see Chapter 2).

On the first question of who, we focus in this chapter on the elected government and look for an articulate will in governing platforms such as coalition agreements, in the governing parties' programs, and in speeches by key government officials (such as the speech to the throne). The current government's platform is spelled out in the Hurdal Declaration (Regjeringen, 2021). It states,

> The government will develop and deepen Nordic cooperation in a range of areas. Nordic and European countries are Norway's most important political and economic partners. The government will stand up clearly in favour of an open and cooperative Europe at a time when authoritarian forces, nationalism and xenophobia are on the rise. The EEA Agreement will form the basis for Norway's relationship to Europe. The government will be working more actively to promote Norwegian interests within the framework of this agreement and the wriggle room in the EEA Agreement is to be utilized in particular to ensure national control in such areas as working life, energy and railways.

The declaration lists several bullet points. The government will do the following:

a) Expand and deepen Nordic cooperation in defence and security policy, economy, technology, climate and infrastructure;

b) Conduct an active Europe policy in a broad field so as to take care of Norwegian interests;
c) Take active part in and influence Europe's climate work and contribute to Norwegian business' ability to position itself to exploit the opportunities this offers;
d) Carry out an evaluation of the experiences of the EEA cooperation during the last 10 years. In that connection, the experiences of countries outside the EU which have alternative arrangements with the EU will be assessed;
e) As fast as possible enter a dialogue with the EU with the aim of ensuring that Norway gets exemptions from the provisions in the EU's fourth railway package;
f) Develop further the cooperation with Great Britain in the fields of foreign and security policy and sustain a broad cooperation across the North Sea;
g) Contribute to a reinforced cooperation in the fields of law and justice to improve the fight against digital and other border-crossing crime (authors' translation).

This declaration is less Europe-focused and places more emphasis on the Nordic region than its predecessor, the Solberg government's governing platform, which stated:

> The European countries and the EU are Norway's close neighbours, friends and most important trading partners. Access to the internal market through the EEA-Agreement provides predictability and market access for goods and services for Norwegian business. That is decisive for ensuring economic growth and welfare in Norway. Norwegian foreign policy must therefore start in Europe. International cooperation is fundamentally important for this government. The government places the EEA Agreement and Norway's other agreements with the EU as the basis for Norway's relationship to Europe. The government will seek improvements within the framework of the EEA Agreement and aims to conduct an active Europe policy aimed at increasing Norwegian influence on decisions affecting Norwegian interests.
>
> *(Regjeringen, 2018)*[5]

In comparison to the Støre government, the Solberg government put more emphasis on international cooperation and emphasised the importance of the EEA. In this connection, it is interesting to note that the first Solberg government had a 'Europe minister'. The fact that this was a minister without a portfolio represented a clear limitation on the minister's practical political importance.

Norwegian governments vary in their EU orientation, with centre-right governments generally more favourable to the EU than centre-left governments. The Støre government, a centre-left coalition, is more focused on obtaining exemptions from the EU than was the centre-right Solberg government, which was more unambiguously in favour of increased European cooperation. Both governments underlined the need to use the wriggle room available in the current EU affiliation framework, and both proposed concrete measures or areas for doing so.

It is obvious that the scope for an active policy at the EU level is more limited for a non-member that lacks formal rights of access to key EU decision-making forums in the Council, the European Council, and the European Parliament than is the case for an EU member state, and the EEA-EFTA countries have never actually exercised the right to exemption in the EEA Agreement. Nevertheless, as the previous chapters have shown, Norway has channels for exercising influence and forums for voicing interests and concerns.

The relevant issue from an autonomy perspective is how and to what extent Norwegian governments actively utilise such channels and seek and articulate opportunities. Norway is, for instance, allowed to send experts to the European Commission, either as affiliated members of Commission expert groups, comitology committees, or in more long-term positions as seconded national experts (SNEs) (the latter posts have a maximum length of six years and are supposed to work solely as loyal civil servants of the Commission). Whereas those attending Commission committees provide relevant sectoral expertise to the European Commission and enable the Commission to learn about the policy views of national administrations, those attending the European Commission as SNEs are included in the Commission services as 'normal' civil servants without any strings attached to their employer at national level.

For Norway to maximise its autonomy, we would expect the government to instruct these experts of any national positions and to monitor their knowledge of and compliance with these. Empirical studies, however, show a different picture. Those attending Commission expert groups and comitology committees tend to participate as independent experts with only vague and ambiguous mandates from their home government, and those attending as seconded experts are 'out of sight, out of mind' vis-à-vis their home government. The latter implies that SNEs behave as independent Commission civil servants and not as 'Trojan horses' of the member states (Trondal, 2010; Trondal et al., 2018). There is little to suggest that a serious change here has taken place in the last few years, which raises the question of the government's actual will to exercise autonomy in relation to the EU.

A passive government stance could come down to lack of faith in the ability to wield any influence on the EU. A useful test of that could be the so-called EEA-EFTA Comments. The European Commission organises public consultations in connection with preparing a legislative proposal, a policy, or a strategy, and the EFTA Working Groups prepare EEA-EFTA Comments in response to these (EFTA, 2023). A recent study of EEA-EFTA Comments between 1995 and the end of 2019 showed that, out of the 242 comments from the EEA countries, close to 40 per cent of the three states' preferences were wholly attended to (Karlsen, 2020). This suggests that there is some resonance within the EU. At the same time, the EEA-EFTA Comments must be agreed among the three EEA-EFTA countries, which presumably limits how extensively Norway can use these to pursue its interests.

In any case, the fact that there is a will to respond to concerns on the side of the EU suggests that there might be other factors accounting for the Norwegian government's passivity in relation to its SNEs. Might there, for instance, be a relationship between the level of active government involvement and the extent to which it is possible to form a unified will? In principle at least, the fewer internal tensions and disagreements within the political system, the easier for the government to take an active stance. The next section looks at the issue of unified will.

A contested relationship

Autonomy of will is much easier to obtain when actors with different interests are able to agree on a unified position. Historically speaking, there has been a recognised need for building cross-partisan consensus on foreign policy issues. In this context, it is important to underline that the issue of Norwegian EU membership has been one of the most politically divisive issues in Norway since at least the EU's inception. The issue activated old and entrenched cleavages in Norway, pitted regions against each other, caused a significant rural-urban split, and caused deep divisions between and within political parties (Valen, 1999). These effects were particularly visible during the two popular referenda campaigns in 1972 and 1994. What is the situation today? A brief survey of the party positions will provide us with a better overview of the range of positions and in what main direction they lean.

The Støre government (2021–present) is a minority coalition between the Labour party (AP) as the senior and the Centre Party (SP) as the junior partner. Thus, given that it is a minority government, it depends on support from the opposition, and the prime minister has pledged to seek support mainly to the left, from the Socialist People's Party (SV). There is, however, no formal agreement with SV in place.

These three parties hold different positions on Norway's EU affiliation. The Labour party underlines that Norway's EU affiliation is foremostly to be based on the EEA Agreement and the consultation arrangements derived from this. The EEA Agreement, the party notes, has served Norway well. The party is a supporter of a strong political cooperation in Europe and notes that, regardless of the EU affiliation, it is in Norway's interest that the EU succeeds in handling decisive challenges such as a responsible climate policy, the defence of democracy, and the rule of law (Labour Party (Arbeiderpartiet), 2023). This position is quite different from that of its coalition partner, the SP, which seeks to replace the EEA Agreement with a set of trade and cooperation agreements. Nevertheless, there are good grounds for saying that the coalition agreement is a form of self-bind in that there is a clear expectation that neither party should actively work to change the status quo. The SP notes that as long as Norway is part of the EEA Agreement, it should exploit the opportunities that the EEA Agreement provides for promoting Norwegian interests. The SP underlines that Norway must resist conferring sovereignty to the EU through the EEA Agreement. The SP is also determined to terminate Norway's role in the Schengen cooperation and reintroduce national border controls (Centre

Party (SP), 2021). Since the minority coalition is committed to look to the left for parliamentary support, we include the Socialist Left Party here. This party is determined to terminate the EEA Agreement and opt for less binding alternatives. It justifies its stance with reference to the notion that the EU is too market-liberal.

This brief overview shows that the parties that govern together from late 2021 are quite divided on the EU issue. What about the opposition? Is it more united or less united? Red, with some of its roots in a former Marxist-Leninist Party, advocates for abolishing the EEA Agreement and replacing it with a mere free-trade agreement. The party's stance is that the EU is far too market-liberal; and hence, an unravelling of this relationship is necessary. The Christian People's Party has historically been the most consistent and ardent supporter of the EEA Agreement and argues that it preserves national action space in important issue-areas, as well as ensures Norway's access to the EU's internal market, which is very important for Norway's economy. The Christian People's Party is thus a defender of the status quo but also notes that the collaboration with the EU ought to be strengthened in those areas where Norway has special interests and priorities (Christian Democratic Party (KrF), 2023). The Greens is committed to a debate on Norway's EU affiliation. The party program does not explicitly state that the party is in favour of EU membership, but the party's national convention in May 2022 clearly points it in the direction of eventual accession. The Greens are committed to close cooperation with the EU on climate issues and a fossil-free Europe within 2040. It will also, with its European sister parties, work to reform and democratise the EU. (Green Party (MdG), 2023). The Liberal Party has, in recent years, turned towards support for Norwegian EU membership over time (Liberal Party (Venstre), 2020). The Conservative Party has long been a supporter of EU membership, even if the former Solberg government (2013–2021) toned down its support, and underlined the need to preserve the EEA Agreement (Conservative Party (Høyre), 2023). Nevertheless, at the last party convention, a majority of delegates decided that the Conservative Party should work towards EU membership (Kristiansen, 2022). The Progress Party (FrP), as Norway's right-wing populist party, is against Norway becoming an EU member state. The party is committed to renegotiate portions of the EEA Agreement and is critical of the Schengen arrangements, mainly because the party is determined to increase national control of migration. It therefore does not want Norway to be part of EU's common asylum and migration policy (Progress Party, 2023).

If we sum up the positions, we find that there are at least four options in play:

a) Abolish the EEA Agreement, and negotiate a free-trade agreement with the EU.
b) Renegotiate the EEA Agreement.
c) Renegotiate Schengen (with or without changes to the EEA Agreement).
d) Apply for EU membership.

This overview shows that there has hardly been a harmonisation of partisan positions since 1994. We can, from this range of positions, expect governing to involve difficult negotiations and hard-won compromises rather than any clearly articulated will. What is, however, notable is that this situation has given rise to what we may term 'Norway's integration paradox'.

Norway's integration paradox

The paradox states that, whereas the question of EU membership has long been a highly controversial and divisive issue, Norway's comprehensive incorporation in the EU through the EEA Agreement, and a whole host of other arrangements, has profound constitutional democratic implications and yet has sparked surprisingly little controversy (NOU 2012:2); Eriksen and Fossum (2015); Fossum (2019). Rather than wrangling over every Europe-related issue as appears to be the case in Britain since before the Brexit referendum in 2016, the Norwegian political system has effectively removed the contentious EU affiliation issue from the political agenda. The situation is thus *politically deadlocked*.

What this means is that changes from the status quo of the EEA Agreement plus – either towards a less binding affiliation or towards full EU membership – have effectively been taken off the political agenda. The current affiliation with the EEA Agreement, at the core, is considered as the compromise that ensures access to EU's internal market and other EU programmes (a key concern for EU membership supporters) and, at the same time, helps preserve national sovereignty (a key concern for EU membership opponents). The effect of this is to clear the path for the rapid and dynamic EU adaptation that Norway has experienced since the EEA Agreement's inception. Some parties (especially the Labour party) are deeply divided and seek to limit the political fallout by keeping the contentious EU membership issue off the agenda. The parties recognise that they cannot allow the EU issue to block the functioning of parliamentary democracy. All parties have then also served both as opposition parties and have had shorter or longer stints in government or have supported governing parties during the period in which the EEA Agreement has been in place.

The main mechanism that Norwegian political parties apply to lock down the status quo is through 'gag rules'.[6] Such gag rules are to be found in government declarations or coalition agreements, which specify the government's commitment to maintain the present arrangement with the EU, through the EEA Agreement. We have referred to two of these declarations earlier. Norway has, as the overview of partisan positions shows, a multiparty system. The proportional electoral system places a high bar against any one party obtaining a majority of seats in parliament (Regjeringen, 2017). Hence, every government is a (minority or majority) coalition government, and the structure of EU support/opposition is such that every coalition will consist of parties in favour of EU membership and parties in favour of a less committing affiliation than the present. Thus, to avoid the highly contentious EU affiliation issue from destroying the climate of cooperation, each coalition agreement (including the present, as noted in the quote from the Hurdal Declaration) contains a statement to the effect that the coalition will govern on the basis of the EEA Agreement.

The implication is that a political party that seeks to alter the status quo – actively seeking EU membership or revoking the EEA Agreement – will violate the coalition agreement, even if that is not stated explicitly in the agreement. Especially for the large parties, it is a Hobson's choice: if you seek to change the EU membership status quo, you will no longer be able to govern. Such agreements have even been labelled 'suicide clauses'. Gag rules ensure that the status quo is retained; and in so doing, they facilitate the ongoing and dynamic Norwegian incorporation in the EU, through the EEA Agreement as the core. In this context, the formal status of non-membership is politically important. It provides symbolic reassurance of constitutional-democratic sovereignty and enables the no-parties to reassure their voters that they have successfully managed to keep Norway out of the EU. That the agreement can be understood to reconcile these two different sets of concerns would appear to be an important reason for why voters do not want Norway to be an EU member state.

Autonomy foregone

We noted earlier that autonomy requires knowledge of the different available courses of action. With regard to Norway's relationship to the EU, that relates, for example, to relevant changes in the EU that affect the affiliation, whether directly or indirectly. Directly affecting changes could be EU treaty changes, such as the gradual and stepwise incorporation of much of the Schengen Agreement in the EU acquis. The same applies to the entry and exit of new members, which alters the nature and composition of the EEA (the EEA-EFTA and EU). We may also include (the broader implications and cumulative effects) those issues that we discussed in Chapter 2 regarding expansion of EU competencies through sectoral spillover or the steady influx of legislation that is part of the consolidation and firming up of the EU's internal market. Of particular importance would be changes in the nature and range of EU affiliations with non-members. Do developments move in the direction of greater EU openness to bespoke agreements, or do they move in the direction of a narrower range of affiliation options?

In the following, we illustrate the difference between autonomy, broadly speaking, on the one hand, and wriggle room, on the other, by outlining an autonomy-maximising strategy: actors that maximise wriggle room do so within the bounds of the existing affiliation; actors bent on maximising autonomy in general are constantly on the lookout for the best possible option, whether that is in the direction of more independence or in the direction of more structured collaboration.

Our expectation is that autonomy-maximising actors will

a) keep closely abreast with EU and global developments and actively consider what implications they have for the current affiliation;

b) keep well-informed of developments in similar comparable countries (members and non-members alike);
c) actively assess and compare own practices with those of comparable others; and
d) develop a monitoring structure that either involves systematic (rather than periodic/episodic monitoring) and/or strategic monitoring with focus on the most consequential events or developments.

Autonomy maximisation would seem to require the near-impossible, that is, the monitoring bodies would be closely linked to decision-makers to ensure that monitoring results are fed into policymaking processes and political (including constitutional) change processes. The autonomy-maximising model is an ideal model. All real-life instances will fall short of that, but it could serve as a useful benchmark for establishing how much of a deviation there is. If we consider the case of Norway, the Foreign Ministry and other parts of government, especially the Norwegian Delegation in Brussels, as well as the parliament's European Consultative Committee, monitor and discuss European developments. Regions and cities also have offices in Brussels to be close to where EU decisions are made. It is, however, fair to say that this information is not systematically assessed with explicit reference to the implications for Norway's current EU affiliation.[7] The NGOs Nei til EU (No to the EU) and Europabevegelsen (the European Movement) do that, but both are advocacy organisations with clear stances on the Norwegian EU membership issue.[8]

There is no government apparatus in place that is explicitly designed with the task of undertaking any form of continuous monitoring of Norway's EU affiliation as compared to other affiliations. Neither was that included in the very comprehensive and incisive White Paper detailing Norway's affiliation that was presented in 2012 (NOU 2012:2). This important report did not spark much debate. The current government is committed to produce a new White Paper at the end of 2023. Neither report was, however, mandated to undertake a full evaluation of possible EU affiliation options.

This brief assessment suggests that there is quite a lot of information available, but it is not tailored to any systematic assessment of alternative options nor possible lessons from comparable countries. The present EEA evaluation has been criticised for only assessing non-members' experiences (Switzerland, UK, and Canada) and not EU membership. However, the mandate includes reference to experiences in Nordic states, the most prominent of which are EU members. The limits to the mandate are hardly surprising if we consider most parts of the political system's inclination to keep the issue of Norway's EU affiliation off the political agenda.

Viewed in this perspective, Brexit represents a unique development and occasion to examine how the Norwegian political system responded.

Brexit as an illustration

An interesting question for this discussion on autonomy is whether Brexit has spurred a reassessment of Norway's EU relationship, and the implications for the EU's relations with affiliated non-members. The centre-right Solberg government (2013–2019) underlined Norway's strong dependence on the EU (Haugevik, 2017). Foreign Minister Ine Eriksen Søreide noted on 20 October 2018,

> A position that we share with the EU is that we are very concerned about the integrity of the internal market, namely that it should not be possible to divide up the four freedoms and as such destroy the internal market [. . .] we are concerned about having a very close relationship to the British and a close trading relationship also after Brexit. But we must at the same time be clear that for Norwegian interests it is readily apparent that preservation of the internal market which provides us with common rules of conduct, market access, common standards etc. is immensely important for Norway given that 80 percent of our exports go to the EU. That includes the opportunity to bring in labour when we need it.
> *(Søreide, 2018)*

Fossum and Vigrestad (2021) show that the government and the major political parties saw Brexit as a challenge to a depoliticised status quo, in other words as we saw from the government declarations, namely a commitment to hold onto the EEA Agreement. Governing authorities rejected proposals for studies to explore the effects of less binding alternative affiliations than the EEA Agreement. In maintaining the EEA Agreement, the government was aligned with public opinion, a clear majority of which supported the EEA Agreement. Some political entrepreneurs sought to change the status quo but did not agree on what they wanted to change. If we consider the options that were discussed, they were as follows: renegotiate the EEA Agreement, renegotiate Schengen, or sign a less comprehensive trade agreement. The actors showed little appetite for a new EU membership debate. What is also notable is that whereas some political entrepreneurs stressed the need for Norway to echo the UK's onus on protecting UK sovereignty (through 'taking back control'), they would not embrace the UK's preferred socioeconomic model, which was far too neoliberal for their liking. Some Norwegian actors expressed concern about the EU's neoliberal turn and the problem of social dumping associated with labour mobility. Whereas this stance appears to dovetail with the Brexiteers' onus on regulating immigration, it was not the immigration-critical, right-wing populist Progress Party that was the most eager to change the status quo, but parties on the far left. The change-oriented Norwegian political entrepreneurs endorsed a socioeconomic model that was much further to the left than are the UK Conservatives (even those in favour of state aid). An important reason for the lack of explicit reference to the UK as a benchmark on the socio-economic dimension is precisely this significant discrepancy in understandings of solidarity and economic justice.

With regard to the implications that we can discern for the EU's relations with affiliated non-members, Brexit thus appears far more as a deterrent than as an inducement for change bent on emulating the UK's path. Whether this is mainly due to the tangled Brexit process or whether, at least for Norway, Brexit left little scope for linking sovereignty to the socioeconomic problems that actors associate with the present EU affiliation requires further investigation. Note that formerly EU-supportive social democrats largely share these socioeconomic concerns. In the Brexit negotiations, concerns with social justice and environmental standards figured strongly in the EU's demands to the UK, but this does not appear to increase Norwegians' support for EU membership.

The upshot is that, whereas the UK's sovereignty stance had some appeal among Norwegians, there was far less support for going in the same socio-economic direction as the UK seemed with Brexit.

Autonomy as ability and capability

Autonomy is, as noted earlier, about will and ability/capability. One set of concerns pertains to the intellectual and material resources that a government has at its disposal to pursue its aims, either alone or in cooperation with others. The other consideration pertains to the obstacles it faces, whether self-imposed or other-imposed, and what type of time frames are involved. We can further distinguish between other-imposed (non-EU) effects resulting from non-members' EU affiliation more concretely and from globalisation and non-members' autonomy in global affairs generally.

To illustrate the difference between resources and obstacles internally in Norway, we may consider procedural constraints associated with changing the mode of EU affiliation. Obviously, the lower the threshold against altering the status quo, the more easily the government can pursue an autonomous course of action. Conversely, the higher the threshold, the less leverage there is for immediate action. A high threshold is likely there because certain actors have found it advantageous. The nature of the threshold will therefore tell us something about the balance of forces associated with upholding the status quo.

How strongly is Norway locked into the current EU affiliation? Here we focus on the procedures Norway has for changing its existing arrangements. We discuss that under the broader heading of autonomy and not wriggle room. As noted earlier, wriggle room is about the scope for change *within* the existing EU-affiliation arrangement; autonomy is about the will and capacity to institute changes tout court.

Procedural constraints

We may start by asking what domestic procedure Norway must use if it wants to leave the EEA Agreement and what procedure it has if it wants to opt for EU membership. These are, of course, self-chosen procedures, even if the choice of procedure reflects the nature of the relationship and the character of the other party. The logic governing the Norwegian Constitution's provisions for change is that the more constitutionally invasive the external affiliation, the higher the procedural threshold for effectuating change. A formal change such as exiting the EEA only requires the government proposal to obtain a simple majority in parliament (the

Storting). Then the government informs the EEA partners, and the 12-month deadline for exiting the EEA is activated. The logic must be that departure from the EEA reverses the situation to status quo ante. That, however, disregards the way Norway has been transformed by its EU affiliation.[9]

With regard to EU membership, that is a clear matter of rescinding constitutional control, hence is subject to a higher threshold. There are two constitutional change procedures that are relevant, Article 121 and 115. Article 115 was used in connection with Norway's entry into the EEA Agreement. The Article states,

> In order to safeguard international peace and security or to promote the international rule of law and cooperation, the Storting may, by a three-fourths majority, consent that an international organisation to which Norway belongs or will belong shall have the right, within specified fields, to exercise powers which in accordance with this Constitution are normally vested in the authorities of the state, although not the power to alter this Constitution. For the Storting to grant such consent, at least two thirds of its Members shall be present, as required for proceedings for amending the Constitution. The provisions of this Article do not apply in cases of membership in an international organisation whose decisions only have application for Norway exclusively under international law.
>
> *(Lovdata, 2023).*

The threshold is high, as it requires a three-quarter majority in parliament. With reference to EU membership, it has become akin to a constitutional convention to arrange a popular referendum. In Norway, popular referenda are consultative only, which brings up the issue of whether parties will accept the outcome. Most parties have declared that they will, but some small parties will most likely not.[10] Nevertheless, all parties would insist on the need for a popular referendum to determine the EU membership issue. Some parties and politicians have also advocated the need for two referenda: one to determine whether Norway should send an application for membership to the EU, the other after the negotiations have been concluded to allow the population to accept/reject the negotiated agreement. The two previous referendums – in 1972 and 1994 – took place after the negotiations had been concluded. There is nothing to prevent a government from holding an EEA referendum, but there has not been any appetite for that within most of the political establishment. The upshot is that the procedures in terms of political practice are lopsided: more arduous to strengthen Norway's EU affiliation than to seriously weaken or abolish it.

A further question pertains to what procedure is required for changes *within* the EEA and Schengen and the other of Norway's EU affiliations.[11] In aspects of the EEA Agreement such as Norway's affiliation with the EU's system of financial supervision, Article 115 was used; this Article (and its predecessor Article 93) was not used in connection with any other element of the EEA nor with the Schengen association agreement. Legal experts have criticised the government for using the less arduous Article 26 in a whole range of issues, which have constitutional implications (Holmøyvik, 2015).

174 Autonomy under complex interdependence

The assessment of procedural constraints shows that it matters in what direction change are sought, since the procedures are lopsided: much higher with regard to opting for EU membership than for abolishing the EEA Agreement.

Competence and capacity

Autonomy entails capacity and capability that are readily available to the government. This can be both material-tangible and more immaterial and take the form of trust. In terms of the latter, an important trait of Norway is the public's high level of trust in government (Olsen, 2017, p. 107). That does not appear to have declined through Norway's process of adaptation to EU laws and rules. As Fossum (2019, p. 20) has noted, 'It is interesting to note that the EU-sceptical Norwegian population has been saddled with much of the EU's socioeconomic model and regulatory style, but that has not reduced trust in government'. The reasons for this situation help to account for the paradox of public hostility to EU membership yet acceptance of dynamic EU adaptation. The possible reasons for this are beyond the scope of this book. Suffice to say that trust can represent a legitimacy buffer that prevents negative experiences from rubbing off on the public's conception of the state's role in society. Norway has, more than the UK, been willing and able to compensate for negative effects of EU adaptation through a well-functioning state; a very comprehensive public welfare system and social security net; a comprehensive system of regulations and policies to ensure gender equality; and a very substantial fiscal buffer (the large pension fund is a case in point). Norway's close EU affiliation has meant that the state's role in the process of accumulation has been reduced, but not so in social protection and 'compensation'.

With regard to the more tangible forms of capacity is domestic public administration as an essential tool for good and efficient governance of autonomy. The overall well-being of citizens is shown to be nurtured by societies administered by 'impartial' public bureaucracies (Rothstein, 2012). Independent administrative capacities are more generally associated with what makes 'good' and 'living' political orders (March and Olsen, 1989). As noted earlier, Norway has a highly competent and professional public administration with a, generally speaking, high problem-understanding and problem-solving capacity (Christensen et al., 2018). That is clearly an autonomy-enhancing feature of Norway.

Europeanisation through Norway's wide range of EU affiliations challenges us to understand the effects of shared capacity across levels of governing. A government whose administration is tied up with other administrations can get access to much more capacity insofar as it is able to direct such a system of multilevel administration (Trondal et al., 2021). Conversely, if there is a system of multilevel administration developing that escapes government control, the state will be able to partake in multilevel problem-solving, but without much of a nationally elected governmental imprint. That will most likely be autonomy-reducing. The issue is therefore not only the government's possession of capacity, but the government must have a demonstrated ability to give direction to and exercise control of that. Norway's situation as a closely affiliated non-member is particularly precarious here.

As will be argued in the following, executive integration at the EU level biases and reduces the autonomy of will of national governmental institutions. Executive European integration has been pictured in the literature as a 'multilevel and nested network administration, where administrative bodies at different levels of government are linked together in the performance of tasks' (Hofmann and Turk, 2006, p. 583). Empirical studies of executive integration have focused on the emergence and consequences of regulatory agencies, European administrative networks, and how vertical and horizontal interconnections of regulatory bodies give rise to 'double-hatted' national agencies. Studies of EU agencies have documented their varied origins, how they are situated closely to the European Commission, and how they contribute to autonomise national regulatory agencies, making them double-hatted vis-à-vis both the European Commission and domestic ministerial departments (Bach et al., 2015; Egeberg and Trondal, 2017). This literature has, moreover, examined the role of EU-level agencies in policy uploading and policy implementation (Egeberg and Trondal, 2009b; Groenleer, 2009; Levi-Faur, 2011; Rittberger and Wonka, 2011), the interconnected nature of policymaking between EU-level and national-level ministries and agencies (Bach and Ruffing, 2018; Curtin and Egeberg, 2008; Egeberg and Trondal, 2009; Maggetti, 2014; Maggetti et al., 2021; Trein and Maggetti, 2018), and consequences for administrative autonomy (Bach and Ruffing, 2018; Bach et al., 2015; Trondal, 2010). Studies of European administrative networks show how they emerge largely from pre-existing network formations, how internally connected they have become, that is, in bridging the gap between levels of governance, and how they manage to influence regulatory governance, for example by providing knowledge exchange and facilitate learning (Polman, 2020; Schrama et al., 2020; Trondal and Peters, 2013). One distinct body of literature has focused on what is termed 'multilevel administration' (MLA), featuring particular institutional constellations and configurations that span across levels of governance. This line of research has been interested in understanding *patterns or processes* of integration of public administration institutions – not their outcomes (Benz, 2015). Administrative integration is thus conceived of as processes of European administrative capacity-building (Rittberger and Wonka, 2011) and processes of multilevel administrative governance of ministerial departments and regulatory agencies (Bach et al., 2015; Curtin and Egeberg, 2008; Egeberg, 2010; Egeberg and Trondal, 2009).

Ultimately, administrative integration may contribute to the transformation of administrative governance, measured by patterns of administrative autonomy. The MLA literature has argued that administrative integration across levels of governance in Europe essentially involves the rise of relatively autonomous administrative capacities at European level; that is, the permanent governing institutions that operate relatively autonomously of pre-existing political institutions at the national level (Matthews, 2012). Studies suggest that the European Commission has requisite capacities to influence governance processes within EU agencies as well as national agencies, making national agencies 'double-hatted', serving both as national and EU-level regulatory bodies. Further, studies demonstrate that the European Commission has administrative capacities to influence everyday governing activities of domestic agencies – making them, in practice, partly European and partly national (Egeberg and Trondal, 2017) as well as making them semi-autonomous vis-à-vis their parent ministries (Bach et al., 2015). As such, executive integration at the EU level has biased and reduced the autonomy of will within domestic government institutions.

Autonomy or wriggle room: the 'NAV scandal' interpreted

In 2019, the so-called 'NAV scandal', or social benefits scandal, shook Norwegian society. In Chapter 7 we discussed this as an instance of failure to comply with the free movement principle in the EU Treaty. In this chapter, we discuss the matter further, but now to highlight the analytical differences between autonomy and wriggle room. What we do in the following is to shed light on the non-compliance of NAV as an interesting case to illustrate the scope for interpretation regarding whether something falls under the heading of wriggle room or autonomy. One possible explanation could be that it was an attempt at exercising or expanding wriggle room. An alternative explanation sees it as a manifestation of 'autonomy in action'. We therefore present two possible accounts of how this scandal can be interpreted, in part drawing on previous research and evaluations of it. Our concern is not to give a full or complete empirical account, but rather to discuss two plausible interpretations utilising the distinction between autonomy and wriggle room.

The wriggle room account. The point of departure for this account is that there is a recognised set of EU rules that regulate activities in the social benefits issue-area. The relevant rule is Regulation 883/2004, which addresses coordination of social security systems across the member states. The regulation explicitly falls within the framework of free movement of persons. As a regulation, it is directly applicable and should be transposed as Norwegian law and implemented accordingly. The scandal, then, pertains to the lack of enforcement of this regulation in Norway. The wrongful implementation of Regulation 883/2004 lasted for more than a decade. Pavone and Stiansen (2021, p. 329) document that around 2400 cases were handled by NAV in violation of the principle of free movement and EEA rules with 78 individuals convicted of social security fraud and 48 individuals sentenced to jail time. The principle of free movement is akin to a constitutional principle of EU law and at the core of the EEA Agreement. It is, then, highly interesting that a government agency failed to comply correctly to the most significant EU regulation in the field of social security. The regulation goes back to 1971 when its first iteration was introduced exactly to safeguard the non-discrimination of European citizens that exercised free movement to work and live in other member states of the European Community.

Central as both the regulation is and the framework of basic individual rights that it builds on, EU member states and EEA states, in theory, should have little to no wriggle room in legal terms to circumscribe its application in practice. Yet NAV did exactly this. This can be interpreted as Norwegian authorities entering a form of 'blind-zone' of rule implementation, as the expert evaluation of the scandal coined it (NOU 2020:9). The interpretation of the regulation and free movement rights was narrow, with an administrative understanding of portability that excluded a range of unemployment and 'out-of' employment-related benefits. The rationale was that the recipient should be resident in Norway so that relevant NAV offices could monitor progress and follow up any specific measures taken in an individual case. This narrow interpretation can be understood as bent on exercising a perceived as well as willed wiggle-room. Seemingly, NAV and successive Norwegian governments have understood free movement to narrowly mean the exercise of mobility across intra-EU and EEA borders to work or study. This utilising of wriggle room has, then, not fully taken in the fact that mobility in European integration has long since expanded beyond work to be based on personhood: thus, free movement of *persons*.

The autonomy account. The point of departure for this account is that the NAV scandal is not only a case of legal wriggle room but also a matter of political autonomy. Here two versions can be found. One version would see the NAV scandal as a case of lack of capacity. The implication is that the otherwise very competent Norwegian administrative system lacks the necessary competence in European issues and therefore produces fallacious decisions. This account is premised on the assumption that it was the intention to comply with EU rules but there was a lack of adequate knowledge. An alternative account would hold that there was an attempt to hold onto Norwegian law even if that was in contravention to what relevant EU-incorporated law prescribed. This latter account refers to a practice that, at a minimum, straddled the legal boundaries of EU law and policy. Pavone and Stiansen (2021) highlight from document research and policy debates how the legal practice of NAV was paralleled by a discourse on so-called welfare tourism from the government. The portability of social benefits for EU and EEA citizens working and residing in Norway was widely debated at the beginning of the 2010s. This issue was linked to the sustainability of the welfare state in government-appointed public commissions and can be seen as indicative of increased gatekeeping from Norwegian governments on access to national territory, its welfare community, and, ultimately, to citizenship (Olsen, 2019a, 2019b). In the autonomy perspective, then, the NAV scandal could be indicative of a will to pursue a policy that is reflective of national concerns and places these ahead of EU regulations and their correct implementation. This can, moreover, link to the issue that the EU lacks administrative capacity of oversight and, therefore, ability to detect this form of wrongdoing. Tellingly, Pavone and Stiansen's (2021) main point and analysis succinctly highlight how the Norwegian authorities changed policy on the portability of social benefits only after it came under 'the shadow of the court', in this instance the possibility of an infringement procedure by the EFTA Court.

This all may come down to an instance where the Norwegian administrative and political system has shown the burdens of seeking to navigate a system marked by what we have called complex interdependence in this book. The NAV administration did not understand that they were operating under conditions of complex interdependence and seemingly operated based on assumptions of sovereign autonomy that link up with the political and public debates on the welfare state, migration, and welfare tourism.

Government-society links and interactions

The analysis thus far has shown that the EU affiliation issue remains a divisive matter in Norway, one that has prompted the political system to lock in the current affiliation. That has bearings on autonomy as it represents a form of self-bind that limits the scope for autonomy, especially in terms of assessing alternatives and seeking information on other members' and non-members' experiences.

This situation reflects for Norway a rather anomalous state-society dynamic. Most analyses of the Norwegian state would underline how embedded it is in society and how close the links are between state officials and interest organisations. Norway is quite typical of that category of states labelled as societally corporatist. The political system's depoliticisation of the EU affiliation issue effectively links (aspects of) the state much closer to the EU than the rest of society. The lack of Norwegian formal representation in the EU's governing bodies means that society is not 'woken up' by periodic EP elections and compelled to keep abreast with EU developments in the manner that the citizens and organisations of EU members must be (Fossum, 2023).

That in turn is likely to have autonomy implications. For instance, can we, in line with two-level bargaining theory (Putnam, 1988), posit that an alert and critical society can provide state officials with added bargaining leverage? EU member states, when negotiating in the European Council and the Council formations, can point to the difficulties of getting proposals past a sceptical domestic public opinion and, through that, obtain bargaining concessions. For affiliated non-members such as Norway, there is no such leverage due to lack of access to negotiating forums at the EU level. In this case the government is better off with a depoliticised society that does not question its actions. The implication is that the Norwegian government obtains more action leverage in its EU relations the less attentive and linked-in society is. But that comes with a cost: society is not involved in the making of the decisions and therefore does not in the same way feel ownership of them. From a legitimacy perspective, the existing affiliation would then appear precarious, which in turn places an even higher premium on the government not rocking the boat by discussing alternative affiliations.

Autonomy in Norway's/associated members' relation to the world

Is there an articulated autonomy of will and capacity to exercise this will regarding Norway's relationship to the wider world while living in the shadow of the external relations of the EU? The issue of external relations is relevant because autonomy is not only about Norway's relationship to the EU but also about whether Norway articulates an autonomous policy towards the wider world or whether its relation to the EU sets determinants for Norway's external relations. This was an issue covered in several of the chapters in this book (see Chapters 4, 5, and 6).

The distinction between autonomy of will and autonomy of action is particularly interesting with regards to Norway's and other associated members' relations to the wider world. Norway tends to align closely with the EU's foreign policy decisions. Yet, when Norway's preferences diverge from the EU's, Norway does not have enough capacity to act autonomously or counter EU proposals in multilateral fora. The EU is an actor that shapes important aspects of global politics, especially in the realm of global trade (Bradford, 2020). Meunier and Nicolaidis (2006) characterise the EU as 'one of the major actors shaping the multilateral trade agenda'. Damro (2012) points out how 'market power Europe' uses the size and harmonisation of its common market to influence international politics in its favour. The EU relies on pre-negotiated compromises when they arrive to make decisions in multilateral institutions such as the OECD and WTO, thus pre-empting disagreements between member states. While Norway has articulated an autonomous will (will-formation is intact), it lacks the capacity to exercise this due to the EU's power and negotiating clout internationally. In other words, Norway arrives too late to the decision-making table to influence the will-formation of its European allies.

Britain, after Brexit, has found itself in the same outsider's trap. Regaining status as a global power on the world stage featured prominently in the leave campaign's justifications for Brexit. Yet after Brexit, we have seen a Britain that has shown autonomy of will to stake out its own course in trade but lacking the capacity to exercise such autonomy. The failed trade negotiations with the US serve as a prime example. Boris Johnson's push towards the US quickly faded, and a UK-US free-trade agreement seems far away from becoming a reality. The Johnson government seems to have been more concerned about showcasing their autonomy of will than serving as an agitator for free trade (Heron and Siles-Brügge, 2021).

The result is that non-members' autonomy is constrained. Their will-formation remains intact; however, their autonomous capacity of action, when their position differs from that of the EU, becomes difficult to exercise.

Conclusion

This chapter focused on the broader issue of autonomy. As such, it focused on the two core components of autonomy: will and ability. The first part of the chapter spelled out what is meant by will or interest when talking about autonomy. One aspect that was underlined was commitment to pursue a self-chosen goal (an interest or set of values) and course of action. In a context of complex interdependence, this does not necessarily mean go-it-alone. In the context of complex interdependence, autonomy cannot be gauged simply with regard to whether a state is independent of the EU; it is equally a matter of assessing to what extent it can recompense for the limits that the EU affiliation imposes through the ability it has to co-decide issues with others in structured collaboration. Autonomy of will thus depends on establishing what one's interests are and be committed to pursuing them and having knowledge of the options available and power over relevant tools to pursue these options. The chapter underlined that autonomy presupposes keeping abreast with developments and identifying and evaluating possible alternative courses of action.

The application of the analytical framework to Norway showed that successive governments were primarily concerned with preserving the status quo. The Norwegian political system contained a range of mechanisms bent on keeping the EU affiliation issue off the political agenda. That gave rise to Norway's integration paradox which states that whereas the EU membership issue has long figured as a highly controversial and divisive issue, the country's comprehensive EU incorporation has sparked surprisingly little controversy. That can only be fathomed if we take the active measures to depoliticise the EU affiliation into consideration. The instance of Brexit did nothing to change that.

The chapter proceeded to consider autonomy with reference to *capacities and capabilities* for dealing with complex interdependence and queried what capabilities – fiscal, administrative, legal, educational, and so forth – the government would have for pursuing. We have focused on administrative competence and shown how Norway's incorporation in the EU renders those parts of the administration 'two-hatted', in a vertical sense. Such incorporation in an emerging European multilevel administrative order can be capacity-enhancing, but it comes with the cost of loss of national control. The chapter also considered autonomy in relation to *internal and external constraints* on the government. It showed that there are not only internal procedural obstacles to change the EU affiliation, but these were lopsided, much higher in the direction of membership than in the direction of leaving the EEA.

The chapter also briefly considered state-society dynamics and found that a depoliticised domestic scene would likely provide Norway with greater action leverage than a politicised domestic scene. Nevertheless, the role of societal constraints differs to EU member states. An EU member state that faces a recalcitrant society can use that as a leverage in interstate negotiations; there is no similar effect for Norway. Hence, Norway's EU affiliation is structurally biased in the direction of executive dominance.

Notes

1 This book focuses mainly on EU influence on third countries. A useful approach for studying third countries' influence on EU is found in Lavenex and Öberg (2023).
2 The EU is treaty obligated to include non-members in structured cooperation. Article 21.1 TEU states that '(t)he Union shall seek to develop relations and build partnerships with third countries, and international, regional or global organisations which share the principles referred to in the first subparagraph [democracy, the rule of law, the universality and indivisibility of human rights and fundamental freedoms, respect for human dignity, the principles of equality and solidarity, and respect for the principles of the United Nations Charter and international law]'.

3 There are treaty-based limits to what the EU can do, even in relation to members. The principle of conferral and Article 4 TEU.
4 Consider the famous 'Barnier staircase'. Available at: Slide presented by Michel Barnier, European Commission Chief Negotiator, to the Heads of State and Government at the European Council (Article 50) on 15 December 2017 (europa.eu) (Accessed 30.01.2023).
5 Regjeringen (2019) Granavolden-plattformen, *Regjeringen*, 17 January, p. 81. Available at: www.regjeringen.no/no/dokumentarkiv/regjeringen-solberg/andre-dokumenter/smk/2019/politisk-plattform/id2626036/?q=plattform (Accessed 30 January 2023).
6 For this notion, see Holmes (1995). For an application to Norwegian political parties, see Fossum (2010, 2019).
7 The Foreign Ministry in particular was heavily criticised by EU opponents in 1972 for advocating in favour of EU membership. See Gleditsch et al. (1974).
8 These two NGOs are explicit on their stances towards Norwegian EU membership. 'No to EU works to ensure that Norway does not become a member of the European Union. . . . No to EU works to prevent that Norwegian laws and rules – through our EEA-membership and in other ways – are adapted to the EU's internal market in contravention to the majority's basic views during the popular referenda in 1972 and 1994' (Nei til EU, 2023) (Authors' translation). No to EU does not explicitly state that Norway should leave the EEA. During the 1994 referendum campaign, the No side was divided on this issue. Conversely, Europabevegelsen 'works towards Norway becoming a full-fledged EU-member' (Europabevegelsen, 2022) (Authors' translation).
9 The Norwegian procedure does not pick up on the fact that the EU acquis should be understood as a distinct form of material constitution. The Norwegian Constitution has, in some respects, notably with regard to rights, been upgraded to reflect the situation of international rights granting entities (notably the ECHR) but has not, in contrast to member states' constitutions, been equipped with provisions to authorise European integration. For the latter, see Fossum and Menéndez (2011).
10 See discussion of this in Fossum (2019).
11 An overview is provided here (Stortingsbiblioteket, 2021).

References

Arbeiderpartiet (2023) *EU*. Available at: www.arbeiderpartiet.no/politikken/eu/ (Accessed 25 January 2023).
Bach, T. and Ruffing, E. (2018) 'The Transformative Effects of Transnational Administrative Coordination in the European Multi-level System', in Ongaro, E. and Van Thiel, V. (eds) *The Palgrave Handbook of Public Administration and Management in Europe*, Houndmills: Palgrave Macmillan.
Bach, T., Ruffing, E. and Yesilkagit, K. (2015) 'The Differential Empowering Effects of Europeanization on the Autonomy of National Agencies', *Governance*, 28(3): 285–304.
Benz, A. (2015) 'European Public Administration as a Multilevel System Administration: A Conceptual Framework', in Bauer, M. W. and Trondal, J. (eds) *The Palgrave Handbook on the European Administrative System*, Houndmills: Palgrave Macmillan.
Bradford, A. (2020) *The Brussels Effect. How the European Union Rules the World*, Oxford: Oxford University Press.
Christensen, T., Egeberg, M., Lægreid, P. and Trondal, J. (2018) *Sentralforvaltningen. Stabilitet og endring gjennom 40 år*, Oslo: Universitetsforlaget.
Curtin, D. and Egeberg, M. (2008), 'Tradition and Innovation: Europe's Accumulated Executive Order', *West European Politics*, 31: 639–661.

Damro, C. (2012) 'Market Power Europe', *Journal of European Public Policy*, 19(5): 682–699.
EFTA (2023) *EEA EFTA Comments*. Available at: www.efta.int/EEA/EEA-EFTA-Comments-1339 (Accessed 9 February 2023).
Egeberg, M. (2010) 'L'administration de l'Union Européenne: niveaux Multiples et Construction D'un Centre', *Revue Française d'Administration Publique*, 133(1): 17–26.
Egeberg, M. and Trondal, J. (2009a) 'Political Leadership and Bureaucratic Autonomy. Effects of Agencification', *Governance*, 22(4): 673–688.
Egeberg, M. and Trondal, J. (2009b) 'National Agencies in the European Administrative Space: Government Driven, Commission Driven, or Networked?', *Public Administration*, 87(4): 779–790.
Egeberg, M. and Trondal, J. (2017) 'Researching European Union Agencies: What Have We Learnt (and Where Do We Go from Here)', *Journal of Common Market Studies*, 55(4): 675–690.
Eriksen, E. O. and Fossum, J. E. (eds) (2015) *The European Union's Non-members: Independence under Hegemony?*, London: Routledge.
Europabevegelsen (2022) *Politisk program 2022–2023*. Available at: www.europabevegelsen.no/wp-content/uploads/2022/09/Politisk-program.pdf (Accessed 25 January 2023).
Fossum, J. E. (2010) 'Norway's European "Gag Rules"', *European Review*, 18(1): 73–92.
Fossum, J. E. (2019) 'Norway and the European Union', *Oxford Research Encyclopedia of Politics*, 28 August. Available at: https://oxfordre.com/politics/display/10.1093/acrefore/9780190228637.001.0001/acrefore-9780190228637-e-1043;jsessionid=05D44C57 26D193B86B6E0CB58C246C63 (Accessed 9 February 2023).
Fossum, J. E. (2023) 'The Norway Model and the UK Post-Brexit', in Fossum, J. E. and Lord, C. (eds) *Handbook on the European Union and Brexit*, Cheltenham: Edward-Elgar, pp. 362–383.
Fossum, J. E. and Menéndez, A. J. (2011) *The Constitution's Gift*, Lanham: Rowman and Littlefield.
Fossum, J. E. and Vigrestad, J. (2021) 'Is the Grass Greener on the Other Side? Norwegians' Assessments of Brexit', *Politics and Governance*, 9(1): 79–89.
FrP (2023) *Norge og Europa*. Available at: www.frp.no/var-politikk/utenriks-og-forsvar/eu-og-eos. (Accessed 25 January 2023).
Gleditsch, N. P., Østerud, Ø. and Elster, J. (eds) (1974) *De utro tjenere. Embetsverket i EF-kampen [The Unfaithful Servants. The Norwegian Civil Service in the Common Market Struggle]*, Oslo: PAX.
Groenleer, M. L. P. (2009) *The Autonomy of European Union Agencies*, Delft: Eburon.
Haugevik, K. (2017) 'Hva Betyr Brexit for Utenforlandet Norge?', *Internasjonal Politikk*, 75(2): 152–166.
Heron, T. and Siles-Brügge, G. (2021) 'UK-US Trade Relations and "Global Britain"', *The Political Quarterly*, 92(4): 732–736.
Hofmann, H. C. H. and Turk, A. H. (eds) (2006) *EU Administrative Governance*, Cheltenham: Edward Elgar.
Holmes, S. (1995) *Passions and Constraint*, Chicago: Chicago University Press.
Holmøyvik, E. (2015) 'Norway's Constitutional Acrobatics Under the EEA Agreement', in Eriksen, E. O. and Fossum, J. E. (eds) *The European Union's Non-members: Independence under Hegemony?*, London: Routledge.
Høyre (2023) *EØS*. Available at: https://hoyre.no/politikk/var-politikk/naeringspolitikk/eos/ (Accessed 25 January 2023).

Karlsen, O. J. (2020) *Decision-Shaping from the Outside: Measuring and Explaining the Degree of Preference Attainment in the EEA EFTA Comments* (Master's thesis), University of Bergen, Norway.

KrF (2023) *EU*. Available at: https://krf.no/politikk/utenriks-og-forsvar/eu/ (Accessed 25 January 2023).

Kristiansen, A. A. (2022) 'Landsmøtet vedtok EU-debatten Erna Solberg ikke vil ha', *Aftenposten*, 3 April. Available at: www.aftenposten.no/norge/politikk/i/47AmOE/landsmoetet-vedtok-eu-debatten-erna-solberg-ikke-ville-ha (Accessed 25 January 2023).

Lavenex, S., & Öberg, M-L. (2023). Third Country Influence on EU Law and Policy-making: Setting the Scene, *Journal of Common Market Studies*. Available at: https://onlinelibrary.wiley.com/doi/10.1111/jcms.13490

Levi-Faur, D. (2011) 'Regulatory Networks and Regulatory Agencification: Towards a Single European Regulatory Space', *Journal of European Public Policy*, 18(6): 810–829.

Lovdata (2023) *The Constitution of the Kingdom of Norway*. Available at: https://lovdata.no/dokument/NLE/lov/1814-05-17#KAPITTEL_6 (Accessed 25 January 2023).

Maggetti, M. (2014) 'The Rewards of Cooperation: the Effects of Membership in European Regulatory Networks', *European Journal of Political Research*, 53(3): 480–499.

Maggetti, M., Di Mascio, F. and Natalini, A. (2021) 'National Regulators, Regulatory Networks and European Agencies: Connecting the Dots', *Public Policy and Administration*, 36(3): 275–280.

March, J. G. and Olsen, J. P. (1989) *Rediscovering Institutions*, New York: The Free Press.

Matthews, F. (2012) 'Governance and State Capacity', in Faur, D. L. (ed) *The Oxford Handbook of Governance*, Oxford: Oxford University Press.

MDG (2023) *Europapolitikk*. Available at: www.mdg.no/europapolitikk (Accessed 25 January 2023).

Meunier, S. and Nicolaidis, K. (2006) 'The European Union as a Conflicted Trade Power', *Journal of European Public Policy*, 13(6): 906–925.

Nei til EU (2023) *Om Nei til EU*. Available at: https://neitileu.no/Om-oss (Accessed 10 February 2023).

NOU 2012:2 (2012) *Utenfor og innenfor: Norges avtaler med EU*, Oslo: Ministry of Foreign Affairs. Available at: www.regjeringen.no/contentassets/5d3982d042a2472eb1b20639cd8b2341/no/pdfs/nou201220120002000dddpdfs.pdf (Accessed 25 January 2023).

NOU 2020:9 (2020) *Blindsonen – Gransking av feilpraktiseringen av folketrygdlovens oppholdskrav ved reiser i EØS-området* [The Blind Zone: Investigation of the Malpractice over the National Insurance Law's Residence Demands for Travels Within the EEA Area], Oslo: Ministry of Labour and Social Inclusion & Ministry of Justice and Public Security. Available at: www.regjeringen.no/no/dokumenter/nou-2020-9/id2723776/?ch=1 (Accessed 9 February 2023).

Olsen, E. D. H. (2019a) 'Welfare State Discourse and Citizenship Politics: From "Silent" Policy to Steering Logic', in Engelstad, F., Aakvaag, G. C. and Holst, C. (eds) *Democracy and Institutional Change in the Nordic Model*, The Hague: Brill, pp. 76–93.

Olsen, J. P. (2017) *Democratic Accountability, Political Order, and Change*, Oxford: Oxford University Press.

Olsen, J. P. (2019b) 'Sentraladministrasjonen i en utfordrende æra: tid for ettertanke', *Norsk Statsvitenskapelig Tidsskrift*, 35(1): 4–27.

Pavone, T. and Stiansen, Ø. (2021) 'The Shadow Effect of Courts: Judicial Review and the Politics of Preemptive Reform', *American Political Science Review*, 116(1): 322–336.

Polman, D. (2020) 'Participation of Implementing Agencies in European Administrative Networks', *Journal of Common Market Studies*, 58(4): 818–835.

Putnam, R. D. (1988) 'Diplomacy and Domestic Politics: The Logic of Two-Level Games', *International Organisation*, 42(3): 427–460.

Regjeringen (2017) *The Main Features of the Norwegian Electoral System*. Available at: www.regjeringen.no/en/topics/elections-and-democracy/den-norske-valgordningen/the-norwegian-electoral-system/id456636/ (Accessed 25 January 2023).

Regjeringen (2021) *Hurdalsplattformen for en regjering utgått fra Arbeiderpartiet og Senterpartiet 2021–2025*. Available at: www.regjeringen.no/contentassets/cb0adb6c6fee-428caa81bd5b339501b0/no/pdfs/hurdalsplattformen.pdf (Accessed 25 January 2023).

Rittberger, B. and Wonka, A. (2011) 'Introduction: Agency Governance in the European Union', *Journal of European Public Policy*, 18(6): 780–789.

Rothstein, B. (2012) 'Good Governance', in Faur, D. L. (ed) *The Oxford Handbook on Governance*, Oxford: Oxford University Press.

Schrama, R. M., Martinsen, D. S. and Mastenbroek, E. (2020) 'Going Nordic in European Administrative Networks?', *Politics and Governance*, 8(4): 65–77.

Senterpartiet (2021) *EU og EØS*. Available at: www.senterpartiet.no/politikk/A-Å/politisk-sak/eu-og-eøs (Accessed 25 January 2023).

The Solberg government´s governing platform (2018) 'Politisk plattform for en regjering utgått av Høyre, Fremskrittspartiet og Venstre', Jeløya, Norway.

Søreide, I. M. E. (2018) *Møte i Europautvalget* [Meeting in the European Affairs Committee]. Stortinget. Retrieved from https://www.stortinget.no/no/Saker-og-publikasjoner/Publikasjoner/Referater/Europautvalget/2017-2018/refe-201718-09-20/?all=true

Stortingsbiblioteket (2021) *Myndighetsoverføring og EU*. Available at: www.stortinget.no/globalassets/pdf/eu_open/faktaark_myndighetsoverforing.pdf (Accessed 25 January 2023).

Trein, P. and Maggetti, M. (2018) *Reasserting the Center of the Nation State: How Supranational Institutions Reshape the Public Sector*, unpublished paper, University of Lausanne, Switzerland.

Trondal, J. (2010) *An Emergent European Executive Order*, Oxford: Oxford University Press.

Trondal, J., Haslerud, G. and Kühn, N. S. (2021) 'The Robustness of National Agency Governance in Integrated Administrative Systems. Evidence from a Large-Scale Study', *Public Administration Review*, 81(1): 121–136.

Trondal, J., Murdoch, Z. and Geys, B. (2018) 'How Pre- and Post-Recruitment Factors Shape Role Perceptions of European Commission Officials', *Governance*, 31(1): 85–101.

Trondal, J. and Peters, B. G. (2013) 'The Rise of European Administrative Space: Lessons Learned', *Journal of European Public Policy*, 20(2): 295–307.

Valen, H. (1999) 'EU-saken post festum' [The EU Issue Post Festum], in Aardal, B., Narud, H. M. and Berglund, F. (eds) *Velgere i 90-årene*, Oslo: NKS Forlaget.

Venstre (2020) *Venstre sier ja til EU*. Available at: www.venstre.no/artikkel/2020/09/27/venstre-sier-ja-til-eu/ (Accessed 25 January 2023).

9
NOT MUCH WRIGGLE ROOM
Brexit and the Norway model

When, in January 2013, David Cameron started the Brexit process by committing the Conservative Party to an 'in-out' referendum on the UK's continued membership of the EU, he made a point of criticising 'those who suggest we could turn ourselves into Norway or Switzerland with access to the single market but outside the EU'. As he put it, 'Norway sits on the biggest energy reserves in Europe, and has a sovereign wealth fund of over 500 billion euros'. Yet he continued, Norway finds itself a part of the EU's single market with 'no say in implementing its rules. It has to implement its directives'.[1]

In lavishing such criticism on the Norway model, Cameron was plainly trying to present Norway's relationship with the EU as a kind of *reductio ad absurdum* where arguments for Brexit would negate themselves. Just look at Norway, Cameron seemed to be saying, if you want to see how European countries outside the European Union just end up following EU policy and law without full participation in its making. On that interpretation, autonomy, sovereignty, and control of laws were to be found more inside the European Union than outside it.

As the referendum approached, the British government made a further attempt to suggest that if the UK voted to leave, it would have to consider a relationship similar to that between Norway and the EU. When, in March 2016, it published a report on 'alternatives to membership', the UK government listed the Norway model as the first of three possibilities. The second possibility was bilateral treaties. Those could, in turn, be multiple bilateral treaties like EU-Switzerland or a single bilateral Treaty like EU-Canada. The final possibility was no relationship at all with the Union beyond shared membership of third bodies such as the World Trade Organization. The Johnson government would later describe the latter as the Australian option. So, from closest to furthest from the membership that the UK was giving up, four country comparisons were used to understand ways in which the UK could relate to the EU from the outside: Norway, Switzerland, Canada, and Australia.

Once, however, the 2016 referendum decided that the UK should leave, the Norwegian option largely disappeared from British public debate. Apart from an issue of the *Economist* (2017) and a cross-party group of just four members of Parliament, few have made a case for the UK adopting the Norway model since 2016 or even said very much about it at all, apart, perhaps, to dismiss it as unsuited to the UK or to Brexit. That is also confirmed by Asimina Michailidou's work in collecting data for the Benchmark project from parliamentary and media debate in the UK. What was widely thought to be the main alternative to membership before the referendum largely disappeared from political debate after the referendum.

Some might feel that puzzle is not a puzzle at all. The referendum itself removed the 'Norwegian option' from the UK's political agenda. The Norwegian option hardly seems compatible with a referendum famously won by a campaign to 'regain control' of the UK's 'laws, money and borders'. Take laws. Norway applies a lot of European law, 75 per cent of it by some counts, which may even mean that, as a non-member, it applies more Union law than the UK did as a member. Take money. Norway pays into several EU programmes (see Chapter 1 and Four). Take borders. As outlined in Chapter 1, Norway is associated with the EU's Schengen agreements on the management of internal and external boundaries. Through the EEA Agreement and EFTA, Norway and the EU have even developed something of a shared political and legal order.

Hence, many have questioned whether the Norway model would be a form of Brexit at all. In Johnson's words, it would have kept the UK in the 'EU's orbit'. Developing a relationship similar to that between Norway and the EU would probably have provoked widespread outrage amongst leave voters who would have seen it as an elite trick to reverse the outcome of the referendum by keeping the UK in a strange kind of membership without membership, with its obligations but not its decision rights.

Yet huge difficulties also follow from not adopting the Norway model. The core problem is that a part of the Norway model corresponds to the institutions, policies, and laws needed for a non-member to participate in the EU's single market. It was not in the June 2016 referendum that the UK decided to leave the EU's single market. It was when it decided not to adopt the Norway model that even allows a non-member to participate in the single market from the outside. Given the conceptions of sovereignty, autonomy, self-rule, and control that come closest to providing Brexit with its common core, it is hard to see how the UK could have adopted the Norway model.

However, not adopting the Norway model means withdrawal from the single market at considerable risk to the political economy of the UK. It even entails problems for the territoriality of the UK. Although it has so far been rejected, the Norwegian option remains at the centre of a trilemma in Brexit. The Norwegian option is i) hard to reconcile with expectations created by the referendum of regaining control of laws, boundaries, and money. Yet it is the only means by which the UK can ii) participate in the EU's single market as a non-member. Excluding the Norwegian option also iii) limits scope for a form of Brexit based on a compromise between the territorial parts of the UK.

That difficulty is especially acute in the case of Northern Ireland, which is even a trilemma within a trilemma. Within the trilemma between i) regaining control of laws and boundaries, ii) a single market, and iii) a Brexit that could work for all parts of the UK, there was, in the case of Northern Ireland, the further difficulty that Brexit would unavoidably require a choice between i) a boundary within the island of Ireland; ii) a boundary between Northern Ireland and the rest of the UK; and iii) a boundary between the Republic of Ireland and the rest of the EU. Any, including the latter, could unsettle the territorial settlement of the British state itself.

That 'double trilemma' illustrates how little wriggle room there has been in Brexit, as defined in this volume, as choice and flexibility beyond what is needed to specify the EU's external affiliations legally. Thus understood, lack of wriggle room in Brexit had much to do with the nature of the EU, its law, its Customs Union, and its single market. But a need for a legal relationship that left little room to wriggle also had much to do with low trust of how British governments would behave after Brexit, and with difficulties in reconciling the Brexit project with hard choices over markets, boundaries, and the territorial settlement of the UK. Only the Norwegian option could have kept the UK in the single market. Only 'Norway plus' – keeping the UK aligned with the EU's Customs Union as well as its single market – or a version of 'Norway plus' scaled down to keeping just Northern Ireland aligned with the single market and Customs Union would have avoided any 'within Ireland' boundary as a consequence of the UK leaving the EU whilst the Republic of Ireland remained. But as seen, Norway, let alone Norway plus, was not regarded by Brexiters as a Brexit at all. As for a Northern-Ireland-only solution, they regarded that as dividing the UK.

The core compromise was, of course, the protocol that kept Northern Ireland aligned with the EU's single market and Customs Union. That may have been a 'poor man's' Norway model, without the governance structures of the latter. But, without an agreement on Northern Ireland, the EU would probably not have approved a withdrawal agreement at all. What had the last two and a half years of continuous wrangling been all about if not a need for some legal guarantee to avoid a border within the island and Ireland? The Northern Ireland protocol was, therefore, also the basis for Johnson's claim in 2019 to have 'got Brexit done' by negotiating a form of Brexit acceptable to the EU. Once, however, withdrawal from the EU was complete, the Johnson government threatened to withdraw unilaterally from the Northern Ireland protocol unless the EU agreed to changes. The UK government even accepted that would be a breach of international law. The Brexit project – which had begun as a promise to regain control of laws – was at risk of turning the UK into an outlaw. That might suggest a lot of wriggle room in exiting the Union to the point at which a leaving state can disregard any continuing obligations it has agreed with the EU or at least threaten to do so. But to the contrary. We have defined wriggle room in this book as room for manoeuvre within legal agreements. It cannot mean breach of legal obligations.

Understanding that lack of wriggle room in Brexit requires three things that have not so far been investigated together. First, an analysis of just what would be involved in the UK adopting the Norway model (Section 1). Second, an understanding of how the EU is constrained in the relationships it can offer to non-members, and why, therefore, the Norway model is probably the only basis on which it can let outsiders participate in its single market (Section 2). Third, an analysis of both the territorial and economic predicaments the UK faced in exiting the Union (Section 3). All that reveals two further things. First, how the UK has been constrained even in its own exit, even in defining its own *non*-membership, even in its own recovery of control. Second, avoiding the Norway model has not allowed the UK to avoid the main feature of the Norway model: namely some convergence with EU policy and law, let alone selective application of something like the Norwegian model.

The Norwegian option

It is not hard to understand why many believed that if the UK left the Union, it would have, at least, to consider a relationship similar to that between Norway and the EU. Norway is one of the few highly developed European democracies that have long chosen not to be a member of the EU. That, however, has not stopped Norway from developing an elaborate and ambitious relationship with the EU that can be seen as 'state of the art' in how far a European democracy can cooperate with the Union without being a member of it. As argued throughout this chapter, the Norwegian option is most obviously state of the art in including those institutions and laws needed for a non-member to participate in the EU's single market. That is not just a matter of the contingent political preferences of the main players and of what they happen to require in return for creating and sustaining a single market that covers much of Europe. Rather, it is a matter of what is logically entailed in creating a single market. All that is crucial, since access to markets has always defined the UK's understandings of how it should relate to European cooperation or integration. Brexit is no exception.

Building on Chapter 1 (with reference to Fossum, 2023), we take the Norway model to consist of:

a) Norway's membership – along with Iceland, Liechtenstein, and the EU27 – of the European Economic Area (EEA);
b) multiple other cooperations based on 70 further agreements with the EU;
c) a parallel Nordic model of politics and society; and
d) a distinctive political compromise within Norway itself.

The aim here is not to detail i)–iv) in full, given that other chapters in this volume do that. Rather this section introduces i)–iv) in ways aimed at understanding what might be involved in the UK developing a similar relationship with the EU.

i) The EEA

This is not a static relationship in which commitments are 'nailed down' to what is fully and explicitly specified in a founding treaty. Rather, in the matters it covers, the EEA aims at dynamic convergence, or continuous updating, of laws. Yet there is a crucial asymmetry. As noted in Chapter 1, a proposal for an EEA law is only made insofar as the EU itself legislates. Thus, there is a sense in which EEA law follows EU law. Dynamic convergence is on EU law, albeit with opportunities for Norway, Iceland, and Liechtenstein to shape new proposals for EU law.

What it would be for the UK to develop a similar relationship with the EU requires understanding of the scope and institutions of the EEA. The EEA was mainly intended as a means of including non-members in the EU's single market. However, the single market is itself hard to demarcate, free of multiple spillovers to contiguous policy areas. So energy, environment, and climate are also covered by the EEA and its commitment to convergence in laws. Even agriculture, fisheries, and trade policy with third countries are affected by the EEA, although formally excluded from it (see Chapter 4; Fossum, 2023). Two things follow for democracies that participate in the EEA without being members of the EU.

First, decisions about markets are also decisions about allocations of value, life chances, power relations, and conditions for democracy. Markets are semi-spontaneous orders. They are invisible hands that develop in response to the individual decisions of millions of producers and consumers mostly unknown to one another. Yet they are also creations of politics and law (Reich, 2015). The EU's single market – extended to the EEA – is a clear example. How well they work together through the EEA to develop and enforce shared rules on state aids, market concentration, public procurement, collective goods, and externalities will depend on how well participating democracies can provide free and competitive markets without monopoly rents, market failures, or forms of market power that can dominate the democratic process. Achieving those things no longer depends just on their decisions as single democracies but on their joint actions and collaborative rulemaking through the EEA.

Second, and closely connected to the last, a single market is necessarily a huge undertaking in shared law-making. Crucial is how a single market is so different and so very much more than a free-trade area. The second aims to remove tariffs or 'at-border' obstacles to trade. The first to remove 'non-tariff' or 'behind-border' obstacles to trade. Hence, a single market is a far more ambitious exercise in market creation and even a form of joint rule insofar as removing non-tariff barriers requires shared laws. Around 6000–10,000 EU/EEA laws – many of them linked to the single market – are in force in member states. Even national laws are then constrained by an obligation to interpret them consistently with EU/EEA acts aimed at market creation. It is largely because of the single market that the EU and the EEA have become important in how citizens are governed.

Consider John Rawls' (1999, pp. 7–10) observation that political rule and its fairness is a question of how laws, policies, institutions, and economic and social opportunities all hang together as an overall structure and 'scheme of cooperation' under which citizens can live their lives. It would be hard to argue that the overall structure of laws and of economic and social opportunities under which citizens live is unaffected by EEA law. Free movement of persons, mutual recognition of professional qualifications, rules for supervising and bailing out banks, regulation of data are all single market principles and laws with huge implications for citizens' lives. Yet they are all matters where the balance of rights and obligations, of permissions and prohibitions, is significantly governed at the European level. Participation in the single market – whether as a member of the EU or as a non-EU member of the EEA – also constitutionalises economic and social models. It constrains how easily laws regulating market structures can be changed through any one election at the national or European level and, therefore, through normal democratic processes of political competition.

Its institutions confirm the EEA as a significant form of political rule. It may not be fair to describe Norway as a 'fax democracy' that receives its laws by fax from Brussels. Yet, through their membership of the EEA, Norway, Iceland, and Liechtenstein plainly do decide many of their internal laws through the procedures of a political and legal order they share with the EU. Those procedures amount to a distinctive distribution of agenda-setting powers, veto powers, and adjudicative powers. In an important sense, Norway, Iceland, and Liechtenstein are brought within the European Commission's agenda-setting powers – its exclusive right of initiative – on EEA matters. If the European Commission makes a proposal, Norway, Iceland, and Liechtenstein have to respond as a group in spite of the perils of any of them rejecting a proposal, about which more in a moment. The three are likewise constrained in how far they can amend the European Commission proposal. In practice, there is much suppleness in the EU system. The European Commission voluntarily adopts many suggestions made by others, including non-EU members of the EEA which have a formal and institutionalised right to participate in the shaping of European Commission proposals. But since, as seen, any proposal is for how the EEA should align with EU legislation, there are limits to how far choices can be other than 'take-it-or-leave-it', making it all the more important that the EEA countries should be able to shape initiatives even before the EU itself legislates. If, finally, the European Commission makes no proposal, there will be no change from the *status quo*. Fritz Scharpf (2009) identifies why that is a problem even for EU members. As he puts it, the EU's consensus decision-rules only 'work first time round'. Once a law is made, formal or informal consensus can become an obstacle to amendment. Member democracies can end up burdened with unwanted laws. The more EU and EEA law cumulates over time – with EEA countries applying 75 per cent of the acquis – the more that becomes a problem.

For sure, Norway, Iceland, and Liechtenstein also retain veto powers, jointly and individually. Yet those veto powers are, in turn, constrained. In evidence to a House of Commons report on what the EEA and other ways to relating to the EU from the outside might mean for the UK, Jóhanna Jónsdóttir (2013a) – who has worked for EFTA and contributed to the academic literature on the EEA – questioned both of the mechanisms by which the sovereignty of the non-EU members of the EEA is supposedly safeguarded: namely their right to agree between themselves not to adopt a Union law into the EEA and the right – in the absence of any direct effect – of their national parliaments not to ratify laws proposed for incorporation into the EEA. As she put it, those mechanisms do not 'confer much real veto power'. Each EEA-EFTA government and parliament knows that – under A102 of the EEA – the EU can respond to any refusal to incorporate an EEA relevant law by suspending that part of the EEA to which it relates. As Jónsdóttir (2013b, p. 67) continues, 'There is a real fear that the entire EEA agreement' would collapse were A102 ever to be used. Given that the EEA-EFTA states would then lose their access to the single market' it is 'difficult if not impossible' for the EEA3 to say 'no' to Union legislation.

Finally, adjudicatory powers lie with the EFTA Court. But the latter aims at consistent interpretation with the CJEU (Fredriksen, 2015). The EEA is also committed to the EU's four freedoms of goods, services, capital, and labour. Nor could things be otherwise, given that the EU has partially constructed the single market from the four freedoms.[2] Yet that is a form of market creation that is premised on core principles developed by the Union. All that draws Norway into the EU's political and legal order as well as its single market.

ii) Multiple further cooperations based on separate bilateral treaties

The EEA is a multilateral relationship between three non-EU democracies and the Union. However, Norway also has, as noted in Chapter 1, more than 100 bilateral treaties and multiple informal or ad hoc cooperations with the EU. Some have claimed that Norwegian governments aim to cooperate as closely as possible with the EU short of membership, and to do that across the range of policy. So Norway's relationship with the EU consists of a pre-commitment to *integration* through shared law-making in matters covered by the EEA and a wider openness to forms of *cooperation*. However, it may be a mistake to assume that the latter will always be less entangling than the first. If Norway aims to cooperate across the range of policy, the scope of its cooperation with the EU will obviously be shaped by the scope of the Union's own cooperation. Here the Union is itself a mix of integration and cooperation, sometimes using its own powers to make its own laws (the Community method), sometimes coordinating the powers of member states through Union institutions (the Union method) (Bickerton et al., 2015).

Crucially the latter often involve instances where member states may find it hard to use and nurture their own core state powers (Genschel and Jachtenfuchs, 2014) – of internal and external security or of taxation, borrowing, and spending – without coordination at the European level. Even if each national government chooses how it will cooperate, subsequent choices may be constrained by previous ones. For sure, it is up to each government to decide whether they are going to use the Common Security and Defence Policy to develop defence capabilities or to divide labours in ways that allow all to benefit from specialisation. But once they decide, that constrains the capabilities and the partnerships that will be available to them in the future. So even where a non-member cooperates on a voluntary and ad hoc basis, that may still affect its core state powers and put subsequent constraints on how they can be employed.

iii) and iv) Internal roots of the Norway model

Even if history had been different and the UK had adopted a relationship similar to that between Norway and the EU as part of an amicable solution all round – without any rupture from the EU or any disagreement in British politics on how to relate to the EU from the outside – the UK would still have found it difficult to operate the Norway model. The latter requires a commitment to political compromise not just in response to a past experience with a divisive referendum but as a continuing way of doing politics. The EEA especially requires low politicisation (see Chapter 8 and Norway's integration paradox); or, better still, forms of trust, cooperation, and communication that ensure disagreements are anticipated when the Norwegian government is still able to do something about them through its participation in shaping Union policy. Several factors make that work. A political culture that rewards compromise. An electoral system that requires parties to work together in coalitions that are most likely to include at least one pro-European party and at least one more reserved party (Fossum, 2022). Divisions within and between the parties that create stand-offs more than confrontations (ibid). In contrast, the UK has a famously adversarial politics. At 40 per cent – or a mere plurality and not even a majority of the vote – the electoral system can allow a winning party to take all. Much beneath 30 per cent, a party can dice with annihilation (unless its support is regionally concentrated). The result is an extraordinarily competitive system with strong incentives to politicise and seek controversy. Maybe that is one more reason for doubting whether there was ever really a Norwegian option in Brexit.

Far from the EEA being a solution to Brexit, spill-back conflicts from the UK's adversarial politics might only have destabilised the EEA (Fossum and Graver, 2018). Recall that the non-EU members of the EEA must agree proposals and to do so as 'one'. Otherwise, they risk suspension of parts of the agreement.

That leads to the important question of how far developing a similar relationship would have required the UK to adopt all features of the Norway model set out in i)–iv) above and in the same way as Norway itself. If Norway has wriggle room in its relationship with the EU (see other contributions in this book), could the UK have wriggle room in adopting only some aspects of the Norway model? We take it that i) – joining or replicating the EEA – is the essential feature, without which it would make little sense to speak of the UK adopting the Norway model as opposed to some other way of relating to the EU from the outside. Yet it is not hard to imagine why adopting i) might also require ii) and iv). Remaining in a single market adds to common vulnerabilities that call for security cooperation; and, as just seen, it is hard to see how the EEA can work where it is not also a basis for domestic political compromise. So maybe there is not much wriggle room in the model itself. But maybe the EU could offer single market on some other basis than the EEA? Maybe there is wriggle room there?

The EU and the problem of non-membership

It might be objected that it is a failure of logic or of imagination to assume that existing examples – the Norway model included – exhaust all possible ways the UK might now relate to the EU from the outside. That argument might run as follows. The UK will have more options and more bargaining power than existing European non-members. It will not need to reproduce existing models. Rather, it will redefine what it is to be a non-member and possibly even do so for the benefit of others, like Norway. The UK might be in a better position than Norway and Switzerland themselves to use, adapt, discard, or go beyond aspects of the Norway and Swiss models in ways that contribute to a more balanced and comprehensive settlement between all European democracies that are EU 'ins' or 'outs'. And, even if all that fails, the UK will be able to ignore the EU by developing more global relationships. Europeanisation is the past. Globalisation is the future.

To argue that the UK has the bargaining power to insist on access to the EU's single market on better terms than the EEA is plainly different from arguing that the UK could manage or prosper outside the single market. For the moment, though, we want to concentrate on a weakness in the first of those arguments: namely, its mistaken assumption that the problem is only one of power relations. Not all constraints on the relationships the EU is willing to offer outsiders have to do with asymmetries in power between the Union and non-members. The EU is, in many ways, a 'vulnerable hegemon' (Fossum et al., 2020). We need to understand not just the Union's hegemony as the main framework of integration and cooperation in the European region. We also need to understand the Union's acute vulnerability as a non-state, multi-state, multi-democracy political order charged with the difficult task of providing multiple different club goods and international public goods from beyond the state, without the coercive means or resources of a state, whilst all the time depending on the active cooperation of states.

Take the following challenges in creating a single market between democracies:

a) As seen, a single market goes well beyond a free-trade area as a form of market creation. It aims to remove 'behind-border' and not just 'at-border' restrictions to trade.
b) Dealing with differences in laws that are 'behind-border' restrictions does not just require democracies to make some of their laws together. It also requires them to interpret and administer laws together.
c) A single market for some markets but not others creates problems of efficiency and fairness. A single market for capital but not labour increases the bargaining power of the first at the expense of the second.
d) A single market needs to work over time. Markets are intertemporal. Democracies seeking to construct a single market between themselves need to make credible commitments that rules will operate effectively and predictably in the future.
e) 'Good' and 'bad' externalities can be involved in creating a single market. If designed well, it can create substantial positive externalities. Each participating democracy will benefit not just from its own efforts – but those of all the others – in creating the single market. Rules can also be agreed for avoiding negative externalities. On the other hand, democracies can also make themselves more vulnerable by creating a single market. They may be more exposed to others free-riding on their provision of positive externalities. Failures to avoid negative externalities may be more acute within a single market. For example, negative externalities from negligent supervision of banks prior to the banking crisis in 2008 spread quickly throughout the EU's financial single market.

All that has implications for the institutions needed to create and sustain a single market. Point a) confirms earlier suggestions that a single market will need to be an ambitious undertaking in shared law-making. Yet b) means that it will not be enough to make law together. Democracies creating a single market will also need to 'subject themselves' to some mutual surveillance in the day-to-day implementation of laws and to some shared adjudication of laws. C) and d) imply they will need to commit to doing all that over time and over a range of different markets. E) implies they will need means of excluding free-riding and of enforcing rules aimed at avoiding negative externalities. Taken together, a)–e) are likely to require significant shared institutions and law: significant elements of shared political and legal order.

The forms of political and legal order they need to develop to sustain a single market between themselves, in turn, limit the conditions under which EU members can extend the single market to non-members. As Sieglinde Gstöhl (2023) puts it, the EU can only extend its single market to non-members by minimising a whole series of gaps: in the substance of market rules; in the time between their adoption by the EU and the EEA; and in the administration and interpretation of the rules. Hence the two distinctive institutional features of the EEA: first institutions that aim at real-time updating and convergence of laws; second, isomorphism with matching institutions on both sides (ibid) for deciding, surveillance, interpretation, and adjudication (see Chapters 1 and 2 in this volume).

Whilst, though, extending the single market to non-members requires equivalent obligations, it cannot involve equivalent decision-rights. That sometimes cruel asymmetry is the core predicament. The single market may be a collective good with positive externalities and agreed rules for avoiding negative externalities. But, as with any other collective good, it depends on exclusion. It depends on being able to limit benefits to those prepared to pay the cost of providing them. Since rules and laws are constitutive of the single market and defining of its positive and negative externalities, the key benefit of membership is rights in the deciding of single market laws. The costs then include any sovereignty costs needed to sustain a single market such as majority voting, the jurisdiction of a shared Court, commitments to sustain a single market over time in spite of some fluctuations in domestic politics, and obligations to participate in the single market as a whole without cherry-picking. Limiting the full benefits of full decision-rights to those prepared to pay the sovereignty costs is a condition for creating a single market at all.

Hence, only members can have votes or vetoes, or even rights to be present and participate in deliberations at the moment decisions are made.[3] Exclusion from final decisions yet participation in their preparation and cooperation and mutual surveillance in their implementation is the most that can be offered to non-members where the benefits of shared provision depend on everyone incurring the sovereignty costs of collective provision. It is no surprise that is the institutional form of the EEA. Hence our claim throughout that the EEA component of the Norway model amounts to that set of legal and institutional arrangements needed for a non-member to participate in the single market. Inclusion requires a non-member to commit to shared making, interpretation, and administration of laws, as well as dynamic convergence in all those things over time.

Nor is it a coincidence that the EU developed principles to guide relations with non-members at the same time as it began the single market programme, and that those principles have remained the same. The Interlaken principles (1987) included the priority of the Community's internal integration, the preservation of its decision-making autonomy, the maintenance of a balance of benefits and obligations (De Clercq, 1987, cited in Gstöhl, 2023); the integrity of the internal market, no 'cherry-picking' and a level playing field. More than 30 years on, the same principles guided negotiations of Brexit and of alternatives the EU was prepared to offer the UK to membership.

So when the Union insists there are not many ways in which it can structure its relations with outsiders – or that working together with non-members should largely be done its way, or that non-members should have equivalent obligations to members – it is not necessarily being doctrinaire or unimaginative, or even trying to drive a hard bargain, let alone dominate anyone. Rather, as the example of the single market illustrates, it is safeguarding what is required for its own member democracies to associate together to provide themselves with club goods or international public goods or even to make certain kinds of choice at all. Nor is the problem just a functional or technical one of how to provide certain collective goods or manage particular externalities. It is also one of rights and values. Requiring non-members to agree rights and values if they are to participate in Union decisions may be a condition if the Union and its member democracies are to base their own decisions on those rights and values. As remarked during the Brexit process (Barnier, 2021), there are limits to how the Union can include outsiders in its decisions without ceasing to be the EU. Again, there is vulnerability as well as hegemony in all that (Fossum, 2023).

Membership and non-membership, therefore, shape one another. The kinds of relationship that the EU can offer non-members depend on what positive externalities its members are trying to provide and what negative externalities they are trying to avoid through their membership of the Union. Conversely, forms of non-membership will affect judgements of whether it is better for a European democracy to seek solutions to collective action problems from inside or outside the EU.

This section suggests rather little wriggle room. There just are some things that will need to be done and some relationships and behaviours that will need to be excluded if the EU and other European democracies are to manage collective action problems. Yet such wriggle room as there is will not necessarily follow power. There may even be a paradox of weakness. The EU may be less vulnerable to including smaller non-members in its policies and institutions precisely because they are less likely to disrupt its complex and delicate systems of politics, laws, markets, as well as its means of providing positive externalities and avoiding negative externalities between its own members.

The Norway model and the UK's Brexit predicaments

Maybe the Norway model is a bit like a child who has inherited some of the most distinctive features of both its parents. It is a product of Norwegian politics and society and of the EU's distinctive political and legal order. For Norway, it is a form of domestic political compromise. For the EU, it is a relationship that it can offer non-members that is shaped by the Union's own role in providing its members with collective goods and means of avoiding negative externalities. In contrast to the first, UK domestic politics are adversarial. In tension with the second, the UK is an ex-member that gave up its membership because it seemingly had insufficient control of its own laws. How, then, can it accept a form of non-membership that necessarily involves many of the same laws but fewer decision-rights and, therefore, less control? Close investigation of how the Norway model works for Norway and the EU only reinforces doubts that it can be made to work for the UK.

Yet the UK also faces unresolved problems in *not* adopting the Norway model. That will become clearer if we briefly consider how this model did not entirely disappear from the politics of Brexit after 2016. Even after the probability of the UK adopting it was supposedly laid to rest by a referendum won on a promise to regain control of British laws, the Norwegian option might have been raised from the dead as part of a compromise solution, a temporary solution, or a partial solution. Above all, even if the UK has nothing to do with it, the Norway model will remain a benchmark against which Brexit needs to be compared and evaluated.

The Norway model as compromise

Just as there were aspects of the referendum outcome that seemed to rule out the Norwegian option, there were others that argued for considering it. The narrowness of the result (52:48 per cent) and the fact that two parts of the UK (Northern Ireland and Scotland) had voted against leaving the Union might have suggested a questionable mandate for a hard Brexit and a need to compromise on a soft Brexit, defined either as a Customs Union or the Norwegian option of remaining in a single market with the EU. The referendum had decided neither how the UK should leave the EU nor any alternatives to membership. The alternatives – the Norway model included – needed to be democratically debated and decided in relation to one another. Whether that ever happened comes down to a judgement about the 2017 and 2019 elections – which were the main opportunities that the public had to decide the form of any Brexit – and parliamentary debate in between. Was the rather slender consideration of the Norwegian option a failure of public debate or part of a well-thought-out understanding that it was not worth exploring as a plausible basis for compromise?

As a form of social compromise, the Norway model may even have been well suited to Brexit. A large part of the leave vote believed that the UK's economy and society had become fundamentally unfair through its membership of the Union. Parts of the UK had grown rich. Others had been left behind. Whether, however, the whole complex of institutions, policies, and laws that define a country's participation in the single market creates fair opportunities is not just a product of European single market law. It also depends on how national policy and law works alongside, filling some of the gaps in single market law and counterbalancing some of its problems. The Norway model acknowledges precisely that. Norway is a highly open and strongly competitive market economy. Yet rules of production and exchange are expected to cohere with the social entitlements and protections of a still-ambitious welfare state. Norway has matched participation in the EU's single market rules with 'flanking' policies aimed at compensation, adjustment, and avoiding any 'falling behind' (see also Chapter 8). Compensatory policies at the national level accompany European commitments to single market rules. If Norway has found scope for autonomy for domestic policy within its single market commitments, could the UK achieve something similar by adopting the Norway model?

Perhaps the main obstacle was that it was less obvious the Norway model would have been a constitutional compromise within the UK on questions of sovereignty. Yet even that is not entirely implausible. At the same time as it cooperates widely and closely with the EU, Norway avoids several important commitments to the EU's political and legal order and to the process of integration. There is no primacy of EU law over Norwegian law. Nor is there direct effect of EU law in Norway. Nor is there a commitment to a form of political association aimed at 'ever closer Union' through a process of continuing and cumulative European integration. Norway is a non-member state and is, therefore, of course, not in the Eurozone.

Moreover, the Norwegian option was not entirely implausible from a point of view of developments in the British constitution between 1973 and 2020, especially in rights jurisprudence and in the territorial (re)settlement of the UK. Precisely because it started off from such a strong conception of parliamentary sovereignty, the UK went further than most in using membership to transform its own internal political order. The UK used EU membership to develop rights that had previously been hard to guarantee in a system of parliamentary sovereignty and to entrench a new territorial settlement through devolutions of powers to Northern Ireland, Scotland, and Wales. A political system that had already qualified parliamentary sovereignty in relation to the EU could more credibly commit to not using parliamentary sovereignty to alter rights or devolutions of power to Northern Ireland, Scotland, and Wales at the whim of changing majorities in the Westminster Parliament.

Of the forms of 'non-membership' of the EU available to the UK, the Norwegian option was the least likely to depart from the partially Europeanised constitution that the UK developed as a member state. EEA law gives individuals standing (see Chapter 7). They can use EEA law against their own governments. Norway's participation in the EU's single market is through its commitment to the EU four freedoms and principles of non-discrimination or, in other words, precisely the European law which British Courts used before 2016 to develop rights law. If the willingness of the UK Parliament to limit its sovereignty in favour of the EU helped reassure devolved governments within the UK that Westminster accepted limits to parliamentary absolutism, might not willingness to limit sovereignty in favour of the EEA offer similar reassurance? In contrast, leaving the single market by leaving the EEA poses its own difficulties for the UK's devolution settlement. The reversion of internal market powers to Westminster means that Scotland and Northern Ireland are now at the mercy of largely English majorities on questions of market regulation.

For sure, adopting the Norway model would even have been a provocation, not a compromise, for those who believed that shared law-making through EU institutions and procedures – let alone their EEA equivalents – had become incompatible with the *overall* sovereignty of the British state. Yet foregoing the Norway model also weakened other compromises important to the territorial parts of the British state (Keating, 2021). Avoiding a border on the island of Ireland was crucial to the peace process and even to maintaining consent to Northern Ireland itself. For many in Northern Ireland, consent was premised on an agreement to hold a vote on Irish unification should there ever be evidence that it would be supported by a majority. A physical border would challenge the credibility of that commitment. As seen, that predicament could only be avoided by keeping the whole of the UK in a Customs Union and a single market in Goods with the EU, or by just keeping Northern Ireland in a Customs Union and single market with the EU. The first was the May deal. The second was the Johnson deal. Both overlapped with the Norway model since both contained some element of alignment with the single market. There was little wriggle room in the negotiations. The EU insisted the UK should choose the one or the other.

Indeed, the May deal was itself at, or even beyond, the limits of any wriggle room. Since it would give the UK significant access to the Customs Union and single market without the full obligations of EU membership, the May deal was almost as deeply disliked by the EU as by many in May's own party. A further problem – which shows how lack of trust diminishes wriggle room – was that the EU also had to allow for the possibility that the UK might unilaterally withdraw from any Customs Union. That seemed likely if May was replaced by a hard Brexiter or if a future Conservative government lost control of European policy to multiple veto holders, including, of course, those opposed to remaining in a Customs Union or a single market for goods. But if the UK backed out of an all-UK Customs Union and single market in goods, the EU and the Republic of Ireland could then be forced either to create a within-Ireland boundary after all or to introduce restrictions between Ireland and the rest of the EU. Ireland would then, in effect, have been forced out of full participation in the EU's single market and Customs Union by Brexit. Hence, the EU's initial response to May's proposal for an all-UK Customs Union and single market with the EU in goods was not to regard it as an alternative to only keeping only Northern Ireland aligned with the single market and Customs Union but as something that would be needed in addition. In what came to be known as 'the double back stop', the EU wanted Northern Ireland to remain aligned as an insurance against any breakdown in the wider agreement to keep the whole of the UK in a Customs Union and single market in goods with the EU until both sides could agree that new technologies made it possible to track all trade without a physical boundary in the island of Ireland. Although the EU dropped it as a 'headline demand', a double backstop, arguably, remained implicit in the detail of May's withdrawal agreement with the EU.

However, it was, of course, the Johnson deal, and not May deal, that was ratified by both sides. But, once again, there was little wriggle room. The EU was only prepared to negotiate a different deal by reverting to its own original proposal for keeping Northern Ireland alone aligned with the single market and Customs Union. But if he agreed that divided the UK – that the UK was not exiting as one – Johnson could only secure wriggle room by presenting the deal as an 'oven-ready Brexit', by winning a majority for it in an election, and then by unilaterally reopening the deal once it had been ratified, about which more in the conclusion.

The Norway model as benchmark

However, even without being adopted, the Norway model also remains central to Brexit as a benchmark. Catherine De Vries (2017) argues that Brexit creates a counterfactual to European integration: an example of a major European democracy outside the Union that makes it easier to compare non-membership with membership.[4] Yet the Norway model is, in turn, a counterfactual to the hard form of Brexit eventually adopted. It is a softer form of Brexit that 'might have been' and against which harder forms of Brexit may need to be justified. It is the decision not to adopt the key component of the Norway model by also leaving the EEA that tests how well the UK can manage outside the single market. Just what follows from not using the Norway model to remain in the single market can only be understood historically as the latest episode in a 70-year struggle by the UK and its governments to decide how best to combine markets, sovereignty, and autonomy once access to markets in their most immediate neighbourhood came to be governed by the rules of a shared European political order which increasingly had its own constitutional principles, laws, institutions, and decision rules. The UK has always had a markets/sovereignty predicament in its relationship to European integration. Both the UK's rejection of the Norway model – and the UK's attempts to find wriggle room for market access without using the Norway model to remain in the single market – require a brief sketch of how the UK's markets/sovereignty predicament had evolved over time and how it eventually shaped Brexit.

Sovereignty was important to the UK's 'absence from the creation' (Lord, 1996) of the European Communities in the 1950s. Access to markets was crucial to the UK's decision from 1961 to seek membership of the European Communities after all. So much so that three years earlier, the Prime Minister, Harold Macmillan, had even considered sanctions and a review of the UK's commitment to NATO if the newly formed European Communities did not also form a free-trade area with the UK (Milward, 2002). Part of that despair was a structural difficulty that has always dogged relations between EU 'ins' and 'outs'. As seen, creating a shared market – whether the original common market aimed at removing tariffs or the more ambitious single market aimed at removing non-tariff barriers from the 1980s onwards – is a club good. In an ideal world, democracies would be able to form as many clubs as they want. But if the optimal scale only allows for one club, any club that emerges may be a natural monopoly, even without anyone intending it. The EU has, arguably, been the dominant club for market integration in Europe since its inception. That makes things hard for any European democracy that is divided within itself on any institutional and constitutional principles on which an integrated European market is based. If they go in, they may have to adopt unwanted rules and accept institutions designed by early movers. If they stay out, they may have limited means of forming alternative clubs to provide some crucial goods. Remaining outside would be a competitive disadvantage. Going in would risk domestic disagreement on the legitimacy of the shared market and of the laws, procedures, and institutions that define it.

After 1973, the UK was, however, at least able to manage that predicament from inside the EU. Shaping how markets and sovereignty would relate to one another as a member with full decision rights was quite different to doing so as a supplicant for membership. Before, however, identifying how UK governments came by (2016) to combine sovereignty and markets, we need to say some more about the centrality of markets to UK policy on European integration. It is hard to understand UK accession in 1973 – and its confirmation in a referendum in 1975 – without also understanding a near obsession with the idea that the UK had been in long-term relative decline since the 1870s. Nor is it possible to understand the hegemony of neoliberalism in British economic thinking since the 1980s apart from a belief that decline had been reversed by Thatcher's economic policies. Yet the EU's single market and Thatcher's structural reforms at least complemented one another. Some (Campos and Coricelli, 2017) have even suggested that ever closer access to European markets – first as a result of accession in 1973 and then through the Single Market programme from 1986 – contributed even more than Thatcher's own domestic reforms to the regeneration of the British economy.

Later, the financial single market contributed massively to the UK's tax base (Armstrong, 2016) without which it would have been hard for the UK to sustain a financial sector that was five times GNP. The single market created a virtuous circle between the economies of scale and scope of the UK's financial sector, UK tax revenues, and the ability of the UK to guarantee its financial system. As a former member of the Bank of England's Monetary Policy Committee (Buiter, 2008) has put it, the UK role as a 'floating hedge fund' was only as good as the solvency of its governments. The single market even enabled the UK to emerge as the financial centre of the Eurozone without being a member of the single currency (Jones, 2015). The single market, arguably, became indispensable to the political economy of the British state.

Meanwhile, the UK famously developed its own form of membership with several opt-outs (and even some opt-ins). Still, in one crucial respect, the UK was firmly on the side of constraint and uniformity. It sought neither exception nor differentiation from the single market and insisted none should be given to others. The UK's former Permanent Representative, Sir Ivan Rogers (2017), would later claim the UK had developed a 'single-market-only' form of membership. For sure, the UK had other commitments as a member of the Union. But the single market was plainly what it valued most. Even if it is generally justified, the idea that the UK was an 'awkward partner' (George, 1998) was a caricature when it came to single market. The same goes for the idea that the UK invariably favoured intergovernmentalism or the Union method (unanimous voting + no exclusive Commission initiative + consultation only of the European Parliament + restricted CJEU jurisdiction) over supranationalism and the Community method (majority voting + exclusive Commission initiative + Co-decision with EP + CJEU jurisdiction) (Bickerton et al., 2015). The UK found much to support in the supranational aspects of the Community method as a means of market creation. At one stage, during the Thatcher years, the UK even favoured a stronger role for the Court of Justice in sanctioning infringements of single-market rules. Thatcher famously accepted majority voting in single-market questions, and not just as a reluctant compromise needed to secure agreement but as a necessity for getting the single market done: As she put it (1993, p. 553):

> I had one overriding positive goal. This was to create a single market. . . . What remained were so-called non-tariff barriers. The price which we would have to pay to achieve a single market with all its economic benefits was more majority voting in the Community. There was no escape from that, because otherwise particular countries could succumb to domestic pressures and present the opening up of their markets. It also required more power for the Commission.

However, the idea that the single market was the one matter on which it was worth paying the 'sovereignty costs' of supranational institutions and law-making became contentious within the Conservative Party. Many had believed that the main threat to the UK's continued membership would be the inability of the UK either to join the single currency or share a EU with a monetary union that could become a union within a union. However, it was the sovereignty implications of the UK's own enthusiasm for the single market that eventually destroyed its membership.

Since, as seen, a single market removes behind-border and non-tariff barriers, it is necessarily a massive undertaking in shared law-making. It was largely on account of the single market that the EU and its law became a significant component of how the UK and its public were governed. Moreover, it was precisely the sovereignty claims of the EU that made it uniquely suited to constructing a multistate internal market. The priority of EU law and the monopoly final interpretation of EU law by its Court facilitated certainty and coherence in the creation of a single market through a mixture of politics, law, economic competition, and cross-border transactions. This was a pooling of sovereignty to which British governments bound themselves at least as enthusiastically as other members. Even when the Cameron government (2010–2016) made a point of voting more frequently against proposals, it only opposed 12 per cent of measures. Otherwise, the UK was just like any other member state hardly voting against proposals at all (Mattila and Lane, 2001).

Yet initial agreement did not mean absence of subsequent constraint. Once passed, single market laws could not be changed by the UK on its own. They constitutionalised particular economic and social choices by removing them from the scope of political competition within the UK. The single market eventually required a level of shared and binding rulemaking which clashed with important conceptions of what it is for the UK to control its own laws. It was the accumulation of single market and other laws (Brouard et al., 2012; Töller, 2010) – as well as the commitment to free movement as a part of the single market – that made it possible to win a referendum on the claim that the UK needed to leave the EU to take back control of its own laws and borders.

The foregoing highlights why it is crucial to the case for Brexit that the UK should leave the single market by not exercising the Norwegian option. But do those arguments identify the full difficulties of leaving the single market? It is important to note pro-Brexit arguments that technological change and transformations in the global economy give the UK a unique window of opportunity to manage, and even prosper, outside the single market and by differentiating British laws from it. But the gamble in leaving the single market is also clear. For sure, the proportion of UK trade within Europe has been declining since the 1990s. But the UK's trade with the EU is still 44 per cent of the total, rising to 50 per cent when trade with the EEA and EFTA – both trading systems that are closely connected to the EU's single market – are included. The EU remains the world's largest internal market. The EU is, crucially, also a bloc negotiator in questions of international trade. It is trade that makes the EU an economic giant even if it is otherwise a political dwarf. Finally, as seen, the political economy, and tax base of the UK state, has benefitted from the single market in ways that will now require the UK to develop sufficient alternative markets to fund the promises of Brexit itself to regenerate 'left-behind' areas, all of that without hurting more prosperous – and usually older – voters who were also essential to the leave vote.

The gravity theory of trade (Tinbergen, 1962) continues to predict that countries are most likely to trade with their neighbours, especially where they have similar levels of GNP and, therefore, similar patterns of supply and demand. Clearly, then, a lot depends on the claim that trade is about to overcome geography: That, in providing many future services, any person sitting behind a computer in any part of the world will be able to trade easily with anyone else as if the two of them were in the next room. However, the argument that the UK needs to leave the EU in order to trade more globally may be one of history's great *non sequiturs*. The contrary may even be true. The UK's trade beyond Europe may depend on its trade within Europe. Hopes of trading more globally may benefit – and even depend upon – building up comparative advantage within a large, competitive, and well-managed internal market within the European area. On that understanding, not using the Norway model to remain inside the single market may be a drag on the UK's global trading ambitions.

The difference between trading services and goods is also at the core of the problem. The UK is overwhelmingly a service economy. Yet it is a single market – with a focus on removing non-tariff and 'behind-border' barriers, as opposed to tariff barriers at borders – that is needed for trade in services. So as long as the UK avoids constructing single markets with others, it will be in the odd position of mainly promoting free-trade in goods, which is more its competitors' comparative advantage than its own. The TCA is an example. By concluding what was overwhelmingly a free-trade agreement in goods, the UK has already conceded what its European trading partners most need without securing the freer trade in services its own economy needs. On the other hand, free trade in services, as just said, requires single markets, So the UK would be back to making laws with others; and if those others are to include European neighbours, participation in the EU's single market from outside the EU would require something like the Norwegian option after all. Nor, as seen, is it just political preferences or Euro-dogma that requires the kind of institutions, laws, rights, and obligations found in the Norway model if non-member democracies are to form a single market with the EU. Convergence of laws is simply what a single market is.

Conclusion

The question of whether the UK should adopt a relationship similar to that between Norway and the UK has been a predicament without much wriggle room. The predicament arose twice over: in relation both to the territoriality and political economy of the UK after Brexit. Keeping Northern Ireland aligned with the EU's single market and Customs Union may have been a 'poor-man's' version of 'Norway plus'. But, apart from keeping the whole of the UK in a Customs Union and a single market for goods, it was the only way of avoiding a boundary on the island of Ireland. However, that, in turn, was seen as dividing the UK by many Brexiters in the Conservative Party. Johnson would later seek scope for autonomy room by threatening to rewrite the withdrawal agreement unilaterally. But, as the government itself admitted in the House of Commons, that could only be done by breaking international law. A form of Brexit premised on signing trade agreements would start by breaking an international agreement.

So the predicament that gave the UK little wriggle room in questions of its own territoriality connected to the predicament that gave it little wriggle room on questions of political economy. Given conceptions of self-rule that form the core of Brexit, the UK cannot easily use the Norway model to participate in the EU's single market as a non-member. Yet it is hard to see how any non-member could participate in the EU's single market without the elements of shared political and legal order with the EU that Norway and others have developed through the EEA. Much will, therefore, depend on whether the UK can manage without participation in the world's largest single market that happens also to cover the UK's immediate neighbourhood. If there is any wriggle room, it is perhaps to think differently about sovereignty: to see both the EU and EEA as two different ways of pooling sovereignty in which closely interconnected democracies create ways of exercising their sovereignty together, achieving some things together that they cannot achieve apart, retaining their ultimate rights to withdraw, yet binding themselves, as long as they remain in a relationship, to its agreed rules. But all that is another discussion for another time. For the moment it is enough to doubt that it is the kind of wriggle room available to those who took the UK out of the EU. Theirs was not a vision of sovereignty pooling.

Notes

1 Speech by David Cameron on the Future of Europe 23 January 2013. For the full text, see the *Guardian* (23 January 2013). Available at www.theguardian.com/politics/2013/jan/23/david-cameron-eu-speech-referendum (Accessed 30 January 2023).

2 Fossum (2022) notes that the EU's single market with the four freedoms is polity constitutive for the EU.
3 For some of the trade-offs and dilemmas involved, see Fossum (2022).
4 As noted in Chapter 8, Fossum and Vigrestad (2021) discussed whether Brexit could serve as a benchmark for Norway's relations with the EU and concluded that it was not considered as such.

References

Armstrong, A. (2016) 'EU Membership, Financial Services and Stability', *National Institute Economic Review*, 236(1): 31–38.
Barnier, M. (2021) *La Grande Illusion: Journal Secret du Brexit (2016–2020)*, Paris: Gallimard.
Bickerton, C., Hodson, D. and Pütter, U. (eds) (2015) *The New Intergovernmentalism. States and Supranational Actors in the Post-Maastricht Era*, Oxford: Oxford University Press.
Brouard, S., Costa, O. and König, T. (2012) 'Delors' Myth: The Scope and Impact of the Europeanization of European Law Production', in Brouard, S., Costa, O. and König, T. (eds) *The Europeanization of Domestic Legislatures. The Empirical Implications of the Delors Myth in Nine Countries*, New York: Springer, pp. 1–19.
Buiter, W. (2008) 'Why the United Kingdom Should Join the Eurozone', *International Finance*, 11(3): 269–282.
Campos, F. and Coricelli N. (2017) 'How EEC Membership Drove Margaret Thatcher's Reforms', *VOX EU/CEPR*, 10 March. Available at: https://cepr.org/voxeu/columns/how-eec-membership-drove-margaret-thatchers-reforms (Accessed 18 February 2022).
De Vries, C. (2017) 'Benchmarking Brexit. How the British Decision to Leave Shapes European Public Opinion', *Journal of Common Market Studies*, 55(Supplement 1): 38–53.
Economist (2017) *Norway's Deal with the EU Still Holds Lessons for Britain*, 4 February. Available at: www.economist.com/europe/2017/02/02/norways-deal-with-the-eu-still-holds-lessons-for-britain (Accessed 9 February 2023).
Fossum, J. E. (2022) 'The EU and Third Countries: Consequences for Democracy and the Political Order', *Journal of Common Market Studies*. https://doi.org/10.1111/jcms.13421.
Fossum, J. E. (2023) 'The Norwegian Model and the UK Post-Brexit', in Fossum, J. E. and Lord, C. (eds) *Handbook on Brexit*, Cheltenham: Edward Elgar, pp. 362–383.
Fossum, J. E. and Graver, H. P. (2018) *Squaring the Circle on Brexit – Could the Norway Model Work?*, Bristol: Bristol University Press.
Fossum, J. E., Quesada, M. G., Zgaga, T. and Wolff, G. (2020) 'The Key Principles, Underlying Logics and Types of Affiliation', *EU3D Report 1*, Oslo: ARENA. Available at: www.eu3d.uio.no/publications/eu3d-reports/eu3d-report-1-20.html (Accessed 25 January 2023).
Fossum, J. E. and Vigrestad, J. (2021) 'Is the Grass Greener on the Other Side? Norwegians' Assessments of Brexit', *Politics and Governance*, 9(1): 79–89.
Fredriksen, H. (2015) 'The EEA and the Case Law of the CJEU. Incorporation Without Participation', in Eriksen, E. O. and Fossum, J. E. (eds) *The European Union's Non-Members. Independence under Hegemon*, London: Routledge.
Genschel, P. and Jachtenfuchs, M. (eds) (2014) *Beyond the Regulatory Polity? The European Integration of Core State Powers*, Oxford: Oxford University Press.
George, S. (1998) *An Awkward Partner: Britain in the European Community*, Oxford: Oxford University Press.

Gstöhl, S. (2023) 'The Pattern of Affiliations between the European Union and its Neighbours. Normative, Market and Governance Power Europe', in Fossum, J. E. and Lord, C. (eds) *Handbook on the European Union and Brexit*, Cheltenham: Edward Elgar.

Jones, E. (2015) 'Forgotten Financial Union. How You Can Have a Euro Crisis Without the Euro', in Matthijs, M. and Blyth, M. (eds) *The Future of the Euro*, Oxford: Oxford University Press.

Jónsdóttir, J. (2013a) *Written Evidence from Jóhanna Jónsdóttir, Policy Officer, European Free-trade Association*, London: House of Commons.

Jónsdóttir, J. (2013b) *Europeanisation and the European Economic Area: Iceland's Participation in the EU's Policy Process*, London: Routledge/UACES.

Keating, M. (2021) *State and Nation in the United Kingdom. The Fragmented Union*, Oxford: Oxford University Press.

Lord, C. (1996) *Absent at the Creation: Britain and the Schuman Plan 1950–2*, Aldershot: Dartmouth.

Mattila, M. and Lane, J.-E. (2001) 'Why Unanimity in the Council? A Roll-Call Analysis of Council Voting', *European Union Politics*, 2(1): 73–97.

Milward, A. (2002) *The Rise and Fall of a National Strategy 1945–1963. The United Kingdom and the European Community Volume 1*, London: Routledge.

Rawls, J. (1999) *The Law of Peoples*, Cambridge, MA: Harvard University Press.

Reich, R. (2015) *Saving Capitalism, for the Many, Not the Few*, London: Icon Books.

Rogers, I. (2017) 'The Inside Story of How David Cameron Drove Britain to Brexit', *Prospect Magazine*, 25 November. Available at: www.prospectmagazine.co.uk/politics/the-inside-story-of-how-david-cameron-drove-britain-to-brexit (Accessed 9 February 2023).

Scharpf, F. (2009) 'Legitimacy in the Multilevel European Polity', *European Political Science Review*, 1(2): 173–204.

Thatcher, M. (1993) *The Downing Street Years*, London: Harper Collins.

Tinbergen, J. (1962) 'An Analysis of World Trade Flows', in Tinbergen, J. (ed) *Shaping the World Economy*, New York: Twentieth Century Fund.

Töller, A. E. (2010) 'Measuring and Comparing the Europeanisation of National Legislation. A Research Note', *Journal of Common Market Studies*, 48(2): 417–444.

UK Government (2016) *Alternatives to Membership: Possible Models for the United Kingdom Outside the European Union*, London: HM Government.

10
CONCLUSION

The book's main aim was to increase our understanding of the relationship between the EU and its affiliated non-member states, the implications of such relationships for different policy areas, and, based on these insights, extract lessons for the UK. To address this aim, the book, on the one hand, focused on the triangular relationship between Norway, the UK, and the EU, and, on the other, developed a theoretical framework for analysing EU-third country relations under conditions of complex interdependence and harnessing lessons therefrom.

The next section provides a brief summary of the main arguments in the book. Thereafter we summarise the findings from the substantive chapters. These findings are derived from the application of the analytical framework to the different policy areas that the book covers. The final section contains reflections on the way forward.

Overview of the book's main arguments

The first conclusion we may draw from the analyses that have been conducted in this book is that European interstate relations have changed as a result of Brexit. An important observation that has been documented in considerable detail throughout the book is that the UK's departure from the EU has repercussions for the EU's relations with other third countries, which find themselves situated in between changing EU-UK relations post-Brexit. In other words, the dynamic nature of EU-UK relations have spillover effects on EU-Norway, as well as Norway-UK, relations. That does not, as is underlined in Chapter 8, mean that the UK's experience serves as any benchmark for third countries to follow. Neither does it mean, as is underlined in Chapter 9, that the Norway model has thus far had much traction in the UK debate. That does not, however, rule out that some of the features that mark

Norway's EU affiliation may not yet again crop up on the UK political agenda. What is clear is that the triangular EU-UK-Norway relations have become more volatile and unpredictable than was the case whilst the UK was an EU member. The main source of volatility thus far has come from the UK; Norway has sought to align closely with both the EU and the UK and has sought to reduce uncertainty as much as possible.

That brings up a point that is indicated in Chapter 9 and is worth considering in more detail as the triangular EU-UK-Norway relations develop, namely the importance of state size and power. Small states recognise their vulnerability and are therefore more likely to accept EU rules-based hegemony than larger states with self-conceptions as being more powerful. The UK, as a former global hegemon, clearly sees itself as more powerful and in a different league from Norway and is therefore less willing to submit to EU rules-based hegemony than Norway. The detailed analyses of Norway versus UK wriggle room and autonomy in Chapters 3 through 6 show a more complex and nuanced picture to suggest that size and power need not always directly translate into more autonomy. That, in turn, suggests the need to distinguish between power to disrupt versus power to produce decisions that are in line with one's interests.

The second conclusion that the analyses in this book have confirmed pertains to the need for rethinking core analytical categories to understand the nature and dynamics of EU–third country relations under conditions of legally regulated complex interdependence. The book has confirmed the need for an analytical framework that is sufficiently tailored to this circumstance, a set of terms that help to uncover not only the power relations but also the dilemmas, trade-offs, and conundrums involved. Sovereignty has figured centrally in the debates but is of limited usefulness since it is about the legal right of final decision. It refers to a distinct status of being recognised by other states as sovereign and says basically nothing about a given state's actual power. The near-equivalent and far more power-sensitive term 'independence' is about the absence of reliance or dependence on others. Complex interdependence entails almost, by definition, a delimitation of independence. The general line of thinking has been to establish how much independence a state is able to retain under conditions of complex interdependence. That, however, weights the scales in favour of independence without taking into consideration the reasons why states join together in binding cooperation in the first place. To capture costs and benefits of binding cooperation, the obvious approach would be to clarify the relative salience and costs/benefits of self-rule versus shared rule. That equation is, however, less relevant for Norway because it, through its EU affiliation, basically forfeits shared rule. It also, as the book has shown, has given up on elements of self-rule, and independence, the magnitude of which cannot be assessed if we simply consider the issue of sovereignty.

The term we settled for in this book was 'autonomy', which we defined as having choices and ability to will choices. Autonomy directs us to actor attributes such as their goals, values, and interests and the ability (capacity and capability) they have for realising these. In that sense, autonomy is more amenable to the analysis of the domestic politics of third states since it directs us to focus on how actors perceive and relate to the situation of complex interdependence. Autonomy is also interesting for understanding complex interdependence; the term opens up for considering whether the contact and cooperation involved is autonomy-reducing or autonomy-enhancing.

The book's main theoretical aim was to shed new light on the nature of and conditions for autonomy in a context of complex interdependence. This particular challenge, the book shows, requires further fine-tuning autonomy as a conceptual tool. It is well-known and recognised that law is a key driver of the European integration process. What this book has shown has bearings on how we understand and analyse autonomy: it was necessary to develop a specific subcategory of autonomy that we label wriggle room to capture the nature and scope for autonomy under conditions of binding international collaboration. Wriggle room refers to the scope for autonomous choices within formal legal commitments and constraints. Chapter 2 unpacks the notion of wriggle room and suggests eight subtypes: i) wriggle room in relation to new legislation; ii) wriggle room in relation to existing legislation; iii) wriggle room under conditions of dynamic homogeneity; iv) wriggle room in the context of agencification and administrative interweaving; v) wriggle room in relation to sanctioning and compliance mechanisms; vi) wriggle room for third states in between EU and UK agreements; vii) wriggle room in agreements regulating members exiting from the EU; and viii) the EU-external dimension of wriggle room. Some of these categories reflect traits that will mark all legally regulated EU–third country relations (i, ii, v, viii); others reflect the specific features of Norway's (and the other EEA-EFTA states) situation (iii, iv), and the distinct conditions surrounding the UK's situation of departing from the EU (vii).

After unpacking wriggle room, Chapter 2 and Chapter 8 proceeded to unpack autonomy more generally. Under the heading of capacity/capability, it singled out forms of political and institutional autonomy; legal autonomy; economic autonomy; cultural autonomy; and epistemic/knowledge/expertise-based autonomy. This list of traits to be associated with autonomy shows that, in addition to autonomy being a broad concept, several factors need to be accounted for in order to understand the implications of autonomy (in relation to states). Autonomy-relevant traits of third countries are, for instance, Norway's political system, its political culture, its public administration, and its society.

The book shows that the scope for autonomy is shaped by each actor's will and ability to pursue a course of its own choosing, as well as by the nature of the relationship: how binding or compelling it is, that is, if the contract is open-ended or highly specified, and whether it is symmetrical or asymmetrical. The EU is, legally speaking, a highly regulated political system.

Taking a step back to consider what all this means for autonomy in the context of complex interdependence, the book has shown that the overall scope for autonomy refers to the will and ability to pursue one's interest and stake out one's future; how and to what extent a third country is able to compensate for the negative effects of constraints imposed by the form and contents of the legally binding EU affiliation; and the capacities and capabilities as well as social support that a third country has for staking out its own desired course regardless of the formal EU affiliation.

The book has applied this framework to a range of issue-areas to determine the relationship between autonomy, broadly speaking, and wriggle room, more specifically. This is done with reference to Norway's affiliations with the EU: how much wriggle room Norway has in its relationship with the EU, how Norway's wriggle room has been changed by Brexit, and what lessons follow for the UK.

In the following we present an overview of the findings in the different substantive chapters.

The scope for autonomy and wriggle room: a summary of the empirical investigations

Chapter 3 shows that the UK has increased its autonomy and wriggle room post-Brexit in the climate and energy sector, although less than it wishes to convey. Norway's autonomy and wriggle room is, by contrast, more restricted, as a consequence of the country cooperating closer with the EU on climate policy. However, in both cases, the type of wriggle room varies in line with many of the types of wriggle room introduced in Chapter 2.

Referring to the first type of wriggle room, that is, *new legislation from the EU*, we find that the scope for UK influence has decreased dramatically. The UK no longer has those continuous negotiations and discussions with the other EU member states, and its possibilities to influence policymaking during the initial stages are limited. In contrast, Norway experiences more leeway than the UK – it has more experience as a 'corridor diplomat', and as an EEA member, it participates in expert groups when proposals are being developed. However, the European Green Deal and the REPowerEU plan challenge Norway's wriggle room because of the speed and cross-sectoral nature of legislative developments.

Wriggle room in terms of existing legislation has, on the one hand, increased in the UK because it no longer needs to adhere to EU environmental, climate, and energy legislation. On the other hand, the TCA restricts this wriggle room via the non-regression clause. Moreover, the withdrawal from the Single Energy Market, the EU's Emissions Trading Scheme, and the EU Environment Agency might also hamper the UK's possibilities of reaching its climate targets, as these policy tools are important for contributing towards the green energy transition. In Norway, wriggle room related to existing legislation has become more limited as non-compliance might be met by enforcement by ESA. However, its wriggle room has also increased as the climate cooperation with the EU awards Norway increased flexibility in how it reaches its climate target.

In terms of *dynamic homogeneity*, the UK's wriggle room has expanded post-Brexit, but not without limits due to for example the TCA's non-regression clause.

Both within climate and energy policy, Norway has entered into voluntary agreements that are not required as part of the EEA Agreement. Given the holistic and cross-sectoral approach of the European Green Deal, spillovers from one policy area (such as climate or energy) might reduce the wriggle room in other areas where Norway, in theory, should have full autonomy (such as within agriculture).

Addressing differences and similarities between *the Norway-EU and the Norway-UK formal affiliations* and following the UK's exit from the EU's electricity market, we find instances of more limited wriggle room for both the UK and Norway due to the costs of less efficient electricity trading. These issues decrease the UK's wriggle room as the country depends on electricity trading to meet its objectives of electrification and reducing emissions. Moreover, in the negotiations with the UK, the EFTA countries aimed for an agreement similar to the EEA Agreement and at least as good as the TCA but were unsuccessful on the issue of non-regression, which would have required Norway to give further concessions in, for example, agriculture. It is also worth noting that in the EFTA-negotiations, the UK was more interested in expressing its autonomy gains rather than binding itself to climate goals through a trade agreement. However, Brexit also impacted Norway's wriggle room due to the rules around country origin in the TCA, which defines Norway as a third country. For example, Norway now faces an additional customs duty on the export of batteries to the UK via the EU.

Concerning the *EU-external dimension of wriggle room*, both the UK and Norway enjoy more wriggle room than EU member states, as they – as non-members – can form their own trade (and other) agreements with countries outside the EU. In the UK it is an unsolved question as to how Brexit and future trade agreements will affect the wriggle room of the devolved nations. To what extent will, for example, the national government, in negotiations with other countries, take into account matters where the devolved nations have stricter rules than at the national level? The UK will have more wriggle room than Norway as it will not be part of the Carbon Border Adjustment Mechanism (CBAM), which is currently being decided in the EU. The aim of CBAM is to prevent 'carbon leakage' by subjecting the import of certain groups of products from third (non-EU and non-EFTA) countries to a carbon levy linked to the carbon price payable under the EU Emissions Trading System (ETS) when the same goods are produced within the EU.

In Chapter 4, we examined Norway's and the UK's autonomy and wriggle room in primary industry policies. Our point of departure is that Norway wanted to use its non-member status in the EU to have autonomy to develop and implement its own policies within the areas of agriculture and fishery. These concerns were important for why Norwegians voted no to EU membership in 1972 and 1994, and for why agriculture and fishery are both outside the EEA Agreement. However, political decisions such as the implementation of the international law of the sea (UNCLOS) and the EEA Agreement have drawn Norway closer to the EU in these policy areas. In fisheries, the management of shared fish stocks has led to cooperation and limited wriggle room in some areas, while Norway has retained autonomy in relations with third countries and in domestic policymaking. The current situation is that Norway has considerable autonomy to decide its own agricultural policies. However, the need for market access for Norway's large and growing seafood export has tied both policy areas closer to policymaking in the EU. Two examples illustrate this development particularly well. First, in 1998, the EEA Agreement was expanded to include the whole EU acquis on hygiene and veterinary rules (the SPS framework). Although there still are some tariffs, Norwegian seafood has, by this, gained easier access to the EU market. Second, by contributing to regional development in the EU, Norway has retained significant tariff-free quotas for seafood in the EU. Thus, Norway still has considerable autonomy within some areas of agriculture and fishery policymaking, while in other areas there is only some wriggle room within Norway's formal EU affiliation.

Brexit means that the UK has experienced the opposite development. The UK was, as an EU member, subordinated to the EU's Common Fisheries Policy and Common Agricultural Policy. This meant limited autonomy, but the UK had considerable leverage to influence EU policymaking and wriggle room in the implementation of its domestic policies on agriculture and fisheries. The TCA means that the UK has gained considerable autonomy in both policy areas. However, the gains within fisheries have been smaller than imagined before the signing of the TCA. This is due to both obligations in the UNCLOS agreement and the EU's negotiating power in the free trade part of the negotiations. Finally, the UK has gained tariff- and quota-free access to the EU market for all goods, including agri-food and seafood products. However, since it has insisted on staying outside the EUs Customs Union, single market, and the SPS framework, UK food exports are subjected to substantial border controls with the costs being covered by fishers, farmers, exporters, and UK consumers.

In Chapter 5 we analysed Norway's and Britain's wriggle room and autonomy to stake out their own course in the realms of global trade and development. At first sight, these policy areas allow non-members significant wriggle room compared to members of the Union because the EU has exclusive competence in trade, and the European Commission has, over the years, developed a federating role over the members' development policies. Using this wriggle room, Norway has concluded free-trade agreements bilaterally and, together with the EFTA, states that it would not have been able to do as an EU member. Similarly, the UK has, post-Brexit, managed to conclude trade agreements with third states. Yet, despite this legal wriggle room, non-members' autonomy is constrained by their relationship to the EU. For Norway, this is manifested by the EU's dominant role and presence in multilateral institutions such as WTO and the OECD-DAC. Norway does not have enough power or negotiating clout to counter EU proposals in multilateral fora. In addition, Norway often negotiates global agreements in parallel with the EU, something which makes it difficult to act in a radically different way than its European counterparts. The reluctance to move ahead on the deal with Mercosur and Norway's acceptance of the elimination of export subsidies on agricultural products in the WTO and the acceptance of the EU's proposal to establish a task force on policy coherence in the DAC exemplify this. The EU arrives in international organisations with prior negotiated and accepted positions, something which makes it difficult for associated non-members to influence the outcome. Britain, after Brexit, faces a similar conundrum. Although Brexit provided the UK wriggle room both in global trade and development, the EU's position as a bloc negotiator limits the UK's autonomy more broadly. While autonomy was a significant justification for Brexit, we see that the UK is not able to fully realise their newly gained autonomy. Rather, they have spent their efforts on securing the trade benefits lost by Brexit. Hence, while one would expect Britain to be better equipped than Norway to stake out their own course in global trade and development due to its power and bargaining clout at the international stage, so far, the results for Britain have been minimal. Thus, we conclude that Brexiteers enjoy autonomous will-formation, but their capacity to act autonomously is constrained.

The focus of Chapter 6 is the scope of autonomy and wriggle room in the area of foreign, security, and defence policy. The field of foreign, security, and defence policy, as underlined in Chapter 1, is marked by EU–third country relations that are not formalised and regulated by treaties but are shaped and conditioned through practical cooperation and political compromises. This leaves scope for both Norway and the UK to cooperate closely with the EU on foreign, security, and defence policy insofar as they want to. The limited legal constraints here ensure that they can cooperate with the EU without ceding their ability to determine their own political, economic, social, and cultural development.

In the extension of this, we see from Norway's experience that it is possible to develop a foreign, security, and defence relationship that is flexible, allows for a substantial amount of wriggle room, and retains formal sovereignty. At the same time, what has emerged over time is a below-the-radar wide-ranging patchwork of cooperation between Norway and the EU which is autonomy-reducing. Conversely, the UK became hostage to the Brexit process, and this issue-area was not included in the formal agreement with the EU. As the Brexit dust gradually settles, the wider security situation, the EU's development as a foreign, security, and defence actor, and domestic appetite are all factors that will determine how third countries like Norway and the UK will cooperate with the EU in foreign, security, and defence policy. The inclusion of the UK in PESCO adds to the empirical track record in this regard. In relation to this, it is significant to also consider what we find to be gradually diminishing Norwegian autonomy due to a changing geopolitical context and the spillover across a range of policy areas to the domain of foreign, security, and defence policy.

Despite the failed attempt to include foreign, security, and defence policy in the formal Brexit process, the UK is not cut off from the European security order. Yet it chose not to build a strong foreign, security, and defence relationship with the EU. The Norway model, which is based on a typical EU approach to third countries, may prove illustrative for the UK in the longer term. For Norwegian officials, the main problem associated with a close non-member relationship with the EU in this area is that it is not always possible to get as close to processes as possible. Yet, at the same time, Norway is free to opt in or out across the whole spectrum of EU initiatives, ranging from declarations and sanctions to crisis management operations. If the UK would choose to engage more actively at some point, the Norwegian experience is testament to how that is possible without having to compromise on some of the core values that drove the Brexit process in the UK, yet that would have to be consolidated in the domestic debate. Both at home and in relation to power symmetries, Norway and the UK are quite different cases of EU partners in this regard.

In the European foreign, security, and defence architecture, NATO is the prime territorial defence institution, and the EU has been increasing its efforts to support NATO and carve out its own contribution. Due to the complexities of current security threats and imaginaries, the EU is building a framework that cuts across traditional policy areas. This emerging and complex architecture both provides some wriggle room and ability for states to retain autonomy but, as we have seen, potentially contributes to limit it.

Chapter 7 charted citizenship developments in Norway as an EEA-EFTA state and the UK as an EU-exited state from the theoretical vantage point of citizenship as a status of rights (private autonomy) and political participation (public autonomy). This chapter thus shifts the focus on autonomy from the state to the individual.

In so doing, the chapter underlined that the issue of autonomy in processes of Europeanisation is not only about state autonomy and wriggle room but also concerns individual autonomy. A main aspect of the chapter was highlighting how the public and private autonomy of citizenship is not seamlessly linked to national citizenship. Through EEA citizenship, Norwegian citizens have gained in private autonomy as individuals in society and the marketplace, yet they have lost in terms of public autonomy, leading to a form of depoliticisation of citizenship that dovetails with what Chapter 8 has shown of how Norway's political system deals with the EU affiliation. In the case of Brexit, we have shown that the UK could have chosen the path of the Norway model post-Brexit. The choice not to do so has significant consequences for citizenship. UK citizens have become partly disenfranchised in a Europeanised sense. In addition to this loss in political rights, they have lost civil rights and social rights that follow from EU citizenship. Thus, the form of affiliation chosen by a third country to the EU has significant effects for the rights of national citizens and the role of citizenship in the political community. In a complex and interdependent world with high degree of cross-border integration, with the EU as a 'vanguard', citizenship cannot be isolated as a 'purely internal' institution. It is always affected by political choices in terms of a state's international relations as well as by its affiliation with EU institutions in the European context. Norway and the UK are two states that have taken different paths, with different consequences for citizenship. How we conceptualise these differences will differ based on the understanding of what citizenship is as well as what European integration entails. Yet the facts lay bare: in affiliating with the EU, non-member states will experience that a gain in autonomy in one may lead to a loss of autonomy in another. In terms of citizenship, this means that there is no uniform balancing between private and public autonomy.

Chapter 8 returned the focus to the state level and thus complements Chapters 3 through 6 by focusing on the broader issue of autonomy, which naturally shifted the locus to issues of the state's will and ability to pursue an own or self-chosen course of action. An important question in this chapter is to establish how self-chosen the course of action really emerges, and the actor's ability or capability to stay that course. The chapter assesses Norway with a view to clarify whether the government has a clear stance on what it sought to achieve in relation to the EU and, if so, actively sought knowledge and information on the range of options that might be available. In this context, the chapter identified what it refers to as Norway's integration paradox, which was defined as follows:

> Whereas the question of EU membership has long been a highly controversial and divisive issue, Norway's comprehensive incorporation in the EU through the EEA Agreement, and a whole host of other arrangements, has profound constitutional democratic implications, and yet has sparked surprisingly little controversy.

To reach there, the Norwegian political system has effectively depoliticised Norway's EU affiliation, which ensures rapid and smooth EU adaptation. Rather than active search for options and lessons from others, the political system has become effectively deadlocked in the preservation of the status quo. The chapter proceeded to the capacity or capability aspect of autonomy and noted that this consists both in material and immaterial factors, an important aspect of the latter being high levels of trust in government, which still is a hallmark of Norway. On material forms of capability, the chapter highlighted fiscal clout and administrative competence. Both have played a role in sustaining trust through, for instance, the will and ability to compensate 'losers' of Europeanisation to prevent legitimacy losses. The chapter also looks at procedural constraints for autonomy and found that the legal procedures for changing the status quo were lopsided, far higher for Norway seeking EU membership than for Norway leaving the EEA. That might be a further reason for the onus on depoliticising the EU affiliation.

The chapter also examined the autonomy implications of state – society dynamics. The conventional approach to state autonomy that we find in the comparative politics literature highlights autonomy in terms of the state's relative autonomy towards society. When considering autonomy in interstate rather than state-internal relations, it was noted that an alert society capable of giving the government input on how best to manage its EU affiliation can help to empower the government, and even a Eurosceptic society can provide the state leverage in interstate negotiations. For Norway, however, the EU affiliation effectively prevents the Norwegian government from bringing Norway-internal conflicts or grievances to the EU level.

The implication is that the Norwegian government obtains leverage when society is de-coupled from European developments. A society out of touch with European developments has tangible and legitimacy costs and risks.

Chapter 9 considers the role and status of the Norway model in the UK debate and in the constraints that the UK faced when seeking to exit from the EU. It shows the relevance of the Norway model in relation to the role and status of Northern Ireland and the political economy of the UK after Brexit. Keeping Northern Ireland aligned with the EU's single market and Customs Union may have been a 'poor-man's' version of 'Norway plus'. But, apart from keeping the whole of the UK in a Customs Union and a single market for goods, it was the only way of avoiding a boundary on the island of Ireland. However, keeping only Northern Ireland in the EU's single market and Customs Union was seen as dividing the UK by many Brexiters in the Conservative Party. Johnson would later seek wriggle room by threatening to rewrite the withdrawal agreement unilaterally. But, as the government itself admitted in the House of Commons, that could only be done by breaking international law. A form of Brexit premised on signing trade agreements would start by breaking an international agreement.

So the predicament that gave the UK little wriggle room in questions of its own territoriality connected to the predicament that gave it little wriggle room on questions of political economy. Given conceptions of self-rule that form the core of Brexit, the UK cannot easily use Norway model to participate in the EU's single market as a non-member. Yet it is hard to see how any non-member could participate in the EU's single market without the elements of shared political and legal order with the EU that Norway and others have developed through the EEA. Much will, therefore, depend on whether the UK can manage without participation in the world's largest single market that happens also to cover the UK's immediate neighbourhood. If there is any wiggle-room, it is perhaps to think differently about sovereignty: to see both the EU and EEA as two different ways of pooling sovereignty in which closely interconnected democracies create ways of exercising their sovereignty together, achieving some things together that they cannot achieve apart, retaining their ultimate rights to withdraw, yet binding themselves, as long as they remain in a relationship, to its agreed rules. But all that is another discussion for another time. For the moment it is enough to doubt that it is the kind of wriggle room available to those who took the UK out of the EU. Theirs was not a vision of sovereignty pooling.

This chapter thus provides new insights into a special and clearly under-investigated form of wriggle room: wriggle room in the process of exiting a legal arrangement. This is about residual ties, but also about the procedures through which exit takes place.

The way forward

The ways forward are plenty for the study of autonomy and wriggle room under conditions of complex interdependence. In closing the book, we outline four avenues for future research: there is a need for both comparative, longitudinal, and interdisciplinary studies. First, while this book has empirically examined the complex puzzles of autonomy and wriggle room with a focus on the triangular relationship between two states and the EU, a more encompassing research design would be to include more cases of third countries that have different degrees and forms of affiliations towards the EU. Autonomy and wriggle room might be subject to more fine-grained analysis based on more data and observation points but also by including different scales of EU involvement or EU affiliation for different types of actors.

Secondly, there is a need for longitudinal studies of autonomy and wriggle room in contexts of complex interdependence. This book has highlighted how the triangular relationship between Norway, the UK, and the EU is dynamic and subject to both endogenous and exogenous shifts, for example, partly driven by the dynamic elements in the contracts/treaties as well as driven by exogenous events. To better understand the dynamic elements, future studies should examine individual and collective actors' autonomy and wriggle room over time. In doing so, we would be better equipped to conclude how robust and sustainable autonomy and wriggle room are, and to understand under which conditions they are likely to change or not.

Third, the study of autonomy and wriggle room would need interdisciplinary research teams to uncover the many faces of the puzzle. Future research should not only be interested in the political and administrative element of autonomy and wriggle room as this book has primarily been but also include the economic and cultural aspect of it. Such studies could also examine the complex interrelations between political, administrative, economic, and cultural autonomy and wriggle room, for example, how changes in political autonomy ('Brexit') may unintendedly play into other segments of society.

Fourth, the main thrust of the discussion of autonomy in this book has focused on states. However, as shown in Chapter 7, there is a further body of literature on individual autonomy that is relevant here, not the least because the EEA Agreement effectively makes EEA-EFTA citizens economic citizens of the EU (Olsen, 2014; see also Chapter 7). Further research should consider the interaction between state and individual autonomy under conditions of complex interdependence.

BRITAIN AND NORWAY LOST ON VOYAGE

A Postscript

Andrew Duff

EU membership is difficult

On 22 January 1972, Prime Minister Trygve Bratteli signed Norway's treaty of accession to the European Community. The ceremony at the Palais d'Egmont in Brussels was joined by the leaders of Denmark, Ireland, and the United Kingdom who likewise had secured a membership agreement with the six member states of the Community. Entry negotiations had taken over a decade. The door was opened at a summit held at The Hague in December 1969: the first enlargement of the Community would be accompanied by completion of the common market and a deepening of integration: '*achèvement, élargissement, approfondissement*'. German Chancellor Willy Brandt, who had spent much of the '30s in exile in Norway, said that the breakthrough anticipated 'a future federative system' of Europe.[1]

Some hope. Having had second thoughts, Norway rejected EU accession in the referendum of September 1972 – and repeated the '*Nei*' in 1994. Denmark, Ireland, and Britain made it into the Community in 1973 but ran into trouble. Denmark rejected the Treaty of Maastricht at a referendum in 1993 and was bought off with fudges and opt-outs. Ireland rejected both the Treaty of Nice in 2001 and the Treaty of Lisbon in 2008 before being pacified by similar concessions. The UK launched a first renegotiation of its terms of membership in 1975 and demanded (and won) important opt-outs from successive EU treaties and abatements from its budgetary contributions. After an unsuccessful second renegotiation and a referendum in 2016, the UK left the Union altogether in January 2020 [Duff (a)]. Britain has joined Norway, lost on the voyage towards European unity.

The facts on the ground belie the simplicity of Article 49 of the Treaty on European Union (TEU) which says, welcomingly enough, that 'Any European State which respects the values [of the Union] and is committed to promoting them may apply to become a member of the Union'. The rhetoric from Brussels may be seductive, but the actual accession process is long, complex, and arduous. When the full implications of membership became clear to Iceland and Switzerland, they withdrew their applications. If joining the Union is difficult, sustaining the membership criteria after entry also proves a challenge. As Freedom House reports, in the last twenty years, only two new member states (Estonia and Lithuania) have avoided democratic backsliding.[2] Greece, next to join in 1981, struggled to shoulder the burden of membership, even risking the collapse of the euro. Hungary and Poland, entrants in 2004, now jeopardise the rule of EU law. Bulgaria and Romania, joining in 2007, have struggled for years to shed the systemic corruption that is their legacy from Soviet times. Sweden finds it impossible to fulfil its treaty obligation to join the single currency. Cyprus has neglected its commitment to reunite the island. These are only the most egregious examples of the difficulties faced by new member states in meeting the expectations of EU membership.

For the Union's institutions, therefore, enlargement is a great challenge. New member states change not only the size of Europe's emerging new polity but also its shape: new frontiers mean new neighbours, sometimes troublesome. Newcomers disturb the EU's internal balance of power as well as its budget. The presumption that further widening of membership would always be accompanied by reforms aimed at deeper political integration has proven to be mainly false. The Treaty of Lisbon was signed as long ago as 2007 and is overdue for revision, but no agenda for constitutional change is yet agreed.

Current candidates for membership range from Turkey and the Western Balkans to the three East European states with association agreements, Ukraine, Moldova, and Georgia. None of the candidates, however, are close to meeting the EU's formal accession criteria – or of winning the unanimous agreement of all 27 member states they need before crossing the threshold. The Union is badly divided on questions which, from an accession country's point of view, can seem intractable: migration, taxation, foreign policy, corruption, the rule of law. With such internal divisions and with integration stalled, the prospectus of membership begins to look less than scintillating. This is a very unsatisfactory situation at a time of rising instability across the wider Europe – especially for those applicants (not all) who are genuinely in want of Union membership. Discouraging and deceiving progressive forces in the Balkans and Ukraine discredits the Union.

Did Norway get off lightly?

In these circumstances, Norwegians may feel they had a lucky escape. A bipartisan mood seems to have settled over Norway's earlier fierce debates about Europe. The European Economic Area agreement of 1991 and the subsequent supplementary agreements, not least on joining the Schengen Area in 1996, seem to have left Norway's politics becalmed. Neither the pro or anti-European forces of the left or right find it in their own interests to reopen the discussion about EU membership. The pact behind the EEA holds, and the arrangement proves flexible enough to permit the gradual Europeanisation of Norway without provoking a nationalist reaction. Although Norway, as a member state, would play a vital role in EU foreign and security policy and aid and development policy, it is undeniable that Norway has established a reputation as a reliable arbiter and peacemaker in international affairs precisely because it is not an EU member state.

The fact that Norwegians can travel for study and work across the EU mitigates the effect of non-membership for individual citizens. Likewise, Norway is home from home for its many resident EU citizens. That Norway accepts the EU's SPS regulations draws Norwegian farming and fisheries towards the EU despite its formal exclusion from the CAP and CFP. Even though Norway is not a member of the EU Customs Union, the EU's clout in all matters of international trade, including the OECD and WTO, obliges Norway to act in parallel with EU trade policy and not to contest it. The norm is political alignment between Oslo and Brussels. As this book explains very well, Norway may have next to no influence over EU policy making, but it maintains a certain flexibility – 'wriggle room' – when it comes to implementing EU law and operating EU policy. Norway has never seen fit to use its veto under the EEA Agreement – and the EU has never had cause to suspend the agreement in whole or in part. Where disputes arise, they are dealt with in and by the courts: government and Storting in Oslo tend to stand clear.

As we know, the 'Norway model' played a big walk-on role in the Brexit drama, but it was much misconstrued. This book will help to dispel the misunderstandings – not least in making clearer the difference between the paradigms of free-trade agreement on the one hand and regulatory alignment on the other. As with Switzerland, there is free movement of people between Norway and the EU, but goods and services face customs controls and border checks. So Norway's relationship with the Union requires Norwegians to be patient and agile as well as essentially unambitious.

Britain and Norway: the unlikely couple

The comparison often drawn with Britain is exaggerated. For one thing, there is the difference in size – 5.5 million Norwegians against 68.8 million Brits. Size matters. Where Brussels may turn a blind eye towards minor transgressions of its internal market agreement with Norway, it cannot afford to do so in the case of post-Brexit UK – especially where Northern Ireland, which remains in the EU market for goods, is concerned. The UK economy is much broader and more service orientated than Norway's, which is why the loss of a customs union agreement with the EU simplifying rules of origin is so acutely felt by post-Brexit British traders.

Brexit has disrupted trade way beyond the Strait of Dover. The triangular relationship of Norway, Britain, and the EU has suffered. It was nonsense to argue, as some did, that Norway should welcome Brexit. On the contrary. It is in Norway's interest to preserve the single market intact with its balance of rights and obligations, especially freedom of movement. As Stefaan De Rynck records, Oslo actually discouraged Michel Barnier from creating a 'bespoke EEA' for Britain, with fewer obligations. The idea that the UK could simply join up with EFTA and the EEA as an alternative to the EU was allowed to gain too much traction in the Brexit debates: in fact, were London to propose such a thing, another long and complex triangular negotiation would have to take place.

As Brexit plays out, the contrast between the UK and Norway becomes even clearer. Britain's neoliberal socio-economic model offers next to no attraction for social democratic Norway. And as Norway continues to converge with the EU in new policy areas, such as energy and climate change, the UK diverges. The bilateral trade agreement between the UK and Norway is worse for the latter than the deal pertaining under the EEA. Harmonised rules of origin have disappeared. Norway continues to apply over 75 per cent of EU law as the UK government seeks to jettison all its retained EU law by the end of 2023.

The only field where Britain and Norway, both founding members of NATO, move closer together is security and defence policy. The UK, as an EU member state, long resisted the development of an autonomous EU security policy. France, for opposite reasons, was also complicit in keeping the EU and NATO apart. President Macron, however, now works to ensure better systemic collaboration between the two Brussels-based organisations. And Britain has surrendered its veto against such alignment. The appearance in 2022 of the conference of the European Political Community brings Norway and Britain together in an EU-led geopolitical forum whose agenda is firmly established by Russia's invasion of Ukraine. Norway has negotiated its way into EU defence funding mechanisms and commits its troops to EU battlegroups: this can be a practical example to the UK should it wish to follow. NATO membership for Finland and Sweden accentuates the strategic importance of the High North. By contrast, the UK's attempt to reorientate its defence effort East of Suez has been blown out of the water by Putin.

Where next for Brexit Britain?

The future of British European policy is as murky as ever. Opinion polls suggest that a growing number of leave voters now regret the clumsy, hard Brexit with which the Conservatives have lumbered the country. But this does not equate with a majority for rejoining. That truth, no doubt, informs the very cautious policy of partial re-engagement with the Union adopted by Keir Starmer, Labour leader and likely next prime minister. Starmer also knows that, as far as the EU is concerned, the prospect of having to receive a prodigal Britain back into the fold is troublesome. As the Conservative government tries to wriggle out of its post-Brexit agreements, mistrust between London and Brussels deepens.[3] Any new government will take years to rebuild the confidence of Brussels. The most one can expect if the Tories are ousted at the next election, scheduled for 2024, is a joint review of the Trade and Cooperation Agreement.[4]

A good starting point for the review will be to resurrect the Political Declaration on the future relationship which was signed by Boris Johnson in October 2019 and then discarded by him.[5] Accommodation in several practical matters can be reached fairly easily in the short term, for example, over food safety and plant and animal health.[6] EU policing of trade in and out of Northern Ireland – which remains in the EU single market for goods – can be made less rigid if the UK authorities become more cooperative. The arrangements made in the Withdrawal Agreement for EU citizens resident in the UK can be fully respected. The new UK government can drop threats against retained EU law and renew guarantees on international law, including the ECHR. All this would seem to be Labour's policy, and in this they would be supported by the minor opposition parties, the Liberal Democrats, Greens, and Scottish and Welsh Nationalists. The pragmatic spirit behind Norway's association agreements with the EU, explained so well in this book, can teach the British how to do it.

Nevertheless, longer-term settlement of Britain's vexed relationship with Europe will only become possible once the UK recognises that, as a borderland state, it is fully interdependent with the Union. Just as Brexit meant the erection of borders, interdependence means their dismantling. The first concrete step to structural convergence should be to negotiate a new customs union with the EU.

Without doubt, however, the end goal for any pro-European UK government will be to reintegrate with the EU single market. It was the very creation of the internal market in the first place that was the principal prize and purpose of British membership. Returning to it will require anew from the UK the commitment to the four principles of free movement of goods, services, capital, and people – precisely that which Brexit ruptured. A new treaty will be needed to establish a deep and comprehensive free-trade area dedicated to dynamic alignment with the evolving *acquis communautaire*. A useful template is the Ukraine Association Agreement of 2014 whose governance institutions are similar to that of the Withdrawal Agreement – with dispute mechanisms subject to the oversight of the European Court of Justice – rather than those weaker organic links of Johnson's Trade and Cooperation Agreement.

Affiliate membership

Going further, I have argued that a new category of affiliate EU membership should be created to cater for a repentant UK [Duff (b)]. This would allow British ministers a vote in the Council – without a veto – on relevant single market legislation and on EU trade treaties. As such, it would constitute a significant upgrading over and above Norway's position as a consultative associate under the EEA arrangements. The concept of affiliate membership would enhance the EU's capacity to act effectively across its wider neighbourhood and could be used either as a staging post on the way to full membership or as a long-stay parking place. If Hungary and Poland continue in their illiberal ways, relegation to affiliate membership may also be tempting.

The initial concept of association was invented by Jean Monnet once it became clear that the UK was not going to join the European Coal and Steel Community. Affiliate membership with strong institutional linkage should be the contemporary equivalent – not only extending the EU's normative power but also furbishing its democratic credentials. Without a return to some form of democratic co-decision, I do not think it possible for the UK to take that important step back into the orbit of the European Union. What was acceptable to Norway in 1991 in terms of democratic deficit would not be acceptable today to the British. The typical British sneer about Norway being a 'fax democracy' will resonate long after everybody has forgotten what a fax was.

The European Union should not be surprised by this. If Brexit was ever more than a populist spasm among ill-informed and badly led British voters, it sprang from a feeling that native national British democracy was somehow superior to the supranational continental type. If the EU is to avoid a future deployment of Article 50 TEU by another member state, it had best use Brexit to instigate a period of serious self-criticism. The fact is that the EU is no longer well governed, and its constitution is out of date. The Union finds itself trapped between a confederal past where national sovereignty is stoutly defended and a future where pooling those sovereignties is taken to its logical conclusion with the installation of an accountable, discernible, and effective federal government, respecting subsidiarity and enjoying wide competences.

Such radical reforms, of course, require at least one revision of the EU treaties, possibly several, step by step. There are indeed many reasons to reopen the Lisbon Treaty, not least to reduce the use of the national veto and to advance qualified majority voting in the Council plus full co-decision with the European Parliament. Britain and Norway will find themselves united in a desire to get as close as possible to the work of a new constitutional Convention (Article 48(3) TEU). Clearly, neither country is yet ready for such an exercise. Britain is still in post-Brexit intensive care. Beyond a desire to be informed and consulted, Norway has no strategy of its own on the question of Europe's future. The EU itself still needs to work out how best to deploy differentiated integration across the wider Europe. In the context of heightened tension in Ukraine, Moldova, and the Western Balkans, EU enlargement policy deserves an urgent, rational, and honest review.

The addition of a new category of affiliate membership would enlarge the options available to the Union and its autonomous but interdependent neighbours. The birth of the European Political Community is welcome evidence of a willingness to experiment: if the conference were to transmute into a European security council including all EU and NATO states, it would be a big boost to Europe's strategic autonomy. No matter how the political geography of Europe changes, however, the EU institutions at its centre must be strong enough and democratic enough to manage the process. Britain and Norway, with the benefit of all their experience, would be wise to nudge things forward in that direction.

Notes

1 Willy Brandt to the Bundestag, 6 November 1970.
2 Freedom House, *Nations in Transit 2020: Dropping the Democratic Façade*, May 2020.
3 EU-UK Withdrawal Agreement, Official Journal L 29, 31 January 2020.
4 EU-UK Trade and Cooperation Agreement, Official Journal L 149, 30 April 2021.
5 EU-UK Political Declaration on the framework for the future relationship, Official Journal C 384 I, 12 November 2019.
6 See *Where Next? The Future of the UK-EU Relationship*, UK in a Changing Europe, 20 January 2023.

References

De Rynck, S. (2023) *Inside the Deal: How the EU Got Brexit Done*, Newcastle upon Tyne: Agenda.
Duff, A. (2022a) *Britain and the Puzzle of European Union*, London: Routledge.
Duff, A. (2022b) *Constitutional Change in the European Union: Towards a Federal Europe*, Cham: Palgrave Macmillan.

INDEX

ACER *see* Agency for the Cooperation of Energy Regulators
administrative interweaving *see* agencification
Africa 127; African Commonwealth nations, trade negotiations with EU 112; EDF financing of 117; EPAs with 99; EU Emergency Trust Fund for Africa 109; EU migration deals 116; Nordic Plus countries and 107; SACU 101
Africa, Caribbean, and Pacific Group (ACP) 117
agencification (EU) 11; administrative interweaving and 25, 42, 209; wriggle room in context of administrative interweaving and 29–31
Agency for the Cooperation of Energy Regulators (ACER) 57
agricultural exceptionalism 85, 100–101, 105
agriculture 7; autonomy and wriggle room for Norway regarding 84–87, 91, 97, 211–212; Brexit and 78–79; CFP and 71; EEA and 189; EGD and 56; ESR and 55; Norway EU affiliation and 9–10, 14, 18, 55; Norway and EEA Agreement and 29, 69, 84; Norway FTA with EU and 58, 80; Norway as being outside EU to protect 48; Norwegian Agricultural Agency 68;
Norwegian Food Safety Authority 88; origin check for products 15; SPS acquis, implications for 88; TCA and 73; WTO agreement for 70; *see also* Common Agricultural Policy (CAP)
Amazon, deforestation of 33, 103, 105
American Revolution 148
anti-dumping measures against Norwegian seafood 82–83
anti-piracy operation, Somalia 127
anti-smuggling initiatives 109
aquaculture 69, 70, 82–83, 75
Arctic cod 82
Arctic Strategy 131
Arctic, the 137
Argentina 103
asylum, agreements on 8, 12
asylum policies, institutions and practices in European migration system 149–150; EU common policy 167
asylum seekers 116, 145, 150
Atalanta anti-piracy operation 127
AUKUS 136
Australia 108, 112, 113, 136, 186
Australian option 185
Austria 83, 104, 108
autonomous: action 24, 37, 109–110; agenda-setting 7; choices 3; development policy 106, 113; fishery and agricultural policies outside EU, Norway's pursuit

of 79; global actor, Norway as 99–100; institutional resources 37; interest 5; legal action outside EU affiliation 40; role 38; will 28; will-formation 98

autonomy: Britain regaining autonomy via Brexit, question of 110; broad conception of 34–39; defining 33; dimensions of (five) 39–41; legal 40; of Norway, in relationship to EU 134–135; Norway's capacity to act with 99–100; of UK, post-Brexit 63, 111, 113–115; temporality and 34, 40; translating legal wriggle room into 97–119; as will or pursuit of own goals 33–36; wriggle room and 23–42; *see also* Norway; wriggle room

Baltic Sea 60
bank bailouts 190
banking crisis of 2008 194
Bank of England 201
Barnier, Michel 221
Barnier staircase 18n6, 181n3
BEIS *see* Department for Business, Energy and Industrial Strategy (BEIS)
Belgium 52, 59, 77, 104, 108
Belt and Road initiative, China 98
Benchmark project 186
Bergmann, J. 116
Bolsonaro, Jair103, 119
Brandt, Willy 218
Bratteli, Trygve 218
Brazil 103–16, 112, 119
Brexit (UK) 1–6; agriculture and 78–79; autonomy of Britain regained via 110; Britain and EU in global trade after 110–111; CETA and 2; climate and energy policy post-Brexit in the trilateral relationship 59–61; Common Fisheries Policy (CFP) and 69–70, 73, 75, 220; EEA and 2, 193; EU relations, post-Brexit 14; fisheries and 75; foreign, security, and defence policies in Brexit process 135–137; Freedoms Bill 50, 53,'global Britain' and 33; hard 136, 151, 197, 199; Leave campaign 73, 78, 110, 137, 179, 221; 'normalisation' of UK, post-Brexit 113–116; Norway-EU relationship and 170–172; Norway-EU relationship and implications for climate and energy policy post-Brexit 54–57; 'Norway model' and 1, 17, 185–204, 220; Norwegian lessons for UK, post-Brexit 69–70; post-Brexit climate and energy policy 48–63; post-Brexit EU members 9; post-Brexit Norway 24, 54–59; Remain campaign 4, 73; securing trade benefits (UK) lost after 111–112; soft 151, 156, 197, 200; Swiss Model and 1; Taking Back Control' UK Leave slogan 3–5, 145, 156; Trade and Cooperation Agreement (TCA) and 76–78; trying to punch over its weight (UK) after 112–113; UK as autonomous actor in EU, shift in position following 113–115; UK–EU relations in primary industries before and after 73–79; Withdrawal Agreement 75–76; wriggle room, lack of 188; UK-EU relationship and implications for climate and energy policy post-Brexit 50–54; UK-Norway relationship and implications for climate and energy policy post-Brexit 57–59

Brexiters 1, 33, 154, 156, 187; Conservative Party 204, 216
Brexit Freedoms Bill 50, 53
Britain: aid used to control migration to UK 116; autonomous will formation of, showcasing 117; Department of International Trade, leaked document from 59; as 'Dirty Man of Europe' 50; EEA Agreement and 58; EU and, in global trade 110–117; as market for Norwegian exports 102; Norway and 118, 164, 168, 218–224; securing trade benefits lost with Brexit 111–112; trying to punch above its weight 112–113; wriggle room and autonomy in policy areas of global trade and development 97–99, 110–119, 212–213; *see also* 'Global Britain' debate; United Kingdom
Brundtland Commission report 54
Bulgaria 219

Index **227**

Cameron, David 18n2, 185, 202, 204n1
Canada: United States-Mexico-Canada free trade agreement 112
Canada free-trade agreement (CETA) 1–2
CAP *see* Common Agriculture Policy
capability/capacity 5–6, 23, 36–39, 180, 208, 209–210
capacity: action 41, 109; autonomous will and 28, 34, 42, 98, 160; autonomy and 162; autonomy-enhancing 35; capability and 5–6, 23, 36–39, 180, 208, 209–210; competence and 174–176; operational 117; will-formation and 100
Carbon Border Adjustment Mechanism (CBAM) 53, 211
CBAM *see* Carbon Border Adjustment Mechanism
CETA *see* Canada free-trade agreement
CFP *see* Common Fisheries Policy
Chile 101, 102
China 33, 112, 119; Belt and Road initiative 98; EU-China investment agreement 103; Iceland's FTA with 102; Norway's FTA with 103; Xi's leadership of 98
citizenship: Aristotle's *Politics* on citizenship 143; Brexit's impact on 151–156, 157; defining and conceptualizing 143–144; EEA 153; EEA citizenship and Norway citizenship 144–149; EEA citizenship and UK citizenship 154–155; EU 141–142, 150; inclusive/exclusive aspect of 143; market citizens 146; political 145; semi- 152; transnational, EU and EEA 144–145; transnational, UK 152; UK 142
citizenship, migration, and mobility 17, 141–157
Clean Development Mechanism, Kyoto Protocol 55
Clean Energy Package (EU) 55
climate and energy policy post-Brexit, EU, UK, and Norway 7–8, 17, 29, 39, 48–63; EEA and 189, 211; EU-UK relationship and 50–54; Hurdal Declaration (Norway) regarding 163–164; Norway-EU relationship and 54–57, 166–167; Norway-UK relationship and 57–59; Norway wriggle room regarding 131–132;
trilateral relationship between EU, UK and Norway post-Brexit 59–61, 63; UK wriggle room regarding 210
climate actor, EU as 106
climate and forest initiative (Norway) 103
climate change 17; EU as international leader on 48; global fight against 103
Climate Change Act (CCA)(UK) 50
climate leader, Norway as 54, 55
Climate Settlements (Norway) 54
co-determination, as opposed to self-determination 148–149
Colombia 101
colonialism and neocolonialism: British 111, 113, 117, 152; European 99, 116–117
Common Agricultural Policy (CAP) 8, 69, 70, 79, 84–85, 87, 220
Common Fisheries Policy (CFP) 69–70, 73, 75, 220
Conservative Party (Norway) 90, 102, 128, 167
Conservative Party (UK) 50, 113–114, 171, 185, 199, 202, 204, 216, 221
Cotonou Agreement 117; post-Cotonou agreement 117
COVID-19 61, 63, 115, 127
Customs Union (EU) 2, 8–9, 14–15; British exit (Brexit) from and decision to remain outside 2, 14–15, 92, 111, 151, 187, 188, 197, 199, 212, 222; EEA-EFTA countries not part of 9; Northern Ireland and 187, 199, 204, 216; Norway not part of 14–15, 55, 220; Norway plus option 187, 204, 216; South African Customs Union (SACU) 101
Cyprus 219

DEEU *see* Department for Exiting the European Union
deforestation *see* Amazon, deforestation of
Denmark 59, 60, 72, 75, 77, 108, 116, 128, 218
Department for Business, Energy and Industrial Strategy (BEIS) 52
Department for Exiting the European Union (DEEU) 111
De Rynck, Stefaan 221
Development Assistance Committee (DAC) (OECD) 98, 108–109, 114, 212–213
Dublin I, II, and III agreements 8, 12, 150

Dublin Regulation (Dublin III) 150
Dublin System 145, 150
Duff, Andrew 2, 218–223
dynamic homogeneity 25, 28–29, 42, 131, 209–211

ECJ *see* European Court of Justice
economic autonomy 40, 209; *see also* autonomy
economic citizens of EU 6, 217
economic integration, of EFTA and EU 86
economic migrants 150
Economic Partnership Agreement (EPA), EU 99, 112
economic rights 143, 144, 147–148, 153
economic sanctions, EU against Russia 127
EDA *see* European Defense Agency
EDF *see* European Development Fund
EDIDP *see* European Defence Industrial Development Programme
EEA *see* European Economic Area
EEA-EFTA states: Comments 26; dynamic homogeneity and 28; EEA Agreement and 13; EEA rules, compliance with 9; establishment of 19n13; EU economic citizenry of 6; EU law and 32; EU participation of 13; institutions 28; Norway 14, 27, 118, 156, 214; Schengen, not empowered inside 12; trade and other agreements with countries outside EU 33; transnational citizenship of members states of 152
EEAS *see* European External Action Service
effort-sharing regulation (ESR) 55–56, 61
EFTA *see* EEA-EFTA states; European Free Trade Association
EFTA-Mercosur Agreement 33, 101, 103–106
EFTA Surveillance Authority (ESA) 9, 31–32, 56, 61, 88, 155, 210
EGD *see* European Green Deal
Egypt 101
Emergency Trust Fund for Africa (EUTF) 109
emission cuts 39, 56
emissions allowance 61
Emissions Trading Scheme (ETS)(EU) 51, 54–55, 57, 61, 210–211
ENGO *see* environmental non-governmental organisation
Environment Agency, EU 51, 210

environmental non-governmental organisation (ENGO) 49, 51–54, 59–61
Erasmus+ 13
ESA *see* EFTA Surveillance Authority
ESR *see* effort-sharing regulation
ETS *see* Emissions Trading Scheme
EU *see* European Union
EUNAVFOR 127
EU-Norway relations and affiliations 6, 7, 25, 129; agreements, overview of Schengen and beyond 11–17; defining features of 8–11; in fisheries 79–81; primary industries 79; unidirectionality of 25; wriggle room in 6
European Coal and Steel Community 223
European Commission 2, 11, 13, 16, 62; *de jure* right of initiative of 26; CFP and 71–74, 77, 79, 81; Directorate General for Fisheries established by 71; EFTA and 82; EU agencies and 30, 175–176; EU legislation, involvement with application of 29, 55; as federator of EU member states' development policies 114; Norway's foreign/security/defence relationship with EU and 126, 131; Norway's ability to send experts (SNEs) to 165; Norway wriggle room and 28, 61; regulation of energy market, rethinking by 60; UK and Norway and 57; UK opposition to 115; *see also* REPowerEU plan
European Court of Justice (ECJ) 62, 147
European Defense Agency (EDA) 127
European Defence Industrial Development Programme (EDIDP) 128
European Development Fund (EDF) 116–117, 128; budgetisation of 117
European Economic Area (EEA) 81, 189; Brexit and citizenship, lessons from 151–152, 193; citizenship in, depoliticization as key feature of 153–154, 192; citizenship in, Norway as case example of 148; Committee of the Parliament 148–149; Council 26; distinctive institutional features of 195; EU citizens' rights in 142, 144–148; European Commission and 30; free movement of persons central

to 155–157; individuals given standing under EEA law 198; 'mobile membership' in 155; non-European Union members of 142, 191; Norway as member of 55, 62, 149; as rights-based legal order 141

European Economic Area Agreement (EEA Agreement) 211, 217; agriculture as being outside 29; Article 19 69, 86; Article 102 27; commitment to EU made explicit in 13; design and purpose of 8–11; dynamic homogeneity and 28–30; EFTA-Mercosur not bound by 105; issues area excluded from 28; fisheries and 81–82, 83; overview of 7; as legally regulated straitjacket for countries outside EU–Norway 6; market core of 154; Norway and 13–14, 56, 79, 99, 102, 124–128, 130–134, 144–148, 163, 166–177, 180, 186, 203–204; Norway as market citizen of 146; Norway model and 2, 189–191, 198, 198; Norway's scope of decision-shaping 24–27; Norwegian Official Report assessment of 12; Protocol 3 (three) 86; Protocol 9 (nine) 82; right to exemption, per 165; singing of 83; SPS framework and 70, 87, 91; TCA compared to 14–17, 58, 90; trade and agricultural products covered by 69; wriggle room of Norway per 24–39, 61–62, 69–70, 84, 86, 88; *see also* EEA-EFTA

European External Action Service (EEAS) 127

European Free Trade Association (EFTA): agricultural exceptionalism and 100–101; China and 102; EFTA Court 11, 31, 43n10, 155, 177, 191; EFTA-led trade agreements with Norway 117; EFTA-Mercosur Agreement 33, 101, 103–106; EFTA Surveillance Authority (ESA) 9, 31–32, 56, 61, 88, 155, 210; EU development and 82, 84; EU and, economic integration with 86; EU and, free trade agreements 87; Norway and 99–101, 110, 117, 186, 209; seafood trade within 81; UK and 221; UK and, free trade negotiations with 90, 211

European Green Deal (EGD) 48, 210–211; CBAM 53, 322; EEA and 56; foreign supply chains and 60; Norway and 61–62

Europeanisation 9, 18n8; negative effects/consequences of 36, 40, 108–109, 116

European Political Community, birth of 223

European Union: Arctic Strategy 131; Battlegroups 127, 128, 221; as climate actor 106; difficulty of membership in 218–223; Effort-Sharing Regulation 55; Environment Agency 51, 210; environmental and energy *acquis* 55; EU27 189; EU-ACP relationship 117; EU-Canada 1, 185; EU-China investment agreement 103; EU-derived legislation, sunset clause in 50; EU-driven reform processes 34; EU Emergency Trust Fund for Africa (EUTF) 109; EU-external wriggle room 33–34, 42, 97, 100, 209, 211; EU-Japan deal 113; EU-internal and EU-external wriggle room 24; EU-level agencies and regulatory bodies 175–177; EU-Mercosur agreement 103–106, 119; EU-sceptical Norwegians 174; EU-style regulations 106; EU-Switzerland bilateral treaty 185; EU-third country relations 2, 3, 5, 23–24, 29, 31, 33–36, 137, 157, 207–211, 213–214; Maritime Security Strategy 131; monetary union, EU and UK 202; problem of non-membership in 193–197; Space Strategy 131; Strategic Compass document 124; WTO and 179, 212, 220; *see also* agencification; EU-Norway relations; EU-UK relationship; EU-UK-Norway relationship; EU-UK Trade and Cooperation (TCA) Agreement

EUTF *see* Emergency Trust Fund for Africa

EU-UK-Norway relationship 24, 60, 132, 207–208; climate and energy policy post-Brexit in the trilateral relationship 59–61; in primary industries after Brexit 88–91;

triangular relations and dynamics of 7–8
EU-UK relationship 7, 15, 18, 59; in agriculture 78; after Brexit 70; dynamic nature of 207; fisheries 73–79; future cooperation on foreign, security, and defense issues 125, 128, 132, 135, 137
EU-UK Trade and Cooperation (TCA) Agreement 1–2, 6–7, 14–15, 58–59; ambiguity and openness associated with 32; barriers to trade in 79, 90; Brexit and 136; EEA agreement compared to 7; fisheries and 73, 75–79, 89–91; foreign security and defense not included in 126; governance arrangements 16–17; influence on primary industries in the UK 70, 73; non-regression in 62, 210; 'paradox' of 53; rules around country origin in 56, 118; TCA-like agreement between Norway and UK 32; UK autonomy to make own rules in SPS area, per 91; UK-Norway Agreement mirroring 6
exclusive economic zones (EEZ) 70–75, 77, 80–81, 89–91

Farstad, Fay Madeleine ix
Farsund, Arild ix
FCDO see Foreign, Commonwealth and Development Office (UK)
fisheries 7–9, 14, 17–18, 29, 48, 55, 69–83, 88–92; Brexit and 75–76, 88–89; EEA Agreement and 81–82; EU Agreement on fishing and 80; EU–Norway relationship in 79–81; EU–UK relationship in 73–75; International Council for the Exploration of the Sea (ICES) and 71, 73; market access and 83–84; maximum sustainable yield (MSY) 71, 73; Regional Fisheries Management Organisations (RFMOs) and 71; TCA and 16, 76–78, 89–90; Total Allowed Catch (TAC) 71; UNCLOS and 70–71, 80–81, 89, 91, 211–212; UN Fish Stock Agreement 1995 and 71; wriggle room of UK before Brexit 73; see also Common Fisheries Policy (CAP)

Foreign, Commonwealth and Development Office (FCDO) (UK) 115
Fortress Europe 150
Fossum, John Erik ix, 9, 18n5, 19n16, 43n3, 168, 171, 174, 189, 205n2
four freedoms, principles of 13, 146, 171, 191 198, 205n2
Fox, Liam 111–112
France 75m 77, 104, 108, 221
Fredriksen, H. H. 12
free movement: of capital 8; of goods, services, capital, and persons 15, 222
free movement of persons 176–177, 190; borders and 155; Brexit and 155–156; EEA Agreement and 157; exercise of right of (UK) 151–152, 154; Norway and EU 220–221; principle of (EU Treaty) 176; right of (EEA) 142, 146; right of (EU) 144–145, 146, 149–152, 176–177
Free Trade Agreement (FTA) 58–59; EFTA-Mercosur 103; Iceland-China 102; Norway-China 103; United States-Mexico-Canada 112; see also EFTA; NAFTA
FTA see Free Trade Agreement

GATT 80, 85–87
GATT/WTO 87
Georgia (country of) 118, 219
Germany 52, 59, 77, 104, 107, 108, 218
'Global Britain' debate 33, 52, 110–111, 136–137; Global Britain in a Competitive Age (UK strategy document) 137
Global Europe Instrument 117
global financial crisis 50
Global South 107
global trade and development 97–119
Graver, H. 9, 18n5
green agenda, von der Leyen commission 56, 77
Green Deal, Europe see European Green Deal (EGD)
green energy transition 51, 63n1, 210
greenhouse gas (GHG) 54
Green Investment Bank 50
Greenland 81
Green Party (Norway) 102, 167, 222
Greenpeace NGO 103
Gstöhl, Sieglinde 18n5, 194–195
Gullberg, A. 55–56

Herfkens, Eveline 107
High North 137, 221; *see also* Arctic
High Representative of the EU for Foreign Affairs and Security Policy (HRVP) 127
homogeneity 8; dynamic 25, 28–29, 131, 209–211; legal 11
homo oeconomicus 149
HRVP *see* High Representative of the EU for Foreign Affairs and Security Policy (HRVP)
human, animal and plant health, protecting 85, 87
humanitarian superpower ambitions of Norway 97, 99, 106–107
human rights 17; activists 102; China 102, 103; European Convention on Human Rights 147
Hungary 219, 222
Hurdal Declaration (Norway) 163–164, 168

Iceland 9, 11–12, 59, 90, 97, 101–102, 116, 189–91, 219
ICES *see* International Council for the Exploration of the Sea
Indonesia 101
International Council for the Exploration of the Sea (ICES) 71, 73
Internal Market Bill (UK) 62
Ireland: election laws and voting rights 153–154; Northern Ireland 33, 153, 187–188, 197–199, 204, 216, 220, 222; Northern Ireland Protocol 51, 76; Republic of Ireland 72, 74, 77, 104, 106, 108, 154, 199, 218; unification vote 199; *see also* Northern Ireland
Isaksen, Thorbjørn Røe 102, 104
Israel 101

Japan 108, 113
Johnson, Boris 107; Australian option and 185; Brexit and 18n2, 53, 112, 116, 135–136, 187–188, 204, 222; free trade under 179; Global Britain speech 110; Norway option and 186, 199; Political Declaration of 2019 222; Ten Point Plan for a Green Industrial Revolution 50; Truss and Sunak's succession of 49; Withdrawal Agreement and 76–77, 216
Johnson, Hilde Frafjord 107

Jordan 101
juridification 148

Korea (South) 101, 108
Kyoto Protocol 55

Land Use, Land Use Change and Forestry (LULUCF) Regulation 55
Laval case 147
Lebanon 101
Leiren, Merethe Dotterud ix
Lichtenstein 9, 11, 58, 90, 101–102, 189–191
Lisbon Treaty 72, 128, 147, 218, 219, 223
Liu Xiaobo 102
Lord, Christopher ix
Lula *see* Silva, Luiz Inácio 'Lula' da
LULUCF *see* Land Use, Land Use Change and Forestry (LULUCF) Regulation
Luxembourg 104, 108

Maastricht Treaty 43n3, 145, 150; Denmark's rejection of 218
Macri, Mauricio 103
Macron, Emmanuel 221
Malta 128
maritime law, international 70; *see also* UNCLOS
Maritime Security Strategy (EU) 131
market citizens 146
Marshall, T. H. 143
maximum sustainable yield (MSY) 71, 73
May, Theresa 18n2, 53, 76, 112, 135–136
Mercosur 105–106, 118, 119n2; EFTA-Mercosur Agreement 33, 101, 103–106; EU-Mercosur agreement 103–106
Michailidou, Asimina 186
migration and migration policy: Brexit and 142, 151–156; Britain 15, 116, 142; EU 145; EU common asylum and migration policy 167; EU transnational 143–144; India 112; internal EEA 34; intra-EU 142, 145; Norway 142, 146–150, 167; root causes of 109; weaponization of 133
Military Mobility project 128
Moldova 219, 223
Monetary Policy Committee, Bank of England 201
monetary union, EU and UK 202
Monetary Union (Schengen) 154

Monnet, Jean 223
Morocco 101
MSY *see* maximum sustainable yield

NAFTA *see* North American Free Trade Agreement
Nationally Determined Contribution (NDC), Norway 54
NATO 127–128, 133, 136, 138, 200, 214, 221
NAV *see* Norwegian Labour and Welfare Administration
NAV social benefits scandal 31, 149, 176–178
NDC *see* Nationally Determined Contribution
NDICI *see* Neighbourhood, Development, and International Cooperation Instrument
Neighbourhood, Development, and International Cooperation Instrument (NDICI) 117
net zero carbon targets 50–51, 59, 60, 63n2
New Zealand 108, 112
non-discrimination 142, 144–146, 176
Nordic model 40
Nordic Plus countries 106–107
Nordics, the 106–107
Nordlinger, Eric 35
North American Free Trade Agreement (NAFTA) 112
Northern Ireland: Customs Union and 187, 199, 204, 216; EU citizenship claims by UK citizens living in 153; Irish citizens living in, denied EU voting rights 154; legislatures 1998 75; special circumstances of (Brexit) 33, 187–188, 197–199, 216, 220, 222; trilemma posed by 187–188
Northern Ireland Protocol 51, 76
North Sea 49, 57–60, 81, 89, 164
North Sea Link project 57–58
Norway: autonomy and wriggle room of ix, 4–7, 23–42, 69–70, 81, 83–84, 86, 88, 91, 97–110, 117, 124–138, 142, 148–149, 157, 160, 169–170, 172, 176–178, 185–204, 209–217, 220; Centre Party (SP) 166, 171; climate and energy policy post-Brexit, Norway-EU relationship and 54–57; climate and energy policy post-Brexit, Norway-UK relationship and 57–59; as climate leader 48; Conservative Party 90, 102, 128, 167; Customs Union, not part of 14–15, 55, 220; DG SANCO 88; EEA Agreement and 125; EU affiliation of and dependence on 7, 170–171, 174, 185; EU Emergency Trust Fund for Africa (EUTF) and 109; EU-Norway-UK relations in primary industries after Brexit 88–91; Europeanisation of 174, 220; Food Safety Authority 88; Green Party 102, 167, 222; humanitarian superpower ambitions of 97, 99, 106–107; Hurdal Declaration 163–164, 168; Labour Party (AP) 166, 168; Nationally Determined Contribution (NDC) 54; Norway-China FTA 103; Norway-EU and Norway-UK affiliations, differentiating between 32, 42, 211; Norway-EU relationship, Brexit and 170–172; Norway-EU relationship, implications for climate and energy policy post-Brexit 54–57; Norway-EU relations in foreign, security, and defence policy 124, 127, 129; Norway-EU relations in primary industries 79–89; Norwegian lessons for UK, post-Brexit 69–70; parallelism and coherence with EU 101–103; post-Brexit 24, 54–59; Storting (Parliament) 54, 173, 220; strong development and humanitarian identity of 107–108; third-country status of 40, 56, 87, 124–125, 130, 211; trilateral relationship between EU, UK-Norway relationship and implications for climate and energy policy post-Brexit 57–59; as welfare state, Norway as 177–178, 197; WTO and tariff-free seafood access 83–85; *see also* European Economic Area Agreement (EEA Agreement); NAV social benefits scandal; Solberg; Støre
Norway model: Brexit and 1, 17, 138, 157, 185–204, 220; dense affiliations as sum total of 12; EEA Agreement as core of 2, 151; UK debate over merits/drawbacks of 4; UK's Brexit predicament and 196–204
Norway plus option 187, 204, 216

Norway – UK free trade agreement 90–91, 100–102, 106
Norwegian Labour and Welfare Administration (NAV) 147; social benefits scandal 31, 149, 176–178
NOU 10

ODA *see* Official Development Assistance
OECD 98, 220; Development Assistance Committee (DAC) 98, 108–109, 114, 212–213
Olsen, Epsen D.H. ix
Official Development Assistance (ODA) 108

Palestine Authority 101
Paris Accords/Agreement 17, 52, 54, 59, 98; climate targets 39
Paris Declaration of Aid Effectiveness 108
PEM convention 118
Permanent Structured Cooperation (PESCO) 126, 128, 136, 138, 213
PESCO *see* Permanent Structured Cooperation
Plender, R. 146
Poland 219, 222
policy coherence for development 108–109, 213
Putin, Vladimir 221

Raab, Dominic 110
Regional Fisheries Management Organisations (RFMOs) 71
renewable energy/power sector 50, 56, 60–61
REPowerEU plan 53, 56, 61, 62, 210
RFMOs *see* Regional Fisheries Management Organisations
Riddervold, Marianne ix
Romania 219
Rüffert case 147
rule-shirking/undermining 31, 32, 34
Russia: gas from 61; Norway's agreements with 81; war on Ukraine 105, 119, 125–127, 133–135, 211

SACU *see* South African Customs Union
Saltnes, Johanne Døhlie ix
Scotland 62, 197, 198; legislature 1998 75
Schengen Area 150, 219
Schengen association agreements and system 8, 11–14, 24–25, 154, 186; Dublin system and 145; EEA Agreement and 169, 171, 173; as part of EU *acquis* 34, 169; guillotine clause 31, 43n12; Mixed Committee of 11–12; Monetary Union 154; Norway's foreign policy and 133–134; Norway's Progress Party criticism of 167; Norway's role in, SP's determination to terminate 166; Norway's wriggle room regarding 131–132; supranational logic of common norms and rules applied to 145
Schengen Information System (SIS) 11
sector-specific policy initiatives 34
Short, Clare 107
Silva, Luiz Inácio 'Lula' da 105
Simmonds, Mark 114
single energy market, EU 51
single market: challenges of creating 194–196; EEA-EFTA states quandary regarding 10–11; Northern Ireland and 188; Norway's EU affiliation and 8, 18, 34, 55, 83–84, 185–191, 198; Thatcher and 202; UK's exit from 2, 14, 76–79, 92, 151, 186–187, 193, 197, 199–204
Single Market Scoreboard (EU) 31
SIS *see* Schengen Information System
Skocpol, T. 35
solar power 50
Solberg, Erna 164, 167
Somalia 127
Søreide, Ines Eriksen 171
South African Customs Union (SACU) 101
Spain 75, 77, 81, 82, 108
stability versus instability 34
Starmer, Keir 221
Støre, Jonas Gahr 103, 134, 164–166
Storting (Norwegian Parliament) 54, 173, 220
Strait of Dover 220
Sunak, Rishi 18n2, 49–51, 53, 115
Svendsen, Øyvind ix, 18n5
Sweden 83, 108, 219, 221
Swiss model 1, 16, 193
Switzerland 56, 219–221; agricultural treated as special industry by 84–85; EU affiliation of 1–2; EU budget contributions 13; free-trade agreement with China 102; free-trade agreement with UK,

post-Brexit 90; OECD-DAC and 108; as potential model for UK treaties with EU 185–186, 193; Schengen Mixed Committee member 11; sectoral bilateral agreements of 9, 16, 185; *see also* Swiss model

'Taking Back Control' UK Leave slogan 3–5, 145, 156
taxation 8, 13, 148, 192, 219
Team Europe 107, 116
TEU *see* Treaty on European Union
Thatcher, Margaret 201–201
third countries: autonomy of, vis-à-vis the EU 129, 134; EEA Agreement and 6, 28; EU and 2, 3, 5, 23–24, 29, 31, 33–36, 137, 157, 207–211, 213–214; migration by nationals of 145, 151, 156; Norway as 40, 56, 87, 124–125, 130, 211; security and defence 18n5; TEU and 180n1; wriggle room for third countries in between EU and UK agreements 32, 70, 130; UK as 76, 125, 156
Thomas, Gareth 114
Tories 221
Trade and Cooperation Agreement (TCA) *see* EU-UK Trade and Cooperation (TCA) Agreement
Treaty of Maastricht *see* Maastricht Treaty
Treaty of Lisbon *see* Lisbon Treaty
Treaty of Nice 218
Treaty on European Union (TEU): Article 4 181n2; Article 21.1 180n1; Article 49 218; Article 50 223
Trevi Group 145
triangular relations and dynamics 7–8
Trondal, Jarle ix
Trump, Donald 112
Truss, Liz 18n2, 49–51, 53
Tunisia 101
Turkey 101, 118, 219

Ukraine 101, 118, 219
Ukraine Association Agreement 2014 222
Ukraine war 1, 49, 53, 56–57, 60–63, 105, 119, 125–127, 221; EU enlargement policy and 223; NATO response to 133; Norway's response to 134–135
UNCLOS *see* United Nations Convention on the Law of the Sea

United Kingdom: Benchmark project 186; CCA 50; Conservative Party 50, 113–114, 171, 185, 199, 202, 204, 216, 221; Customs Union, no longer a member of 2; environmental commitment, history of 50; Foreign, Commonwealth and Development Office (FCDO) 115; Internal Market Bill 62; Tories 221; UK-EU relationship and implications for climate and energy policy post-Brexit 50–54; zombie legislation 49–50, 62; *see also* Cameron; Johnson; May; single market; Sunak; Thatcher; Westminster
United Nations 115; Charter 180n1
United Nations Convention on the Law of the Sea (UNCLOS) 70–71, 80–81, 89, 91, 211–212
United Nations Fish Stock Agreement 1995 71
United States: GATT and EU negotiations 80; UK free trade agreement negotiations, post-Brexit 92, 112; Trump and UK trade negotiations 112; United States-Mexico-Canada free trade agreement 112
Uruguay 119n2; *see also* Mercosur
Uruguay round, GATT 85–86

Viking case 147
von der Leyen, Ursula 56 77

Wales 198
Weber, Max 37
welfare fraud *see* NAV social benefits scandal
welfare rights 143
welfare state, Norway as 177–178, 197
welfare tourism 177
Western Balkans 101, 118, 219
Westminster Parliament (UK) 62, 129, 198
Wieczorek-Zeul, Heidemarie 107
wind energy/power 49, 50, 56, 59, 61
wriggle room: autonomy and ix, 3, 4–7; 23–42; Brexit and Norway model and 185–204; concept of 23; EU and 2; EU-external dimension of 33–34; global trade and development and 97–119; Norway and 4–7; in primary industry policies (agriculture, aquaculture,

fisheries) 69–92; sanctioning and compliance mechanisms 31–32; temporality and 34; third country 32; under conditions of exiting from system of legally binding cooperation 32–33; unpacking 24–34

World Trade Organization (WTO): Dispute Settlement Mechanism 83; elimination of export subsidies on agricultural products in 106, 213; EU and 179, 212, 220; GATT/WTO 87; Norway tariff-free seafood access and 83–85; SPS agreement in 70, 91; UK trading on terms defined by 111

WTO *see* World Trade Organization

Xi (President, China) 98

zero carbon emission *see* net zero carbon target

zombie legislation (UK) 49–50, 62

Printed in Great Britain
by Amazon